THE ORDEAL OF PEACE

Historians know a great deal about how wars begin, but far less about how they end. Whilst much has been written about the forces, passions, and institutions that mobilized societies for war and worked to sustain that mobilization through years of struggle, much less is known about the equally complex processes that demobilized societies in the wake of armed conflict. As such, this new book will be welcomed by scholars wishing to understand the effects of the Great War in its fullest context, including the reactions, behaviors, and attitudes of 'ordinary' Europeans during the tumultuous events of the years of demobilization.

Taking a transnational perspective on demobilization this study demonstrates that the experience of mass industrial war generated remarkably similar pressures within both the defeated and victorious countries. Using as examples the important provincial centers of Munich and Manchester, this book examines the experiences of European urban-dwellers from the last year of the war until the early 1920s. Utilizing a wide variety of sources from more than twenty archives in Germany, Britain, and the United States this book recovers voices from the period that are often lost in conventional narratives, capturing the richness and diversity of the ideas, visions, and conflicts engendered by those difficult and tumultuous years. The result is a book that paints a vivid picture of the difficulties that peace could bring to economies and societies that had rapidly and fully adapted to the demands of industrial world war.

About the author

Adam R. Seipp is an Assistant Professor of History at Texas A&M University, USA

The Ordeal of Peace

Demobilization and the Urban Experience in Britain and Germany, 1917–1921

ADAM R. SEIPP
Texas A&M University, USA

ASHGATE

Birmingham Studies in First World War History

Series Editor

John Bourne
The University of Birmingham, UK

The First World War is a subject of perennial interest to historians and is often regarded as a watershed event, marking the end of the nineteenth century and the beginning of the 'modern' industrial world. The sheer scale of the conflict and massive loss of life means that it is constantly being assessed and reassessed to examine its lasting military, political, sociological, industrial, cultural and economic impact. Run in conjunction with the *Centre for First World War Studies* at the University of Birmingham, this new series offers a platform for the publication of international research on all aspects of the Great War. Whilst the main thrust of the series is on the military aspects of the conflict, other related areas (including cultural, political and social) can also addressed. Books published will be aimed primarily at a post-graduate academic audience, furthering exciting recent interpretations of the war, whilst still being accessible enough to appeal to a wider audience of educated lay readers.

Also in this series

Doctrine and Reform in the British Cavalry 1880–1918
Stephen Badsey

'A Student in Arms'
Donald Hankey and Edwardian Society at War
Ross Davies

British Generalship during the Great War
The Military Career of Sir Henry Horne (1861–1929)
Simon Robbins

Published by
Ashgate Publishing Limited
Wey Court East
Union Road
Farnham
Surrey, GU9 7PT
England

Ashgate Publishing Company
Suite 420
101 Cherry Street
Burlington
VT 05401-4405
USA

www.ashgate.com

British Library Cataloguing in Publication Data
Seipp, Adam R.
The ordeal of peace : demobilization and the urban experience in Britain and Germany, 1917–1921. – (Birmingham studies in First World War history) 1. World War, 1914–1918 – Peace – Social aspects 2. World War, 1914–1918 – Veterans 3. Manchester (England) – Social conditions – 20th century 4. Manchester (England) – Economic conditions – 20th century 5. Munich (Germany) – Social conditions – 20th century 6. Munich (Germany) – Economic conditions – 20th century
I. Title
942.7'33083

Library of Congress Cataloging-in-Publication Data
Seipp, Adam R.
The ordeal of peace : demobilization and the urban experience in Britain and Germany, 1917–1921 / Adam R. Seipp.
p. cm. – (Birmingham studies in First World War history)
Includes bibliographical references.
ISBN 978-0-7546-6749-0 (hardcover : alk. paper)
1. Reconstruction (1914–1939)–England–Manchester. 2. Reconstruction (1914–1939)–Germany–Munich. 3. Manchester (England)–Social conditions–20th century. 4. Munich (Germany)–Social conditions--20th century. 5. Manchester (England)–Economic conditions–20th century. 6. Munich (Germany)–Economic conditions–20th century. I. Title.

D659.G7S35 2009
940.3'1440942733–dc22

2009004628

ISBN 978 0 7546 6749 0

FSC Mixed Sources
Product group from well-managed forests and other controlled sources
www.fsc.org Cert no. SGS-COC-2482
© 1996 Forest Stewardship Council

Printed and bound in Great Britain by
TJ International Ltd, Padstow, Cornwall

Contents

Series Editor's Introduction *ix*
Acknowledgments *xi*
Abbreviations *xiii*

Introduction: Munich, Manchester, and the Demobilization of Europe, 1917–21 1

1 Manchester, Munich, and Urban Europe in 1914 25

Section I Visions of the End: 1917–18 and the Beginnings of Demobilization

2 "Do Something!:" Manchester in Transition and War, 1917–18 47

3 An Immeasurable Sacrifice of Blood and Treasure: Munich at War, 1917–18 91

Section II "The Man Afterwards Changed Completely:" Demobilizations, Homecomings, and Transformations

4 "The Fabric of Europe and the World was Being Remade:" The Armistice and After in Manchester 131

5 "We Don't Want Gratitude, We Want Our Rights:" Demobilization, Violence, and Politics in Munich, 1919 165

Section III "The Dregs of this Bitter Chalice:" Crisis and the End of Demobilization, 1920–21

6 Ordeal by Peace: Manchester, 1920–21 203

7 Scapegoats for a Lost War: The Crisis of Demobilization in Munich, 1920–21 233

Conclusion: Ending and Beginning Again 261

Bibliography *267*
Index *285*

Series Editor's Introduction

Few subjects have received more attention from students of modern history than how wars begin. Few subjects have received less attention than how wars end. During the great wars of the twentieth century states succeeded – or failed – in large measure through how effectively they "mobilized" their economies and societies. Mobilization did not only drive – or fail to drive – military power, but also became an engine of social change, which could include social dissolution. Political solidarities could be strengthened but they could also be destroyed. Nor did these complexities and ambiguities end with the onset of "peace." Re-sheathing the double-edged sword could be as problematic as forging it in the first place. This process was, perhaps, especially true of the First World War, whose "ending" was far from clear-cut and where great states had also to wrestle with the consequences of defeat and "regime change." As Adam Seipp writes, "The end of the First World War was not an event, but rather a process. Understanding how this process worked can tell us a great deal about the evolving relationship between war, the state, and civil society in the modern world." This innovative, perceptive and subtle study of the transition from war to peace in two contrasting but comparable regional cities, Manchester and Munich, is a welcome addition to the *Birmingham Studies in First World War History* series.

John Bourne
Director of the Centre for First World War Studies
The University of Birmingham

Acknowledgments

This book is the result of many years of work, during which time I have incurred intellectual and personal debts that I can only hope to one day repay. In North Carolina, I had the opportunity to work with outstanding mentors who pushed me to think about how history should be written and taught. I am particularly grateful to my doctoral advisor, Konrad H. Jarausch. Thanks also go to Richard Kohn, Tami Davis Biddle, Christopher Browning, Alex Roland, Jay Smith, Richard Soloway, and Gerhard Weinberg. This project would have suffered without the friendship and camaraderie of people like Bruce Baker, Michael Meng, Kathy Nawyn, Brian Puaca, Paul Quigley, and Mike O'Sullivan.

I have been fortunate to work for the past few years in an exciting and energetic Department of History at Texas A&M University. Special thanks go to R.J.Q. Adams, Walter Buenger, Chip Dawson, Sylvia Hoffert, Walter Kamphoefner, Arnold Krammer, Brian Linn, David Vaught, and the Junior Faculty Reading Group.

Research for this project was funded by the German-American Fulbright Commission, the German Marshall Fund of the United States, the Melbern G. Glasscock Center for Humanities Research, and the Office of the Vice President for Research at Texas A&M.

In Germany and Great Britain, I benefitted from the help of some truly extraordinary archivists and scholars, many of whom took time to help a PhD student navigate the mazes of archival research. Particular thanks go to Martin Geyer and Alan Kidd. Duncan Broady of the Greater Manchester Police Archive, Ulrike Trummer of the Stadtarchiv München, and Achim Fuchs of the Bavarian War Archive also deserve my gratitude for their competence, patience, and extraordinary knowledge of the collections they help manage. My time in Europe was greatly enriched by the hospitality of friends and family, particularly the Quigley and Sears families. Dario, Tullio, and Laura Vittori have been our family in Europe for a long time and hopefully will be for years to come.

This project, and so much else, would not have been possible without the lifelong support of my family. I cannot thank them enough. Nor can I say too much about the contributions of my best friend, patient travelling companion, and sometime editor Leslie Seipp. As this book neared completion, we were joined by Rowan Kane Seipp. To them, in the hope of further adventures to come, I dedicate what follows.

Abbreviations

BA-R	German Federal Archive, Imperial Section
BAMA	German Federal Military Archive
BHStA	Bavarian Main State Archives
BVP	Bavarian Peoples' Party
CO	Conscientious Objector
CPGB	Communist Party of Great Britain
CWS	Co-operative Wholesale Society
DAP	German Workers' Party
DDP	German Democratic Party
EW	Einwohnerwehr (Citizen Militia)
ILP	Independent Labor Party
IRA	Irish Republican Army
IWMA	Imperial War Museum Archives
KPD	German Communist Party
MEN	*Manchester Evening News*
MG	*Manchester Guardian*
MSPD	Majority Social Democratic Party (See SPD)
NA	National Archives (Great Britain)
NARA	National Archives and Records Administration
NSDAP	National Socialist German Workers' Party
NSF	National Shell Factory
Pmf	Powder and Munitions Factory
SJFB	Statistisches Jahrbuch für den Freistaat Bayern
SJSM	Statistisches Jahrbuch der Stadt München
SPD	Social Democratic Party
SSS	Socialist Sunday Schools
StaMu	Munich Municipal Archives
USPD	Independent Social Democratic Party

Introduction
Munich, Manchester, and the Demobilization of Europe, 1917–21

> The Prince of Darkness receives word that the Thirty Years War is ended and that peace on Earth is greeted with the joyous singing of 'Gloria in excelsis' and 'Te deum laudamus.' This news drives Lucifer almost insane with rage. He lashes out at various devils for having wasted their chances through laziness. But Belial points out that peace also produces a respectable crop of vices and that all is not lost.
>
> Grimmelshausen, *Simplicissimus*[1]

In the history of Europe's twentieth century, November 11, 1918 stands out as a watershed moment. As the guns fell silent along the line of trenches that ran from the Swiss border northwest toward the coast, great empires buckled and swayed under the pressures of revolution, and the fires that defined the deadly century to come burned brightly across the continent. That moment at which, as Robert Graves pithily suggested, "the kitchen clock had stopped at eleven o'clock in the morning and the household was uncertain as to when the potatoes should be put on to boil…" seemed to mark an extraordinary psychological and military chasm.[2]

As with many moments of apparently dramatic rupture in the historical narrative, the reality of that November day and its consequences was far more complex. Whether they celebrated victory, lamented defeat, mourned for lives lost, or shrugged with indifference on November 11, tens of millions of Europeans awoke on November 12 to face the same bureaucratic, administrative, and legal machinery with which they had dealt during the war. Rationing, legal restrictions on speech and behavior, men serving in conscript armies, and the other manifestations of a highly mobilized society at war persisted for months, and in some cases years. The apparatus of mobilization did not end with the war; it had to be dismantled over time. In victorious Britain or in a Germany teetering on the edge of collapse, the machinery that sustained the war effort played a role in the lives of ordinary Europeans for a long time to come.

Second, while the cease-fire agreed to by the warring states proved durable, this was by no means clear at the time. It was, after all, only an Armistice. There was a good chance that it would not hold until a more permanent peace arrangement

1 Jakob Grimmelshausen. *Simplicius Simplicissimus*, trans. George Shulz-Behrend. (New York: Bobbs-Merrill, 1965), 333.

2 Robert Graves and Alan Hodge, *The Long Week-End: A Social History of Great Britain, 1918–1939* (New York: Norton, 1940), 7.

could be made. In any case, much of Europe and the wider world remained in a very real state of war. In the East, a swirling and interconnected set of civil wars set national armies, nationalist insurgents, and armed bands against one another in bloody fighting across vast swaths of territory. In western Germany, occupation troops took up positions in the face of a sometimes hostile population. In western Asia, the demise of the Russian and Ottoman Empires created a fragmented and highly fluid situation in which thousands of troops from Germany, Britain and their allies found themselves embroiled. For millions of Europeans, violence continued to be a very real facet of their daily lives long after the Armistice. Many who did not face physical violence had reason to believe that they might. Just because revolutionary violence took place in Budapest, Berlin, or Munich and not in London, Paris, or Manchester does not mean that reasonable people in the postwar years did not believe that such a spasm was possible or even likely.

Finally, if the peace came after the surprisingly quick collapse of the German military in the Fall of 1918, Europeans had been talking about the end of the war since it began four sanguinary years before. While diplomats and senior policy makers debated war aims, an equally important set of discussions took place in civil societies across the combatant states. Fueled by wartime propaganda but also stemming from grassroots commitment to the war, European societies discussed and debated the world after the war long before the end of the conflict was in sight. Given the divisions in prewar societies, the extraordinary mobilization of combatant societies and the length of the conflict, these visions of the future were often contradictory or mutually exclusive. They were nonetheless profoundly believed and when they were not realized, disappointment and disillusionment resulted.

On European home fronts, the war mobilized populations like no other conflict in the continent's history. In Britain, 6.2 million men were called the colors, while 13.2 million male Germans served. More than 45 percent of Frenchmen wore a uniform at some point in the war. More than 9 million people died, and hundreds of billions of dollars had been spent or lost by combatant states.[3] At home, millions more entered into new labor arrangements under increasingly strict state control, including a dramatic influx of women. Mobilization for war shaped the experience of a generation and was not reversed simply because the guns ceased to fire. The mobilization of European societies in a time of war could not be undone quickly in either the defeated or victorious states of Europe. The end of the First World War was not an event, but rather a process. Understanding how this process worked can tell us a great deal about the evolving relationship between war, the state, and civil society in the modern world.

This book is a study of how the transition from war to peace took place in two important European regional cities. The south German royal city of Munich and the northern English industrial conurbation around Manchester are and were very different cities with distinct historical trajectories, but both were swept up in and

---

3 Statistics from Roger Chickering, *Imperial Germany and the Great War, 1914–1918*, 2nd edn (Cambridge: Cambridge University Press, 1998), 192.

transformed by wartime mobilization. Both emerged from the war to face challenges that, while shaped by historical contingency, suggest that the experience of mass industrial war produced commonalities that are critical if we are to understand the transformative power of armed conflict in the twentieth century. While victory or defeat in war clearly shaped the options available and the outcomes of choices made, every combatant state faced the challenges of managing the transition from war to peace at the end of the conflict, and the results that followed were by no means predetermined by the end of the war.

This book makes two larger arguments about the end of the First World War and the early postwar period. First, it argues that there was a period of demobilization experienced across the combatant states and lasting from 1917, when the principal combatants began to invest significant bureaucratic resources in planning for the end of the war, until about 1921. This demobilization period saw the whole or partial dismantling of wartime institutions, practices, and attitudes within a framework of intense and sometimes violent negotiation between states, local and regional authorities, and European civil societies.

Second, this study argues that the demobilization period was defined by a crisis of reciprocity that emerged from the specific conditions of mass industrial war in the early twentieth century. Contemporaries knew, and historians of mobilization have demonstrated, that the processes of physical, institutional, and cultural mobilization and self-mobilization demanded and justified enormous sacrifices among combatant populations.[4] Civil societies in combatant states expected that their sacrifices would be rewarded in the wake of the war. While combatant populations expected and hoped for eventual victory, the experience and subsequent memory of sacrifice dominated political discourse at the end of the war. Men and women, combatants and non-combatants, could claim that they had willingly paid the costs of the war and deserved to be compensated in political and material ways. The visions of the future that emerged in the last years of the war were often conflicting, contradictory, or impossible given the postwar situation in victorious and defeated states. This did not make them any less compelling for those who believed that they deserved to come to fruition in the postwar world. This language of reciprocity framed debates about the transition from wartime to postwar social order.

Domestic politics, economics, and international affairs were inextricably linked during the demobilization period. As diplomats tried to reconstruct or rehabilitate Europe, they did so in the context of a network of domestic crises and near-crises across the continent. The tension between crisis and rebuilding lay at the heart of Europe's

4 Very good examples can be found in John Horne, "'L'impôt du sang': Republican rhetoric and industrial warfare in France, 1914–18," *Social History*, vol. 14, 2 (May 1989), 201–23 and Richard Bessel, "Mobilization and Demobilization in Germany, 1916–19" in John Horne, ed. *State, Society, and Mobilization in Europe During the First World War* (Cambridge: Cambridge University Press, 1997), 212–22.

varied and uneven "twisted paths" between the World Wars.[5] For the diplomats who tried to find international solutions to these multiple crises, it was a moment of opportunity as well as anxiety, which Zara Steiner has called a "moment of maximum dislocation in the international order."[6] Perhaps nowhere were the international effects of domestic problems so apparent as in the linked and mutually reinforcing networks of the global economy. The vulnerabilities in domestic economies in the years after the war catalyzed problems elsewhere, further emphasizing the need to understand the demobilization years in international perspective.[7]

The demobilization of European societies was neither smooth nor uncontested. Demobilization took place in the context of enormous social tension that contemporaries often understandably mistook for the stirrings of revolution. Across a band of Central Europe, chaos seemed to be stalking the land and emerging both in ancient capitals and rural villages. In Berlin, the Kaiser fled into exile ahead of a violent and chaotic revolution from below. Other German cities swiftly followed at a pace that surprised even the German Socialists whose efforts had helped make the revolution. German soldiers in the East found new battles with nationalist militias in the Baltic and Poland as their old army held increasingly precarious positions in a region that they would soon lose at Versailles.

In the dissolving Austro-Hungarian Empire, there was a scramble for territory as a patchwork of ethnic identities tried to resolve themselves into coherent national states. While there were scattered acts of violence and land seizures, much of this transformation occurred peacefully. This was not the case in Hungary, where national independence swiftly turned violent as early attempts at Social Democracy gave way to the brief regime of Béla Kun and the subsequent interwar autocracy. As Ivan Behrends has noted, while a distinct variety of postwar right-wing backlash thrived in East-Central Europe, the real or perceived retrograde developments at the end of war had echoes across the continent.[8]

5 Robert Gerwarth, "Introduction" in Robert Gerwarth, ed., *Twisted Paths: Europe, 1914–1945* (Oxford: Oxford University Press, 2007), 10.

6 Zara Steiner, *The Lights that Failed: European International History, 1919–1933* (Oxford: Oxford University Press, 2005), 604.

7 Probably the most influential study of postwar economic reconstruction is Charles Maier's study of "corporatism" and the reordering of European economies, *Recasting Bourgeois Europe: Stabilization in France, Germany and Italy in the Decade After World War I* (Princeton: Princeton University Press, 1975). See also Gerald Feldman, ed. *Die Erfahrung der Inflation / The Experience of Inflation* (Berlin: de Gruyter, 1984) and Susan Armitage's excellent *The Politics of Decontrol of Industry: Britain and the United States* (London: Weidenfeld & Nicholson, 1969). Another economic treatment of this process is Daniel Silverman, *Reconstructing Europe after the Great War* (Cambridge: Harvard University Press, 1982).

8 The best account of East Central Europe during the postwar period, and Hungary specifically, can be found in Ivan Behrends, *Decades of Crisis: Central and Eastern Europe Before World War II* (Berkeley: University of California Press, 1998), 116. A broader discussion of the region during this period can be found on pp. 115–54.

It was not just in the defeated nations that the end of the war brought turmoil and upheaval. In Britain there were almost 1,400 strike actions in 1919, which affected more than 2.5 million workers. This figure is all the more impressive when compared with the far smaller figure of 1.46 million striking workers in 1912, a year then considered the benchmark for labor militancy.[9] In France, citizens who had for patriotic and economic reasons invested in bonds found their investments undercut by inflation and the Republic's enemies had new reasons to accuse the state of betraying their interests and their wartime sacrifices in the name of debased stability.[10] Italy was the most vivid example of the sometimes spectacular problems of victory after 1918. Having been on the winning side of the war, many Italians felt aggrieved when their victory was "mutilated" by the peacemakers and the country seemed unable to translate its battlefield resolve into tangible gains. By the middle of 1919, labor unrest had reached unprecedented levels across the country, where more than one million workers struck in 1919 alone. The economic and political chaos of the "postwar crisis" helped to establish the conditions under which parties like the Fascists could establish themselves as forces of order.[11]

Even neutral countries found themselves drawn into and profoundly affected by the events of the war. The Netherlands, fearful of attack from either side of the conflict, experienced something approaching total war without warfare. The government faced the task of demobilizing a highly mobilized society that had not fought.[12] Switzerland, with its firm but uneasy neutrality, was not immune from what seemed to be looming continental conflagration. Having safely seen off many of its resident Bolsheviks-in-exile after 1917, the Swiss still faced a crippling General Strike in November 1918.[13] In Spain, neutrality only served to weaken the power of the governing alliance and usher in an era of mass politics. "Spain did not enter the war," one recent historian of the period observed, "but the war entered Spain."[14]

If the dreaded Russian-inspired social revolution did not happen in Western Europe, it is equally clear that something important did, in fact, take place during

9 Co-Operative Press Agency, *The People's Year Book, 1922* (Manchester Co-Operative Wholesale Society Press, 1922), 255.

10 Eugen Weber, *The Hollow Years: France in the 1930s* (New York: Norton, 1994), 27.

11 Philip Morgan, *Italian Fascism: 1919–1945* (New York: St. Martin's Press, 1995), 3–59; Spencer M. DiScala, *Italy: From Revolution to Republic, 1700 to the Present*, 3rd edn (Boulder, CO: Westview, 2004), 223–9.

12 Maartje M. Abbenhuis-Ash, *The Art of Staying Neutral: The Netherlands in the First World War, 1914–18* (Amsterdam: Amsterdam University Press, 2006).

13 Alfred Erich Senn, *The Russian Revolution in Switzerland, 1914–1917* (Madison: University of Wisconsin Press, 1971) and E. Bonjour, ed. *A Short History of Switzerland* (Westport: Greenwood Press, 1985), 343–56.

14 Francisco J. Romero Salvadó, *Spain 1914–1917: Between War and Revolution* (London: Routledge, 1999), ix. See also Sebastian Balfour, *The End of the Spanish Empire, 1898–1923* (Oxford: Clarendon Press, 1997).

those immediate postwar years. These events, and countless others large and small, happened in the context of the largest demobilization to date in European history. Neither national history nor the history of the continent can be properly written without understanding this framework of social transition and transformation.

This book fundamentally argues for a more nuanced understanding of the relationship between armed combat and the history of European society in the age of mass industrial war. Demobilization is a set of processes that bridge the chasm between "wartime" and "postwar," effectively extending the lived experience of societies at war beyond the conclusion of hostilities and the diplomatic agreements that periodize warfare in the historical consciousness.[15] The vastness and complexity of modern war, particularly in the era of the World Wars, generated pressures upon and from within European societies that took years to resolve, and then often unevenly and with destabilizing consequences. Roger Chickering ends his masterful study of the German city of Freiburg during the war years with the observation that the armistice "brought no interruptions of the usual business."[16] For historians of this war, and of modern war more generally, this presents a significant definitional problem. For many Europeans, warfare ended on November 11, 1918, but the war did not.

In their penetrating and erudite survey of the First World War, Stéphane Audoin-Rouzeau and Annette Becker identify what they consider one of the paradoxes of the First World War: that it was "*accepted* in 1914–18, and much later *rejected*."[17] This "rejection" has informed our fundamental understandings of the multiple crises of interwar Europe and the rise of extreme ideologies during the twenty years that followed 1918. Scholars have looked at the war as a wellspring of "brutalization" or the birthplace of an irony-laden "modern age."[18] By emphasizing the war, this approach overlooks the critical importance of the myriad ways in which peace returned and Europeans struggled with the problems of transition. If Europeans in both victorious and defeated states came to later reject the First World War, it was in large part because of their bitter disappointment at the events that followed.

We know a great deal about how wars begin and the forces that mobilize societies for the conduct of interstate conflict. We know far less about how wars end. While we accept that mobilization is a complex phenomenon with bureaucratic, military,

15 Tony Judt has argued for a six decade "post-war" in Europe after 1945 in which the Cold War stifled any efforts to resolve the conflicts and silences still left in the war's "long shadow." Tony Judt, *Postwar: A History of Europe Since 1945* (New York: Penguin, 2005), 10.

16 Roger Chickering, *The Great War and Urban Life in Germany, Freiburg, 1914–1918* (Cambridge: Cambridge University Press, 2007), 568.

17 Stéphane Audoin-Rouzeau and Annette Becker, *14–18: Understanding the Great War*, trans. Catherine Temerson (New York: Hill and Wang, 2002), 170.

18 Fussell, Paul, *The Great War and Modern Memory* (London: Oxford University Press, 1977) and George L. Mosse, *Fallen Soldiers: Reshaping the Memory of the World Wars* (New York: Oxford University Press, 1990).

and cultural elements, there has been far less systematic study of the myriad ways in which states and societies manage the transition required after the end of hostilities. As the capacity of modern states to mobilize for war expanded and the totalizing tendencies of war transformed the nature of armed conflict, the question of postwar transition became increasingly important and deserving of study.

While our understanding of mobilization has benefited greatly from the insights of the new cultural history and the cultural history of politics, definitions of demobilization remain overwhelmingly focused on bureaucratic and institutional change. Historians use the term in a number of ways, but it remains principally wedded to the traditional definition associated with the study of military institutions. A turn-of-the-century German military reference volume defines demobilization as "… the dissolution of war formations, the furlough of personnel, the sale of military horses, and the handover of … weapons and munitions."[19] One recent and widely-used reference work defines the term as "the release or draw down of wartime military forces as the nation resumes peacetime status following a war or major buildup. It is, then, the opposing process of 'mobilization'…. The extent of the process of demobilization depends upon the mobilization that preceded it."[20] A recent German volume yields the more expansive "conversion of a society from a wartime situation to one of peace."[21]

The first two of these definitions are incomplete because they assume that demobilization is simply the mirror image of mobilization, when, in fact, as we will see demobilization is fraught with its own tensions and complications. The third is unsatisfactory because it implies a linear continuous motion in which a society can be said to be "mobilized" or "demobilized." The reality on the ground after the First World War was much more complicated.

Far more than simply the opposite of mobilization, demobilization is in reality a nexus of interests, contingencies, and competing visions that can tell us much about both societies at war and broader trends in the history of war and society. The period of demobilization at the end of and following the war has been little explored as a discrete phenomenon.[22] In structural terms, this period witnessed the dismantling of some or all wartime regulations, restrictions, and bureaucratic entities that had been created to manage the war. Just as important for the longer term was the persistent centrality of the war in the political culture of formerly combatant states. The wartime propaganda that had been so central in creating and maintaining wartime mobilization stood in marked contrast to the inability

19 Hermann Frobenius, ed., *Militär-Lexikon: Handwörterbuch der Militärwissenschaften* (Berlin: Martin Oldenbourg, 1901), 134.

20 John Whiteclay Chambers, ed., *The Oxford Companion to American Military History* (New York: Oxford University Press, 1999): 208.

21 Gerhard Hirschfeld, et. al. eds, *Enzyklopädie Erster Weltkrieg* (Paderborn: Schoeningh, 2003), 427–30.

22 There is a good discussion of the "sketchy knowledge of the demobilization" in Audoin-Rouzeau and Becker, 166.

or unwillingness of state and local authorities to provide the tangible rewards that societies had been promised for their years of service and sacrifice.

National history is of crucial importance here. The two cities under discussion had their own unique histories and were part of national political and organizational cultures that helped to shape the range of outcomes possible after the war. The contingencies of wartime, which in the end saw Germany defeated and Britain victorious, are also too critical to simply gloss over. That we can speak of a common set of debates going on across the combatant states suggests that the particular demands of mobilizing and sustaining mobilization for mass industrial war generated similar pressures on societies at war that can best be explored through a transnational approach to the problem. Demobilization after the First World War was rooted not only in the unique national experiences of combatant states but in the transnational influence of mass industrial war and the conflicts and compromises required to mobilize sophisticated urbanized societies to sustain interstate conflict.

Demobilization was a vast set of socio-cultural processes that derived from the unprecedented penetration of wartime into the everyday lives of ordinary Europeans and the governments at all levels that tried to survey, cajole, coerce, or compromise with them over more than four years of war. To understand the experience of demobilization and the boundaries of the demobilization period, we need to try to reconstruct the collisions that took place during those years and then, like those who attempted to plan and carry out the demobilization, to pull apart those collided bodies and try to make sense of what happened. If we understand demobilization simply from the perspective of those who made and tried to carry out policy, we will never really grasp how profound the experiences of demobilization really were.

For the purposes of this study, demobilization will be defined as the whole or partial withdrawal of the legal claims of a warring polity, generally a state, on the physical, economic, and cultural resources of that polity with regard to the planning and execution of armed conflict. I would suggest that demobilization in the context of modern industrial war has four components. Physical demobilization refers to the release of some members of the armed forces during wartime and the transition of armed forces at the conclusion of armed conflict. Economic demobilization is the reduction of any state controls on production, wages, labor, and pricing designed to produce materiel for armed conflict. Bureaucratic demobilization is the dismantling of regulations and institutions intended to survey and control civil society during wartime. The final facet, cultural demobilization, is the most diffuse. It refers to both the ending of state-sponsored or supported advocacy designed to develop and maintain popular enthusiasm for armed conflict and the recognition among civil society that the need for such enthusiasm has ended. This last process, which has received a good deal of scholarly attention in the past few years, was the longest-term of the four. The cultural demobilization of the later 1920s and 1930s was fundamentally shaped by contingent developments in the first few years after the war.

One critical feature of demobilization that is often overlooked is that it is an ongoing process whose beginning is nearly simultaneous with mobilization and whose endpoint is not necessarily distinct or apparent. Wounded or otherwise incapacitated troops need to be demobilized regularly, requiring plans and facilities to deal with them and their needs. The possibility of hostilities concluding unexpectedly cannot be ignored, so military and civilian planners normally pay some attention to this potential problem throughout the course of the conflict. At the end of conflicts, even defeated states are not generally completely stripped of their armed forces, so some element of remobilization must be considered in any demobilization planning. Another complicating factor in defining the process of demobilization is that states and their militaries do not actively plan to lose wars. Demobilization planning is therefore carried out with no certainty as to when the conflict will terminate and an expectation that the outcome will be favorable. If Britain emerged victorious from the First World War, while Germany experienced the traumas of defeat and domestic unrest, this was by no means clear until late in the war. Any effective study of demobilization must take these factors into account.

Demobilization occurred along three axes, in a triangle bounded by the national state, local and regional authorities, and civil society. This in no way suggests that any of these bodies acted in a unitary way, but it is critical to understand that no participant in this story was simply an actor and none was merely a bystander or acted upon. Just as there had been in wartime, demobilization was shaped by a push and pull of power and authority that did not simply move from the top down or from the center toward the periphery, but in a variety of ways and emerging from a variety of places. If the Ministry Offices, City Halls, and Army Corps headquarters of Europe were essential sites in the shaping of demobilization, then so were the unemployment lines, food queues, and factory floors of the continent's cities.

The academic study of the First World War has been transformed and energized by a series of new impulses since the early 1990s.[23] As historians have grappled with new cultural history of the war and its impact on the twentieth century, they have become increasingly interested in the ways in which ordinary Europeans experienced and found meaning in the trauma of mass industrial war. This fruitful line of debate has been catalyzed by innovative readings of older sources and the successful mining of archival material that provide insight into the relationships between authorities and civil society in Western Europe.[24] Recent studies of

23 This cultural turn in First World War Studies was a truly international project. Three of the outstanding early exemplars were Gerhard Hirschfeld, Gerd Krumeich, and Irina Renz, eds, *Keiner fühlt sich hier mehr als Mensch : Erlebnis und Wirkung des Ersten Weltkriegs* (Essen: Klartext, 1993); Mosse (1990); and Jay Winter, *Sites of Memory, Sites of Mourning : The Great War in European Cultural History* (New York: Cambridge University Press, 1995).

24 Belinda Davis, *Home Fires Burning: Food, Politics, and Everyday Life in World War I Berlin* (Chapel Hill: University of North Carolina Press, 2000); and Niall Ferguson, *The Pity of War* (London: Penguin, 1998).

violence and the legacies of conflict have moved toward a nuanced approach to wartime violence that takes into account exceptional regional variation and the importance of gender as a category of analysis.[25]

Out of these distinct but related fields of inquiry has emerged an interest in what Francophone historians have called *culture de guerre*, the study of how contemporaries during and after the conflict represented, discussed, and found meaning in the shared experience of mass industrial war. This interest in war culture has diffused throughout the international community of scholarship on the First World War.[26] Advocates of studying war culture have been criticized for ignoring or marginalizing the social, economic, and military history of the war, a charge is that is not wholly unfounded, but it is clear that the war's social and cultural historians have much to share with each other. At the very least, historians have acknowledged that the battle lines and the home front cannot be understood in isolation from each other.

This focus on the war as a lived experience and the relationship between front and home front leads to broader interpretive questions of consent, dissent, and enthusiasm in wartime societies. This apparent disjuncture between the obvious horrors of the war and the widespread support that it enjoyed during most of its course has fostered a fruitful inquiry into the ways in which states and societies negotiated the increasing totality of the war. The behaviors that Pierre Purseigle and others have termed "belligerence" were not axiomatic; they had to be created and fostered.[27] Issues of mobilization and motivation, which circumscribe the ability of governments and societies to prepare for and sustain armed conflict, have received a great deal of scholarly attention.[28] Janet Watson, in her study of

25 See Dirk Schumann, "Europa, der Erste Weltkrieg und die Nachkriegszeit: eine Kontinuität der Gewalt?," *Journal of Modern European History* 1 (2003) and *Politische Gewalt in der Weimarer Republik: Kampf um die Straße und Furcht vor dem Bürgerkrieg* (Essen: Klartext, 2001). John Horne approaches the subject of violence and conflict from structural and ideological perspectives in "War and Conflict in Contemporary European Society, 1914–2004," *Zeithistorische Forschungen / Studies in Contemporary History* 3 (2004). Karen Hagemann and Stephanie Schüler-Springorum, eds, *Home/Front: The Military, War, and Gender in Twentieth-Century Germany* (Oxford: Berg, 2002); Bernd Weisbrod explores the "acceptance of illegal political violence" in interwar Germany in "Gewalt und der Politik. Zur politischen Kultur in Deutschland zwischen den beiden Weltkriegen," *Geschischte in Wissenschaft und Unterricht* 43 (1992): 392.

26 Leonard Smith, "The 'Culture de guerre' and French Historiography of the Great War of 1914–18," *History Compass*, 5/6 (2007), 1967–1979.

27 Pierre Purseigle, "Warfare and Belligerence: Approaches to the First World War" in Pierre Purseigle, ed. *Warfare and Belligerence: Perspectives in First World War Studies* (Leiden: Brill, 2005), 18.

28 N.F. Dreiziger, ed., *Mobilization for Total War: The Canadian, American, and British Experience, 1914–1918* (Waterloo: Wilfred Laurier University Press, 1981); John Horne, ed., *State, Society, and Mobilization during the First World War* (Cambridge: Cambridge University Press, 1997); and Jeffrey Verhey, *The Spirit of 1914: Militarization,*

the war experience in Britain, suggests that gender and class differences so marked contemporary understandings of the conflict that Britons might be said to have been "fighting different wars" between 1914 and 1918.[29]

It is all the more remarkable that more attention has not been paid to the demobilization, which occurred at the end of the war. The various formal agreements that brought the conflict to an end have been extensively debated by historians of European diplomacy.[30] The economic and political crises of the 1970s inspired an earlier generation of historians to examine the aftermath of the war in terms of economic and structural transformation and the "revolutionary" character of postwar dissent.[31]

Historical studies of the end of the First World War, and indeed of war termination in general, are still closely tied to national boundaries.[32] Largely due to the traumatic memory of the interwar period, historians of France have been responsible for pushing the boundaries of the study of the First World War's aftermath.[33] John Horne has explored the process of "cultural demobilization" that took place between 1918 and 1933 as French men and women reinterpreted and revisited the war years, broadly challenging and contesting its meaning.

Myth, and Mobilization in Germany (Cambridge: Cambridge University Press, 2000). For two interesting discussions of the self-mobilization of intellectuals, see Becker and Audoin-Rouzeau as well as Martha Hanna, *The Mobilization of Intellect: French Writers and Scholars During the Great War* (Cambridge: Harvard University Press, 1996).

29 Janet S.K. Watson, *Fighting Different Wars: Experience, Memory, and the First World War in Britain* (Cambridge: Cambridge University Press, 2004).

30 Recent contributions to this voluminous literature include Manfred F. Boemeke, Gerald D. Feldman and Elisabeth Glaser, eds, *The Treaty of Versailles: A Reassessment After 75 Years* (Cambridge: Cambridge University Press, 1998); Gerd Krumeich, ed., *Versailles 1919 : Ziele, Wirkung, Wahrnehmung* (Essen: Klartext, 2001); and Margaret Macmillan, *Paris 1919: Six Months that Changed the World* (New York: Random House, 2002).

31 See, for instance Charles Bertrand, ed., *Situations Révolutionaires en Europe, 1917–1922: Allegmagne, Italie, Autriche-Hongrie* (Montreal: Centre Interuniversitaire d'Études Européenes, 1977), the proceedings of a conference on the subject. Albert Lindemann's *The Red Years: European Socialism versus Bolshevism, 1919–1921* (Berkeley: University of California Press, 1974) offers an international perspective on a specific range of political movements.

32 Two very different but outstanding examples are Richard Bessel, *Germany After the First World War* (Oxford: Clarendon, 1993) and Michael Gambone, *The Greatest Generation Comes Home: The Veteran in American Society* (College Station: Texas A&M Press, 2005).

33 In addition to titles above, see Stéphane Audouin-Rouzeau, *Cinq deuils de guerre* (Paris: éd. Noêsis, 2001); Annette Becker, 'Du 14 juillet 1919 au 11 novembre 1920, Mort où est ta victoire', *Vingtieme Siècle*, 49, 31–44; Antoine Prost, "Les représentations de la guerre dans la culture française de l'entre-deux-guerres," *Vingtième Siècle*, 41, 23–31 and *In the Wake of War: 'Les Anciens Combattants' and French Society, 1914–39* (Providence: Berg, 1992). Also Daniel J. Sherman, *The Construction of Memory in Interwar France* (Chicago: University of Chicago Press, 1999).

This "cooling of passions," Horne argues, was part of a broader "demobilization of the mind" that necessarily followed the industrial slaughter of the First World War.[34] Bruno Cabanes's recent work on the varied and problematic experiences of French troops returning home or on occupation duty after 1918 reminds us of how complex a process it is to demobilize an army, the importance of cultural demobilization, and the crucial role played by returning troops in shaping the narrative of the war experience.[35]

The past decade has seen an explosion of comparative and transnational studies of the war, driven by unprecedented interest in the war and its impact on Europe's twentieth century.[36] As military historians begin to grapple with the transnational dimensions of war, it is becoming clear that we cannot hope to fully understand modern war as an accretion of national phenomena but only as a complex and interconnected network of national, subnational, and international experiences.[37] As the recent work of Maria Bucur and others demonstrates, historians of gender are now beginning to consider the transnational dimensions of warfare by exploring the relationship between gender, sacrifice, and identity in the era of the world wars.[38]

Urban histories of "everyday life" during wartime have greatly enhanced our understanding of how the experience of war was lived by large numbers of Europeans.[39] Some of this work has been transnational in scope, suggesting that there are important commonalities across the urban landscape that transcend national boundaries.[40] Transnational history offers a way for historians to understand how events are experienced across national borders without eliding the very real

34 Horne and others involved in the "Demobilizing the Mind: Culture, Politics, and the Legacy of the Great War, 1918–33" conference in Dublin in 2001 pioneered the use of the term. See John Horne, "Presentation," *14–18 aujourd'hui*, 4 (May 2002): 48.

35 Bruno Cabanes, *La Victoire Endeuillée: La Sortie de Guerre des Soldats Francais, 1918–1920* (Paris: Éditions du Seuil, 2004).

36 Manfred Boemeke, Roger Chickering, and Stig Förster, eds, *Anticipating Total War: The German and American Experiences, 1871–1914* (Cambridge: Cambridge University Press, 1999) as well as the other volumes in the excellent series of publications on the concept of total war sponsored by the German Historical Institute.

37 An excellent summary of this argument can be found in Ute Frevert, "Europeanizing German History," *Bulletin of the German Historical Institute*, 36 (Spring 2005), 12–15.

38 Maria Bucur, ed. *Gender and War in Twentieth-Century Eastern Europe* (Bloomington: Indiana University Press, 2006). Also Hagemann and Schüler-Springorum.

39 Among many examples are Chickering; Davis, *Home Fires Burning*; Maureen Healy, *Vienna and the Fall of the Hapsburg Empire: Total War and Everyday Life in WWI* (New York: Cambridge University Press, 2004).

40 Marcus Funck and Roger Chickering, eds, *Endangered Cities: Military Power and Urban Societies in the Era of the World Wars* (Boston: Brill, 2004) and Jay Winter and Jean-Louis Robert, eds, *Capital Cities at War: London, Paris, Berlin, 1914–1919* (Cambridge: Cambridge University Press, 1997).

differences of national political and organization cultures.[41] The experience of war in the age of the nation-state offers a particularly rich opportunity for transnational history since it is self-evidently a set of events and processes that occur more or less simultaneously across a number of national states. The fundamental question in the construction of transnational models for understanding war rests on the issue of identifying discreet units of analysis that can be productively examined across national boundaries. While military institutions offer an obvious avenue for transnational or comparative study of war, understanding the behavior of societies at war proves considerably more diffuse.

In recent years, historians have begun using subnational units like cities and regions to further refine the methodology of transnational history and to try to avoid the lack of precision and specificity that bedeviled more traditional models of comparative history.[42] Philipp Ther has argued that comparative urban history offers, among other things, a way for historians to discuss issues across national boundaries without falling prey to the problem of making claims based on large and unwieldy units of analysis like national states.[43] War is a transnational event that is experienced at the national, regional, and local levels. Such a pervasive and complex phenomenon calls for an effort toward what Roger Chickering memorably termed "total history."[44]

While Chickering's total history must necessarily rely on the sort of thick description and archival breadth that he employed in his study of a German city at war, these problems can usefully be addressed transnationally. The war, both as a moment of tremendous violence and a transformative experience on the home front, lies at the center of such an analysis. The industrial societies of Western Europe, despite broad national differences, entered the second decade of the twentieth century facing a range of problems that were not only similar, they were related. The challenges of working-class politics, economic interdependency, an arms race on land and at sea, and the questions of urban reform in Europe's

41 Deborah Cohen, "Comparative History: Buyer Beware," *Bulletin of the German Historical Institute*. 29 (Fall 2001): 26. See also Deborah Cohen and Maura O'Conner, eds, *Comparison and History: Europe in Cross-National Perspective* (New York, Routledge, 2004) and Kiran Klaus Patel's perceptive *"Nach der Nationalfixierheit: Perspektiven einer transnationalen Geschichte"* (Antrittsvorlesung: Humbolt-Universität zu Berlin, January, 2004), 11.

42 Michael Schäfer, *Bürgertum in der Krise: Städtische Mittelklassen in Edinburgh und Leipzig, 1890 bis 1930* (Göttingen: Vandenhoeck und Rupprecht, 2003) and Andreas Wirsching, *Vom Weltkrieg zum Bürgerkrieg? Politischer Extremismus in Deutschland und Frankreich 1918–1933/39. Berlin und Paris im Vergleich* (Munich: Oldenbourg, 1999). A recent summary over the literature on East-Central Europe can be found in Alena Janatkov and Hanna Kozinska-Witt, eds, *Wohnen in der Großstadt 1900–1939: Wohnen und Kultur in Östlichen Mitteleuropa* (Stuttgart: Franz Steiner, 2006).

43 Philipp Ther, "Beyond the Nation: The Relational Basis of a Comparative History of Germany and Europe," *Central European History* 36, no. 1: 72.

44 Chickering, *The Great War and Urban Life*, 2.

burgeoning cities were not bounded by national borders. These initial conditions into which European states and societies embarked on the project of mass industrial war suggest that the conflict generated broadly similar sets of crises within these societies and a correspondingly limited range of options for dealing with those that emerged from the war years.

Comparing two cities in peacetime is difficult, all the more so when those cities are part of vast national war efforts. Decisions normally made in city halls were now made in offices and army headquarters often far from the places where their effects would be most directly felt. The historian's task becomes all the more complicated when it was sometimes even unclear to participants just who had the authority to resolve crucial disputes over housing, wages, labor, or food. The team assembled by Jay Winter and Jean-Louis Robert and the French scholar Pierre Pursiegle, among others, have recently grappled with the tremendous archival and interpretive problems of looking comparatively and transnationally at cities as units of analysis that reveal much about the impact of war on urban communities.[45] This study argues that such comparisons are equally useful in understanding the years after the war, when many of the mechanisms involved in national mobilization reversed, even if slowly and sometimes haltingly.

Munich and Manchester were and remain very different cities, with distinct historical trajectories. Comparisons between Britain and Germany, two of the most successful industrial powers in the world at the turn of the century, have long wrestled with the very real differences in political, historical, and organizational culture in those two powers.[46] Nonetheless, these two urban areas shared certain important and reasonably obvious features. Munich and Manchester were and are regional political and economic centers, geographically removed from their national capitals and offering counterweights to the power of the national state. Each had been shaped by the explosive expansion of industrial and urban Europe in the nineteenth century, giving them populations shaped by the experience of migration and urban development.

While historians have long debated the "exceptional" nature of Britain or Germany, these cities were exceptions (and proudly so) within their national communities.[47] Identity as a Mancunian or a Münchner/in was based in large part on not being from the distant national metropolis. This self-conscious local or

45 Pierre Purseigle, "Mobilisation, Sacrifice et Citoyenneté. Contribution à l'histoire des communautés locales face à la guerre. Angleterre – France, 1914–1918." PhD Diss. University of Toulouse II, 2006; Winter and Robert.

46 The long list includes Deborah Cohen, *The War Come Home: Disabled Veterans in Britain and Germany, 1914–1939* (Berkeley: University of California Press, 2001; Jan Rüger, *The Great Naval Game: Britain and Germany in the Age of Empire* (Cambridge: Cambridge University Press, 2007), and Schäfer.

47 David Blackbourn and Geoff Eley, *The Peculiarities of German History: Bourgeois Society and Politics in Nineteenth-Century Germany* (Oxford: Oxford University Press, 1984).

regional particularism had important political consequences in wartime, when the legal reach of those distant capitals grew exponentially at the real or perceived cost of local interests. As will be developed much more fully in Chapter 1, bureaucrats and political leaders in both cities had made urban reform a priority in the decades before the war. This conscious consensus-building forged political cultures that both reflected and diverged from national trends. The upheaval of war stalled or reversed much of this and set the conditions for the emergence of a very different postwar politics.

The primary axis of comparison in this book is the interaction between these local/regional institutions, civil society, and the state. This story is as much about the perception of power as it is about the machinery of authority. Wartime blurred the lines of responsibility that had developed in the course of the long nineteenth century. The war years saw the creation of multiple layers of bureaucracy and authority that then transformed or dissolved when the war ended. At precisely the same time that the vast majority of combatant populations came to believe that they were owed tangible rewards for their years of service and sacrifice, the mechanisms for achieving those ends changed dramatically once more.

The result of this was a crisis, felt across the former combatants, over the reciprocal relationship between the state, local and regional authorities, and various elements within civil society. Reciprocity has three implicit components: obligation, expectation, and outcome. Obligation is critical because all parties in a reciprocal relationship must believe that it is not only desirable but necessary to satisfy the needs of the party that has provided them with benefit. Each party must expect that they will receive the concessions they desire from the other parties in order to provide the needed incentives to make the sacrifices demanded by the relationship. Finally, since reciprocity is a positive feedback loop, all parties must be able to identify quantifiable outcomes of the relationship that in turn engender further reciprocal action.

In the case of European states and societies in the wake of the First World War, the obligatory function was a product of the war years. Repeated evocations of the "Thanks of the Fatherland" and a land "Fit for Heroes" were so often repeated (and proved so manifestly inadequate) that they have become clichés. However, mobilization during the long years of war was not just a top-down process. The self-mobilization of European societies was, as we shall see in this study, also predicated on the idea that the world after the war would be better than the one before. Between state-sponsored mobilization and self-mobilization lay the consensus that sacrifice was necessary for the common good. In contradistinction, dissent and dissenters rejected that common purpose and acted either on behalf of the enemy or against the interests of the national community.

Expectation became increasingly important as the war entered its remobilization and concluding phases. Since the rhetoric of impending victory became less efficacious with the passing of years, the hope and language of "holding on" characterized the terrible late war years, particularly in Germany. This served in no small part to detach obligation from victory. The act of endurance, rather than the potential outcome of triumph, became the basis for the relationship of reciprocity. This was a crucial step, since it assured that citizens of a defeated and exhausted Germany could stake just as clear a claim on the postwar political community as could their former enemies in a victorious and exhausted Britain.

The end of the war and the first few years of peace witnessed a wide variety of outcomes in former combatant states that reflected real efforts at reform. Women voted for the first time in several countries, including Britain and Germany. Housing reform became a real priority and for many, living standards improved. Despite seemingly overwhelming challenges, millions of men returned home from military service and economies haltingly converted to civilian production. Yet these were also years of intense crisis in large part because the successes seemed to pale in comparison to the challenges left outstanding.

The European crisis of reciprocity can be best understood as an agglomeration of national, regional, and local experiences. Yet the widespread dissatisfaction, commonly referred to as "disillusionment" in the wake of the war was a fact of life in victorious and defeated states alike within a few years of the conflict's end. The scale of the promises made by states during wartime and understood by populations encouraged to express their own visions of the future proved simply too great and all too often mutually contradictory. However profound the actual outcomes were, they could not be enough to prevent the evident failure of reciprocity.

While it would be simple to attribute the stability of the postwar regime in Britain to the fact of victory and the concurrent instability in Germany to defeat, there were processes at work in both places that can tell us much about the nature of "total war" and the relationship between the conflict and its aftermath. As this study will demonstrate, the different character of the failure of reciprocity in Britain and Germany was rooted in different approaches to a set of wartime challenges. While many Germans and Britons grew disillusioned in the wake of the war, the illusions which proved to be false or impossible were different in important and instructive ways.

In Britain, the state based its wartime mobilization strategy for much of the war on a minimally intrusive approach in which local officials played a critical and public role in decision-making. Elements within civil society at the local level knew or believed that they could appeal to local officials for redress of grievances, and the not infrequent victories of protestors suggested that the apparatus of mobilization was flexible in its responses to pressure. In the wake of the war, when authorities did not respond adequately to demands for reform, protestors came to believe that those authorities were *unwilling* to live up to wartime promises. The solution, therefore, was to compel authorities to live up to their reciprocal obligations, but to do so largely within a system-supporting framework. To do otherwise, many reasoned, risked forfeiting the legitimate claims that they had. Radicals who urged a rejection of the system had difficulty because those whom they were trying to convince believed that the system was capable of producing the outcome they desired.

On the other hand, in Germany the system of wartime mobilization created the impression that officials were unresponsive to local conditions. As the state put itself forward as the ultimate arbiter of political and economic life, then singularly failed to adequately provide for the material needs of its population, dissenters found purchase with calls to replace the state. When postwar authorities proved no less capable of resolving the crises of demobilization, dissenters who argued that those authorities were *unable* to live up to their reciprocal obligations gained legitimacy. The result was the widespread and increasing legitimation of alternative ideas and political constellations which promised radical revision of the terms of demobilization.

This crucial distinction between inability and unwillingness was not simply a product of the war's outcome. It was rooted in the different approaches to wartime mobilization and the strategies these states employed in sustaining wartime consensus. Choices made in wartime circumscribed the paths available during the postwar transition period. "Total war" did not and could not end with the cessation of hostilities, precisely because the explicit and implicit promises made by wartime states proved so difficult to fulfill in the wake of victory or defeat.

In a time of war, in which the state assumed ever greater authority to manage the war, the persistence of local and regional authority mediated between the power of the state and the demands of civil society. This was particularly true in debates over the issues traditionally managed by municipal authorities, like housing and the provision of public welfare. However, the increasing demands of the state frequently limited the ability of municipal authorities to carry out these tasks or, as frequently happened in the case of housing, halted or reversed the efforts of local governments to manage these conflicts.[48]

During the period of demobilization, as the state surrendered some of the power it assumed during the war, local and regional authorities found themselves trying to balance between restive populations and the planning and execution of the postwar transition. In both victorious and defeated states, demobilization was often every bit as much a surprise as mobilization had been. National priorities, which in both cases included the maintenance of employment and the safe reduction of the armed forces, proved formidable to put into place at the local level.

These challenges can be seen most clearly at points of conflict, so it is these nexuses that I use to organize much of this volume. Across Europe, this was a time of demonstrations. Freed from wartime restrictions on speech and assembly, the "politics of the streets" in Europe centered on tangible gains owed to European populations in the wake of the war.[49] Crowds assembled to protest rations, to

48 For a robust critique of the idea of total war as an instrument of complete national mobilization, see Roger Chickering, "World War I and the Theory of Total War," in Roger Chickering and Stig Förster, eds, *Great War, Total War: Combat and Mobilization on the Western Front, 1914–1918* (Cambridge: Cambridge University Press, 2000), 35–53.

49 Thomas Lindenberger, *Strassenpolitik: Zur Sozialgeschichte der öffentlichen Ordnung in Berlin 1900 bis 1914* (Bonn: Dietz, 1995).

demand better housing, to urge an end to the war or to show their support for it. They welcomed heroes and hurled abuse at those who they believed had failed them. In the years after the war, a new and dangerous language of social revolution crept into their banners and written demands. In their calls for reciprocity, we can see the European dimensions of the crises of demobilization. To whom did they address their sometimes competing claims? What did they hope to achieve? What kind of language did they find effective and why? How did authorities deal with this challenge and what can those responses tell us about the postwar world?

We cannot understand demobilization simply as a postwar phenomenon. It had its origins in the events of the war years. Demobilization began long before the end of the war as planners, bureaucrats, and ordinary Europeans discussed and debated the postwar future. As authorities struggled to manage the demands what John Horne has called the "remobilization" of 1917 and 1918, they began to consider the transition that would follow the end of hostilities.[50] These visions of demobilization were necessarily predicated on the victory of the national polity. Coordinating with military and national/imperial authorities, local bureaucrats focused on managing the economic and social transformation that would inevitably follow when the industrial arrangements of the war came to an end and on the potentially dangerous return of soldiers and sailors intent on getting their old jobs back.

At the same time, debates within civil society over the future drew from wartime rhetoric of sacrifice that would lead to real reforms in the wake of the victorious conclusion of hostilities. Governments at all levels promised a better world in the wake of the war, and these promises were echoed and amplified within combatant societies as different visions emerged and competed with each other. Adding to this complexity was the emergence of significant cracks in the wartime consensus in 1917 and 1918. As conditions worsened at home, the fragile social peace of the war years began to splinter.

This book is organized chronologically and comparatively, in order to emphasize the important role played by contingency and context in shaping the narrative. The first chapter of this book provides background material on the two cities under discussion and a broad overview of European urbanism in the early twentieth century. This is critical because, as I argue, the debates that shaped demobilization were shaped by pre-existing trends in European urban politics. While conflicts over housing, labor rights, and the growing power of working-class political organizations were not completely suspended during the war, they were circumscribed by wartime demands and often formally restricted by emergency legislation. Wartime propaganda intended to foster and maintain mobilization often directly addressed these prewar concerns and the postwar conflicts over reciprocity had their roots in these debates.

The three sections that follow track each city through the lens of several key themes. The first section deals with the last year of the war, the second the instability

50 John Horne, "Remobilizing for 'total war': France and Great Britain, 1917–1918", in Horne, ed., *State, Society, and Mobilization*, 195–211.

and uncertainty of 1919, and finally the normalization period of 1920 and 1921. It begins during the last years of the war, when both sides had ample reason to believe that they would emerge from the conflict triumphant. As planning staffs worked to ensure a workable machinery of demobilization, wartime populations seriously debated the postwar future. While the experience of defeat obviously limited both the viability and the legitimacy of wartime planning in Germany, the circumstances of the end of hostilities and the very uncertainties of victory paradoxically heightened the feelings of disillusionment among those ostensibly on the winning side.[51]

Section I examines the problems of mobilization and remobilization during the last of the war. Each chapter outlines the problems of economic mobilization, food distribution, popular culture at war, and evolving debates over the postwar future in both cities. These chapters demonstrate the central relationship between the ways in which governments and societies managed wartime mobilization and the multiple crises of the postwar world.

This period was defined by a growing uncertainty on the part of combatant governments that their populations were going to be able to stand the strain of more years of war. Domestic propaganda, always a crucial part of the war effort, increased dramatically and shifted focus to emphasize the virtues of endurance rather than the assurance of victory. Real cracks emerged in domestic consensus as the margins of dissent mobilized against the war. Demobilization became a central discussion in political life in large part because wartime governments felt that they had to discuss the postwar world in order to suggest a better future to societies whose continued cooperation was far from certain.

This period was also marked by growing unrest over the effects of the war on consumer society. This unrest was not typically outside of a framework of loyalty to the state, but as authorities began to see dissent in every act of protest, they became more likely to see disloyalty and hidden hands in every angry food line. These wartime developments, particularly the radicalization of dissent and counter-dissent, shaped the course of the years to come. The revolutions in Russia provided a new and radical language that could be deployed by both protestors and authorities, effectively reducing opportunities for compromise between them.

The war's end ushered in a year of dramatic and sometimes violent change across these two cities, their respective states, and indeed Europe. Section II examines the year that followed the Armistice, during which the apparatus of demobilization first envisioned during the last years of the war lurched into operation as postwar transformation affected victorious and defeated societies alike. These chapters look at postwar political transition, the return of the troops, the demobilization of the economy, and the growth of radical challenges to the postwar order.

In Munich, regional and imperial authority collapsed within days of each other, ushering in a period of political turmoil that culminated in the bloody collapse of a

---

51 This idea is developed in Samuel Hynes, *A War Imagined: The First World War in English Culture* (London: Atheneum, 1991).

radical government. This story is the familiar one for Munich, a city on its way to the Beer Hall Putsch of 1923 and the eventual rise of Nazism. However, to focus only on those sanguinary and sometimes surreal events misses the larger context in which they happened. The end of the war brought tens of thousands of troops home, changed the industrial landscape of the city once again, and fundamentally altered the lives of the urban population. While the apparent "self-demobilization" of the German armies alleviated some of the pressure on planners, the postwar government of Munich and Bavaria faced considerable challenges in effectively managing the return of the troops and their peaceful reintegration into society.

Manchester saw the same sort of pressures but with a government that could take the credit for a long-hoped-for victory rather than the blame for defeat. This was, however, by no means clear at the time. If there was no violent conflict in the English Northwest that year, such an outcome was not unthinkable to many watching events on the ground. Discussions of the end of the war were suffused with the language of inequality and injustice even before the celebrations that marked the Armistice fully ended. The planned industrial and economic reconfiguration of the city and region proved extraordinarily painful in the short term as national and regional authorities negotiated the dismantling of wartime economic institutions. Organized protests which had been limited by emergency legislation during the war re-emerged in the streets to challenge what was widely perceived to be uneven and unfair demobilization planning.

Throughout this process bureaucrats and civic leaders faced the challenge of ensuring a peaceful transition from wartime to postwar. Growing fears of radicalized veterans, while more acute in unstable Munich, were a common feature of European urban life after the war. When combined with economic uncertainty, postwar unemployment, and the growing assertiveness of labor and women's organizations, 1919 proved to be a year of instability and the real and imagined threat of violence.

Section III examines the two years that followed. This period saw the stabilization of postwar political life and the dismantling of most of the remaining wartime institutions and restrictions. In both cities, this period was marked by the juxtaposition between a return to normality and a set of related crises both within and from outside that threatened the precarious peace of the postwar order. The results of these crises were very different and had enormous implications for the subsequent histories of Munich, Manchester, and their respective national polities.

The return of formal political life was a critical component of this process of normalization. As governments and civil societies debated the scale and scope of postwar reforms, issues stemming from demobilization remained at the center of political life and language. Gradually, debates over the war shifted in focus from efforts to address specific issues emerging from the end of the conflict to a contest over the war's meaning and who possessed the legitimate right to commemorate and memorialize the war and its dead. In this section, I will examine the role the war played in fostering the growth of extremist groups and political parties.

These, in turn, helped to foster a climate in which people used rhetorics of violence to discuss politics, polarizing already divided societies even further.

Manchester witnessed the full flowering of what is perhaps the most important paradox of demobilization: that winning the war ultimately made it more difficult for people to accept the limits of reconstruction and postwar reform. Having endured a war in which the state promised extensive housing and labor reforms, the chronic unemployment and slow progress of new construction was a bitter pill for many Mancunians. At the same time, the civil war in Ireland spilled over into the immigrant communities of the Northwest, starting a cycle of sporadic but escalating violence that called into question the solidity of postwar English industrial society.

In Munich, despite episodic political instability like that engendered by the Kapp Putsch in early 1920, this period was marked by an uneasy return to normalcy after chaos of the immediate postwar period. A series of large and well-organized public demonstrations challenged the new order from various points along the political spectrum in postwar Germany. While this period witnessed the emergence of a new strain of German right-wing politics that eventually coalesced into a powerful electoral force, such an outcome was not apparent in the first years of the 1920s. What is clear in the multitude of political positions being espoused on the streets of Munich during those years was the struggle to claim ownership of the suffering of the war years.

By examining the experiences of these two cities side-by-side, we can see the remarkable degree to which they shared the challenges of preparing for and adjusting to the world after the war. Despite obvious and often instructive differences, patterns emerged that can tell us much about the transnational character of demobilization, mass industrial war, and European society in the twentieth century.

The physical demobilization of returning troops offers an interesting point of comparison between the two localities. On the surface, there could not be a clearer contrast between the slow but ordered draw-down of British armed forces and the chaotic self-demobilization of the Imperial German Army and its component parts. However, it is clear that urban authorities in both places looked with considerable trepidation at the returning troops, who themselves had good reason to want order maintained to speed the process of transition.

The self-demobilization of the German armed forces at the end of the war did much to relieve the postwar government of the responsibility for bringing troops home to be paid and disarmed. It also created a vacuum in both security and legitimacy that provided ample space for militia formations. While local and national authorities believed themselves to be in control of those formations, in a number of instances this did not prove to be the case. The result was a wave of paramilitary activity that typified the perilous security situation in interwar Germany. In Britain, the fact of victory made the initial physical demobilization that much more difficult as soldiers and sailors balked at long waits to return home. The resulting strikes, which spread from France to the north of England, seemed to suggest a kind of assertiveness that posed a threat to the civilian control of the military. In both cases, the greatest fear among authorities was of a violent and chaotic homecoming by troops that might threaten civil order and the rule of civilian law. Paradoxically, and despite anxieties to the contrary, this aspect of demobilization proved in many ways easier in defeated Munich than in ostensibly victorious Manchester. Victory raised expectations far beyond what the wartime and postwar governments could provide.

It is in the realm of economic and social policy that we can most clearly see parallels between the two postwar situations. Both societies faced similar pressures in finding work for returning troops, finding a way to deal with the vast number of women who had entered the formal political and economic sphere during the war, and in withdrawing controls on civil society without causing chaos. These issues faced any postwar government, regardless of victory or defeat, and proved all but intractable in both circumstances. The key difference was that in Manchester, local authorities turned to the private sector for much of the impetus to recreate economic stability, while successive local and regional governments in Bavaria took much of the task of managing the postwar economy on themselves. Both approaches proved to be problematic. In Manchester, authorities appeared uninspired and heartless in their engagement with the problem of unemployment. In Munich, the worsening economic situation simply proved to be overwhelming, linking the government with failure. Housing was an acute problem, at least in the short term, in both cities. The manifest inadequacy of both wartime and postwar housing plans further undermined public confidence in government. While meaningful housing reform became a reality later in the decade, the widespread expectation that the end of the war would bring an end to the substandard housing that was an inescapable fact of life in European cities proved to be a source of bitterness in victorious and defeated states.

The sphere of cultural demobilization was the most diffuse of the facets discussed here. In both cities, we have seen the profound effect of the war on political language, concerns about public morality, and the individual mentalities of warriors and those whose lives had been shaped by the conflict. There was widespread agreement that the war had fundamentally undone something in what contemporaries would have called "civilization" or "culture." Both state-sponsored and privately-generated propaganda encouraged combatant populations to despise their nation's enemies, a list that grew to include social revolutionaries who seemed to be lurking around every corner. Popular perceptions of rising crime and deviant sexual behavior manifested themselves in nativist groups who blamed the war and its consequences for the increasing presence of immigrants and social undesirables. That such xenophobia flourished in the last years and aftermath of the conflict suggests how profoundly Europeans internalized the wartime debates over masculinity, race, and exclusionary nationalism. These developments were the hardest to roll back when the fighting came to an end.

This is not an effort to explain the exceptional path taken by the German state in the interwar period, or to rationalize Munich's emergence as the "Capital City" of the National Socialist movement. Nor does it intend to validate the survival or parliamentary government in Britain despite the challenges of war, turmoil, and Depression during the same years. Rather than to vindicate or attack the idea of a "*Sonderweg*" (special path) in British or German history, I propose that a victorious and a defeated state and its citizens in the wake of the First World War faced a remarkably similar set of choices, problems, and constraints in the postwar period. In the end, Munich emerged from the postwar period with wide space and real legitimacy available to radical groups of a variety of ideologies and affinities. In Manchester, much of that space was closed off or limited by 1921. This outcome was also not apparent to anyone in 1918. To understand how these two urban sites and the people who lived in and around them, emerged from the postwar period, we must examine the complex story of demobilization and the transition from war to peace.

The lens through which I tell this story is the lived experience of the men and women living in two European cities. Conditions on the ground were shaped by policies being made and interpreted by authorities at the national, regional, and local levels, while the streets often served as a place where crowds could voice their displeasure or dissent against those policies. Telling this story requires a focus on the interaction between civil society and bureaucracy, a relationship that is often difficult to untangle from readily available sources.

The expansion of wartime bureaucracies with their mandate and mania for social control makes this task quite a bit easier for the historian. This is particularly true in Germany, where the preparation of "mood reports" (*Stimmungsberichte*) was a regular function of factory inspectors, police, and military intelligence personnel. There is no equivalent to these rich texts in Britain, though the intense interaction between officials of various ministries and local bureaucrats produced a good deal of detailed surveillance of industrial and military facilities. The popular press provides important sources for the period, though it must be recognized that for much of the time under discussion regulations attempted to control what the public could read.

While archival source material generated by the wartime bureaucracies are almost unwieldy in the depth of their reportage, they must be used with great care. Often they tell far more about the *mentalité* of minor functionaries than they do of the ordinary people who were the subject of the reports. This is not necessarily a terrible hindrance, since it was precisely the interaction between these bureaucrats and the great mass of the population that shaped the stories being told here.

The experience of demobilization, rooted in the events of wartime, helped to shape the conflicts and consensus of the 1920s. Demobilization was neither a wartime or a postwar phenomenon. It bridged the apparent caesura of November 11, 1918 just as the war connected the long nineteenth and short twentieth centuries. Demobilization was a complex and contested process, negotiated between societies and states engaged in bitter conflict. Even in the darkest days of war, there were visions of a coming peace. In late October 1918, Clementine Churchill wrote to her husband, then in France, about her present anxieties and, more hopefully, about a world beyond war:

> It is a rather awful spectacle, two great Empires cracking, swaying & on the verge of toppling into ruins – If only these things could happen gradually and tidily… Meanwhile my Darling do come home and look after what is to be done with the Munition Workers when the fighting really does stop…. I have got a plan – Can't the men Munition Workers build lovely garden cities & pull down slums in places like Bethnal Green, Newcastle, Glasgow, Leeds, etc. & can't the women munition workers make all the lovely furniture for them – Baby's cradles, cupboards, etc.?[52]

The end of the First World War took place at the intersection of visions like Clementine Churchill's and the political and economic realities of a continent engaged in a prolonged and devastating war. To understand the genesis of these postwar visions, we must begin with the dynamic, vibrant, and fractious story of urban Europe on the cusp of the largest war the continent had yet seen.

52 Mary Soames, ed., *Winston and Clementine: The Personal Letters of the Churchills* (New York: Mariner, 2001), 216.

Chapter 1
Manchester, Munich, and Urban Europe in 1914

Before the war came the skylines. In 1867 and 1868 respectively, Munich and Manchester began construction of new homes for their city governments. While Munich's *Rathaus* took nearly four decades to complete compared to Manchester's speedier nine-year building process, both of these new buildings symbolized broader trends in European urban architecture and life. These sweeping gothic revival structures deliberately evoked the majesty and power of medieval town governance, self-consciously asserting the prosperity and authority of urban governments. For Mancunians, the new Town Hall on Albert Square symbolized the power of the municipal corporation and its autonomous identity. In Munich, Georg von Hauberrisser's building on the *Marienplatz* seemed calculated to remind the inhabitants of the royal *Residenz* a few blocks away of the assertiveness and economic power of the bourgeois nineteenth-century social order.[1]

If we concentrate only on the profound changes that the postwar period witnessed across the continent, we ignore the very real sense in which the war was a parenthesis in the much longer story of urban development in Europe. While the history of European industrialization and urbanization was uneven and highly geographically specific, it is clear that significant trends emerged by the second half of the nineteenth century that make it possible to consider urban development as a transnational or continental phenomenon.[2] Trends that were evident in the prewar urban landscape did not vanish into the maw of the war. Instead, they were temporarily halted, diverted, or mobilized into the national war effort and emerged after the war.

Three such trends are critical to examine here, since they helped to determine the shape, scope, and ultimate outcome of demobilization in Munich and Manchester. First was the changing face of urban politics in early twentieth-century Europe. As working-class political parties across Western Europe transformed, haltingly and unevenly, into local and national governments, the nineteenth-century bourgeois political order appeared increasingly imperiled. Second was the changing face of Europe's industrial cities as they drew migrants from within and outside the national state. Finally, urban reform movements attempted to address the evident

---

1 Alan Kidd, *Manchester* (Edinburgh: Edinburgh University Press, 2002), 153 and Richard Bauer, *Geschichte Münchens* (Munich: C.H. Beck, 2005), 130.

2 Sidney Pollard, *Peaceful Conquest: The Industrialization of Europe, 1760–1970* (Oxford: Oxford University Press, 1981), 84–7.

inequalities and inefficiencies of city life. Ultimately, these issues had to do with identity and obligation. Who comprised the urban community and what role should state, local, and regional governments play in fostering economic development and quality of life in urban areas?

Europe's population soared during the second half of the nineteenth century, with urban areas in the front rank of expansion. Between 1880 and the end of the First World War, the population of the continent rose from 356 million to 487 million as death rates fell and migration from the countryside expanded.[3] England, typically seen as the exemplar of urbanization, witnessed perhaps the most dramatic urban–rural transformation, from a strongly rural society in the mid-nineteenth century to one in which nearly three-quarters of the population lived in urban areas by century's end.[4] Critically, migrants tended to cluster in urban areas, differentiating themselves by regional or ethnic markers. This had profound implications for political life in the cities, fostering highly focused, interest group based political constellations that both mirrored and challenged national trends.

This expansion created a more or less permanent and cascading problem of municipal services. Any real efforts to deal with the provision of housing stock had to contend with related problems of moving workers between their homes and places of employment. Publicly funded efforts to build and maintain housing in Europe's cities was still relatively novel at the end of the nineteenth century, with cities like Berlin, Birmingham, and London leading the way.[5] When the war broke out in 1914, there was an almost universal backlog of affordable housing construction in European urban areas. The nearly complete suspension of civilian construction due to shortages of funds and labor only put these schemes further behind.

The second half of the nineteenth century saw the flourishing of the city as a site for study and reform. Sociologists like Durkheim, Simmel, and Weber began to probe the meaning of the city and the relationship between spatial orientation and social relations. Related, though distinct, social reformers like Lincoln Steffens, Ebenezer Howard, and James Hobrecht tried variously to reveal or fix the crippling problems of overpopulation, inadequate housing, and insufficient sanitary provisions in urban areas.

The picture of urban Europe at the turn of the century is one of transition and uneven development. Europeans across the political spectrum were increasingly aware that urban life and living conditions cried out for reform, but there was no agreement about the best ways to accomplish these tasks. Assertive and empowered city governments sought autonomy within national states and to seek accommodation with the new political realities in urban spaces. Europe's cities were dynamic places in 1914, when the war began to transform the language and

---

3 John Reader, *Cities* (New York: Atlantic Monthly Press, 2004), 160.

4 John J. Macionis and Vincent Parrillo, *Cities and Urban Life*, 4th edn (Upper Saddle River: Pearson, 2007), 212.

5 James E. Vance, Jr. *The Continuing City: Urban Morphology in Western Civilization* (Baltimore: Johns Hopkins University Press, 1990), 443–4.

possibilities of formal politics. We can only contextualize what happened after the war by understanding the urban world in Munich and Manchester on the cusp of a world-altering conflict.

Beyond Cottonopolis: Manchester in 1914

Manchester's prewar development shaped and conditioned its wartime experience. The industrial and political constellations that emerged from the war years reflected pre-existing trends and tensions in the city and region. If the war transformed Manchester, that transformation occurred in the context of the city's historical development in the half century before 1914.

The city and its surrounding communities were a complex mosaic of economic and social interests in the prewar period and conflicts over power and political legitimacy were shaping a new future for the city and the region. The tensions of the prewar years did not wholly vanish in the rush to the colors in 1914, and the war exacerbated some of these conditions even as it improved others. The city of Manchester, wrote H.M. McKechnie in 1915, was a place with a "somewhat chequered and not always entirely respectable past. There is seen to have been all along a kind of difficulty in telling what Manchester would do next."[6] Manchester, along with its surrounding towns and Salford, its sister city across the river Irwell, was the scene of one of the most profound industrial transformations Europe had ever known.[7] Its remarkable eighteenth- and nineteenth-century history, well rehearsed elsewhere, is important here, because this study will focus on Manchester at a moment when external and internal forces were bringing its golden age to an end, and the community was in the process of re-forming and re-imagining itself as something other than the mighty textile-dominated urban sprawl of the Industrial Revolution.

A.J.P. Taylor, whose family made its money in the cotton trade in Manchester, wrote elegiacly in 1976 "There was a time when Manchester was the centre of a new civilization."[8] Indeed from the late eighteenth century until about 1921, the story of Manchester was more or less one of hyperbolic growth and

6 H.M. McKechnie, *Manchester in 1915* (Manchester and London: The University Press, 1915), 8.

7 To clear up an important point of nomenclature before proceeding: for the purposes of this study, I will use the shorthand "Manchester" to refer to the urban center and its surrounding communities, including Salford, unless otherwise noted. There are compelling historical grounds to treat Manchester and Salford separately, but much of the literature on the region in the twentieth century has treated the two as one extended unit. It would be more precise to call this urban area Greater Manchester or the South Lancashire Conurbation, but I choose not to do so for the sake of readability.

8 A.J.P. Taylor, "Manchester" in *From Napoleon to the Second International: Essays on Nineteenth Century Europe*, ed. Chris Wrigley (New York: Viking, 1994), 401.

untrammeled urban development, which turned a corner of northwest England into a metropolis. Population statistics provide a rough guide to the explosive growth of urban Manchester. In 1801, there were about 77,000 inhabitants of the (later demarcated) city of Manchester. In 1915, the combined population of Manchester and Salford was around 946,000.[9] A number of factors explain this phenomenal urban development. While historians have traditionally approached Manchester as a city of smokestacks and mills, recent scholarship has begun to see the city as something more complicated than the standard "Cottonopolis."

Manchester, perhaps the most readily-identifiable industrial center in the world, was very much a product of the late nineteenth century. With a location well-suited to take advantage of the trade in wool and linen, particularly that coming from Ireland, Manchester began the industrial revolution at a point primed for take-off. In the second half of the nineteenth century, the face of the city transformed as businesses, warehouses, and factories displaced residents in the city center and sprawling new communities sprung up to accommodate those displaced by the city's economic growth. The great city that replaced the narrow streets of early industrial Manchester housed one of the largest and most dynamic urban economies in the world, and decisions made there had repercussions across the globe.

The city's economy was always relatively diverse, even more so when one looks at Salford as well. For regional towns like Bolton, Manchester was a marketing center for textile products. Manchester responded to the need to store, process, and distribute the region's textiles, giving rise to what Kidd calls a "warehouse town." The expansion of the tertiary sector proved vital to the growth of the city, as opposed to the standard narrative of factories and the "dark satanic mills" that have come to shape the image of industrial Manchester.[10] The need for large numbers of trained workers, the relatively easy availability of coal from the nearby Lancashire coal fields, and the mechanization of the factories bolstered and created a wide range of industries, including chemicals, rubber, brewing, metal works, and specialist engine and machine tooling plants.[11] This diversity was important because it allowed Manchester to survive potentially serious crises like the "Cotton Famine" of the early 1860s that resulted from the blockade of Southern ports during the American Civil War. Another important aspect of this diversity, which we will explore in more detail later, was that it created a network of labor interests, not always compatible with each other, which prevented any of Britain's rising trade unions from establishing a dominant influence in the area.[12]

---

9 McKechnie, 9 and Alan Kidd, 22.

10 Kidd, 24.

11 Gary Messinger, *Manchester in the Victorian Age: The Half-Known City* (Manchester: Manchester University Press, 1985), 116.

12 For a discussion of this phenomenon in the coal industry, see David Howell, *The Politics of the NUM: A Lancashire View* (Manchester: Manchester University Press, 1989), 6.

This would prove particularly significant in the postwar period when trade union membership surged to all-time highs.

The completion of the Manchester Ship Canal in 1894, which linked the city with the river Mersey and the coast, bolstered the city's commercial horizons, capturing about 5 percent of Britain's imports and 4.4 percent of its export trade within 20 years of its completion.[13] With the Ship Canal came the development of the Trafford Park industrial estate, which began to attract concerns like Ford to the region in the years before the war.[14] But cotton still played the decisive role in shaping the local economy. The region's textile producers reached the peak of their global influence in 1913. Lancashire cotton cloth exports totaled 7.1 billion yards and represented 65 percent of the world's total. These extraordinary figures, though, concealed important weaknesses. Export-driven, the cotton industry was vulnerable to any disruption of the international shipping system, and a disproportionate amount of the cloth produced, about 45 percent, went to India, a dangerous over-reliance on a single consumer.[15] Competitors in East and South Asia, particularly Japan and the growing indigenous Indian cloth industry, were already waiting in the wings to claim a greater share of worldwide trade. The shortage of raw cotton in England during the war accelerated this trend rapidly. The Bombay area alone had 114 mills with almost 2.5 million spindles in 1888. That figure rose to 261 mills and 6.65 million spindles in 1916. According to a wartime report on the future of the industry in Lancashire, Indian cotton was "well placed in regard to the markets of the Far East, Africa, Asiatic Turkey, and Persia, and is likely to replace Manchester goods in these markets."[16]

Immigration fueled the economic and geographic growth of Manchester and its region. Manchester was one of the centers of Irish immigration in England. In 1891, 4.6 percent of the population was Irish-born. They brought with them the increasingly volatile conflicts of Irish politics, which played out dramatically after the war. It is important to note, however, that the Orange–Republican conflict in Manchester was far less serious than it was in nearby Liverpool, where conflict between these groups led to periodic mob violence.[17] Irish voters played a critical role in local elections, and local parties rose or fell on their ability to mobilize various components of the Irish community. The Liberals, badly divided over the Irish question in the last decades of the

13 John K. Walton, *Lancashire, A Social History: 1558–1939* (Manchester: Manchester University Press, 1987), 209.

14 Stuart Hylton, *A History of Manchester* (Chichester: Phillimore, 2003), 183.

15 Walton, 198 and Kidd, 184.

16 "Replies to Reconstruction Department Questionnaire II." July 3, 1917, NA MUN 4/176

17 See John Belcahm, ed., *Popular Politics, Riot, and Labour: Essays in Liverpool History, 1790–1940* (Liverpool: Liverpool University Press, 1992) and Frank Neal, *Sectarian Violence: The Liverpool Experience, 1819–1914: An Aspect of Anglo-Irish History* (Manchester: Manchester University Press, 1988), 9.

nineteenth century, fought particularly hard for Irish votes in Manchester and its surrounding communities, with mixed success.[18]

Jewish immigration from Eastern and Central Europe dramatically increased in the late nineteenth century. While it is difficult to establish with any precision how many Jews settled in Manchester, it is clear that Jews set up relatively homogenous communities north of the center of Manchester and in Salford. Significantly, many Jewish immigrants brought skilled trades with them, allowing them to more readily escape the economic marginalization that faced early Irish immigrants. About 29 percent of German Jewish immigrants, for instance, were involved in tailoring.[19] Some members of the economically important Jewish middle class in the city began to form Zionist groups in the 1880s. Among these was the chemist Chaim Weizmann, one of the leading figures in the Zionist movement, who lived in North Manchester until the war years. There were also significant numbers of German and Austrian immigrants in the area, both Jewish and non-Jewish.

The immigration boom also worsened the city's significant housing crisis, a blight on industrial Manchester made famous by a long line of critics and reformers that included Friedrich Engels, whose observations on industrial poverty were gleaned from the Ancoats slum. While there was little disagreement that there was too little housing stock, and too much of that was substandard, successive city governments found different ways to deal with the problem. Some emphasized the refurbishment of existing housing stock, while others, particularly at the turn of the century, launched limited schemes of new construction like the Blackley estate. Between 1901 and the beginning of the war, the Corporation demolished some 25,000 homes and did much to alleviate the notorious "back-to-back" housing that created the terrifying and insalubrious warren of narrow alleys in Manchester's slums.[20] Reform was slow and uneven, with many districts remaining mired in fairly dire conditions. Charles Taylor, recalling his turn-of-the-century boyhood in Hulme, described a neighborhood of narrow alleys, paraffin lamps, and smoke from coal fires. Every morning at 5:00, a local figure called the Knocker-Up walked the streets carrying a bamboo pole with wires protruding from top, tapping on the windows of his clients in order to rouse them for their shift at the mills.[21]

The picture of public health in Manchester was decidedly mixed at the turn of the century. Despite decades of effort that yielded a sharp decrease in deaths due

18 Steven Fielding, "Irish Politics in Manchester," *International Review of Social History*, xxxiii (1988), 261–94. For an examination of how the process worked in one immigrant family, see Lawrence W. McBride, ed., *The Reynolds Letters: An Irish Immigrant Family in Late Victorian Manchester* (Cork: Cork University Press, 1999).

19 For a demographic breakdown of the community, see the Appendices in Bill Williams, *The Making of Manchester Jewry, 1740–1875* (Manchester: Manchester University Press, 1976) and Edward Royle, *Modern Britain: A Social History 1750–1997*, 2nd edn (London: Arnold, 1997), 75.

20 Kidd, 126–7 and Hylton, 184.

21 Typescript of Charles W. Taylor, IWMA 01/8/1.

to water-borne pathogens like cholera, life in urban Manchester could be brutally short. Death rates in the late Victorian city were roughly average for a European urban area of the time, 26.6 per 1,000 residents. While new water schemes slashed the incidence of deadly cholera, poor housing and endemic poverty rendered residents of districts like Ancoats susceptible to malnutrition and opportunistic killers like tuberculosis.[22] Beginning in the late 1860s, municipal government began to take active measures to improve working-class health, connecting the issues of housing and disease prevention. For some, at least, city life became, if not healthier, at least more survivable.

Politically, turn-of-the-century Manchester was contested ground. Just as the city saw the explosive growth of a proto-industrial economy, it also fostered some of the most important and consequential developments in the field of labor relations. From the 1790s, radical reformers found a home and a subject in Manchester. The 1819 "Peterloo" Massacre, the centennial of which fell auspiciously close to the end of the war and provided fodder for anti-government protests, helped to bring Manchester's labor problems to a national and international audience. Some of the most radical members of the Chartist movement in the 1830s and 1840s were workers in the cotton industry in and around Manchester, briefly compelling the dispatch of a large garrison to the city in the wake of the 1842 Plug Strikes. Despite these ominous developments, Manchester entered the second half of the century with a growing reputation for far less contentious labor politics than the industrial centers of the south.[23] In its place grew a political culture based in large part on seeking some sort of consensus in the realm of formal politics, an attitude that served the city and its region well until the early years of the new century. At the center of "class-influenced but not class-based" political arrangement were parties representing a range of cross-cutting political and social interests overlaying the dynamic political and demographic landscape of the city and its region.[24]

As a Liberal bastion in the nineteenth century, Manchester had risen in relative importance as it grew. The *Manchester Guardian*, in large part due to the extraordinary energy of its legendary editor C.P. Scott, became a national voice for free trade. In a country in which political and cultural life was so focused on its massive southern capital, Manchester became "the voice of the provinces against London."[25] The changing demographics of the region, however, effected a series of profound political shifts that threatened at the turn of the century to redefine Manchester's political geography.

---

22 Richard Evans, *Death in Hamburg: Society and Politics in the Cholera Years* (London: Penguin, 2005), 181 and Kidd, 186–7.

23 Kidd, 97.

24 F.M.L. Thompson, ed. *The Cambridge Social History of Britain, 1750–1950*, vol. I (Cambridge: Cambridge University Press, 1990), 410.

25 Alan Kidd, "The Historical Development of Manchester and its Region", in Stanislaw Liszewski and Craig Young eds, *The Comparative Study of Lodz and Manchester: Geographies of European Cities in Transition* (Lodz: University of Lodz, 1997), 38.

Local politics in prewar Manchester and Salford were riven by a variety of tensions, some of which were particular to the area while others represented the broader schisms of English politics. Thanks to the centrality of cotton and other exports, Manchester had long been an area that tended toward Liberalism. However, at the municipal level, the Conservatives dominated local politics in the early twentieth century. Alan Kidd points to the importance of an abiding, Protestant-based "working class Toryism" that saw itself opposed to the influx of Irish immigrants along with the general weakening of Liberal support nationwide in the late nineteenth century.[26]

The fractious ethnic politics of Manchester further complicated this situation, making it difficult for historians to disentangle voting patterns. The city's large Irish population, for instance, was by the beginning of the twentieth century diffused between a number of voting districts. The Irish, as a rule, did not support the Conservatives in national elections because of their uncompromising opposition to Home Rule in Ireland. However, at a local level, the Tories continued to back Church schools, winning them some Irish votes.[27] Manchester's considerable Orange population further complicated voting patterns. Such diversity of opinions makes it all but impossible to identify a clear "Irish" vote in Manchester.

Labour, Britain's newest political party, was solidly represented in the local population within a few years of its establishment, with about 14 percent of local councillors between 1911 and 1913. Many historians of the region have argued that Manchester was one of the more important Labour strongholds in England in the early years of the century. Tony Adams, however, points out that Labour's electoral share in Manchester, while significant, was by no means impressive compared to other industrial centers like Leicester (29.2 percent) or Leeds (27.1 percent). Labour's development in Manchester was impeded by the nature of the local population and the political culture of the English Northwest.

Declan McHugh, examining divisions in the Manchester and Salford Labour Council (which was divided only in 1920), points out that Labour in Salford had a much harder path than in Manchester. Opposition to Labour from both Liberals and Socialists, along with the Protestant working-class conservatism of many Mancunians, meant that any Labour gains were hard won. It was only the postwar division of the party along municipal lines, and the wartime coalition of Labour and Socialists, that allowed Labour to make headway in Salford.[28] The ethnic divisions which encouraged working-class Toryism hindered the rise of Labour in Lancashire. The party had grown in large part by attaching itself to the associations

26 Kidd 2002, 171.

27 Tony Adams, "Labour Vanguard, Tory Bastion, or the Triumph of New Liberalism? Manchester Politics 1900 to 1914 in Comparative Perspective," *Manchester Region History Review* XIV (2001), 32–3.

28 Declan McHugh, "The Labour Party in Manchester and Salford Before the First World War: A Case of Unequal Development," *Manchester Region History Review XIV* (2001), 13–24.

of working-class life. The fractured nature of those structures in the ethnically and religiously divided region made this process all the more difficult. Labour's rise would require a "fundamental reworking of the language of political 'interests' to comprehend labour and related issues."[29]

The proud traditions of the non-conformist North also aided in the fostering of some of the most politically dynamic movements of the late nineteenth and early twentieth centuries. While the region's electoral conservatism remained a powerful force in local politics, radical and progressive strains made significant inroads in the early twentieth century. Manchester became an early home for the Women's Suffrage and Socialist movements, ideas that would have an important influence on city politics during and after the war.[30]

Manchester was an important center for the emerging labor politics of the late nineteenth century. Local branches of the Independent Labour Party (ILP) and the Social Democratic Federation, while far from mass parties, were among the most active in Britain. Sylvia Pankhurst, who was involved with the ILP alongside her parents, remembered meeting celebrated labor leaders like Tom Mann and Wilhelm Liebknecht. She also remembered helping with ILP soup kitchens for the unemployed in the center of Manchester and in some of the more desperate industrial suburbs. "These efforts to alleviate the immediate need were used as a basis for agitation."[31]

Labour arrived with the founding of a local branch of the Labour Representation Council in 1903, three years before the national Labour Party first won significant numbers of parliamentary seats in the midst of a Liberal landslide. In coalition with the Liberals, Labour won important Parliamentary victories in Lancashire in 1906 and 1910.[32] The protean Clarion socialist movement also had considerable success in the area.[33] While it is clear from election results that Labour was able to instantiate itself relatively rapidly into Manchester politics, the impact of the intellectual Clarions is far more difficult to evaluate. What is apparent is that working-class militancy was on the rise

---

29 Trevor Griffiths, *The Lancashire Working Classes, c. 1880–1930* (Oxford: Clarendon Press, 2001), 12. This interpretation owes much to the work of Ross McKibbin, who argued that Labour was restricted in its appeal by divides within its core constituencies. Ross McKibbin, *The Ideologies of Class: Social Relations in Britain, 1880–1950* (Oxford: Clarendon Press, 1990), esp. 40–41.

30 On the Pankhursts, see Martin Pugh, *The Pankhursts* (London: Allen Lane, 2001). See also Jill Liddington and Jill Norris, *One Hand Tied Behind Us: The Rise of the Women's Suffrage Movement* (London: Virago, 1985) and Susan Kingsley Kent, *Sex and Suffrage in Britain: 1860–1914* (London: Routledge, 1990).

31 E. Sylvia Pankhurst, *The Suffragette Movement: An Intimate Account of Persons and Ideals* (London: Longman's Green, and Co., 1931), 129–30.

32 Martin Pugh, *The Making of Modern British Politics, 1867–1939* (Oxford: Basil Blackwell, 1982), 149.

33 Kidd, 174–9.

at the turn of the century and that the organizing principles of various labor groups and parties played a role in that development.

Labor relations during the Edwardian period were worsening as Labour sought and increasingly won representation in Parliament. Rising living costs and low unemployment gave trade unions a wide recruiting base that was becoming increasingly disaffected. Trade union membership rose from 2.5 million in 1907 to more than 4.1 million in 1914, and the number of days lost to industrial disputes peaked at more than 40 million in 1912.[34] Part of the reason for this increase in labor activity was an ideological shift in the fundamental beliefs of labor's leadership. Recent scholarship on "Englishness" and patriotism has helped to illuminate some of these interesting developments, which came to play a role in Manchester's postwar history.

A recent study of the sometimes tortured relationship between patriotism and the Left in Britain asserts that from the 1880s the mainstream Left embraced a self-image as a champion of essentially rural British character against the rising urban tide.[35] During the Edwardian period, burgeoning union memberships and rising living costs catalyzed a series of leadership struggles between the old guard and younger union leaders. Increasingly radical strains in Britain's labor movement, notably the Syndicalists, began to effectively oppose the essentially patriotic, parliamentary methods of the Labour party, establishing the grounds for future conflict.[36]

Manchester saw its share of the emerging labor troubles. There were significant demonstrations by the unemployed in 1905 and 1908 and during the violent nationwide strikes of 1911. The demonstrations, which were largely initiated by the SDF, were not particularly successful and became "a question of public order rather than public policy."[37] It is not entirely coincidental that this apparently unstoppable tide of labor trouble, like the strength of the Lancashire cotton empire, reached its apogee just before the war. The war suspended both activities for several years. Lancashire cotton did not recover, but labor militancy revisited Lancashire even before the guns were silent.

Munich and Bavaria, 1900–1914

It is all too easy to fall into the trap of treating Munich before the First World War in much the way that the city's cultivated public image insists it be treated – as a

34 David Powell, *British Politics and the Labour Question, 1868–1990* (London: Macmillan, 1992), 36.

35 Paul Ward, *Red Flag and Union Jack: Englishness, Patriotism, and the British Left, 1881–1924* (Woodbridge and Rochester, NY: Royal Historical Society and the Boydell Press, 1998), 5.

36 Ibid., 100–101.

37 Kidd, 178.

place of enchanting buildings, *gemütlich* public culture, and fashionable socialists in the coffee houses of Schwabing. In 1914, the city was two years removed from the era still referred to as the "Regency Period," or *Prinzregentenzeit*, after the genial and well-regarded Prince Regent Luitpold who ruled in the stead of the unbalanced Otto I. The end of the regency and the coming of the war represented a caesura for the city, and even at the time many looked to the *Prinzregentenzeit* as the model of a quiet, self-effacing and above all peaceful city free of the social conflicts of the rest of industrial Germany.

There is some truth to this reputation, but to understand what happened during and after the war, it is necessary to examine the forces that shaped prewar Munich and that fundamentally changed the city in wartime. While Munich was a product of a different sort of nineteenth century than that experienced in the industrial north and west of Germany, it was still very much a city in uneven and sometimes problematic transition. Munich's growth came later than many of Germany's other large cities, creating in 1914 a profound gap between old Munich and the new industrial communities whose workers came from the Bavarian hinterland. The clash between the pragmatic conservatism of the royal *Residenzstadt*, the politically engaged artistic community, the mass of Catholic internal immigrants, and the growing self-assurance of working-class politics created new zones of conflict. Under the pressures of war, those conflicts came inescapably to the fore.

While Munich's industrial development occurred along very different lines than in nearby cities like Ingolstadt or Nürnberg, it is important to recognize that the Bavarian capital was a diverse and divided city in the years before the war. These divisions later helped to demarcate the battle lines in contests for power in the postwar context. Munich was unquestionably a city on the rise in 1914, fueled by the same migrations from rural communities that defined the growth of German cities in the nineteenth century. Munich was still relatively small in 1871, with just 167,000 inhabitants. In 1905, there were about 540,000 residents and by 1914 it had a population of 645,000. For perspective, Munich's growth was still far slower than Berlin, which gained around 2 million new residents during roughly the same period and entered the war with a population of around 4 million.[38]

Significantly, and in marked contrast to standard images of the city as a colony of artists and artisans, 47 percent of the city's residents were workers. This figure was only a few points lower than Nürnberg in northern Bavaria, then considered the cradle of industrial development in the state.[39] Munich in the nineteenth century became one of the most important commercial cities in Germany, home to specialized producers in fields like brewing, precision machine-tool production, and railroad cars that manufactured for both domestic and international customers. The city enshrined its evident pride in its technological achievements when it

38 Jay Winter and Jean-Louis Robert, eds, *Capital Cities at War: Paris, London, Berlin, 1914–1919* (Cambridge: Cambridge University Press, 1997), 26.

39 Friedrich Prinz, *Die Geschichte Bayerns* (Munich: Piper, 2001), 401 and Reinhard Bauer and Ernst Piper. *München: Die Geschichte einer Stadt* (Munich: Piper, 1993), 243.

opened the Deutsches Museum, today one of the world's largest technical museums, in 1903.[40] When the war broke out, there were almost 14,000 machinists in the city along with 11,000 in the hospitality trade and almost 14,000 in the building trades. By the end of the war, the number of machinists rose to about 25,000, while the hospitality and building trades shrank in the face of social and economic instability.[41] The last of these was particularly important for the growing city, which suddenly had to deal with an influx of new residents in need of housing. Munich's social reformers, from whom we will hear later, were increasingly concerned at the cramped conditions of the inhabitants of this classical German *Residenzstadt*.

As the urban footprint of the city expanded southward and eastward in the late nineteenth century, both the size of the city and its population grew at a tremendous rate. One of the results was an acute housing shortage that threatened the region's industrial development. Despite the efforts of private developers like Carl von Eichtal, the housing market remained critically under-resourced. At the turn of the century, at least a quarter of Munich's households lived in apartments shared with other families (*Teilwohnungen*).[42] Overcrowding and poor santitary conditions finally alarmed urban authorities, who established a "Society for the Improvement of Living Conditions" in 1899. By 1914, the association had already begun to spearhead efforts to develop new urban communities in areas like Sendling.

If housing construction improved slowly, other urban reform measures proved far more successful. Munich in the nineteenth century was a deadly place, with a mortality rate of more than 30 per 1,000 residents. This was a good deal higher than other major cities in Germany and Western Europe, which averaged in the mid-20s.[43] Thanks to the efforts of physicians and public health officials like Max von Pettenkofer, Munich's traditionally pestilential reputation gave way before a rigorous program of drinking water sanitation and sewage control.[44] Public baths, like the still-extant *jugendstil* Müllersche Volksbad (completed in 1901), offered Munich's growing population places for recreation and hygiene.

Munich developed a reputation as a home for socially progressive thinkers and groups at the turn of the century. Aside from the thriving artistic and cultural scene, which will be discussed below, Munich was host to a variety of politically influential organizations and individuals. Women took a leading role in such organizations, particularly the intimately connected peace and women's movements. The city hosted the 1907 International Peace Congress, and the

40 Eve Duffy, "Representing Science and Technology: Politics and Display in the Deutsches Museum, 1903–45" (PhD diss., University of North Carolina at Chapel Hill, 2002).

41 Statistischen Amt der Stadt München, *Statistisches Jahrbuch der Stadt München* (Munich: J. Lindauersche Universitäts-Buchandlung, 1928), 86–7. After SJSM.

42 Stadtarchiv München, *München wie geplant* (Munich: Stadtarchiv München, 2006), 80.

43 Evans, 181.

44 Prinz, 397–8.

historian and politician Ludwig Quidde was already an internationally known peace activist. Munich women like Margaretha Lenore Selenka led large and well-attended public meetings against the Boer War and were outspoken critics of militarism until silenced by wartime regulations.[45] At the same time, the number of women enrolled at the University increased dramatically, from 198 in 1910 to 694 in 1914. By the middle of the war, more than one-third of female students were studying medicine.[46]

There were undeniably strong connections between Munich and the international Left in the prewar era, a trend accelerated by the city's reputation as a home in exile for those whose politics were a liability in their home countries. Significant numbers of Russians, many of whom were Jews, came to Munich after the failure of the 1905 Revolution. This has caused some traditional historians to argue that the events of the postwar period in Munich were inspired by the revolutionary ideas brought by these Russian immigrants, a suggestion that now seems wide of the mark.[47] The Revolution brought on sizable street demonstrations in Munich against the Czarist treatment of demonstrators on "Bloody Sunday." Demonstrators in Munich included luminaries like Lujo Brentano and Max Haushofer. In 1914, a few months before the outbreak of the war, Rosa Luxembourg gave a speech in a crowded *Kindl-Keller* on "Militarism and the People's Freedom." At least ostensibly, Munich was a city in which opportunities to break or bend the strictures of imperial society abounded.

The impression of Munich as a classless city was not unfamiliar to contemporaries. An American observer in 1909 wrote that in the beer halls "one man is exactly as good as another."[48] The Baedeker's guide published the year the war broke out emphasized that the Hofbräuhaus, perhaps the city's most enduring tourist landmark, was "visited by all of the classes."[49] Important aspects of the rich associational life that characterized Bavarian (and German) civil society during the Empire bridged class divides. Public entertainment, notably theater and musical groups, specialized in regional performances, which appealed to the city's newest residents who had often come from the rural milieu that still characterized much

---

45 Hiltrud Häntzschel, "'Nur wer feige ist, nimmt die Waffe in den Hand:' München – Zentrum der Frauenfriedensbewegung, 1899–1933" in Sybille Krafft, ed., *Zwischen den Fronten: Münchner Frauen in Krieg und Frieden, 1900–1950.* (Munich: Buchendorf, 1995), 18–40. Prinz, 405–8.

46 Statistics from Bayer. Statistischen Landesamt, *Statistisches Jahrbuch für den Freistaat Bayern*, *1919* (Munich: BSL, 1919), 279 (after SJFB). Statistics for the summer *Halbjahr.*

47 See for instance Ludwig Schneider, "Die Russische Studentkolonie und das Echo des Revolutionäre Russland in München von 1914," in Karl Bosl, ed., *Bayern in Umbruch* (Munich: Oldenbourg, 1969), 75–96.

48 Quoted in David Clay Large, *Where Ghosts Walked: Munich's Road to the Third Reich* (New York: Norton, 1997), XIII.

49 Karl Baedeker, *Baedekers Sudbayern, Tirol, Salzburg, usw.* (Leipzig: Verlag von Karl Baedeker, 1914), 4.

of Bavaria. These performances tended to point out the foibles of the prosperous and powerful and appealed to workers and *Kleinbürgertum* alike.[50] Robert Sackett has suggested that the overriding message of these entertainments was a "yearning for a preindustrial community, disdain for Jews, [and] patriotism." Sackett also argues that the views expressed and validated by the popularity of performers like the legendary Karl Valentin and Weiss Pferdl later helped to shape the rejection of the postwar Republic.[51] At the same time, Munich was home to experimental modernist theatrical influences like the circle around Franz Wedekind whose energetic attacks on social conventions placed them at odds with the conservative Catholicism of the Bavarian censors.[52]

The thriving cultural life of Munich was more than mirrored by a surfeit of great and would-be-great artists, writers, and poets upon whom the city's reputation as the "Athens on the Isar" rested. The profusion of intellectuals and artists who made their way through Munich or settled there during the *Prinzregentenzeit* was truly impressive. Thomas Mann, Wasily Kandinsky, Franz Marc, Gabrielle Munter, Ludwig Thoma, Henrik Ibsen, Wedekind, and Rainer Maria Rilke were just some of the luminaries who called the Bavarian capital home for some or all of this period of extraordinary flowering. Groups like the theatrical ensemble the Eleven Executioners, the painters of the Blue Rider, and the notorious Cosmic Circle of writers who hovered around the increasingly bizarre words of Stephan George drew inspiration from and, in turn, influenced artistic life across Europe. The city earned a reputation as a refuge for dissolute and brilliant intellectuals from far beyond Bavaria's borders, who seemed drawn to the artist and student quarter of Schwabing. Some historians have found in the Schwabing culture the roots of the extremist tendencies of the postwar regimes and later the city's honored place in the imagined history of the National Socialist Movement.[53]

Munich was also a center for activist and often controversial journalism. The most famous example was *Simplicissimus*, the satirical magazine that delighted in skewering the pretensions of middle-class German life in the Empire.

---

50 Volker D. Laturell, *Volkskultur in München: Aufsätze zu Brauchtum, Musikalische Volkskultur, Volkstanz, Trachten und Volkstheater in einer Millionenstadt* (Munich: Buchendorf Verlag, 1997), 33–4.

51 Robert Sackett, *Popular Entertainment, Class, and Politics in Munich, 1900–1923* (Cambridge: Harvard University Press, 1982), 5. A slightly different view of popular entertainment in the city, emphasizing the importance of the European colonial experience in the city's spectacles, is Anne Dreesbach and Helmut Zedelmaier, eds, *"Gleich hinterm Hofbräuhaus waschechte Amazonen:" Exotik in München um 1900* (Munich: Dölling und Gallitz, 2003).

52 See Peter Jelavich, *Munich and Theatrical Modernism: Politics, Playwriting, and Performance, 1890–1914* (Cambridge: Harvard University Press, 1985).

53 See especially Large, *Where Ghosts Walked* and Prinz, 428. The passions evoked by the "honorary title" of *Hauptstadt der Bewegung* can still be felt in Munich, as evidenced by the recent exhibition of the same name at the *Stadtmuseum*. Münchner Stadtmuseum, *München – Hauptstadt der Bewegung* (Munich: Münchner Stadtmuseum, 2002).

Ludwig Thoma, one of Bavaria's most beloved writers, was an editor, and T.T. Heine provided the signature look to a magazine whose red bulldog with a broken chain became synonymous with satire that pushed, and sometime overstepped, the legal strictures of the imperial state.[54] The war complicated the cozy satirical word of Schwabing's red bulldog, and by the end Thoma was every bit the nationalist that his magazine took such pleasure in tweaking.

While *Simplicissimus* was the most enduring and famous of Munich's journalistic offerings, it was far from the only one. Others, particularly the conservative *Süddeutsche Monatshefte*, point toward a different sort of Munich than the one suggested by the bohemianism of Schwabing. Particularly with the influx of immigrants from the countryside, Munich remained in many ways deeply conservative and suspicious of outside influences. The Archbishopric of Munich-Freising was one of the largest and most important in Germany and certainly the largest in the Southeast. Confessionally, Munich was overwhelmingly Catholic, counting 89.8 percent of the population in 1916.[55] While these statistics do not necessarily speak to the piety of the citizenry, it is clear that Catholic identity played a major role in politics in prewar Bavaria and Munich and that the contests between Catholic politics and other political actors like labor and agrarian interest groups was one of the central conflicts in urban and regional politics during the *Prinzregentenzeit* and beyond.

Much of the literature on German Catholicism has emphasized a milieu-centered approach to Catholic identity, while recent studies have suggested how porous such a construction really was. In Munich, historians have stressed that Catholics, especially working-class believers, had relatively little trouble seeing themselves as members of cross-cutting political and social groups. As a result, the political landscape in the city and its surroundings was different from other Catholic regions of the German empire. These differences had important consequences for the city's long term development and its relationship with the national state.[56]

Formal politics in Munich in the years before the war centered on continuing efforts to integrate Bavaria politically into the rest of the Reich, a herculean task made all the more awkward by the presence of competing bureaucracies and

54 See Ann Taylor Allen, *Satire and Society in Wilhelmine Germany: Kladderadatsch and Simplicissimus* (Lexington: University of Kentucky Press, 1984).

55 Joachim Seiler, "Statistik des Erzibistums München und Freising in der ersten Hälfte des 20. Jahrhunderts" in *Das Erzbistum München und Freising in der Zeit der nationalsozialistischen Herrschaft* ed. Georg Schwaiger (Munich: Schnell & Steiner, 1984), 287.

56 Good summaries of the literature can be found in Heinz Hürten, *Deutsche Katholiken, 1918 bis 1945* (Paderborn: Schöningh, 1992) and Michael O'Sullivan, "Persevering Piety and Declining Devotion: Popular Catholicism, Secularization, and Everyday Religion in Western Germany, 1918–1965" (PhD diss, University of North Carolina at Chapel Hill, 2006). On Munich, see Derek Hastings, "How 'Catholic' Was the Early Nazi Movement? Religion, Race, and Culture in Munich, 1919–1924" *Central European History* 36, no. 3, esp. 383–5.

incompatible systems of voting. Electoral reforms in 1906 and the ascent of the Center Party moderate Georg von Hertling to the Chancellery in 1912 mollified, but did not silence, the reformists. The constitutional debates emerged again after the war when some of the long-debated reforms came to pass only in the atmosphere of crisis that defined Bavarian postwar political life.[57] These constitutional debates only hint at the complex and changing dynamics of political life in the rapidly modernizing *Landeshauptstadt*.

One of the more readily discernable features of political culture in Munich before the First World War was its relatively non-contentious class politics. While this does not mean that class was unimportant, it does suggest that the radical movements that emerged from the war had an uphill battle to mobilize support. Bavarian electoral politics were in dramatic transition just before the war, as the reliable Catholic support for the Center Party (*Zentrum*) in the traditional Bavarian heartland of *Altbayern* weakened in the face of two new political forces – the newly-legalized Social Democratic Party (SPD), whose support could and did shift the balance several times between the Center Party and the Liberals, and the *Bauernbünde* (Farmer's Leagues).[58] The Leagues, strongest in the East, were dominated by the *eminence grise* of Bavarian politics, the shadowy "Uncrowned King" Dr. Georg Heim. The SPD was by far the most dynamic party in Munich. Since 1887, when they polled just 5.2 percent in municipal elections, the SPD had gained considerable success among the city's workers, largely at the expense of the Center and Liberal parties. In 1902, the SPD captured about a quarter of the municipal vote, and two years later they won a plurality, with 38.6 percent. The Center and divided Liberals split much of the remainder.[59] For the Catholic politicians who easily dominated the electoral map of Bavaria in the late nineteenth century, the rise of working-class politics seemed to be a challenge to the very notions of particularism on which Bavarian self-identity was based. They responded to the challenge by moderating their message to compete for the loyalty of workers.[60]

The political culture of labor politics in Bavaria and Munich was, in some ways, quite different from what was going in Germany's industrial West and agrarian East. While organized labor was active in Bavaria in the years immediately preceding the war, Munich was far from a hotbed of industrial conflict. In 1914, strike activity in Munich accounted for less than 10 percent of industrial conflicts

57 A short but effective summary of the reform debates can be found in Allan Mitchell, *Revolution in Bavaria, 1818–1919* (Princeton: Princeton University Press, 1965), 17–21.

58 A thoughtful discussion of Bavarian electoral trends can be found in Zdnek Zofka, "Wahlen in Bayern, 1849–1994," *Der Staatsbürger, eine Beilage der Bayerischen Staatszeitung*, http://www.stmuk.bayern.de/blz/web/archiv/landtag/artikel.html.

59 SJSM, 307.

60 Norbert J. Mayr, "Particularism in Bavaria: State Policy and Public Sentiment, 1806–1906" (PhD diss., University of North Carolina at Chapel Hill, 1988), 374.

in Bavaria and involved just over 10 percent of striking Bavarian workers.[61] Aside from the relative absence of large firms, Munich also benefited in this regard from a functioning reciprocal relationship between authorities, labor organizers, and the SPD, which stressed pragmatic concerns at the expense of ideological rigidity. SPD leaders like the legendarily moderate Georg von Vollmar complemented a *Land* government that had little interest in the hostility and undeclared warfare that marked labor relations in some other German cities.[62] The relative strength of the SPD among municipal employees also seems to have contributed to this overall spirit of conciliation instead of confrontation.

At the head of the Bavarian monarchy was the eccentric but essentially harmless figure of Ludwig III Wittelsbach. Ludwig was something of a departure from the psychological and architectural excesses for which his family had acquired a reputation. He was a technocrat, largely interested in pursuing his love of innovative methods of milk cow husbandry. His tendency to find comfort on his model dairy farms earned him the lasting sobriquet "*Millibauer*" (Dairy Farmer). He was also a proud and prickly scion of a family that had ruled Bavaria for more than seven centuries and walked with a limp until the end of his life after a wound suffered in battle against the Prussians on the side of Austria in 1866. Ludwig never ceased to remind the famously insecure Prussian Emperor that the Hohenzollerns were mere *parvenus* compared to the durable Wittelsbachs. The Kaiser's erratic mental state elicited comparisons with Ludwig's self-aggrandizing (and mad) ancestor Ludwig II.[63]

Ludwig's country idyll gave him an image of being disinterested and certainly no danger to the democratizing tendencies within Bavarian society. Unlike the Prince-Regent, he had the temperament of a modernizer, and this appears to have placated even Munich's leftist community, who viewed his ascension in 1912 as a positive step.[64] However, the greatest weakness of the monarchy at the time of the

61 SJFB, 307.

62 A good discussion of labor relations can be found in Elisabeth Jungling, *Streiks in Bayern 1889–1914: Arbeitskampf in der Prinzregentenzeit* (Munich: Neue Schriftenreihe des Stadtarchives München, 1986), 207. A counter-example, that of Berlin, is discussed in Thomas Lindenberger, *Strassenpolitik: Zur Sozialgeschichte der öffentlichen Ordnung in Berlin 1900 bis 1914* (Bonn: J.H.W. Dietz, 1995). Sean Dobson presents a different version of worker roles in political life, in which workers below the level of political representation took active roles in advocating political change, in his dissertation "Authority and Revolution in Leipzig, 1910–20" (PhD diss., Columbia University, 1996).

63 Lamar Cecil, *Wilhelm II*, vol. 2 (Chapel Hill: University of North Carolina Press, 1989), 63.; Hans-Michael Körner "Ludwig III: Totengräber oder Monarchie?" in *Die Herrscher Bayerns: 25 Historische Portraits von Tassilo III bis Ludwig III*, eds Alois Schmid and Katharine Weigand (München: C.H. Beck, 2001), 376–90; Alfons Beckenbauer, *Ludwig III von Bayern, 1845–1921: Ein König auf den Suche nach seinem Volk* (Regensburg: Friedrich Pustet, 1987)

64 Ludwig Hümmert, *Bayern von Königreich zur Diktatur, 1900–1933* (München: Ludwig Verlag, 1979), 31.

First World War was precisely that symbolic connection between the monarchy and the older conservative order. Some Bavarian historians have argued persuasively that the legitimacy of the monarchy had been in decline since shortly after their greatest triumph at the end of the Napoleonic Wars, and the Dairy Farmer was clearly not the Wittelsbach to reverse that trend, particularly when confronted with the demands of mass industrial war.[65]

At the war's outset, event the phlegmatic Ludwig seems to have been swept up in the possibilities of victory, envisioning Bavarian territorial claims against France and the possibility of restoring Bavaria to something resembling its former prominence.[66] The dynasty whose fortunes had been made on an unerring ability to side with winners made a critical misjudgment. Ironically, and despite his best efforts, even Ludwig's passion for dairy cows came back to haunt him as a city increasingly cut off from regular milk supplies slowly turned on a monarch whose holdings guaranteed him and his family a steady supply.

Munich, like the rest of Germany, sat on a precipice in 1914. If Munich had a more comfortable seat than other cities in the empire, it was the result of a careful policy of managing conflict and the cultivation of an ostensibly integrated and inclusive "people's culture." The stresses of the war belied these cozy notions of cooperation and conciliation by forcing changes in the structures of social integration that defined prewar Munich. As we will see, the city transformed economically, spiritually, and physically during the war years, and the tensions of those years shaped what was to come.

65 Körner, 377.

66 Prinz, 432.

SECTION I
Visions of the End: 1917–18 and the Beginnings of Demobilization

For Edmund Blunden, like so many of his contemporaries across Europe, the postwar years were haunted by visions of events witnessed or imagined from the front lines of the Great War. In *1916 Seen from 1921*, Blunden captured the guilt of a survivor, the uncertainty of the world beyond war and the terrible nostalgia of the returned warrior:

> Tired with dull grief
> I sit in solitude and only hear
> Long silent laughters, murmurings of dismay,
> The lost intensities of hope and fear;
> In those old marshes yet the rifles lie,
> On the thin breastwork flutter the grey rags,
> The very books I read are there – and I
> Dead as the men I loved, wait while life drags.[1]

Blunden was one of the most celebrated and haunted members of that cohort of writers who formed what Paul Fussell much later called "a virtual allegory of political and social cognition in our time."[2] For Blunden and those around him, the war remained a central reference point around which they arranged their later lives. This insistent reminder that for the generation of men and women who experienced the war first hand, future events would be seen through the lens of that conflict points to critical continuities between Europe's political cultural during the war and in the years that followed. The story of Europe's demobilization began not with the end of the conflict but with the emergence of serious conversation about and planning for a world beyond war. For four reasons, one must begin the story of demobilization in transnational perspective during the violent and turbulent year 1917.

Most broadly, the conditions under which European states demobilized were strongly influenced by the conditions of wartime mobilization. By 1917, all of the

---

1 John Silkin, ed. *The Penguin Book of First World War Poetry*, 2nd edn (London: Penguin, 1991), 112.

2 Paul Fussell, *The Great War and Modern Memory* (London: Oxford University Press, 1975), 35.

combatant states practiced conscription, state control over labor markets, legal measures to control political activity, and legally-mandated limits on consumer society. Following the extraordinary bloodletting of 1916, combatant states began a period of "remobilization," during which the mobilization apparatus assumed greater powers and the impact of mass industrial war became even more inescapably intertwined with the lives of ordinary Europeans.

Second, 1917 saw significant increases in the scale and scope of official and public discussion about the end of the war. For military and civilian planners, this trend was manifested in the expansion of bureaucratic entities dedicated to thinking about issues of transition in the wake of the end of hostilities. These official debates were reflected in discussions within civil societies that envisioned the reforms that were sure to follow in the wake of the war. While these visions were far-reaching, conflicting, and sometimes contradictory, they reflected a growing sense of entitlement that stemmed from the pervasiveness of mobilization. While many of these visions of the postwar world drew from official wartime propaganda, they also reflected the genuine grass-roots commitment of many Europeans to the war effort.

While popular support for the war remained high across the combatant states, 1917 also saw the first significant cracks in wartime domestic consensus in Western and Central Europe. Despite efforts by national governments to regulate labor activism, the third year of the war and the pressures of mobilization drove wide gaps between traditional labor leaders and an increasing number of industrial workers. When workers laid down tools or took to the streets, local and national authorities feared that worse was to come. Since these industrial disputes lay at the center of postwar conflicts over economic recovery and the rights of groups and individuals to be compensated for their wartime sacrifice, it is critical to understand the wartime origins of the postwar debates.

Finally, the influence of the revolutionary experience in Russia on the mentality of authorities and ordinary Europeans cannot be overstated. While Britons and Germans reacted quite differently to Russia's exit from the war, the upheaval in Eastern Europe added a new element of revolutionary language to debates over the war and the postwar future. While there was little evidence of widespread affinity for the Bolshevik revolutionaries in either country, the rhetoric of social revolution served to radicalize debates about quotidian issues like food, housing, and labor.

In the two chapters that follow, I will demonstrate that authorities and civil society in Munich and Manchester during the last two years of the war confronted a similar set of questions, fears, and debates over the course of the war and the world to come after the peace. At the same time, different national approaches to mobilization created varying pressures that later shaped the processes of demobilization. These chapters will concentrate on five critical themes, exploring them in each of the two urban areas under consideration.

First, these chapters contextualize the economic and social mobilization of the urban environments during the first three years of war, focusing particularly on the intensified mobilization strategies of 1917 and 1918. In both cities, mobilization expanded both horizontally and vertically as the war went on, affecting a higher percentage of the population and in increasingly profound ways. As the effective lines between front and home front blurred, ever more members of the population who were not combatants, particularly women, the young, and men whose jobs kept them from active duty service, lived in a world where the realities of war were inescapable.

Food control was, without a doubt, the most critical and public manifestation of the state at war in the urban environment. While Munich had been under some form of rationing since early in the war, Manchester in 1917 witnessed dramatic demonstrations urging rationing as a way to ensure equitable distribution of foodstuffs. Whether real or imagined, food was the primary site at which people in the urban environment perceived injustice and inequitable treatment. Since claims of lack of transparency and fairness were central to criticisms of postwar reconstruction, wartime debates over food were a critical nexus of wartime dissent and an emerging critique of the entire project of mobilization.

As the war progressed, evidence of its disruptive and destructive powers became all the more evident. Urban residents in wartime could not escape state-directed wartime propaganda, a pervasive culture of military imagery and language, or increasingly pervasive fears that the war was breaking down moral and sexual norms by tearing apart the fabric of prewar society. Most important in understanding this culture of wartime was the persistent presence of death in the language of those on the home front. By 1917, Europeans were increasingly accustomed to news of long casualty lists and the sight of the wounded in city streets. This created what Jay Winter has called "communities in mourning" in which widening circles of familial and social kinship both provided comfort for the bereaved and created an ever-expanded number of "victims" of wartime violence.[3] The postwar moral panic, in which critics from across the political spectrum attacked what they imagined to be the collapse of restraint, had its origins in this death-suffused and belligerent wartime culture.

When wartime consensus began to break down, various forms of dissent emerged into public spaces. Despite, and sometimes because of, rigorous police and military efforts to survey and contain such dissent, it was inescapable by the end of 1917. In a crucial predecessor to such protests in the postwar war, dissenters had to carefully balance their criticisms of the wartime state and hopes for the future with a carefully calibrated avoidance of rhetoric that seemed treasonous or likely to hinder the war effort. The boundaries of loyal dissent hindered the ability of protestors to press their demands, while the wartime state reserved the right to crack down on protest with considerable legal force. As the experience of revolution in Russia echoed across the combatant states, dissenters and authorities negotiated over visions of a fairer, more equitable world after the war.

---

3 Jay Winter, *Sites of Memory, Sites of Mourning: The Great War in European Cultural Memory* (Cambridge: Cambridge University Press, 1995), 30.

Such visions are the last, and most diffuse, of the themes in these chapters. The planning for the physical, economic, and bureaucratic facets of demobilization took place between London and Manchester and Munich and Berlin. Planners, assuming that their state would emerge victorious, focused on maintaining order and delivering stability in the wake of the end of the conflict. Since no one knew when that event would come, or under what circumstances, such plans were, by nature, subject to constant revision. At the same time, debates within civil society drew from prewar visions of urban social reform and wartime rhetoric of the rewards of victory to imagine a future in which mobilized societies would see their sacrifices reciprocated by a grateful state. The inability and unwillingness of European states to realize those visions was the greatest source of postwar bitterness. Without an understanding of how those hopes formed and the agents who shaped them, we cannot fully grasp how profound the postwar disappointments, in victorious and defeated states, really were.

These two sites represented two different approaches to the similar set of challenges engendered by mass industrial war in the early twentieth century, and that that the responses to those challenges conditioned the postwar outcomes in these cities. In the north of England, local initiative, agency, and structures both played and, more important, were widely perceived to play an important role in setting the conditions under which society mobilized. While the deepening crisis of the last years of war broke down the fragile domestic consensus, dissenters tended to believe that they could positively influence authorities and thus had every reason to work within a framework of loyal opposition in order to avoid violating the terms of the wartime reciprocal relationship.

In Munich, a very different dynamic emerged in which local structures were subsumed into a larger Bavarian/Imperial war effort that left far less room for responsiveness on the part of local and regional officials. The harder the state worked to assure it citizenry that it and it alone had the answers to the problems of wartime society, the more self-evidently false those claims became. The result was an outbreak of dissent in late 1917 and early 1918 that looked increasingly to the destruction of wartime order. Even before the Kaiser's armies were defeated in the field, there were real questions as to whether the imperial German order had the capacity to hold up its end of the wartime social bargain.

Chapter 2
"Do Something!:"
Manchester in Transition and War, 1917–18

On the bitterly cold afternoon of January 16, 1918, four thousand munitions workers in the Openshaw and Gorton districts just east of central Manchester put down their tools and, led by factory bands, marched toward the center of the city. Initially, witnesses said that most of the marchers were men, but as the crowd grew, more women emerged from plants and joined the march. As they marched north along Oxford Road, there were cheers from the long lines of women who waited in the cold outside food shops.

When the procession, now swelled with workers from other factories, arrived in Albert Square outside the Town Hall, they were met by the Lord Mayor, Sir Alexander Potter, and a number of local leaders. The Lord Mayor, flanked by the head of the Food Control Committee, addressed the crowd, promising that, "everything possible was being done to relieve the food situation." He was greeted by shouts of "No!" from a crowd that, as one reporter described it "could not stand the conditions much longer." There were rumors of food hoarding and profiteering, and the march's leaders demanded that the city government establish a sensible rationing plan, something which had been heretofore rejected. The crowd was calm, but even casual observers could detect an ominous and threatening note in the attitude of some of the labor representatives, one of whom told the Lord Mayor and his delegation that, "If nothing was done to remedy the state of affairs the workers' committees would not be responsible for anything happening in the shops."[1]

We can see how seriously the city government took the threat of worker discontent in the vital munitions industry by the fact that this remarkable and largely unprecedented protest succeeded in the greater part of its objectives. That afternoon, the Lord Mayor announced that tea, butter, and margarine would be rationed beginning in early March. This dramatic change in policy in the face of coordinated protest seems sudden, but it must be considered in context. The early days of 1918 were, in the minds of many, a period of grave danger for Britain and its war effort. A German offensive in the West seemed ever more likely, and demonstrations like this one seemed to be spreading from city to city. The political truce that sustained Britain through three years of war seemed to be on the verge of collapse.

---

1 Descriptions taken from *Manchester Evening News* (*MEN*), January 16 and 17, 1918.

Yet even in this moment of apparent crisis, the demonstrators on that cold day went to Albert Square believing that their elected officials could and would do something to alleviate the problems in the food supply. For Manchester, and for the broader story of the mobilization of British society during the hard years of war, this expectation proved critical. Rationing policy, like so much else in the British wartime state, developed slowly and haltingly over time. For many ordinary Mancunians, the very *ad hoc* nature of mobilization suggested that they could influence the wartime government and win concessions in exchange for remaining loyal partners of the state and it mobilization efforts. It is not remarkable that demonstrators in an urban area of a combatant state took to the streets in January 1918 to protest over food control. It is remarkable that they walked away with clear concessions. This belief in a functioning reciprocal relationship lay at the heart of the mobilization of British society.

"The war has overcome every other activity," wrote Manchester Liberal leader Arthur Haworth in 1916, "and stayed for the moment those movements to which we gave our earnest thought before the fateful days of 1914."[2] The broad political coalition forged in 1914 formed the bedrock of British politics during the war. It was a truce that survived military defeat and a change of government in 1916 and one that would survive, albeit in rump form, the end of the war. At the end of 1916, after the military catastrophe of the summer and the fall of the Asquith government, Manchester's Liberals argued that "the government of the day should receive the cordial support of all its citizens in its efforts to prosecute the war to a successful conclusion." They pledged again to "co-operate loyally and whole-heartedly in the struggle to maintain the freedom of Europe against the arrogant claims of Prussian Militarism."[3]

However, underneath the surface of national consensus, currents circulated that would not be stilled by a rhetoric of national unity. The last two years of the war saw the domestic consensus challenged repeatedly in the streets and market places of Britain. While party leaders disavowed the normal cut and thrust of formal politics, events on the ground made it abundantly clear that for many Britons, the war crystallized prewar resentments, added new complaints, and called into question the reciprocal relationship between the state and its political citizenry.

This chapter will examine the ways in which authorities at the municipal and national levels tried to channel these concerns into a discussion of the reshaping of postwar society. The need to maintain an artificial and often visibly false image of a nation together-in-arms radicalized any form of dissent, bequeathing a potent brew of disquiet to the postwar world. This juxtaposition between rhetoric and reality in the streets became more pronounced as the war went on, reaching its

2 Clipping "Manchester Liberals: Trade Policy after the War," *Manchester Guardian* (*MG*), March 25, 1916. Unpaginated. Scrapbooks of the Manchester Liberal Federation. Manchester Archives M/283/1.

3 Minutes of the Executive Committee, Lancashire, Cheshire, and North Western Liberal Federation. December, 1916. Manchester Archives, M/390/1/3.

noisy apex in the winter of 1917–18. Crucially, the government's response to this marked increase in dissent was "never obvious and seldom heavy-handed."[4] This light touch, which mirrored the minimally intrusive overall mobilization strategy, helped to diffuse what might have been a dangerous situation.

At the same time, as the demonstrators on that January day in 1918 proved, the nature of the mobilization effort in Britain unintentionally created space for dissent. Compared with its continental rivals and allies, the mobilization of British society proceeded slowly, haltingly, and sometimes in defiance of the nation's strategic needs. The decision of successive wartime governments to pursue a minimally invasive strategy had important consequences for the relationship between the state and society.[5] Since massive state intervention came late, local institutions played a visible role in the war effort. Britons, and Mancunians among them, experienced mobilization as a national experience mediated by the persistence of local centers of power. These local institutions proved responsive to claims by those who felt ill-served by the wartime social order. While this relationship helped to limit the extent and efficacy of dissenting voices during the war, it also created and fostered expectations for the postwar world that proved beyond reach.

Mobilizing for War in Manchester, 1914–1917

The war came to Manchester, as it did across Britain and Europe, as a sudden cataclysm, a rush of activity and a break from the routines of modern life. The unprecedented expansion of the British army during August 1914 could be seen at Heaton Park, suddenly converted into a training ground for the Manchester Regiment. Difficult as it is to believe given the horrors that the Regiment went through, there is probably a great deal of truth to the claim that in those early days "The irresistible wave of volunteer patriotism, the faith in the righteousness of their cause, overcame all individual interest and personal consideration."[6]

The beloved Salford memoirist Robert Roberts remembered that on August 5, 1914, he and his mother saw a neighbor and South African War veteran, Mr. Bickham, returning from the recruiting office:

> ... He stopped by my mother as she hung washing across the street. "Turned down!" he said disgustedly – "Bad teeth! They must want blokes to bite the

---

4 Brock Millman, "HMG and the War Against Dissent, 1914–18," *Journal of Contemporary History* 40, no. 3 (2005): 413.

5 An excellent discussion of the conscription debate can be found in R.J.Q. Adams and Phillip Poirier, *The Conscription Controversy in Great Britain, 1900–1918* (Columbus: Ohio State University Press, 1987).

6 *Sixteenth, Seventeenth, Eighteenth, Nineteenth Battalions: The Manchester Regiment (First City Brigade): A Record: 1914–1918* (Manchester: Sherratt and Hughes, 1923), 6.

> damned Germans!' She laughed, sympathizing as Mr. Bickham went on his way. "They'll be pulling me in, though," he called over his shoulder "before this lot's done!" By 5 August, 1915 he had been lying dead three months in France.[7]

The crisis of war had come, with effects that could never have been predicted in the late summer days of 1914. The war, and the peace that followed, had profound repercussions for the politics, economy, and social order of Manchester and its region. "The Great War tested the administrative machinery of Manchester very rigorously," acknowledged an official history, "The city was quite unprepared to withstand such a protracted strain. To make matters worse, both the central government and municipal authorities at first held mistaken views about the probable economic effects of the conflict."[8] For local government, part of dealing with this strain was to abrogate certain responsibilities altogether, allowing for, and indeed requiring, high levels of input and initiative from the citizenry at large.

Local government came to rely on private charity to an extent that was neither anticipated nor desired. Following a request to limit petrol consumption by the City Treasurer in April 1918, the Superintendent for Baths and Wash Houses replied that to keep hospitals supplied with clean linens, his department had already "been compelled to appeal to the goodwill of a private car owner, and at present we are indebted to the gentleman for some gallons of spirit, with no prospect of returning them."[9]

The labor market, not just in Manchester but all over Britain, had been co-opted by the national government through a series of agreements and acts, notably the 1915 Munitions of War Act. This piece of legislation allowed the government to ban labor activity in certain factories. At the same time, regulations required written authorization for workers seeking to leave employment or change jobs in designated critical industries.[10] The Defence of the Realm Act, or DORA, gave teeth to many of these regulations, and the government proved willing to use DORA prosecutions to stop all sorts of potentially disruptive or subversive activity.

While significant numbers of skilled male workers were protected from service, many other trades ground almost to a halt during the war for lack of available labor. When the Macfadyen Memorial Church and School tried to solicit bids to install new lighting in mid-1918, most contractors were simply unable to consider doing the work, owing in large part to "have[ing] had so many of my men 'called up',"

---

7 Robert Roberts, *The Classic Slum: Salford Life in the First Quarter of the Century* (Manchester: Manchester University Press, 1971), 150.

8 Arthur Redford, *The History of Local Government in Manchester*, vol. 3 (London: Longmans, Green, and Co., 1940), 205.

9 Letter from J. Derbyshire to J. Williams, April 1917. Corporation of Manchester – Treasurer's Department. Ministry of Munitions – Consumption of Petrol. Manchester Archives M610.

10 David Powell, *British Politics and the Labour Question, 1868–1990*. (London: Macmillan, 1992), 60.

"the reduction of our staff," or "the pressure of extremely urgent war work."[11] Either by enlistment, conscription, or the carrot of lucrative war work contracts, the state's wartime power transformed the economic landscape. For many people, this was welcome news. Robert Roberts remembered one neighbor in Salford who benefited not only financially but also found the experience of living without her soldier husband curiously liberating:

> Many wives of fighting men discovered that they could manage far better on government allowances than they ever did on their breadwinner's meager wage. Mrs. Cassidy with a young brood in a house near the shop now drew nearly three times the amount her usually drunken husband had brought home. "They can keep Mick for ever!" she said, delighted.[12]

"It has been said," wrote H.M McKechnie in 1916, "that the present war constitutes a definite fissure in the modern world's continuity – a sort of geological 'fault' in the stratification of time. Already Manchester is becoming acclimatised to war and 'twelve months ago' begins to look antiquated, almost antediluvian." McKechnie's description, if a bit overwraught, captures the very real sense among many in Manchester, and in Britain, that something had changed. Aside from the "street lamps muffled like highwaymen and tramway lamps tinted the colour of raspberry,"[13] there was a palpable sense that things after the war would not return to the *status quo ante bellum*. What is all the more remarkable is that few at that point would hazard a guess as to exactly what the postwar world would look like. It was as if the smart money was eschewing precise prediction, waiting to see how the war would end before committing itself to any position or program.

In order to understand the multiple economic crises that later came with demobilization, we must first look at the forces that mobilized the local economy during the war years. The mobilization of the economy in Manchester and its region was, broadly speaking, in line with events in much of the rest of the country. Successive wartime governments initially pursued a mobilization strategy that sought to minimize the amount of dislocation, followed by the realization that the demands of war called for more effective penetration of civil society. Second, mobilization saw a remarkable degree of coordination and cooperation between the state and private enterprise. This was not without its problems, but the transition from peacetime to wartime economy was only possible because of the relative sophistication of local industrial facilities.

---

11 Letters from Rueben Bennett, James Higson, and John Collier concerning Macfayen Church, Manchester Archives M/86/4/2. The church did eventually manage to find a suitable bidder.

12 Roberts, 164.

13 H.M. McKechnie, *Manchester in 1915* (Manchester and London: The University Press, 1915), 16.

Britain's initial problems of shell production helped to spur some of the most dramatic expansion of wartime industry in Manchester. By the middle of 1915, the Ministry of Munitions under the energetic leadership of David Lloyd George conducted surveys of the nation's industrial facilities and implemented a scheme designed to quickly harness available plants for the production of shells. The plan, which called for National Shell Factories (NSF) to be built or installed in areas known to have the available space and labor, was administered by local Boards of Management. These Boards gave the appearance of local autonomy but were actually tightly bound to Lloyd George and the Ministry.[14]

Manchester and surrounding communities quickly moved to become part of this new system. Typically, city or town governments offered municipal facilities, often the spacious tramways sheds, for conversion. They also offered the rail access and often heavy equipment like cranes.[15] Manchester, Bury, and Rochdale, among others, had Boards of Management by the end of 1915. Rochdale was supposed to be able to produce 1,000 6-inch shells each week, but owing to production delays did not start manufacturing until July 1916. Manchester, which was to manufacture 2,000 4.5-inch shells weekly, could only manage 500 and did not reach its target until 1917.[16]

The variety of prewar industries in Manchester allowed a range of wartime industrial conversions. In a complicated series of transactions, Crossley Motors adapted their facility at Heaton Chapel as a National Aircraft Factory in 1917. These large works employed over 1,700 men and 1,000 women, but managers and Ministry inspectors complained about the quality and dedication of the labor force. Many of the workers involved in the plant's conversion were Irish, and one report derided them as "deplorable in spirit and quality."[17] Despite designation as a priority customer for raw materials, the factory was unable to match its promised output of 40 DH9 and DH10 aircraft per week.[18]

In other cases, conversion did not work well because of outdated facilities. H.M. Factory, West Gorton was supposed to use a decrepit dye plant for the production of explosives and caustic chemicals. While managers expressed great satisfaction at the quality of their male and female workers, the plant's equipment

14 R.J.Q. Adams, *Arms and the Wizard: Lloyd George and the Ministry of Munitions*, 1915–1916 (College Station: Texas A&M University Press, 1978), 64–70.

15 See the description of the NSF Hyde Road in NA RECO 1/126.

16 Reports on National Shell Factories found in NA MUN 5/366/1122/90.

17 This actually described workers at the Aintree Facility in Liverpool, but is referred to in the report on the Heaton Chapel plant as being "similar." The Aintree report is in NA MUN 5/365/1122/48.

18 "History of the Heaton Chapel National Aircraft Factory" in NA MUN 5/365/1122/50.

proved a major hindrance. From a high of nearly 1,000 employees in mid-1917, the facility had just 16 workers and ceased production by the end of the war.[19]

Finally, this often uneasy alliance between the government and private enterprise suffered from the persistence of prewar competition between firms. Such competition in Lancashire, concluded a Ministry inspector in 1915, "placed the county as a unit of organization outside of the range of practical politics."[20] The case of J.G.W. Gruban proved an excellent example of the cross-cutting influence of competition between firms, the drive for wartime efficiency, and the prejudices of wartime. Gruban was a manager at W.B. Haigh Gruban, a machine tool manufacturer in Oldham. He also served as the firm's representative on the local Munitions Tribunal. In November, 1915, one Lewis Ransome wrote to the Ministry of Munitions and informed them that Gruban was a recently naturalized British citizen who had been born in Germany. "Although in normal times Mssr. Haigh, Gruban, and Co are competitors of my firm, I hope you will not misconstrue my motives in drawing your attention to this matter."[21] This complaint made it all the way to the desk of Lloyd George's deputy, Christopher Addison. While a junior bureaucrat at the ministry wrote in the margin that he thought Gruban should keep his seat, Addison scribbled emphatically "I think not."[22] A few days later, Gruban resigned his position, politely claiming that "my time is taxed to the utmost."[23]

While the Gruban case points to the self-serving and often petty competition that emerged from the public–private alliance that sustained mobilization, the issue of foreigners was actually a highly visible and troubling one. As with the Gruban case, wartime distrust of immigrants often manifested itself in ways that ran counter to expectations of national unity or of the orderly operation of a wartime economy.

The internment of enemy aliens happened, as it did in much of Britain, in a series of hesitating steps. Manchester had a sizable German and Austrian community, many of whom had been there since the mid-nineteenth century. Public debate over the issue of enemy aliens, and the outbreak of physical violence toward them exacerbated pre-existing tensions across community lines and would have serious repercussions after the war.

According to a recent survey of the problem of enemy aliens in Britain, there were 1,318 Germans in Manchester in 1911.[24] They seem to have been most visible in the grocery and butcher trades, and many central European Jews were involved in the sale and manufacture of waterproof clothing. When the war began, the city

19 "Retrospective Review of H.M. Factory, West Gorton" NA MUN 5/368/1122.7/11

20 "Early History of the Manchester Board of Management" NA 5/363/1121/22/6.

21 Letter of November, 12, 1915 in NA LAB 2/47/MT126/1/1919.

22 Marginalia on opening page of file, ibid.

23 Letter from Gruban to Ministry, September 20, 1915, in ibid.

24 Panikos Panayi, *The Enemy in our Midst: Germans in Britain during the First World War* (Providence and Oxford: Berg, 1991), 19.

imposed a curfew on enemy aliens, and very shortly thereafter began rounding up suspicious males and sending them to internment camps, mostly on the Isle of Man. A butcher named Niebel, for example, was interned despite the fact that he was seriously ill, a British citizen who had lived in Manchester since he was 14, and had three sons serving in His Majesty's Forces.[25]

Phil Glantz, a young boy at the time, remembered with some humor the fate of his father, for whom his time on the Isle was a brief but rare respite from the pressures of work and life with a wife who must have been truly formidable:

> ... my father was interned during the First World War, an Austrian, an enemy alien, I think it was the only time he had any happiness in his life when he was interned on the Isle of Man but it was only for a short time cos my mother (?) to get him out and she did do, and said why are you keeping him, you want uniforms she was saying to the authorities, why are you keeping a skilled tailor on the Isle of Man, he could be here making uniforms, and keeping his family.[26]

What followed proved to be considerably less amusing. In the wake of the *Lusitania* sinking on May 7, 1915, there were serious anti-German riots in Liverpool and Manchester. After a group of female factory laborers attacked a German butcher shop in New Cross, mobs in the city and suburbs attacked and destroyed at least two shops, two more butchers, and several houses. The mobs proved to be less than discriminating in their rampage. According to a damage claim filed several years later, one of the destroyed shops belonged to Clara Fechner, an Englishwoman who had acquired her German last name through marriage. Her small shop on Oxford Road was completely looted and partly destroyed, damage which fell in part to the landlord, who was also English.[27]

Later damage claims totaled £4,375.[28] Police moved in and made a number of arrests, while one officer, Inspector Tongue, was injured by a flying brick.[29] Many of those arrested (40 out of 65 in Salford) were women. Some at the time, notably Sylvia Pankhurst, argued that the disturbances were really hunger riots, as evidenced by the rioters' focus on purveyors of food. More recent scholarship, notably by Panikos Panayi, disputes this, since this was a time of relative prosperity

25 Letter from Annot Robinson to Mr. Middleton, June, 1918. Archives of the Labour Party, WNC 2/3, Labour History Archive.

26 Transcript of interview with Phil Glantz, Manchester Jewish Museum, J94, T1, S1., 6.

27 Letter from law office of Batty, Ford and Buckley to Thomas Hudson, Town Clerk, March 8, 1919. Watch Committee Minutes, 79/5. Greater Manchester Police Archive.

28 Panikos Panayi, "The Lancashire Anti-German Riots of May, 1915," *Manchester Region History Review* II, no. 2 (1988/9), 7.

29 Eric Hewitt, *A History of Policing in Manchester* (Didsbury: E.J. Morton, 1979), 113.

and ready availability of foodstuffs.[30] One reason that the mobs targeted butchers and grocers was because they may have been visible manifestations of the German and Austrian presence in the city and would have been commonly associated with this group of immigrants.

This sort of mob violence was certainly not *sui generis*. Wolf Bennington (born Shefinsky) puckishly remembered the incident as another manifestation of ethnic and economic tensions in the city that predated the war:

> You see, of course it only wants something to happen to really, give 'em an opportunity to, but during the First World War there was a big boat, the *Lusitania*, it was sunk in 1915, the *Lusitania*, well the press of course er made a big deal of it and inflamed the people and they went about breaking windows in many shops especially if they thought it was a German or Austrian shop, and I remember many a Jewish shop put a sign in the window "We are Russian." ... I remember it quite distinctly was, it wasn't because they were upset about the *Lusitania*, it was just an excuse to go looting, you see ... Of course this was amongst the lower orders, ha, ha.[31]

In 1917, the Police Department received a War Department directive asking it to draw up a "Grey List" of those who had one or more foreign parent. This rather overwrought document, which appears to have received as much attention as it deserved, asked local police to ascribe to each person on the list a rating between AA (Absolutely Anglicized) and BB (Bad Boche).[32] Curiously, there was little to no guidance as to how one should evaluate the loyalty of such individuals and no indication that this classification system was ever put into place.

The first few years of the war witnessed a large-scale mobilization of the population of Manchester and its surrounding communities. Not only did men march off to war, but women took their places in the factory. Local authorities began to coordinate with national law enforcement to try to contain internal threats. Private enterprise worked in a (sometimes uneasy) partnership with wartime demands. Less tangibly, people felt they were at war and acted accordingly. Germans and Austrians who had once been an integral part of the community were made to feel distinctly unwelcome and on at least one spectacular occasion were the victims of violence. It can be said that total war is something that is perpetually in a state of becoming, an unachievable ideal that exists only in the imagination of planners. What occurred in Manchester after more than two years of war reflected the totalizing possibility of mass industrial war. In 1917, the complicated, difficult

---

30 Panayi. "Anti-German Riots," 9.

31 Transcript of interview with Wolf Bennington, Manchester Jewish Museum, J24, 15.

32 Letter from War Department to Chief Constable. Undated, but summer 1917. General Orders, 1917, 378, Greater Manchester Police Archive.

process of mobilizing society toward the common goal of victory began to yield unexpected and, for authorities, unwelcome results.

The experience of war severely tested the industrial capacities of south Lancashire, a region whose products were vital to the war effort. "Manchester's motto since the war began has been 'Do Something.' It will continue to be 'Do Something' to the end of the war, and afterwards, if necessary," offered a local paper in early 1917.[33] Massive mobilization of manpower and materiel exacerbated existing trends and tensions in the area, provided new sources of resentment, and for some, particularly women, created new opportunities which in themselves threatened to disrupt industrial relations in dramatic ways. The Lancashire cotton industry was already exceptional with regard to women. Female labor had long been a part of mill life.[34] In 1911, 32.5 percent of women over the age of 10 nationwide worked in some capacity. Manchester and its surroundings were well above that figure, with 39.4 percent of Mancunian women employed and just over 50 percent in Bury. Particularly in the surrounding communities, at least a plurality of these women worked in the cotton industry.[35] It was the transition of female workers into other parts of the labor market that was revolutionary.

One of the more unique aspects of the munitions industry was that, because of its relative novelty and rapid expansion, there was plenty of room for ambitious individuals to win promotions, regardless of experience or gender. Of the more than 7.3 million women working by the end of the war, somewhere between 700,000 and 1 million of them were employed in the munitions industry.[36] Maude Mary Spackman (later Dooley), an unskilled worker at a clothing factory, got a job through a Labour Exchange in a shell plant at Belle Vue in 1916. Her memories of her time in the factory are fairly grim but illustrate the possibilities wartime provided. She remembered 18-pound shells rolling off benches onto workers' feet and frequent accidents when improperly stacked shells began to roll, causing nearby workers to "run for their lives." The largely female workforce worked 12-hour days, 7 days a week, with alternate weeks of night work. Spackman often went without sleep during night work weeks, as she had a home and children to look after.

Still, she took advantage of the opportunity afforded by the need for trained shell inspectors, needed, she remembered because "it was alleged that more soldiers were killed by faulty shells than by enemy action." Her notes recalled the relative complexity and difficulty of the training involved, and it was quite an accomplishment for this almost entirely unschooled former laborer to become

33 "Manchester's War Motto," *MEN*, January 16, 1917.

34 Trevor Wilson, *The Myriad Faces of War: Britain and the Great War, 1914–18* (Cambridge: Polity Press, 1986), n. 716.

35 Report on the Cotton Industry in NA RECO 1/768.

36 Figures, and an explanation for the vagaries in the number of munitions workers, see Angela Woollacott, *On Her Their Lives Depend: Munitions Workers in the Great War* (Berkeley: University of California Press, 1994), 17–19.

a qualified examiner.[37] For women like Maude Spackman, the sudden need for semi-skilled labor presented unprecedented opportunities for advancement and for wages that would have been unthinkable without the war.

The Quirk family, which came to Manchester from the Isle of Man before 1914, was also transformed by the war. Sydney Quirk joined the Manchester Territorials and saw service in the Middle East. One sister got a job as a postal inspector, while Gladys Quirk went to work in one of the city's munitions factories. At some point shortly before the end of the war Gladys penned a quick poem called simply "A Munition Girl's Thoughts." While she recorded the uncertainty of the wartime labor market for women and the worsening problems of wartime provisioning, there is no doubt that women like Gladys felt real pride in the work that they did and the role it might play in eventual victory. It read, in part:

> There's a little spot called England
> Where they wait in butter queues
> Also tea, sugar, beef and bacon
> 'till it almost gives one the blues
>
> I'm just a munitions worker
> Toiling 8 hours a day
> Now we are being rationed out
> We'll have to take what comes our way
>
> I'm working my very hardest
> Just going to test a shell
> If I'd Kaiser Bill here for a minute
> I'd just fire him off to H____[38]

The influx of women like Gladys Quirk and Maude Spackman into the workforce was by no means unproblematic or uncontested. Particularly as inspectors from the Ministry of Munitions enforced plans to increase the proportion of female workers, the resentment against women in the factories was palpable and sometimes disrupted production. This put the Ministry in an awkward position, and its responses are instructive in that they point to the compromises that were critical to mobilization.

One of the issues that had to be tackled in First World War Britain was that of "dilution." This refers to the practice of freeing male labor for military service by replacing skilled and factory positions with multiple unskilled or semi-skilled workers. Whatever its efficacy in providing more men for military service, dilution was immensely divisive and unpopular in the workplace. Skilled workers naturally

37 Introductory material, files of Maud Mary Spackman. Compiled by her daughter, Mrs. H. Dooley. MISC 657, Manchester Archives.

38 Files of the Quirk family. IWMA MISC 266/3609.

feared that it would spell the permanent end of their special status and resented the unskilled workers who took their jobs while male workers bitterly resented the influx of female labor. Dilution proved to be perhaps the most contentious aspect of the state's wartime interference in industry.

The Rochdale National Shell Factory was the site of a set of conflicts over dilution that were exceptionally well-documented but do not seem to have been atypical. By early 1917, there were 362 employees, each working a 61-hour (day) or 58-hour (night) week. Women made up more than 62 percent of workers and were employed in every capacity except the tool room and crane operations. Even the Ministry inspectors who insisted on the hiring of women were skeptical of the quality of female labor. "The type of local female labour," wrote one inspector, was too "light" for this type of work. "A heavier type which lived in the Wigan district was the sort of woman labourer required."

Within the factory, women workers were targeted by skilled and semi-skilled male employees. Unknown hands tightened bolts to the limits of their tolerance or deliberately set machines incorrectly. Women were also subject to "abus[e] and annoy[ance]" by their male colleagues. A male worker named Hedan was so singular in his efforts to humiliate and badger the factory's female workers that he earned himself a mention in the official history of the works.

Matters reached a breaking point in April 1917, when Ministry inspectors insisted that the percentage of female workers increase to more than 75 percent, including the replacement of six skilled male workers by nine women and the introduction of women into the previously all-male tool shop. On April 23, the men of the Rochdale NSF refused to work, and there were rumblings that the factory in Bury would join the stoppage. The Board of Management suspended the plan and, after a series of communications with the Ministry, it was halted altogether. The following October, the forced increase in female employment resumed, but by the time its effects could be seen, the war had ended and a new series of problems became far more pressing.[39]

The presence of women in Manchester's factories in large numbers created unexpected problems for some Mancunian businesses. The munitions industry injected large amounts of cash into workers' pockets, which, in turn, created unexpected disequilibrium in services that had once thrived by being positioned close to the industrial heart of the city. A dance hall proprietress in Moss Side wrote to her landlord, explaining that she was unable to pay her full rent.

> I know I promised to pay the sept quarter but unfortunately I have not been able to keep it. Nor can I say what I can do during the war.... No one in the dancing line is doing well except the fortunate few who are near a munition works. None of my clients who used to come from Armstrong and Whitworth come now for the simple reason that they work to [sic] late every evening to come so far.

39 Early History of the Rochdale Board of Management in NA MUN 5/363/1121/22 and the Rochdale National Shell Factory in NA MUN 5/366/1122/90.

> And our dear Tommies cannot. It seems very strange, but no one has more sympathy with my bad trade than the dear boys who are fighting for us.[40]

The expansion of war industries and the manpower needs of the military required a precarious balance between centralized planning and local initiatives. While mobilization in modern society has a profound centralizing effect, the demands of industrial war called for levels of coordination previously unimaginable. It is quite clear in hindsight that neither state nor local authorities had any idea that the war was going to be so long or involve such a level of mobilization and that cooperation between the two should be problematic.

The Food Question and the 'Queue Evil'

"As 1917 wore on," remembered Robert Roberts, "ordinary folk, feeling a deepening weariness of war but not daring to show it too openly, became boldly critical of things about them and especially of those who, they believed, were making huge profits at the country's expense."[41] One should be careful of reading too much into Roberts' accounts of politics, since his memoirs were written fifty years later and with a great deal of hindsight, but his observations as a child watching the neighborhood around his parents' store are priceless in their vivid color.

For the Roberts and their neighbors, the war was a mixed blessing. Price controls and eventual rationing benefited poor consumers, who at least nominally now had access to foodstuffs that were not to be found in Salford stores before the war. Roberts remembers customers becoming "accustomed to the availability of such delicacies as canned lobster or gherkins."[42] This said, however, it was in the area of food supply and price control that the first and clearest collapse of the wartime consensus took place.

Efforts by national and local authorities to mediate in food issues demonstrated in sharp relief the paradox of bureaucratic intervention in the market. The state's efforts to regulate markets originated in a genuine conviction that improving the lives of ordinary people would help the war effort. However, since such efforts also strove to be minimally invasive, they were almost certain to fail in the face of the overwhelming challenges facing domestic production. In the climate of mass industrial war, such pragmatism could easily come to resemble plodding, indecisiveness, and lack of regard for the life of ordinary Britons.

By the middle of the war, the regulation of food became one of great importance in Manchester. Lord Mayor Thomas Smethurst called a "numerously attended"

40 Letter from Ms. Oldbury (Moss Side) to Mr. Maxwell, Finance Comm., M&S Co-operative Society. Undated. Loose papers found in front material, M473/1/2/11, Manchester Archives.

41 Roberts, 170.

42 Ibid., 160.

public meeting at Town Hall as early as November 1916 in response to a public petition protesting against the "flagrant evil" of rising prices and falling supplies. The results of the meeting, couched in the formal language of bureaucracy, were actually fairly radical, in that they acknowledged that large numbers of women and children "were already suffering seriously" from high prices. The council went so far as to call upon the national government to combat profiteering by becoming "the sole purchaser of all imported foodstuffs," commandeering the merchant fleet to control costs, and to take control of the distribution of milk, meat, wheat, oats, barley, and potatoes.[43]

Largely as a result of this sort of agitation, the city set up a Foodstuffs Special Committee, which launched earnest and well-intended projects like educating citizens about home gardening and trying to organize the supply of gardening implements. This was too little, too late, and as an official historian noted "in spite of this abundant goodwill, the practical results of local agricultural efforts were not great when compared with the magnitude of the food problem."[44] The Council set up a local Food Control Committee in August, by which time it was clear that existing measures were totally inadequate. Some suggested that the Committee was aloof from the practical concerns that it intended to solve. The Manchester and Salford Co-Operative Society, representing about 60,000 members in the region, protested strongly that the new body would not include representatives from the Society and that, "on our Municipal council there will be only one official representative of the working class."[45]

Britain held out against rationing until the end of 1917 and did not impose a rigorous rationing regime until early the next year. The rationale for this, as explained in October 1917, was that while the British system was "arduous," it was:

> neither unwieldy or vexatious like the German system of rationing. All who assist in it should be aware of the administrative and commercial difficulties with which the enemy struggles ... . This not only involves the employment of much larger staffs of workers than the British method of food control, but creates disaffection as a result of inter-state rivalries and a contest between urban and rural populations. In this country the use of ordinary channels of supply solves most problems and to the extent that serious disaffection is avoided we shall continue resolute for victory.[46]

---

43 Manchester Council Proceedings, November 29, 1916, 142–3.

44 Redford, 215.

45 Draft of letter to be sent to Lord Rhondda and J.R. Clynes. August 9, 1917. General Board, Manchester and Salford Equitable Co-Operative Society, M473/1/1/22 . Manchester Archives.

46 "News and Comments" *National Food Journal*, October 24, 1917. Unpaginated. M138/box 65. Manchester Archives.

While the assessment of the weaknesses of the German rationing system was not wholly wrong, it defied logic to suggest that because the German system did not function particularly well (under a fairly robust blockade by the Royal Navy) that no rationing scheme was possible.

The louder the government trumpeted its efforts, the more apparent and egregious its failures became. The normally quiescent *Manchester Evening News*, commenting on a visit by Director of Food Economy Sir Arthur Yapp in November, claimed that "the plain man has become bewildered by the multitude of his counsellors on the food question and by the striking contradictions between the actions and words of these gentlemen." Yapp did himself no favors by sitting down to a "comfortable luncheon consisting of soup, fish, meat, potatoes, sprouts, biscuits, and cheese" while many in the city had not enjoyed regular supplies of these items in years. When asked about the eventual demobilization of munitions workers, Yapp assured his audience that "the Government had carefully considered the question of demobilisation, and one of the reconstruction committees had arrived at some very definite conclusions, though a final scheme could not be said to have been absolutely established."[47]

Yapp's visit, and the hostile reception he received, points to a fundamental issue in the British experience of food control. It remained largely in the hands of local officials and structures, who were charged with managing the administration and enforcement of legislation that appeared piecemeal, confusing, and ill-considered. While food control legislation came from London, the population associated the management of the food supply with local authorities.

Part of the problem with enforcement was that it required the cooperation of the police, who, if one carefully reads the reports of the Chief Constable, were not particularly enthusiastic about enforcing the bewildering food orders. Chief Constable Robert Peacock's report on food control orders, filed in January 1918, refers to difficulties in "putting into practice the novel and somewhat complicated provisions" of early food control orders. "The desire of the Police was to get the provisions of the various orders carried out with as little friction as possible...." he wrote, suggesting that the force's command structure was aware of difficulties in asking constables to rigidly enforce complex and intrusive orders. Despite this, the police did take some action against possible food control violators. They made 48,664 visits to businesses during the second half of 1917, resulting in 241 prosecutions, an unspecified number of verbal warnings, and more than 100 official warnings.[48]

The appeals of businesses that had been caught in violation of the food control orders, suggested that the improvised and local nature of both the regulations and their enforcement led to considerable confusion and charges of unfair treatment.

47 "Flat Contradiction," *MEN*, November 13, 1917.

48 Report on enforcement of food control orders, written by Chief Constable Robert Peacock. January 3, 1918. Watch Committee Minutes, 75/124, Greater Manchester Police Archive.

The potato merchant A. Bracegirdle and Son had been driven out of business when a local magistrate ordered them to sell their wares at wholesale prices. His solicitor pointed out that potato vendors in other cities were not under the same restrictions and that other potato dealers in Manchester had been given dispensations by the Food Control Committee to continue to sell at higher prices.[49]

We can learn something more about the enforcement of food regulations from weekly bulletins from the local Food Control Committees, which tracked, among other things, the number of prosecutions for food offenses. For four weeks in early 1918, for instance, there was an average of 50 new cases per week, of which about 90 percent were successfully prosecuted. Unfortunately, these cases were broken down by region, rather than by the nature of the offense. Apparently, some of the most common violations occurred in the cheese, tea, and potato trades, among the most hotly contested of foodstuffs. It is also clear from the Food Control Committee's records that these statistics were well in line with other industrial cities, where there were similar rates of offense and conviction.[50]

The Food Control Committees received a veritable flood of directives from the Ministry of Food, ranging from subtle changes to the byzantine food control orders to suggestions to pass on to the public. The hectoring tone of this suggestion was typical:

> Black puddings are the latest food items to strengthen our National Larder.... These puddings, which are manufactured of pure, wholesome and nutritious ingredients, are submitted to careful scientific test before use. ... They have a higher nutritive value than ordinary pork and beef sausages, as bread is not used in their composition. The Black Pudding has always been a favourite dish among the industrial classes in Lancashire, and North Country folk are sound judges of what is both tasty and wholesome.[51]

The black pudding, indeed a Lancashire specialty, is an offal and blood sausage. It is a fairly grim affair even in the best of times, least of all a period in which the city was taking steps to "salvag[e] condemned meat and fish offal."[52] Despite the promise of a "careful scientific test," one can only wonder how wartime black pudding must have looked and tasted.

Thus could officialdom, in the person of the police and food control bureaucracies, claim that they were taking steps to alleviate food concerns. However, other sources indicated that the public believed that far too little was

49 Letter from Ernest Farrington, esq. to Town Clerk. April 10, 1917. Watch Committee Minutes, 73/153–4, Greater Manchester Police Archive.

50 "Weekly Bulletin of the Food Control Committee" Holdings incomplete. Manchester Archives, M138/box 4.

51 Clipping from the files of the Audenshaw Food Control Committee. Undated. Manchester Archives, M138/Box 66.

52 Redford, 215.

being done and that they were being made to suffer for lack of proper regulation or enforcement. In some cases, prices were too high for many consumers, while in other cases, staple items simply became unavailable. Sometimes, both happened simultaneously, reinforcing the growing idea that the government was unwilling to do anything to improve the lot of urban dwellers.

Potatoes were the subject of one of the earliest food control orders, but that did not stop a collapse in the potato supply during the early months of 1917. Press and food control reports suggested that the tubers were almost impossible to find in markets and shops. A mother of six commented that those who sought to regulate the market on potatoes "are not the people that have a lot of mouths to fill. They have got well-lined pantries while the poor must starve because we can't pay the prices."[53]

In the Spring of 1917, rationing was still something to be avoided in favor of regulated free enterprise. For the *Manchester Evening News*, the problem was not with the system of distribution but rather with those who:

> demand supplies and if they cannot get them think that they have a grievance against the man behind the counter who with very limited stocks at his disposal is doing his best to let all those dependent upon him have their faire share. Unless there is a better compliance by this class of people with the system now in operation .... there can be no doubt that the whole community will have to suffer the inconvenience of compulsory rationing.[54]

Seven months later, the growing "queue evil" forced a turnabout in the paper's stance on rationing. Regular reports of hundreds of poor Mancunians standing in line outside shops waiting to buy food led the editors to conclude that "nothing short of the absolute state control of every article of food right from the source can ease the situation by ensuring the equitable distribution of such supplies are available."[55] After a year of increasing hardship and concerns about the continued quiescence of the population, more and more Mancunians were coming around to the idea of rationing. It was an idea that was also finding favor in local and national government. This turnabout was largely a result of gloomy reports about the attitudes of those unfortunates who found themselves stuck in the food lines.

By mid-1917, there was already a palpable sense that the mood in the food queues was becoming ugly. "People who are reasonably treated generally act reasonably. Unfairness and preference breed irritation ..." claimed the *Manchester Evening News*.[56] A local councillor went further, declaring that the populace was being "robbed by unscrupulous shopkeepers" and that because of this the

53 *MEN*, January 12, 1917.

54 "Compulsory Rations," *MEN*, May 1, 1917.

55 "Manchester Queues," *MEN*, January 1, 1918.

56 "Food Problems," *MEN*, December 20, 1917.

"whole working class population of Manchester is seething with discontent."[57] In December, largely citing the problem of diminishing stocks and increasing lines, the local Food Control Committee finally came around and endorsed rationing schemes. The next month saw the street demonstrations at Albert Square and the final acceptance of local government that rationing was a necessity if civic order was to be maintained.

The issue of food created the greatest challenge to relations between local government and the population. The state, and more directly the city, had failed to adequately address the related problems of availability, price, and quality in any systematic way, leaving it open to charges of unfair treatment. Outrage over this single issue manifested itself in other forms of discontent and protest. The food question became intertwined with other social and moral issues, giving critics of the government new opportunities to find fault with its handling of mobilization of society.

It was possible to piggy-back other issues onto the food crisis. One of the most blatant examples was the temperance movement, which seems to have attracted considerable attention in the Northwest. At a series of open-air meetings, social reformers abandoned traditional anti-alcohol rhetoric about social dislocation or moral degradation to argue that the brewing industry was an inappropriate consumer of foodstuffs in wartime:

> From August 1914 to April 1917 inclusive, £510,000,000 was spent in Drink, 4,400,000 Tons of Grain was used (or wasted) in its manufacture, also 762,000,000 lbs. of Sugar. Is it wise to thus destroy good Food in wartime or at anytime?[58]

In May, 1917, Salford hosted the national conference of the Sons of Temperance. Most Worthy Patriarch W.J. Wrightman told his audience that:

> It was almost incredible that the grain thus saved should be converted into liquor to tempt soldiers and sailors. The liquor trade was using capital, food, transport, coal, buildings and man-power for the making of drink, and there was no denial that the use of liquor spelt inefficiency. Every effort should be made to force the government to prevent the sale, manufacture, and transport of intoxicants during the war, and the period of demobilization. This would mitigate any hardships and would be a means of shortening the war.[59]

Brewers and publicans, already suffering from price control, quality control, and a shortage of ingredients (not to mention drinkers), responded by asserting that they would "cheerfully take their share of sacrifice but let there be common

57 "Rigamarole and Muddle," *MEN*, April 4, 1917.
58 Leaflet "Waste of Food in Wartime," Manchester Archives, M267/5/3.
59 "Sons of Temperance – Drink and the War," *MEN*, May 20, 1918.

sense and fairness in apportioning the sacrifice." Their counter-appeal was solidly grounded in wartime patriotism ("The solider needs it and Army Authorities make sure he gets it.") and the same type of spurious nutritional science applied by the temperance advocates. "Beer economises food because it makes solid food more easily assimilated, and so less of it is needed for nutrition."[60]

Aside from the enormous inconvenience and manifest inequality of the food queues and shortages, there was an evident psychological toll as working- and middle-class consumers found themselves more or less powerless in consumer society. A 1917 advertisement for Chairman Cigarettes expressed this feeling of anomie as power relationships inverted in the face of scarcity:

> I bow before the butcher-man
> I grovel to the grocer
> I swallow all the saucy airs
> With which they answer "No, sir!"
> But what a change to go next door
> And there with head erect
> To buy some CHAIRMAN cigarettes
> And a little self-respect![61]

Public Space and Intimate Space in Wartime Manchester

In July, 1915, a young student at the Seymour Park School, Old Trafford named Edith wrote to her grandmother about wartime life in Manchester. She wrote briefly of the upcoming mid-summer holiday, the recent death in France of school employee Sergeant-Major Mundy, a school employee, and of her hope to begin "in earnest the work of a new standard" in the year to come. Mostly, she wrote about the war. "We believe, however, that we are fighting for right, and so we must fight on till we win whatever the cost." As for her role in this grand story, "there is little else we can do while we are children except to live each day quietly and bravely, being kind and gentle and making those around us as happy as possible."[62]

Edith's letter is a curious artifact. There is nothing personal in the text. Her family is never mentioned, nor does she ever inquire after her grandmother in any way. The language is stilted and the pages are infused with a careful patriotic language. This suggests two options. First, it may be a school exercise in which students wrote to someone about the war. Second, it may represent the actual preoccupations of a young girl at the end of the first year of the conflict. In either case, it helps us to understand how profoundly the war influenced everyday modes

---

60 Anonymous advertisement. *MEN*, March 9, 1917.

61 "Chairman Rhymes, No. 11," *MEN*, November 2, 1917.

62 Letter dated July 15, 1915 in IWMA 248/3441.

of thought and behavior and how profoundly the home front experienced contact with the war.

As a girl, Edith could not aspire to frontline heroism like her male schoolmates. Yet her letter, with its evocation of service on the home front, is a reminder of how quickly and intensely the rhetoric of patriotic service suffused everyday life during the First World War. Stéphane Audoin-Rouzeau, in his study of children in the First World War, has pointed to the creation of a new variety of "child-heroes" whose contribution to the war effort could simply be to suffer loss.[63] While Edith and other girls did grow up during the war with the expectation that they too would someday serve in the armed forces, they were nonetheless mobilized into the evolving culture of wartime. Increasingly, this meant learning to accept the realities of sacrifice and death.

We cannot hope to explain how traumatic the end of the war really was without attempting to grapple with the ways that it transformed the everyday lives of Europeans throughout the combatant states. It created wartime communities in unlikely places like factories, hospitals, schools, and families. These communities were cross-cutting, complementary, and widely varied, but they served the same function. They integrated the home front and the front lines and gave ordinary people a stake in the final victory. They catalyzed the self-mobilization of combatant societies and proved, in some cases, far more durable than anyone imagined at the time.

The war was a confusing experience for many, calling into question established beliefs and limiting choices in ways that went far beyond food lines. Wartime regulations both drew from and created debates over morality and public life, particularly in questions of frivolity or luxury in a time of war. In 1916, the Council's Watch Committee banned films that depicted nightclubs or cabarets as a threat to public morality, pointing particularly to George Sargent's classic *Midnight at Maxim's*.[64] Such intrusive edicts dovetailed with concerns about the war's effect on even the most limited conventions of social life. In 1917, the *Manchester Evening News* wondered about the future of hospitality in an age of rationing. "The interchange of hospitality will perforce have to cease because no householder will be able to acquire more food than is allowed to him on his ration cards." This "social revolution," suggested the paper, would transform the ways in which Mancunians, and Britons, dealt with each other.[65] Such restrictions, real or imagined, suggest the dislocating effects of the war on the home front and the perceived collapse of old certainties. The reality on the ground appears to have been somewhat more complicated.

63 Stéphane Audoin-Rouzeau, *La guerre des enfants, 1914–1918* (Paris: Colin, 2003).

64 Arthur Redford, *The History of Local Government in Manchester*, vol. 2 (London: Longmans, Green, and Co., 1940), 217.

65 "Rationing Effects. Manchester and the Coming Changes," *MEN*, February 19, 1918.

Concerns about public order and public morality point to an interesting conundrum in the wartime history of Manchester and, more broadly, British society. For some, and for some of the time, the war presented undreamed-of opportunities for recreation, release, and fun. Despite wartime restrictions, men and women had cash wages, reasonably-priced if sometimes difficult to acquire supplies of food and drink, and took advantage of what contemporaries perceived to have be a general laxity of prewar sexual mores. In short, there were a significant number of people who seemed to have enjoyed themselves tremendously even as they served loyally and diligently in the war effort.

Rifleman Harold Clegg of the 3rd Battalion, Liverpool Regiment, was one of those people. Gassed at Armentières in 1917 and temporarily blinded, Clegg made his way to Manchester after doctors judged that he had not completely recovered. Tired of "picking up scraps of paper, counting rabbit skins, and other work of national importance," Clegg convalesced at the Heaton Park facility. Wounded soldiers followed a five-stage transition back to full-capacity. When a soldier reached level one, they went back to the front. Clegg seems to have persisted for some time as a category two, which meant that he was subjected to the "hardening camp" in preparation for resuming combat service. He quickly warmed to life in Manchester, recalling that discipline was "slack," and the city welcomed soldiers eager for a good time.

> Manchester was hospitable to us all, we had reduction on fares on the tramway, and reduced prices at places of entertainment. Passes to stay out late were obtained without difficulty, but as pickets were withdrawn at mid-night, many were the figures silhouetted climbing over the walls after that hour. One man would answer several names at roll call. We all enjoyed ourselves in Manchester.[66]

One duty that Clegg and his comrades performed repeatedly during their time in the city was to act as a funeral party. Since he was technically disabled, Clegg was not allowed to help carry the coffin, but participated in the firing of rifle volleys at the ceremony. Even in the poorest parts of the city, he later recalled, the mourners would provide a small monetary gift "to give the lads a drink."

This last duty reminds us that Clegg and those around him lived in a city and country pervaded with evidence of the damage inflicted on the human body by wartime violence. Manchester's hospitals, military and civilian, were constant reminders of the tremendous lethality of the global conflict. Nationally, both civilian and military medicine staggered under the strains of war. The Manchester Medical War Committee was one of the leaders nationally in urging the conscription of medical personnel "which would prove an impossible task if saddled with the voluntary principle."[67] While this proposal never advanced beyond preliminary

66 Manuscript of Harold Clegg, IWMA 88/18/1. [Grammar is in the original.]

67 Cited in Ian R. Whitehead, *Doctors in the Great War* (Barnsley: Leo Cooper, 1999), 271.

stages, it indicated both the problems of mobilizing the medical community and the variety of voices on the issue of military and civilian conscription.

For many wounded soldiers and sailors, women comprised the bulk of their contacts with the medical profession. Despite contemporary debates over how effective the "amateurs" of the Voluntary Aid Detachments (VADs) really were, there is no question that professional and volunteer nurses formed, among themselves and with their patients, extraordinary temporary communities within the wartime experience.[68] The staff at the Manchester Royal Infirmary treated, in addition to their normal caseload of civilian patients, 10,077 war wounded over the course of four years. Without the addition of a detachment of VADs, such an administrative task would have likely proved impossible.[69]

Margaret Kilner, a VAD at the 2nd Western General Hospital, kept an autograph book that recorded, in sometimes intimate detail, the men and women she encountered in her years in the hospital. These included hundreds of Australians wounded at Gallipoli, men from across the country, and other women on the staff. The book is full of slightly lewd verses (many from her fellow VADs), photos of wounded soldiers, and brief expressions of thanks, appreciation, or support from the men in her charge. She must have grown close to many of the British and Australian soldiers, since some of the notes are deeply personal. Perhaps she shared part of her private life with one of them, Private David McDonald of the 1st Seaforth Highlanders. He wrote her a simple aphorism, slightly but appropriately misquoted from *Much Ado About Nothing*, "Sigh no more, lady. Sigh no more. Men were deceivers ever."[70]

While wartime communities were suffused with loss and mourning, the evolving sense of common or national interest also served as an important integrative element. As the lives of ordinary Britons became progressively more entangled in the war effort, sacrifice came increasingly to be defined as integral to the eventual aim of victory. This common vision of victory had two related but distinct components: that the enemy had to be defeated and that the national community could either positively or negatively influence the eventual outcome of the struggle.

The need to achieve victory created and fostered both an inclusive and exclusive sense of community. The First World War's "crusade" existed and survived because people came to believe that they were part of a wartime community that was morally superior to the enemy's and that they needed to prevent that enemy

68 A good summary of recent literature on the experience of women in the wartime medical profession can be found in Janet Lee, *War Girls: The First Aid Nursing Yeomanry in the First World War* (Manchester: Manchester University Press, 2005), 1–22.

69 Letter from Manchester Royal Infirmary, August 29, 1919. Files of Annabella Dawson. IWMA 176/2661.

70 Autograph book of Margaret Kilner. IWMA MISC 122/1884.

from succeeding.[71] Anti-German propaganda permeated the media and found expression in a variety of mediums, with the anti-German riots as an extreme manifestation. Tales of German atrocities were still widely held to be credible and formed an essential part of wartime propaganda. These persistent legends of German cruelty toward civilians and non-combatants legitimized the brutality of war in the minds of many Britons. One recent study has called the atrocity stories of 1914–18 "a vital medium in which myths and other kinds of collective self-suggestion bec[a]me substantive historical phenomena."[72]

There were, in some circles, calls for a more ruthless prosecution of the war. A local church mens' group produced this piece of doggerel in 1918:

> He knows as well as you do
> The Germans must be squashed
> That ere the dove of Peace comes nigh
> The Boche must be out-Boched.[73]

At a time when "the Boche" was widely believed to have been guilty of a variety of horrific offenses against life and property, even this rather light-hearted snippet of verse could easily have been interpreted in an ominous and violent way.

One of the best received films of 1918 was the summer blockbuster "The Kaiser: The Beast of Berlin." Starring Rupert Julian as the Kaiser, it had, according to one Manchester critic, "done much in America to expose the methods of German intrigues."[74] The film's advertising plan was certainly novel:

> Public notice: Any person who resents seeing "The Kaiser: the Beast of Berlin" is an enemy to this country. We have requested people who go see this picture next week at the New Queens Theater, Manchester to instantly report any individual who makes unfriendly or seditious remarks.... We must crush the enemy within our gates. This picture will help seek them out.[75]

This sense of communal striving against a common foe, in which combating the enemy was not just the job of the military, lay at the heart of the vital war bond campaign, an effort that was much stepped up as demand grew toward the end of the war. On print advertisement featured Lloyd-George exhorting that: "your firing line is the works or the office in which you do your bit; the shop or the kitchen in which you spend and save; the Bank or Post Office in which you buy

71 Stéphane Audoin-Rouzeau and Annette Becker, *14–18: Understanding the Great War*, trans. Catherine Temerson (New York: Hill and Wang, 2002), 94–174.

72 John Horne and Alan Kramer, *German Atrocities, 1914: A History of Denial* (New Haven: Yale University Press, 2001), 427.

73 St. Pauls Literary Society. *Odds and Ends*, Volume LXIV (1918), 398.

74 "Film," *MEN*, June 8, 1918.

75 Advertisement found in Ibid.

your bonds.... The road of duty and patriotism is clear before you. Follow it, and it will lead ere long to safety for our people and victory for our cause."[76] The war bond drives, so successful that they later threatened to undermine public finance completely in the postwar years, underscores how deeply this appeal to communal national feeling resonated in the hearts and pockets of ordinary Britons.[77]

The experiences of Edith, Harold Clegg, Margaret Kilner, and Manchester's movie-going population were part of a much more complicated mosaic of wartime life. Together, they remind us of how deeply the mobilization of British society penetrated into the lives of individuals. Despite the atomizing effects of violence and loss, the war also created communities that were at once temporary and durable. Mancunians, like ordinary people across the continent, came to see themselves as living in wartime. Their emotional investment in the war made them willing to sacrifice an extraordinary degree of personal freedom and comfort, and later sharpened their expectations that those sacrifices should be rewarded.

'Industrial Comedy:' Dissent and Mobilization

Workers, like consumers, found themselves caught between legal mobilization, the powerful groundswell of self-mobilization, and a growing sense that the burdens of the war fell unequally. Bound by legal restrictions like DORA and the Munitions Act on one hand and an emerging sense of indispensability on the other, industrial workers began to deploy language very similar to what consumers used in protesting material conditions. The Crossley Employee's Workshops Committee appealed to the city to stop charging war industry laborers for the use of public transportation. "We agree that the worker should pay his quota of the rates, but he is now waking up, and discovers that he is paying more than his fair share."[78] The suggestion here that charging for the use of public transport somehow represented an attempt to deceive workers, and that only by "waking up" could they see the fundamental injustice of the system, is an extraordinary one. It demonstrates, in a small way, how radicalized political language, even in discussions of mundane issues, became during the war years.

These perceptions of inequality and the absence of fair play were particularly evident in the labor movement, where the war years brought a sea change in industrial organization and attitude that would have serious postwar implications.

---

76 Advertisement, "Lloyd-George's Stirring Words to You," *MEN*, June 6, 1918.

77 An interesting and imaginative reading of the triumphs and perils of public war financing can be found in Niall Ferguson, "How (Not) to Pay for the War: Traditional Finance and "Total War" in *Great War, Total War: Combat and Mobilization on the Western Front, 1914–18*, eds Roger Chickering and Stig Förster, (Cambridge: Cambridge University Press, 2000), 410.

78 Letter from T.A. Martin to Lord Mayor, *et al.* Received May 1, 1918. Manchester Council Proceedings, 1917–18, 629.

Perhaps the most important difference between the labor question and food issues was that people were generally aware that food shortages were a manifestation of the wartime economy and the German U-boat campaign. When the war ended, presumably, so would the food crisis. Labor, however, posed a more intractable problem that called for forward-thinking on all sides. Changes in the labor market, particularly those stemming from wartime influx of women into the factories, seemed to threaten to uproot a way of life. Consequently, discontent centered as much on what would happen after the war as it did on alleviating near-term concerns.

In 1917, J.H. Whitley of Manchester University's Department of Industrial Administration, suggested this when asked for his thoughts on industry after the war. "There is no such thing as 'after the war'.... I mean that in our view there ought to be no separation between the problems that had to be tackled during the war and the problems after the war, and that what was right for the one was right in the second case and should be put into operation immediately."[79] In practice, this meant close coordination between the state and private companies, which often fostered a sense among workers that wartime arrangements worked against their interests.

We can see the considerable tensions in this private-public partnership in the meetings of the Manchester Area Armaments Output Committee. This committee, which allowed local Boards of Management to negotiate with officials from the Ministry of Munitions, attempted to act as a mediator between the demands of running the war and local labor issues. In July 1917, the Committee sharply criticized plans to begin paying female workers the same wages as male skilled tradesmen. They suggested that the new rules:

> contained very serious deterrents to efficient organisation and the enforcement of the said Sections is calculated to lead to:
> 1. Decreased output and inefficiency
> 2. Grave unrest amongst skilled, semi-skilled, and unskilled labour
> 3. The refusal of employers to dilute with female labour
> 4. The discharge of female labour already employed under dilution rather than submit to pay the rates outlined in the above order.[80]

In February 1918, facing a steel shortage, the Ministry of Munitions ordered a reduction of shell production. For Manchester and the enormous shell plant at Belle Vue, this would mean large cutbacks in the workforce. The committee, in trying to ensure "the least possible disturbance of labor, and with a view to economy" found itself between two fires. When the committee questioned the

79 J.H. Whitley, "Works Committees and Industrial Councils," in *Labour and Industry* (London: Longmans, 1920), 7.

80 Meeting of the Manchester Area Armaments Committee, July 24, 1917. Manchester Archive MSf 623.4 M1.

cutbacks, the Ministry representative pointedly reminded them that such decisions rested solely with London. A group of Bury sub-contractors suggested a gradual reduction in labor so that workers "especially female labour" would find work in other industries, at which point they were reminded that, owing to the collapse in the cotton supply, the mills were unable to absorb any more workers.[81] As with the food supply, the alliance between the public and private sectors was an uneasy one, often compromised by working at cross purposes.

Labor unions enjoyed some of their greatest successes in the years that immediately followed the war. While there were a number of reasons for this, it is fairly clear that one of them was that, despite being bound by wartime rules, organized labor expended a great deal of energy during the war promoting its visions of what the postwar world would, or should, look like. The experience of Wright Robinson, a local leader of National Warehouse and General Workers' Union and later an important local politician, was indicative of this trend. In a pamphlet that he drew up in 1917, he pointed to the dangers of wartime collusion between employers and the accompanying weakening of organized labor. "Sensible men are asking what is going to happen after the War when millions of war-time workers are thrown on the Labour market? Wise men are organising to meet the situation, and to protect their livelihood."[82]

Robinson expressed his views and his doubts about the possibilities of this renewal of the labor movement in the postwar period in a letter written to a colleague in Summer 1918. "My view is that one large Union boldly called 'The Industrial Workers Union' with an industrial class war basis, politically and industrially well organised, seeking no quarrel or fleeing from none, with an eye to the educative and social value of its basis, is worth hard considering." At this stage, it is important to note, even a committed and experienced organizer like Robinson was uncertain that the confidence expressed to the rank and file could ever match reality after the war. "We shall probably be able to survive in the struggle as the harassed workers survive, but I incline to think we should be able to stake out a future."[83]

Part of staking out a future meant drawing upon the deep well of resentment over wartime sacrifices. Much like the emerging debate over food, organized labor adopted a rhetoric based on the perceived inequality in privation and the demand for reciprocity. When strikes happened, as they did with increasing frequency by the end of the war, the striker's language mirrored those of food protestors. During a brief cotton spinners' strike in September 1918, for instance, Mr. E. Judson of the Cotton Spinners' Association in Ashton-under-Lyme remarked that:

81 Meeting of the Manchester Area Armaments Output Committee, Feb. 12, 1918. Manchester Archvies MSf 623.4 M1.

82 Pamphlet: "A United Warehousing Industry" MWGWU, 1917. Papers of Wright Robinson, M/284/1. Manchester Archives.

83 Letter from Wright Robinson to Mr. Hallsworth, August 31, 1918. Papers of Wright Robinson, M/284/1. Manchester Archives.

> No section of the community of any importance has been hit harder during the war than cotton operatives, but what they feel very keenly is that when equality of sacrifice is called for during these troubled times, all the sacrifices come from the worker and the employers pocket all the handsome profits of the trade.[84]

Labor made its position abundantly clear in May 1917, when Engineers, threatened by dilution, struck in South Lancashire and across the Midlands. Striking engineers, in turn, threatened the ability of almost all industries in the region to keep running. Significantly, this included munitions works and cotton mills. The Ministry of Munitions, concerned about the impact of the strike on the production of artillery and motor vehicles, tried through the second week of May to negotiate with strikers in Manchester and Sheffield. While the ministry tried to appear conciliatory, industry groups felt no such need. A spokesman for the Steam Engine Makers' Society called the unions "wrecking organizations" that were only provoking "social and industrial anarchy, which no civilised and democratic state will in the end tolerate."[85]

Remarkably, the Ministry of Munitions chose at this point to enforce its mandate under the Defense of the Realm Act. On May 18, police raided meeting places in Manchester, Sheffield, and London. In Manchester, George Peat and P.H. Kealey were detained and arraigned a week later with six others at Bow Street in London. While the government chose not to charge the men, the Attorney General promised "no mercy for the next offenders."[86] These arrests were clearly intended to serve as a warning that interference in the war effort would not be tolerated. This policy of toughness tempered by mercy proved less successful than the Ministry of Munitions or the Attorney General might have hoped.

By the middle of 1918, labor trouble became a common occurrence. While the Munitions Act and related legislation capped, but did not completely stop, activity in factories that produced armaments, strikes began to cause considerable inconvenience for ordinary Mancunians. There were two large cotton industry stoppages in 1918. The first of which, in September, shut down 50 million spindles for several days. In August, several thousand municipal employees and the city's carters struck for five days. On that occasion, a number of demobilized soldiers and sailors offered themselves as labor substitutes. As garbage piled up in the streets, the General Secretary of Manchester and District Branch of the National Federation of Discharged and Demobilised Soldiers and Sailors issued a statement that the federations members "will not be used as strike breakers by the Corporation or any private firm."[87]

At almost the same time, the Co-operative Wholesale Society (CWS), one of the largest employers in the city, suffered from widespread strikes over pay.

84 "Cotton Strike," *The Times*, September 19, 1918.

85 "Specious Pretensions," *MEN*, May 12, 1917.

86 "Engineer's Strike," *MEN*, May 23, 1917.

87 "Municipal Strike – Disquieting Conditions," *MEN*, August 13, 1918.

They began at the Society's Longsight printing works and quickly spread to other manufacturing sites. By the strike organizers' own admission, skilled workers in the diverse manufacturing and distribution network mostly remained at work, and the agitation seems mostly to have affected unskilled and semi-skilled labor, who, seemingly, had grown unhappy about continuing low wages for "diluted" labor. Ironically, the Co-operative movement that was accused with increasing frequency of being anti-capitalist and potentially dangerous to civic life faced accusations of being anti-worker, including complaints from the Society's own newsletter.

The Co-operative News counseled patience, in view of the changes in labor policy that were sure to follow the war. "Trade unionism is passing through a stage of transition, and what the ultimate form of organisation may be no one can say. The unions themselves must fight this out until they are taught by experience that only unity can give strength...."[88] In an effort to break the strike, the CWS submitted the dispute for arbitration by the Ministry of Labour but insisted on the resumption of work before negotiations could begin.

The *Manchester Evening News* called the strike and particularly the Society's reaction to it, "an industrial comedy." With no little measure of glee, it remarked that "The co-operative ideal was meant to show to the world that labour and capital need not be opposing factors. To-day not even the most militant body of organised employers would dream of issuing an ultimatum such as that sent to the Ministry of Labour by the Board of Directors who control the CWS."[89] This ambivalent attitude toward organized labor later came back to haunt the co-operative movement and left it open to criticism as it struggled with issues related to the postwar transition.

It is clear that by September 1918, the tenuous peace between labor and industry that dated from 1914 was in tatters. One factor that might help to explain why the fall of 1918 was so contentious is that the pressures of the Spring and Summer had eased, and every day seemed to bring good news from the front. It is also possible that the process mirrored the collapse of confidence in food markets. In either case, the responses of authorities had to change to mirror the increasing volatility of the labor market.

In the event of labor trouble, the police were to be vital in keeping important industries running. Since responses to labor trouble were coordinated from London, this reinforced the subordination of local authority to the national administration. In August 1917, with a possible railway strike imminent, the Home Office ordered the Chief Constable to "preserve order ... and to give protection to men who continue to work" by working with rail company managers and protecting tracks and facilities.[90] Several months later, the Home Office ordered the department to

88 "The Great Strike at the C.W.S," *The Co-operative News*, September 7, 1918.

89 "An Industrial Comedy," *MEN*, August 31, 1918.

90 Order from Chief Constable to Superintendents. August 19, 1917. General Orders, 1918, 62. Greater Manchester Police Archive.

assume a state of "special vigilance" that called for keeping telegraph offices open continuously and possibly using Boy Scouts as auxiliary messengers.[91]

Toward the end of the war, concerns arose about the reliability of the police force. In April, 1918, at the height of the German offensives in France, Chief Constable Peacock sent an extraordinary letter to his men, responding to reports that members of the force were meeting with the Manchester and Salford Trades and Labour Council. These meetings, the beginnings of what would later become the abortive Police Union, struck the Chief Constable as not simply disruptive, but potentially treasonous. He referred to "this critical period of unparalleled crisis" and the force's hitherto "loyal co-operation with responsible authority:"

> The Chief Constable therefore hopes that every member of the Force will, in accordance with his engagement, act in a perfectly loyal manner, so that the good reputation of the Force amongst the citizens of Manchester, and in the country generally, may be fully maintained, and that the splendid work which our men and others are doing at the front shall be backed up by loyalty at home.[92]

For obvious reasons, this fear of plant infiltration by political radicals of all stripes was most acute in the munitions industry. A letter of December 1916, from Lenard Denning of the Ministry of Munitions to Chief Constable Peacock asked for information and surveillance on a number of individuals in Manchester who might seek to disrupt the "output of munitions [that] has been hampered by strikes in different parts of the country, and, though in some cases these may have been purely local in origin, there is without doubt an organized attempt to create trouble in munitions works which has more than local importance." The individuals identified in Manchester included T. Barlass, an "official of ILP and Labour Socialist Club and Institute, Ltd, Higher Broughton Branch" and one "Lyle" who was an "Anarchist – Irishman – connected with Irish rebellion. Chairman of group of anarchists at Oldham."[93]

Aside from the disruption that these strikes caused in munitions production, they were deeply embarrassing to authorities intent on projecting an image of national unity. When a group of allied journalists then touring England proposed to come to Manchester in late May, the local Ministry of Munitions office became concerned that May was "a very bad month for labour troubles" and that scheduling such a visit would invite humiliation. In order that the journalists might "visit the

91 General Order from Chief Constable. April 25, 1918. General Orders, 1918, 164. Greater Manchester Police Archive.

92 General Order, April 25, 1918. General Orders, 1918, Greater Manchester Police Archive, 340.

93 Letter from Lenard Dunning to Robert Peacock, December 22, 1916. General Orders 1917/169, Greater Manchester Police Archive.

Works under the best conditions we can provide," the Ministry rescheduled the trip for June, when it apparently passed without undue incident.[94]

In July, 1918, with the Allied armies in France still trying to contain the German offensives in France, there were further rumors of strikes in munitions plants in Manchester, Coventry, and Birmingham. For authorities, such strikes were not only a danger to industrial policy but treasonous. The Ministry of Munitions sent a message to factories in those industrial centers asserting that "the threatened stoppage of work is not an ordinary trade dispute between employers and workmen, but an attempt to overthrow the policy of the state in a time of national danger. Men who support it are acting under a misapprehension of the real issues."[95]

It is in messages like this one that we can see the potent effects of wartime political culture on the relationship between dissent and authority. As the wartime crisis deepened and the totalizing tendencies within mass industrial war became more pronounced, the space left for dissent shrank and changed. It was obvious in some of the responses to strike actions that were expressed in the media. A common reaction to the strikes was one of indignation; strikes were detrimental to the war effort and weakened the nation's fighting men. Such was the opinion of "Patriot" in September, 1918, "... we struggle on, trying to make the best of it, and our one thought is of the day our dear ones will return victorious. Have these strikers no imagination that they cannot give a thought to what all our brave boys are enduring for their sakes?"[96] "A Gentleman" opined that "many people are tired of the pampering of munitions workers" and that "there would be a big change for them when they were no longer required."[97]

However, emerging from these conflicts over the meaning of industrial action was a new language for describing strikers, one that drew from a new vocabulary of revolutionary dissent. "The sane body of workers do not want these everlasting disputes. It is only the Syndicalists and Bolshevists, a small but exceedingly active section, who delight in causing trouble. Their avowed object is to secure for themselves the control of all industries. They achieved their aims in Russia, and the present state of that unhappy country is an object lesson from the rest of the world."[98] The image of the Bolshevik was firmly entrenched by early 1918 and could be used to represent anyone seen to be advocating social change, no matter how seemingly innocuous.

The Co-operative Society illustrated this trend. This affiliation of stores and manufacturers had been one of the most important employers in the Manchester area, where it was headquartered. Late in 1918, the National Traders' Defence League, a small business association, began to put up posters in Manchester

94 Letter from Eric Davis to D. Caird, Director of Special Intelligence Branch. May 9, 1918. NA MUN 4/4439. See accompanying expense reports for details of the visit.

95 "The Threatened Strike – Notice to Workers," *The Times*, July 22, 1918.

96 *MEN*, September 25, 1918.

97 *MEN*, December 6, 1918.

98 "The Railway Settlement," *MEN*, September 20, 1918.

and other Lancashire towns claiming that the Co-operators' brand of vertical integration was an inspiration for Russian Bolsheviks. The reaction of the Society revealed the problems involved for an organization that sought widespread reform, but wanted to avoid appearing radical or dangerous. While protesting that the Bolsheviks had seized assets belonging to co-operative societies in Russia, *The Co-operative News*, nonetheless, launched an impassioned, if circular, counter-argument. "The Traders' Defense League tries to fix the stigma of Bolshevism upon the Co-operative Movement. But the real Bolshevists ... are the financiers and capitalist classes who foment Revolution." These "real Bolshevists" were in the view of the Society, much closer to home:

> Capitalism was responsible for the all the worst horrors of the Industrial Revolution. It was Capitalism that filled the mills of Lancashire and Yorkshire with the children of tender years, condemned to a pitiless slavery, for pitiful wages, until the Factory Acts brought some amelioration of their terrible lot.... The real fomenters of Revolution are those who uphold Capitalism with its black-stained history of the oppression of labour.[99]

This idea of "hidden hands" at work in the labor market was certainly not novel during the last years of the war, but one thing that became clearer in 1917 and 1918 was that radical dissent now had a face, albeit an indistinct and protean one, in the Bolshevik. This new specter of radicalism did not replace older visions of the fifth columnist in British society but complemented the kind of thinking that spurred the rioters of 1915. Where after the sinking of the *Luisitania*, Mancunians perceived the hidden hand in the work of German and Austrian infiltrators among the immigrant population, events in Eastern Europe added new fears that the national will to fight was being sapped from the inside by revolutionaries. This development in Manchester is roughly consistent with events in London, where the Metropolitan Police strike fueled fears of revolutionaries funded by "Moscow gold."[100] What emerged then was a sharply polarized political landscape, in which groups and individuals tried to place themselves in (or extricate themselves from) the increasingly binary labels of "loyalty" and "opposition."

The remarkably durable conservatism of the Lancashire workers presented organized dissenters with an array of problems. The difficulty in recruiting workers, who clearly supported the war in overwhelming numbers, and in avoiding tension between the leadership of groups on the Left and the rank-and-file, clearly vexed those opposed to the war. Even with the privations of wartime, the conflict remained widely popular. It was difficult, though by no means impossible, to organize successful anti-war meetings in Manchester. These tended to involve the

---

99 "Who Are the Real Bolshevists?," *The Co-operative News*, September 14, 1918.

100 Bernard Porter, *Plots and Paranoia: A History of Political Espionage in Britain, 1790–1988* (London: Routledge, 1992), 143.

highly visible, if small, ILP, which had by 1917 become "the most fertile source of political objection in the First World War."[101]

One attempt in early 1917, loosely organized by a few local politicians like the MP R.L. Outhwaite and Councillor Margaret Ashton, with the support of the ILP, quickly became mired in confusion when the theater that was intended to be the venue refused access. The manager apparently realized at the last minute what kind of demonstration was to take place on his premises. When the demonstrators, mostly female, moved outdoors to Stevenson Square, hecklers appeared and disrupted proceedings so much that the whole affair was called off. Adding to the confusion, former Municipal Councillor Will Phillips was angered that he had not been able to take his turn at the podium before the end of the meeting, a gesture that he blamed on the "ILP'ers, those traitors to the country."[102]

Leftist literature demonstrated these critical ambiguities and tensions within the labor and Left-political communities. It was vital to at least appear to avoid anti-war sentiment. Wright Robinson, the Burnley-born future Lord Mayor of Manchester, signed a statement in 1917 in his capacity as a member of the Liverpool Trades Council, reacting sharply, if somewhat ambivalently, to suggestions in the press that their Treasurer, Fred Hoey, was a pacifist.

> .... The statement that we are a pacifist body, or that we are more concerned with pacifism than trade unionism, is absolutely devoid of truth in spirit and substance, as our records and activities prove.... At the beginning of the War we organized a public demonstration to assist the recruiting campaign...[103]

Since so much of the rank-and-file union membership supported the war effort, the leadership had to tread carefully and make it clear that whatever their personal feelings about the war, the business of the union came first. Significantly, Robinson himself was personally opposed to the war. He had edited an ILP newspaper during his time in Liverpool and took a job as a porter at Manchester University to avoid service.[104] He was also widely seen as a capable and clear-headed labor organizer, as is evidenced by the considerable correspondence in his personal papers between him and factory owners across the northwest of England who sought his advice about labor issues.

The answer seemed to lie in subtle critiques of the war's aims or of the vision of the war promoted by authorities. Labor and anti-conscription appeals almost

101 John Rae, *Conscience and Politics: The British Government and the Conscientious Objector to Military Service, 1916–1919* (London: Oxford University Press, 1970), 83.

102 "Bad Day for Antis – Hall Refused and Meeting Closed in a Hurry" unpaginated news clipping. Loose papers found in M473/1/2/11, Manchester Archives.

103 Announcement from Liverpool Trades Council, "Liverpool Trades Council and Pacifism," August, 1917. Papers of Wright Robinson, M/284/1. Manchester Archives.

104 Introductory biographical material for Wright Robinson Papers, M/284, Manchester Archives.

always contained vaguely worded anti-war messages. One popular tactic was to compare the condition of workers in England with the image of the enemy constructed by government propaganda. One anti-conscription pamphlet railed:

> Down with Conscription!
> Resist Prussianism!
> Your brothers, your husbands, your sweethearts have shed their blood, as they supposed to protect our liberties and crush Prussian militarism. Your rulers are now trying to crush you with British militarism. Now they are demanding Conscription, so as to put the chains more firmly around your necks.[105]

A recruiting advertisement from the Socialist Sunday School movement took this tactic a step further, consciously imitating and parodying the rhetoric of recruiting posters and war bond advertisements:

> Recruits wanted for the Socialist Sunday Schools of Great Britain.
> The enemy is POWERFUL AND UNSCRUPULOUS. He has NO RESPECT FOR TREATIES – or entreaties…
> He can only be crushed by SUPERIOR AND OVERWHELMING FORCE.
> Join at once in the real fight for LIBERTY AND DEMOCRACY.
> Your Kin and Country need you.[106]

Manchester's law enforcement community did not seem to dedicate much time or energy to suppressing anti-war propaganda in the factories. In 1917, the year in which such material boomed in popularity, I could find only one pamphlet, "For You Mr. Worker," which was published by the Socialist Labour Press in Glasgow, that was specifically proscribed without any indication as to it contents.[107] This does not, however, mean that there was not a plethora of anti-war, and particularly anti-conscription, propaganda aimed squarely at soldiers and workers. Examining just a few pieces of broadsheet propaganda demonstrated how vicious some of the anti-war rhetoric had become by the third year of the war and how pervasive the now familiar themes of fairness and equity of sacrifice that had emerged from the conflict over food became.

Propaganda directed at (and possibly composed by) soldiers reflected themes found in the debate over conscientious objectors. Two pieces of doggerel indicated how potent the themes of inequality of sacrifice and coming postwar reconstruction

105 Pamphlet. "Down with Conscription." T.H. Ellison Collection, Working Class Movement Library, General Collection.

106 Advertisment. "Recruits Wanted," *The Young Socialist*, January, 1916.

107 Letter from Chief Constable (Peacock) to Superintendents, June 30, 1917. General Orders, 1918, 6, Greater Manchester Police Archive. This should be compared with the wide range of pamphlets proscribed by authorities in the Munich garrisons and factories.

had become by 1917. "The Soldier's Litany" suggests that soldiers should question the reasons they were given to justify the war, while treading very carefully on the issue of inequality of service. The anonymous author was surely aware that it was counterproductive to be too critical of those with war exemptions in propaganda designed for distribution at home:

> I set small store on medals
> I want no votes of words
> I want a house with a garden
> And a chance to hear the birds
>
> A Man's life and living
> A home, not a nest for germs
> A chance fore the wife and kiddies
> And I want em on decent terms
>
> So fix me a card Shop Steward
> Mark "clear" against my name
> I'm going to butt in with you chaps
> In the great Industrial game.[108]

For many local activists, the issue of conscientious objectors acted as a proxy; a way of criticizing the war effort without explicitly criticizing the war. The draft was a particularly contentious issue in Britain, since it was the only major combatant to enter the war without a conscript army. The BEF fought for more than two years as an all-volunteer force, so the eventual introduction of conscription seemed to be both an indication that the war was going badly and as a particularly egregious extension of state power. Later, the Russian revolutions helped to radicalize debate over conscientious objectors in very direct ways.

Manchester University acquired a reputation during the war as a haven for what a City Council investigation called "unpatriotic and disturbing utterances."[109] It cannot have passed notice that a university employee, Wright Robinson, was actively engaged in protests against conscription. In his role as a trades union leader, he took part in defending three conscientious objectors, including George Benson from Manchester, who complained of being beaten by officers at the Army training facility at Birkenhead in nearby Merseyside. In a typescript essay on the affair, probably intended for publication, he demonstrated the tactic of using anti-conscription rhetoric to criticize the entire war:

108 Broadsheet "A Soldier's Litany" Papers of Wright Robinson. Manchester Archives, M/284/1.

109 "University and Pacifists," *MEN*, May 12, 1917.

> Men enlist, volunteer, submit to conscription for love of country and idealism – and lo their bodies are kneaded into bloody mire to fatten reaction and tyranny at home. They go abroad to fight the enemies of liberty, and the enemy *at home* [hand written, my italics] devours the liberties of their young children and old folks while they are absent.[110]

The death of a young conscientious objector in Salford elicited a similar, if more emotionally overwrought response in early 1917. Hubert Hill, 18, of the Salford Socialist Sunday School died in January of an unnamed illness, "weakened by months of worry over the claims of state for military service." At his funeral, the teacher at the Sunday School, William Watson, made his case for Hill as a martyr, "sacrificed to the barbaric god of War." Hill, Watson told the funeral, had "consecrated the altar of Humanity. We shall think of him always standing proud and defiant against all the forces that sought to drag him down…. So shall it come to pass that when social servitude and suffering shall have passed away, there shall arise a people free and happy, and in their eyes will shine a light such as never yet illumined the portals of humanity."[111]

The problem for conscription opponents was that, particularly in a region as pro-war as Lancashire, George Benson and Hubert Hill made poor martyrs. They were isolated cases, who suffered for refusing to participate in a mobilization that by 1917 had permeated almost all sections of society. Revolution elsewhere, however, turned these lonely figures and their advocates into something far more noble. The overthrow of the Czarist regime and the belated reforms in Berlin as Germany tried to establish a workable wartime government turned conscientious objectors from heel-draggers into the symbolic vanguard of progress. More than ever, anti-war advocates identified conscientious objectors as symbols of their hopes for a society that would reject the continuation of the war. Organized labor and radical politicians stressed their identification with conscientious objectors, and they became "political prisoners."

Despite Britain's alliance with Russia, the Czar was not particularly popular in Britain, particularly in liberal Lancashire. The overthrow of the Romanovs was by no means unpopular, and virtually all of the major political parties and interest groups in Manchester (including the City Council) passed symbolic resolutions congratulating the new government after the Czar's fall. Robert Smillie, the powerful and radical President of the Miner's Federation of Great Britain addressed a rally in Manchester's Free Trade Hall.

> Russia has set free her conscientious objectors (cheers). Do you know that the right to worship God in your own way was secured in this country by the action of conscientious objectors? The conscientious objectors of the past who refused to worship as the King or Government dictated to them, and were imprisoned,

110 Papers of Wright Robinson, M/284/1, Manchester Archives.
111 "Peace – With Honour," *The Young Socialist*, January, 1917.

> and burned at the stake, were them who established your right to worship God as you think fit (cheers). Conscientious objectors really started the Labour Movement, and secured the right to organise into Trade Unions. Many of them were put into gaol, but these were the conscientious objectors of the past, and we honor them.[112]

The Russian Co-operation Committee, which became much more important and visible after the war, started in Manchester. One of their first meetings was held at Milton Hall on Deansgate in June and featured Bertrand Russell and local politicians like Margaret Ashton and R.J. Davies who were known for their anti-war views.[113] The connection between conscientious objectors and revolution emerged at around this time. Literature like "Russia's Charter of Freedom" asserted that Russian political prisoners had been amnestied and called upon Britons to "demand these Liberties for yourselves NOW!" Manchester's workers were not necessarily drawn to Marxist orthodoxies but found the rhetoric of equality and social justice being preached by political radicals far more compelling. What anti-war and anti-conscription radicals advocated in 1918 resonated with their audience, but not necessarily in the ways they intended. As Germany teetered toward collapse, the rhetoric of revolution came to be equated with the promise of peace, a prospect that appealed to a far broader swath of the population than any particular political ethos.

During this tumultuous period, in which accusations of disloyalty and foreign influence flew thick and fast, it is not wholly surprising that the loyalty of Manchester's Jewish citizens was singled out for particular scrutiny. As we have seen, Manchester's large and important Jewish community was caught up in the general anxiety about immigrants in the early years of the war. By the end of the war, Manchester's Jews faced considerable and unwarranted scrutiny from courts, military authorities, the press, and, it appears, popular opinion. Particularly as fears shifted from local Germans, of whom some were Jewish, to Russians, of whom a significant percentage were Jewish, rancor seems to have grown. Wolf Bennison dated his decision to change his name from Shefinsky to his service in a local regiment during the war, when the reading of his name at roll-call earned him the sobriquet "The Russian Jew."[114]

A Manchester businessman named Fred Brocklehurst started a nativist group called "Britain for the British" in 1917, which engaged in local anti-Semitic agitation and seems to have given local hooligans additional incentive to target Jews in the north of the city. There were some high-profile cases of food violations against local Jews, in which stereotypes of acquisitive and hoarding Jews were not far from the surface. A judge described Harry Levi, found with among other things, 368 pounds of sugar and 1,320 pounds of flour, as "a thoroughly selfish man with

112 Broadsheet "The President of the Miner's Federation of Great Britain and Conscientious Objectors." Papers of Wright Robinson, M/284/3. Manchester Archives.

113 "Free Russia." Wright Robinson Papers, M/284/7. Manchester Archives.

114 Bennison transcript, Manchester Jewish Archive.

a very underdeveloped sense of civic responsibility."[115] Anti-Semitic stereotypes merged nicely with pre-existing suspicions of immigrants and growing concerns about political radicalism among Eastern Europeans.

Two conscientious objector cases in April, 1918 further highlighted the issue of the perceived relationship between Jews and potential disloyalty. A group of Jewish men who claimed exemption as members of a religious order were told by a judge that "The books of Moses indicated ... that they had no such objection in those days!" A few days later Julius Allman, a Russian citizen, was admonished that "If you are not prepared to fight for the privilege you enjoy by living in this country you should clear out."[116]

Oddest and most redolent of hoary old anti-Semitic ideas was a rumor circulating in the city at the end of 1918, as the influenza epidemic peaked. Some believed that Jews were suffering less than the rest of the community. A *Manchester Evening News* "investigation" in the Jewish Cheetham Hill district concluded, ambiguously, that there seemed to be no truth to the rumor, but if there was, it might have to do with contaminated bacon.[117] In the politically charged atmosphere, difference led easily to suspicion, which in turn fostered a climate in which those who professed to be "British" could seek to exclude or marginalize those whose Britishness was in doubt.

The fusion of anti-Semitic stereotypes with pervasive anxieties about hidden hands working against (or in the very least, not wholly with) the war effort illustrated the dangerous radicalization in political language that accompanied the war. As we have seen with the anti-German riots in 1915, fierce debates over the nature of loyalty certainly did not rise evenly as the war progressed. What is different about the nature of these debates in the last two years of the war was the context in which they took place. The political and social quiescence that characterized the early years of the war had been replaced by pervasive anxieties about the effect of war on ordinary citizens, large numbers of whom had shed their inhibitions about taking to the streets in protest.

"Comfort is the Surest Prevention of Anarchy:" Visions of the Future

Prior to 1917, the British government had largely avoided the question of what was to be done at the conclusion of hostilities in favor of mobilizing to achieve victory. At the Ministry of Munitions, this began to cause some anxiety by early 1917. "If the war came to a sudden end," the Ministry's statistics chief

115 Bill Williams, *Manchester Jewry: A Pictorial History, 1788–1988* (Manchester: Archive Publications, 1988), 75 and "Hoarded Food: Jewish Family and War Bread," *MEN*, January 18, 1918.

116 "Jewish Conscientious Objectors," *MEN*, April 17, 1918 and "Russian Jew and the Army," *MEN*, April 25, 1918.

117 "Influenza," *MEN*, December 16, 1918.

Walter Layton suggested in January, "there would be something like three months output of munitions in the Factories, in various stages of advancement." The report's authors suggested that the ministry should compel munitions factory to convert to a state of "semi-mobilization" in which they would continue to produce munitions while also manufacturing "vital peace products."[118] No one seemed to know what "semi-mobilization" entailed, a mark of how daunting the postwar economic conversion seemed likely to be.

There were genuine anxieties that a bureaucratic presence dedicated to postwar concerns would exceed its mandate and cause more trouble than it could possibly remedy. Despite such concerns, the Lloyd George government established a Ministry of Reconstruction in August 1917 under former Minister of Munitions Christopher Addison. This represented a major shift in thinking about demobilization. From that point on, there was a permanent, cabinet-level body that could plan and, at the conclusion of hostilities, implement transition policy.[119] This new ministry was both a master stroke and bureaucratic nightmare. It had far more authority to attempt compromise than it did power to make policy, but it did focus thinking at the ministerial level on the military, economic, and bureaucratic levels of the eventual demobilization.

The story of reconstruction and demobilization planning is vast and complex, but it worth considering the dilemma that this new super-ministry found itself in upon its foundation. Upon termination of a conflict the outcome or duration of which was far from clear, the military needed to be scaled back dramatically, all of the industries associated with war production had to be converted, where possible, to peacetime production, and prewar social conflicts that remained unaddressed during the war would rise again. All of these issues needed to be taken into account simultaneously without causing massive social dislocation.

Housing was an excellent example of an issue that bridged prewar social concerns, wartime production demands, and anxieties about the postwar world to come. In the outlying community of Irlam, where Partington Steel and Iron Company had its works, the housing situation had been grim before the war. The Urban District Council's plan to build 200 new homes was interrupted in 1914, and the addition of 1,100 workers caused serious congestion. In a population of about 8,500, 138 houses contained more than one family. Workers had to choose between living in overcrowded conditions or commuting by train.[120]

118 "Demobilisation of Munitions Factories." January 18, 1917. NA MUN 4/3267.

119 See David Englander, "Die Demobilmachung in Grossbritannien nach dem Ersten Weltkrieg", *Geschichte und Gesellschaft* 2 (1983), 195–210; Stephen Richards Graubard, "Military Demobilization in Great Britain Following the Great War", *Journal of Modern History* 19 (December 1947), 297–311; Paul Johnson, *Land Fit for Heroes: The Planning of British Reconstruction, 1916–1919* (Chicago: University of Chicago Press, 1968).

120 Documents related to Irlam Housing Scheme. January 4, 1918, NA T 1/12277.

Addison was insistent that housing concerns, which he believed were the most pressing problem for the coming postwar order, receive priority.[121] For the Ministry, this meant extensive collaboration with local authorities who were much better placed to determine needs and available resources but lacked the resources to carry through housing reform. The result was a hybrid policy in which funding would come from the state, which would retain ownership of new housing stock until the anticipated postwar "transition period" ended.

The Ministry also proved eager to incorporate non-governmental organizations in the consultative process. Even the Co-operative Society, which had a successful house building and financing scheme before the war, became part of the national effort to reconsider postwar housing. At the same time that authorities in Manchester became concerned about the political reliability of the Society, a Co-operative delegation met with Maurice Bonham-Carter in London. The meeting did not go particularly well, as Co-operative delegates were not inclined to surrender the Society's autonomy in the service of the government. The delegates did warn Bonham-Carter about the dangers of wartime and postwar rent increases and that, regardless of who built the new homes, inflation-driven construction costs and wartime rent restrictions would mean that any new homes would have higher rents than existing housing stock.[122] For the new ministry and for people in towns like Irlam, the housing question was both pressing and sisyphean. The problem of postwar unemployment was no less so.

In early December the Ministry of Reconstruction convened a two-day conference of employees, employers, and interest groups at Manchester University, ostensibly to discuss "Problems of Reconstruction." J.L. Hammond, the Ministry representative, left the conference with a deep sense of foreboding. "An official who [is] not thoroughly in touch with working class feeling will only do harm" he wrote in his report. "There is evidently a violent and uncompromising spirit in the workmen's world."

The workers and shop stewards at the conference were manifestly unconvinced by government plans and promises on wages and job security. Shop stewards repeatedly shouted down government speakers, effectively forcing the conference to break up into small groups. The most notable address that day was from a wounded soldier who had resumed his prewar job, only to find that his employer would only pay the wage he had earned when he enlisted. The Gallipoli veteran declared bitterly that he would rather shoot his employer than the Turks.[123] The British state's efforts to shape postwar planning in the public eye, a practice explicitly designed to foster the sense that ordinary Britons were a part of the planning process, now ran into a growing and palpable sense of grievance and

121 Johnson, 108.

122 Meeting minutes in NA RECO 1/479.

123 "Report on the Joint Conference of Employers and Employed and Social Workers at Manchester" NA RECO 1/816.

injustice that helped to foster conflict between government and governed in the last years of the war.

One way to understand the impact of demobilization before the end of the war is to look briefly at some of the emerging visions of postwar society being discussed while hostilities were ongoing. There was clearly a sense, from 1917, that the war was coming to an end and that the end would offer an opportunity to remake society. Sufficient to say, these calls grew stronger as it became clear that the war would end soon. For some, events in Russia gave a messianic caste to their predictions.

Generally speaking, these visions had three things in common. They all assumed that Britain and the Allies would emerge victorious. As we have seen, to make public statements to the contrary was not advisable in Lancashire. All foresaw dramatic changes in the nature of relations between state and society, and all saw a state that was willing and able to reward its citizenry for wartime hardship. The crucial areas of difference came in the means through which such measures would be attained and in the degree of difficulty these changes would require.

Some, like the Socialist Sunday School Movement, looked to a future that would reject war. "Liberty and conscience for every soul will have been won. Woman and man shall stand equally responsible for the making and administration of the laws. Every child over the whole face of the earth shall have its place to grow fragrant as the flowers, and to shine as the stars."[124] This utopian, quasi-eschatological vision of the postwar future was somewhat tempered in this journal by clear evidence that the SSS movement in Lancashire and Cheshire was fast losing active membership. In Rochdale, for instance, average attendance had dropped from 50–60 per week to 30 within a few months.[125]

Richard Newton of the St. Paul's Society offered a somewhat more concrete, if only slightly less hopeful vision of the future. In their small manuscript journal, he offered a blissful vision of a city and a nation that was "living at the end of one stage in the evolution of the social, political, and economic conditions of our country, and entering on a new one."[126] While Newton counted on English temperament to eschew "violent or sudden changes," he, nonetheless, foresaw:

> Better housing, the minimum wage, education from elementary school to university, managing boards of employers and workmen, provision for the sick and the old, maternity provision, arbitration in national quarrels in place of war, access to land for the hitherto hopeless laborer, garden cities, limitation of profiteering, the right to employment – where would the list end?[127]

124 "The Hope of the Future," *The Young Socialist*, January, 1917.

125 "Updates" in ibid., 12.

126 Richard Newton "The New World After the War" in *Odds and Ends*, Volume LXIV (1918) 215. Manchester Archives M38/4/2/64.

127 Ibid., 220.

Needless to say, those whose jobs involved planning policy generally confined themselves to more tangible goals. Even the clearest and most well-intended plans could run into problems in the postwar period. As early as 1917, city planners were aware that something had to be done about the city's chronic housing shortage. The wartime Rent Restriction Act capped rents on scarce housing in an effort to allow war workers, even with their wartime salaries, to afford decent housing near their plants. Still, the city needed a more permanent solution, particularly given an estimated shortfall of 17,000 houses. The council's Housing Conditions Special Committee reported that:

> It is essential that building should be commenced without delay upon the conclusion of peace, as at least one-third of these houses are needed at once; and it is desirable also, in order to utilise the labour which will be made available by demobilisation and to prevent unemployment, that schemes should be prepared; and whilst a high standard of design and lay-out ought to be maintained, economy be carefully studied if a permanent solution of the problem is to be attained.[128]

This sense of faith in the ability of government to improve the lot of vast sectors of society after the war appears to have been widespread. The reasons were not hard to imagine. Government took an unaccustomed role in the running of society for more than four years. Even if the relationship had been uneasy, people looked to government institutions for a wide variety of services that would never have been imagined before the war.[129] This feeling of sometimes panglossian optimism can probably best be seen in predictions about the re-alignment of industry. As early as February, 1918, the editors of the *Manchester Evening News* began to consider the industrial consequences of any peace but were confident in the government's ability to deal with anything that might follow:

> The machinery has been planned for coping with after-the-war problems of resettlement over the whole field of industry…. Nothing could be worse for humanity than that a period of industrial unrest should follow the laying down of arms by the huge forces that are now opposing one another, and all that can be done should be done to avoid a catastrophe of such vast magnitude.[130]

Were these visions put into practice? Did they reflect realistic assessments of existing conditions, or were they mostly wishful thinking? Lord George Askwith, one of the coalition government's leading labor negotiators during the war who spent much of his time dealing with the Lancashire cotton industry, passed on his rather damning judgment several years later:

128 Manchester Council Proceeding, 1917–18, 628.

129 A.J.P. Taylor, *English History, 1914–1945* (Oxford: Oxford University Press, 1965), 1.

130 "Trade After the War," *MEN*, February 18, 1918.

> no statesman had the vision to see or raise his voice to point out that before the final coming of peace there must be delay and uncertainty, but that from the moment of cessation of fighting, reaction must begin; that scarcity existed in the world, and that a devastated and wounded Europe required economy, work, production, and security before it could recover. No warning of shortage of material and food, of weight of national debt, of the evils of inflated currency due to borrowings came from the Government. Unemployment "doles," distributed with amazing laxity, discouraged work and thrift. A state of unpreparedness, lack of leadership, and the example of state extravagance were to lead up to the "land fit for heroes to live in."[131]

Askwith's indictment reminds us that, for all of the conversations going on about the shape of the world to come, very little of the goodwill actually translated into political reality. We will see how this came to pass in the next chapters.

How then do we gauge the political climate in a city like Manchester in the months and years preceding the Armistice? I have pointed to some tensions that were certainly not particular to the end of the war. The mass strikes and politicization of labor in the decades before war point to a period of radicalization that was interrupted by the conflict. The appearance of these issues in 1917 was not novel, but the circumstances in which they re-appeared certainly were.

The fundamental issue in debates over food, labor, and opposition to the war was one of reciprocity. The population had sacrificed comfort, stability, and all too often their own bodies for the war effort, and they began to demand that the state reward them for their sacrifices. National and local governments had established themselves as the arbiters of most disputes and the regulators of essential elements of quotidian existence. In Manchester, they found a municipal government that was often receptive to their grievances and, as in the case of rationing, was willing to interpose itself between national and local demands. While protesters often were not mollified, they at least sensed that institutions existed that would listen to them and that responded to their fundamental demands.

The key issue in wartime protest movements was fairness. Again, this was not in itself particularly novel, but what was new were the stakes. Many saw the war as a turning point. Actors on all sides saw themselves as struggling to establish a place in the new Manchester, and the new Britain, that was to follow the end of the war. Those who criticized local and national government in the last years of the war expected that conditions would improve when hostilities ended. The wartime reciprocal relationship between state and civil society hinged on this sense of possibility. As long as the possibility of a mutually advantageous outcome persisted, dissenters confined themselves to a framework of loyalty. Those who stepped outside of that framework risked marginalization as long as many of

131 George Askwith, *Industrial Problems and Disputes* (London: John Murray, 1920), 467.

their fellow citizens believed that they had a better chance of being rewarded by existing authorities.

After 1917, authorities increasingly began to treat any sort of dissent as potentially "pacifistic" and revolutionary. This conflict between the state's desire to maintain the wartime consensus in peacetime and the emerging streams of dissent will occupy much of the rest of this story. Beginning with the Armistice and the general election that the Government called with what seemed to observers like unseemly haste shortly thereafter, the process of demobilization began in earnest, and the juxtaposition between popular expectation and political reality became progressively more acute. To the extent that the wartime political coalition was able to survive the peace, so, too, did wartime divisions and tensions. These problems coexisted uneasily with the widespread joy and relief that came with the victorious peace that seemed ever closer through the late Summer and early Fall of 1918.

The picture of Manchester in the last years of war offers clues to what would come later in the first years of peace. The omnipresent mobilization of wartime society came late in the war, the result of a wartime system determined to minimize the disruption of consumer society. As a result, the very real stresses of mobilization developed very much in the public eye. Dissenters unhappy with food and labor arrangements managed, on a number of occasions, to influence the development and implementation of policy. As a result, actual and potential demonstrators came to believe that they had a stake and a voice in mobilization. Government institutions like the Area Armaments Output Committee or the Co-operative Society served as conduits through which civil society, the British state, and local bureaucracies could at least be perceived to communicate.

This relationship, understood by all sides to be a reciprocal one, often did not work nearly as smoothly as this description suggests. However, it had a critical outcome that was not present in Britain's continental enemy Germany. As we can see in the earnest but generally unsuccessful efforts of radical groups within Manchester to rally support in the hardest days of the war, the sometimes bewildering flexibility of British mobilization strategy gave a vast swath of the population the sense that they had a stake in the survival of the system. The hesitating and sometimes contradictory mobilization strategy perversely engendered and sustained a sense that state and civil society engaged in a reciprocal relationship in which compromise and flexibility on all sides would and could be rewarded.

On September 12, 1918, as the German armies in France buckled under the great Entente counter-offensive, an ebullient and pugnacious David Lloyd George came to Manchester to receive the freedom of the city. The Prime Minister sounded very much like the confident victor of a long war that day. For the assembled crowd, he sketched in the broadest possible terms his vision of Britain's postwar future:

> To enable the nation to bear the gigantic burden of debt which the war will impose upon it, and the still greater burden of recuperation and reconstruction, we must see that the national resources are developed to the full, and that the State renders all assistance in its power for the attainment of that object. Comfort

> is the surest prevention of anarchy, but comfort involves plenty. How can you ensure plenty? By ensuring the best conditions of production.[132]

The victory, which seemed just over the horizon, reaffirmed wartime rhetoric of equality and reciprocity. Lloyd George's vision was one of cooperation between the state and civil society, an extension of wartime arrangements into the coming postwar period. However, his speech also betrayed the government's anxieties about the possibilities of political radicalism and the potential that these new ideas would disrupt the harmonious vision of a reconstructed Britain.

> If abundance is not there you cannot distribute it. That is an obvious truth which the Bolsheviks seem to have overlooked.... We should shun their teaching like an attack of poison gas.[133]

Here, in one of the great industrial cities of the land, the head of government presented a challenge to the coming postwar society. Reciprocity emerged from the visions of victory and the promises of wartime. It was available to anyone, rich or poor, male or female. But in exchange, the population had to bear the pain of a difficult conversion and they had to endure it without listening to the blandishments of the new radical alternatives that emerged from the years of war. Despite the deprivation and bitterness of the past year, the spirit of the demonstrators who won a victory on the issue of food control ten months before survived. This understanding of the reciprocal relationship between government and governed endured into the postwar period, in marked contrast to the situation in the urban centers of Britain's continental enemy Germany. There, reciprocity took a profoundly different form and produced dramatically different results.

---

132 Manchester Council Proceedings, 1917–18, vol. 1, 553.
133 Ibid., 553.

Chapter 3
An Immeasurable Sacrifice of Blood and Treasure: Munich at War, 1917–18

The policeman stamped his feet to keep warm, braced against the February chill as the winter wind whistled down the broad avenue Tal in the heart of Munich. Passersby had the hard and lean look of people who were still enduring one of the toughest and hungriest years in the modern history of Germany, a time remembered as "the Turnip Winter." The British blockade, labor shortages, and problems with transportation meant empty shelves in the cities and hostile customers standing in the snow. *Bezirkskommissar* Beck was probably too senior a constable to be out here in the cold, but February 7, 1917 was not going to be a good day. Most critically, the trouble was brewing just a few blocks from city hall, so someone had to be responsible for making sure matters did not get out of hand. A local shop, Bronberger, had acquired a supply of sugar, a commodity as prized as it was rare by 1917, and the police expected difficulties with distribution.

By 2:30 the crowd swelled to about 2,000, standing in line in rows of three and four. Beck seemed astonished that people had come from all over the city, from Au, Neuhausen, Giesing, Westend, Schwabing, and other neighborhoods for a chance to buy a bit of sugar. For an hour, a fortunate few were able to buy 200–600 grams before the store ran out. When the shop closed again, Beck and his men faced 1,500 women and children who had waited for nothing. "This is a dirty trick. Why can't the small shops ever get any sugar?" "This is a cock-up. We women can't do anything about it ourselves and our men don't have the heart for it." Beck phlegmatically noted that "A greater law enforcement showing was needed" that day as the women and children turned on him and his men with taunts and insults.[1]

The women and children who shouted at Beck that cold February day were part of an extraordinary process of disillusion and collapsing consensus in German society toward the end of the First World War. These were not revolutionaries or political agitators, but as the war dragged on, authorities tended to read their behavior in those terms.[2] What they were was a crowd of cold, irritated, and

---

1 Letter from Bezirkskommisar Beck to K. Polizeidirektion. February 7, 1917. I b.A.K. 1372, BHStA IV.

2 Here I very respectfully take issue with the Karl-Ludwig Ay's classic study *Die Entstehung einer Revolution* (Berlin: Dunker & Humbolt, 1968). The question of Munich

inconvenienced citizens who demanded in increasingly vocal terms some tangible reward for 2 ½ years of mobilization, deprivation, and sacrifice.

In his recent study of the "world gone wrong" that was Munich in the decade of the First World War, Martin Geyer has made a strong case for placing Munich in the context of an international set of crises by arguing that in the debates over consumption, luxury, and work framed by the decade of inflation make Munich an effective synecdoche for the tensions of modernity and a "watershed" between the nineteenth and twentieth centuries.[3] Munich's tumultuous path after the First World War had its roots in the transformation of the city and urban life that came with the mobilization of its population and resources for the trials of industrial war.

Many of these themes resonate in the British context, and indeed across the combatant states. The relationship between mobilization and demobilization was very different in instructive ways. The legal framework of mobilization, while it theoretically made the process of organizing wartime society easier than in Britain, had important consequences for the ways in which citizens experienced and understood mobilization. The heavy hand of the state, both at the Bavarian and, increasingly, the imperial level significantly reduced the real and apparent authority of local officialdom and created a potential problem for would-be dissenters. If they were willing to challenge the realities of mobilization, to whom would they address their concerns? Was there any hope of successfully asserting the right to legitimate redress of grievances within a framework of loyalty to the state?

Increasingly, protestors found themselves answering the last question in the negative. As the Bavarian and Imperial governments repeatedly and loudly trumpeted their right and ability to manage the war effort and the ordinary lives of their citizens, then publicly failed to do either successfully, the legitimacy of those institutions came under increasing scrutiny. At the same time, a crucial rhetorical shift took place during the hard year of 1917 when state propaganda came to stress "holding on" as the primary duty of the populace. Where earlier propaganda stressed the proximity of victory, this new variety emphasized endurance as material conditions deteriorated.

These two developments; the increasingly evident juxtaposition between the state's claims and its ability to deliver upon them and the transformation of expectation from victory to endurance, left a dangerous legacy in the postwar world. Both emerged from the specific mobilization strategies of the German state and its constituent parts. The very facets of the mobilization of the German empire that made it able to conduct mass industrial war for so long also created

---

as "revolutionary situation" at the end of the war has dominated much of the traditional literature reviewed or cited here, but I will argue that it is not necessary to identify or disprove the existence of such a situation in wartime Munich. Rather I will concentrate on the issues related to wartime expectations. In Chapter 5, I will further explicate the relationship between these expectations and the coup of November 1918.

3 Martin Geyer, *Verkehrte Welt: Revolution, Inflation, und Moderne in München, 1914–1924* (Göttingen: Vandenhoeck und Rupprecht, 1998).

vulnerabilities that could be exploited by a range of dissenters as the engines of mobilization slowed and eventually locked up entirely in the last days of the war. While Germany suffered defeat in 1918, that defeat alone cannot explain what resulted. To do that, we must consider how mobilization took place, the forces that shaped wartime society, and the hopes of civil society for a better world to come.

Munich Mobilizes for War, 1914–1917

The mobilization of society and the German war economy was, at least ostensibly, firmly under the control of military authorities. Under the 1851 Law of Siege, oversight in wartime passed to Deputy Commanding Generals based in regional "fortresses," who in theory had complete and clear authority over their civilian counterparts. This apparent clarity muddied considerably when it ran up against confused and sometimes overlapping political and jurisdictional boundaries. Things became still more confused in regions like Bavaria and Saxony, where the legacies of the uneven nineteenth-century unification of Germany left military bureaucracies who also owed loyalty to their *Land*.[4] In 1914, Bavaria maintained an army of three corps, with headquarters in Munich, Würzburg, and Nürnberg. There were also division commands in Neu-Ulm, Augsburg, Regensburg, and Landau.[5] This military organization became critical later when central authority in Bavaria temporarily disintegrated after the war. Under wartime statutes, authority over much of economic, political, and military affairs passed from the civilian government to Regional Commanders, who were part of both the Bavarian Army and the wider German war effort. It was in the stresses of industrial war that we can see most clearly Wolfgang Mommsen's characterization of the German Empire (*pace* Carl Schmitt) as "a system of skirted decisions."[6]

These skirted decisions now came home to roost as they generated inefficiencies in wartime planning that later became magnified in the demobilization process. The central conflict in the mobilization process developed between the needs of consumer society and the escalating demands of total war. While the German state was comparatively well prepared institutionally to take on the responsibilities of managing mass industrial war, the degree of mobilization required proved well beyond expectations, and the gaps that developed between "front" and "homefront" and between "haves" and "have-nots" fostered resentments that the end of war only worsened.

---

4 Roger Chickering, *Imperial Germany and the Great War, 1914–1918* (Cambridge: Cambridge University Press, 1998), 34.

5 Hermann Frobenius, ed., *Militär-Lexikon: Handwörterbuch der Militärwissenschaften* (Berlin: Martin Oldenbourg, 1901), 144–5.

6 Wolfgang Mommsen, *Imperial Germany, 1867–1918: Politics, Culture and Society in an Authoritarian State* (New York: Arnold, 1990), 5.

The war dramatically sped up the industrialization of Munich and its workforce. From a city of small industrial concerns, Munich grew in three years into a regional industrial dynamo, with some industrial firms continuing to shape the city long after the war ended. A January 1917 survey of factories in the city found that almost half of the producers employed more than 50 workers, and almost 15 percent had more than 100 workers. Many of these factories, particularly plants producing items like leather goods or cigarettes, were struggling with reductions in raw materials as distinctions between "war goods" and "public necessities" (*Volksversorgung*) became progressively more important.[7]

By 1916, new plants produced airplanes, engines, cannon, brakes, and machine tools in the city's suddenly booming industrial suburbs.[8] At their height, designated war industries within the command of the I Bavarian Army Corps employed close to 88,000 workers, 31,000 of whom were female.[9] One of the most important of these concerns, BMW AG, employed about 2,000 workers at its plant in the north of the city.[10] Not only did these plants provide employment and steady wages, but some provided food to employees, a benefit that grew increasingly important as the deprivations of war and blockade settled in.[11]

The dramatic expansion of the city's industrial footprint later had serious consequences during the period of economic demobilization. This was most apparent in the large facilities that could not be readily converted to peacetime use. One of the biggest was the Powder and Munition Factory in Dachau (Pmf Dachau). This facility, whose development was closely monitored by the Bavarian War Ministry and whose records, while limited, are the most extant of any in the city, closely mirrored broader developments in the city and its surroundings during the war.

When construction of Pmf Dachau began in 1915, it was a small factory employing 22 workers. Given the shortage of skilled or semi-skilled construction labor, much of the work had to be done by Russian POWs. At any given time, several hundred prisoners and their guards were on site as the complex grew.[12] As Pmf Dachau grew, it became more difficult to bring workers in from surrounding communities, so ten barracks were hastily built to keep the labor on site. By the summer of 1917, there were more than 300 buildings in the sprawling complex.[13]

7 Survey of 299 facilities. Letter from K.b. Gewerbrat für München to K. Staatsministerium der K. Hauses. January 19, 1917. MKr 17299, BHStA IV.

8 Alois Auer, *Krauss-Maffei: Lebenslauf einer Münchener Fabrik und Ihrer Belegschaft*. (Körsching: 3K Verlag, 1988), 119.

9 SJFB, 169.

10 Caroline Festa, "Als BMW noch in den Kinderschulen Steckte: Die Schwierigen Anfänge eines Symbols der Deutschen Autoindustrie" (MM Thesis: Universite de Nice Sophia-Antipolis, 2001), 82.

11 Ibid., 70.

12 There were 230 working in various buildings in February, 1917. Feldzeugmeisterei 1859, BHstA IV.

13 See map in Feldzeugmeisterei 1856, BHstA IV.

The expansion of the labor pool at Pmf Dachau was as impressive as the growth of its physical plant. From a handful of workers in 1915, the facility drew in a constant stream of workers, reaching its peak in absolute numbers just a few months before the end of the war. Three months after construction started, there were 246 male and 194 female workers. A year later, this figure grew to 2,295 men and 2,486 women. From this point on, more women than men were employed at the works, though these figures obviously do not include the POW construction labor.

Particularly as raw material shortages grew more acute, Pmf Dachau had trouble keeping its daily capacity of 1,000,000 cartridges, though it was far more successful at keeping high levels of powder production. This was hard, dangerous work and accidents, though rare, were dramatic and often deadly. By early 1918, there were 10 recorded major accidents at the plant that killed 7, seriously wounded 6 others, and cost more than 200,000 marks. By far the most serious was an explosion in the powder drying house that killed three, caused nearly 150,000 marks in damages, and destroyed the building.[14]

This industrial boom was not without limitations, particularly as the demand for labor outpaced supply. The building trade outside of war industries declined significantly, just as the need for housing for the city's workers reached its apex. In 1914, about 700 new residences were built in Munich. In 1916, as labor and materials were needed elsewhere, that number fell to 23.[15] According to the city, the occupancy rate at the end of 1916 was roughly 97 percent. Behind that figure was a larger problem. The 2.6–3 percent (depending on the count) of available housing were mostly large (4-bedroom or greater) apartments that were well out of the price range of most ordinary renters.[16] While city officials were aware of the current and looming problems with housing, the city did not set up a distinct office to deal with the housing situation until 1917, when it established the Housing Office (*Wohnungsamt*). "Will our troops return home to find adequate quantities of housing?," asked a report in October, 1917, "If not, what can be done now to address this possibility?"[17]

Managers of industrial concerns tried a number of solutions to this problem, which clearly had the potential to seriously affect production. While Pmf Dachau was able to build barracks to keep vital workers close to the plant, this was possible because they had plenty of space available in less-developed Dachau. Since many of Munich's factories were much closer to the city center, this was not necessarily an option. The Bavarian Gunworks, owned by Krupp, began renting apartments to keep their most important workers close to their facilities in Schwabing.

---

14 Statistics above from Feldzeugmeisterei 1866, BHstA IV.

15 Reinhard Bauer and Ernst Piper, *München: Die Geschichte einer Stadt* (Munich: Piper, 1993), 270.

16 Report "Münchener Wohungszahl vom 1. Dezember 1916." Statistisches Amt der Stadt München. Wohnungsamt 83a, StaMu.

17 "Massnahmen gegen eine Wohnungsnot." October, 1917. Wohnungsamt 83a, StaMu.

One can see how acute this housing problem was by looking at the situation in the districts of Milbertshofen and Mossach. The problem, according to one housing inspector in March, 1917, was not so much a shortage of living space but the concentration of workers in districts where few had previously needed accommodation. In these districts, where there had been fewer than 700 industrial workers before the war, the construction or expansion of ten factories boosted that number to more than 6,500. These included machine shops, chemical plants, an airplane factory, and a furniture maker.[18]

Authorities were keenly aware of the problems inherent in balancing the needs of consumers with those of the war. In public, they spoke of sacrifice and patience, while in private such conversations took on an increasingly panicked tone. While the sometime sunny predictions of authorities about the future of the German war effort now seem absurd, it must be remembered that by 1917 Germany had simply invested too much capital and too many lives in the war for public officials to even countenance anything but victory. In October 1917, as the Italian Army collapsed at Caporetto and the offensive spirit of the Russian Army seemed to reach breaking point, the Bavarian Minister of the Interior spoke at the University about the war economy. "Thanks to God and the German people," Dr. von Brettreich offered the crowd in the Aula, "we can do it!" Despite this optimistic assessment, the manner in which the city and its inhabitants could pull through probably offered little comfort.

> Food, raw materials, and money are important. But something is more important ... the Spirit of the People! The Army that fights out there has to know that at home the people stand behind them.... And so we need once more a spirit of real, right, and loyal People's Community, this consciousness in the depths of disaster or the highest and holiest moments of this time, the consciousness of comradeship in life and death.[19]

The implications here were stark: the government conceded that the balance between consumers and the war effort was to tip irrevocably in the direction of the latter. By the remobilization phase of the war in 1917, this imbalance was familiar to people across combatant societies. Unlike Britain, however, the state claimed the right to manage consumer issues early in the war. When ordinary Germans needed to blame someone for the weakness of domestic production, they had no one to look to but the state.

Had the problem simply been scarcity perhaps this policy would not have inspired the kinds of resentments that ensued. However, at the same time food and consumer goods vanished from shops, the items that remained or their *ersatz* "equivalents" carried price tags that gave even the hitherto comfortable middle

---

18 Letter from Bezirksinspektor Schmidt to Wohnungsamt, March 10, 1917. Wohnungsamt 33, Sta Mu.

19 Speech given October 9, 1917. Underlining in original. Handelsministerium (MH) 15463. BHStA IV.

class pause. Particularly for the unprecedented number of people now employed directly or indirectly in the war effort and thus depended on the state for wages, the widening gap between the costs of daily life and the wages they earned acted as a quotidian reminder of the perceived failures of mobilization.

It is exceptionally difficult to get a measure of the interplay between wages and the price increases that accompanied the privations of war. As a general statement, real wages appear to have kept a ragged pace with inflation and price hikes in consumables through the war years, though as the situation worsened for Germany this became increasingly difficult to achieve. It was only after the war that prices and wages began to diverge completely. Workers at the Munich train depot, which was the marshalling yard for troop trains among others, saw the scope of their work and their wages change dramatically over the war years. When the war began, there were 22 employees working for wages (as opposed to salaries), all of whom were male. This remained relatively constant until 1916, when the Bavarian army became heavily engaged in the battles around Verdun. By early 1917, the depot had 54 employees, of whom 11 were female.

Wages for these employees showed a similar pattern, reflecting both the labor shortages of wartime and wartime price rises. A married male worker in 1914 earned between 3.4 and 4.21 marks per day. That number rose by about 50 pfennigs by 1916, then more than doubled by mid-1918, when the same worker could expect to earn between 7.33 and 9.5 marks. The rise for women was less dramatic, since they began working only in 1917.[20] At Pmf Dachau, while women's hourly wages never came close to those of male workers, the gap between their earnings shrank. In 1916, the highest paid female workers earned more than 60 percent less than their male counterparts. By January 1918, this difference shrank to just over 40 percent.[21] This roughly correlates with the rise in price of items whose prices were regulated by the state. While prices rose sharply in 1917 (25 percent in the case of bread), it was not until 1918 that the real take-off occurred, at which point it was too late for anyone to do much about it. While wages could keep pace, it was much more difficult for those on fixed or investment incomes, and their suffering became part of a general trend toward the economic collapse of the middle class.[22] If women's wages did not rise as dramatically as men's, they generally closed the gap over the course of the war.

Virtually nothing was exempt from the decline in living standards and the needs of the wartime state. During the winter of 1916–17, municipal authorities closed theaters and other forms of public entertainment and reduced the hours of restaurants and bars in an effort to conserve coal. At one point, schools were closed for lack of heating materials. The quality of education overall declined precipitously during the hardest years of the war. With teachers called away to the colors, real shortages of food and necessities like coal, and the ever-expanding needs

20 Report "Statistiken der Depots" Kriegsministerium 17125. BHStA IV.

21 Feldzeugmeisterei 1866, BHstA IV.

22 Geyer, 44.

of industry for labor, Munich's schools functioned on greatly reduced schedules and without many of their students. In 1915, of Munich's 55 *Volkshauptschulen*, 42 operated on a half or one-third day schedule. When school buildings closed, classes were often held in other public buildings. [23]

By 1917, the battle between the war and the consumer clearly favored the former, a situation that would not fundamentally change for some time. The increasing impoverishment of the middle class was a boon for the antiques business as heirloom furniture and other family valuables went to pay for necessities.[24] The contents of peoples' homes were not the only treasures sacrificed during the war years.

The mobilization effort literally changed the soundscape of the city. One of the most publicly noticeable absences of the war years was the ringing of church bells, which the state seized to melt down for shells. In 1917 alone, 35 percent of the city's bells went to the smelter, a process that continued until the end of the war.[25] The bell register at the War Ministry recorded the slow process of identifying, seizing, and destroying the massive bells of the city's churches. In July 1918, for instance, city authorities came for the four bells of the parishes of St. Anna and St. Maximilian. While the brass in the bells, one of which reportedly weighed 3,870 kilograms, was welcome in the shortage-plagued munitions factories, the effects on communities of watching the audible symbols of their faith committed to the increasingly desperate battles in the West can only be imagined.[26] Even the *Münchener Neueste Nachrichten* voiced at least a veiled concern when the army took down the massive Ave Bell from Munich's signature two-domed *Frauenkirche*, pointing out somewhat obliquely that the brass bell bore an inscription proclaiming that it chimed its love for the Virgin Mary. The implication was clearly that this was perhaps not an appropriate item to melt down and turn into shells for the front.[27] While many of the city's bells survived the war to ring in celebration and mourning during postwar public events, the audible landscape of the city must have been profoundly empty. Episodes like the removal of the bells remind us that even in the days of the "total" mobilization of German society, there were limits to what even the most patriotic elements of civil society would endure without criticism. Those critiques might be veiled, but they were clear reflections of discontent at the prospect that there was no end of the war in sight.

---

23 Andrew Donson, "War Pedagogy and Youth Culture: Nationalism and Authority in Germany During the First World War" (PhD diss., University of Michigan, 2000), 221.

24 Bauer and Piper, 250.

25 Richard Bauer, *Geschichte Münchens*. (Munich: C.H. Beck, 2005), 343.

26 "*Verzeichnis der Glocken*" MKr 1325, BHStA IV.

27 "*Das Abnehmen der Kirchenglocken.*" *Münchener Neueste Nachrichten* (*MNN*) June 17, 1917. p. 9.

Feeding the City: Food and Rationing in Munich

At the same time, the price of basic goods and foodstuffs climbed considerably, when they could even be found. Through the course of the war, a half-kilogram of flour rose from 20 to 35 pfennigs, a liter of petrol from 23 to 36, and a cup of coffee, which was a considerable luxury during the war years, from 11 to 40.[28] Beer, sausage, cheese, and other staples of Bavarian life were difficult to obtain and prohibitively expensive. Children in the city were apparently aware of these reduced circumstances and some remember singing an ironic tribute to the increasingly ubiquitous rutabaga called (in Bavarian idiom) "Dotschland, Dotschland über alles."[29] At Julius Fellmeth's *Gaststätte Bauernengl* on April 2, 1917, meat was on the menu but at prices that would have presumably put it all but out of reach of the workers at the depot. Prices were noted in both marks and ration coupons, and the menu, as if by way of explanation, was adorned with an Iron Cross. Smoked ham cost 2.20, the selection of cheese was reduced to Emmenthaler, sausages cost .60 a piece, and there was no coffee. Beer remained relatively cheap, with both golden *Helles* and the maltier *Dunkel* costing about 40 pfennigs a glass. One can only imagine, however, the reaction of customers to what was by 1917 surely the barely-potable *Kriegsbier* ("war beer") of dubious origin and ingredients.

Rationing policies were more important in most people's lives than the cost of restaurant dining. The city's Food Committee was staffed by some of the most energetic and capable politicians in Munich, including the future mayor Eduard Schmid, who was the SPD's food expert. Schmid's introduction to Munich's food problems was quick and confounding. In August 1915, he wrote that "the consumers believe that the wholesalers are the ones driving up prices. The wholesalers allege that milk is being hoarded by the dairies. The small shops say they have to demand more because the wholesalers are raising prices."[30] In this conflict, the Food Committee appeared as little more than an interested observer. No amount of management could allay the problems of supply that grew even as the state intervened more directly in everyday life.

By early 1915, bread and flour required ration cards, a situation that soon expanded to include meat, vegetables, milk, potatoes, and sugar, among others. A particularly cumbersome element of the rationing scheme was that it tied consumers to a merchant through dedicated customer lists (*Kundenliste*). While this was not limited to Munich or to Germany, it was a policy rife with possibilities for abuse and inefficiency. It also did little to address the basic problem of supply,

---

28 SJFB, 601.

29 Christina Böck, "Pikrinsäure und Dotschen: Münchner Frauenalltag zwischen Erwerbstätigkeit und (Familien) Vesorgung im Ersten Weltkrieg" in Sybille Krafft, ed., *Zwischen den Fronten: Münchner Frauen in Krieg und Frieden, 1900–1950*. (Munich: Buchendorf, 1995), 53.

30 Elisabeth Angermair, *Eduard Schmid (1861–1933): Ein Sozialdemokratischer Bürgermeister in schwerer Zeit* (Munich: Stadtarchiv München, 2001), 46.

which by 1916 regularly dipped below what was needed to prevent hunger for more than a few days or weeks.[31] In 1912, slaughterhouses in Munich processed an average of 183 cattle and 606 veal calves a day. By the winter of 1917, those figures dropped by more than 80 percent to 32 and 117 respectively.[32] The city opened municipal *Volksküchen* in an effort to stave off starvation, and these swiftly became a vital source of basic nutrition for many of Munich's citizens.

Authorities also attempted to deal with the problem of supply by addressing the question of demand, a solution bound to make no one happy. There were in some instances legitimate shortages of critical raw materials, most notably coal. Critical for both industrial and home use, the city's supply of anthracite (*Steinkohle*) came almost entirely from beyond Bavaria's borders. Overall supply fell 26 percent in the first two years of the war, largely because of sharp declines in imports from Rhine-Westphalia and Silesia, as well as the near complete termination of imports from Belgium and the Netherlands.[33]

Authorities presented the regulation of essentials in their early incarnations in a way that was almost cheery, in large part because it was expected to be temporary. The journal of the Bavarian Home Economics Center, a women's group, encouraged its patriotic readers embrace the rutabaga (*Dotsch*, in Bavarian idiom) as a "tastier, more agreeable, and more filling" alternative to the ubiquitous potato. "For every housewife now and in the immediate future, the slogan must be: rutabagas instead of potatoes."

Beginning in May 1915, signs appeared in train cars and stations offering suggestions for reducing food consumption, or "saving for the Fatherland." Suggestions included increasing calorie consumption by using sugar, adding buttermilk or low-fat milk to coffee, cutting back on beer consumption, and using things like syrup or marmalade in place of butter. These must have been bitterly ironic for people riding trains in from the countryside bearing quasi-legal or illegally purchased agricultural products. For an increasing number of city dwellers, the only way to supplement wartime diets was to ride out to the countryside in search of food. As they read these signs they were coming home to a city in which coffee, good beer, sugar, or marmalade were increasingly rare, expensive, or simply unobtainable.

These guidelines surely looked more absurd after 1917, when they co-existed with another set of warnings explicitly forbidding such traffic in food from the hinterland.

> Sales of eggs, butter, and similar material by people engaged in agricultural work to private individuals is not allowed, as such foodstuffs must be handed

31 Böck, 41–61.

32 From "Stadt und Land, Bayern und das Reich in der Kriegsernärungswirtschaft," published by K. Bayerischen Landesamt, 1917, 1.

33 Ibid., 5. The pattern was broadly similar for cheaper, less-efficient lignite.

> over to communal authorities. Any other system makes the provision of food to the population, and especially to munitions workers more difficult.[34]

The flyer noted that both the seller and the buyer would be held accountable for food smuggling and that police, gendarmes, and volunteers would keep watch on trains and in stations to enforce compliance. The results of this nationalization of agricultural products and the ostensibly strict efforts to enforce these rules established a system that bred resentment as urban dwellers came to believe, rightly or wrongly, that farmers were benefiting from the black market and at the same time using the black market to deprive cities of precious foodstuffs.[35] Given the close relationship between Munich and its hinterlands, this competition for resources was bound to generate friction, and the results of those tensions long survived the war.

Food smuggling was a fixation for military authorities. In April, 1917, the Bavarian Ministry of the Interior contacted the War Ministry about "organized smuggling" of meat products like salt pork, sausage, and ham from Belgium into Germany. Prussian authorities found evidence of black market pork products, and such goods were reportedly moving as far south as the Pfalz and Nürnberg.[36] Clearly workers in war production facilities had the cash needed to purchase smuggled goods, and farmers in occupied Belgium were doubtless more willing to try their luck with illegal middle-men than they were to turn over their produce at lower prices to German authorities.

Such smuggling went on side-by-side with legal trade in imported foodstuffs, in large part from Holland. Until April 1917, citizens of the Netherlands could legally mail their fellow countrymen in Germany parcels of food, creating opportunities for turning a quick and legal profit. On April 1, the *Ernährungsamt* issued a directive severely restricting the amount of foodstuffs that could be sent (no more than 5kg of butter or 10kg of meat per month, for example) and forcing the sender to sign a pledge that there was no commercial intent.[37]

A group of local grocers petitioned Berlin at roughly the same time to make the case that it was unfair that north German firms got import licenses while Munich, "home of the Krupp Cannon Works, Maffei Machine Tools, Kraus, and countless other armaments factories" did not.[38] Food controls created enormous opportunities

34 "Warnung." April 7, 1917. ZS 221, StdAM.

35 Alan Mitchell, *Revolution in Bavaria, 1818–1919* (Princeton: Princeton University Press, 1965), 22. He argues that the nationalization of the countryside in Bavaria was all but total by 1917.

36 Letter "Einfuhr von Fleisch und Fleischwaren aus Belgien." August 16, 1917. MKr 1325, BHStA IV.

37 "Bestimmungen über die Versendung von Lebensmittel." April 1, 1917. Ernärungsamt 136, Sta Mu.

38 Letter from Morgenroth and Jahn, Lebensmittelversorgungs-GmbH, to Zentraleinkaufsgesellschaft (Berlin). May 30, 1917. MKr 12854, BHStA IV.

for profit, and merchants devised both legal and illegal means to secure access to scarce goods. In a wartime society in which the state claimed absolute authority to regulate private life, the growing indispensability of black and grey market solutions spoke volumes about the limits of such claims.

Price caps were one of the most public manifestations of attempts to regulate food supply. They also exemplify the problems of German economic mobilization, as they were a direct and heavy-handed response to the inflationary pressures of the wartime economy. Such regulation occurred for the most part at the local level, as when the city government announced in 1917 that sauerkraut could cost no more than 12 marks for 50 kilos at wholesale or 17 pfennigs per pound in retail shops.[39] There were also quality controls in place from the beginning of the war, though, as the conflict went on, it must have been more and more difficult to differentiate between adulterated products and the *ersatz* foodstuffs of the day. During the war, there were 2,688 recorded food control law violations, of which by far the largest group, 845 counts, was for selling adulterated milk.[40]

In addition to punishments, which could be quite severe, those who violated emergency food laws were subject to public humiliation. Johann Pfeuffer, along with his wife and "compliant accomplice," Theresa, were convicted of conspiring to fix prices with other retailers. Their case, in which Johann was sentenced to three months imprisonment and a substantial fine, was chronicled in considerable detail in the *Münchener Gemeinde Zeitung*, which called their crime "the worst type."[41] Local government news organs dedicated considerable space to stories like that of the Pfeuffers in an effort to stir vigilance in public employees and to threaten potential wrongdoers with shame or worse if caught. Those who resisted or tried to illegally profit from the mobilization of Bavarian society could expect to be shamed for their efforts. This was, after all, a community at war. That image of a people united by the war effort, however tenuous it was in reality, exercised real power in people's lives as the war years dragged on.

"The Order of the Hour is 'Hold On'" – War Culture in Munich

The attempts to mold the political imagination of Munich's citizenry intensified during the hardest days of the war. As the privations of empty larders, long lines, and *ersatz* food became increasingly intrusive in people's lives, propaganda focused on the new world, which would emerge only in the aftermath of the war. On the last day of 1916, the *Münchener Neueste Nachrichten* enjoined its readers to remember "The long lines of heroes who appear before our eyes, from Moltke and Göltz to the nameless thousands who sleep today beneath the ground or at the

39 "Hochpreise für Sauerkraut." *Münchener Gemeinde Zeitung* (*MGZ*) March 28, 1917, 263.

40 SJFB, 451.

41 "Kriegswucher."(*MGZ*) April 7, 1917, 298.

bottom of the sea. For us! For our land and for our future! For something greater than the destiny of one, for the fate of all!"[42]

A year later, the tone had changed somewhat, reflecting the extraordinary difficulties of the year that had passed between. While joking that the French, British, and American leaders were "sadly not the Three Wise Men," the *Münchener Neueste Nachrichten*'s tone was far more sober than the year before.

> We are full of faith that the Reich's leadership, now headed by a Bavarian statesman, will in the new year fulfill our wish for peace. But we do not just wait and hope, but rather work together, each to his part and each at their post, and so together to carry through to a good end.[43]

The German and Bavarian governments, along with the city of Munich, dedicated considerable resources to surveying and maintaining the enthusiasms of wartime, a task that became all the more difficult as the mobilization effort became increasingly invasive and the double bind of shortages and inflation began to tell. While it is not surprising that authorities at all levels engaged in propaganda work, the types of propaganda deployed are important in understanding the resentments of the postwar period. It is also crucial to understand the degree to which popular culture played a role in creating and sustaining wartime passions. Munich's citizens were literally immersed in a culture of wartime, one in which discussion of the war and its demands permeated civil society and became an inescapable part of everyday life. Norms of behavior, thought, and belief were increasingly bound into the demands of a society at war. Everywhere they looked, they could readily detect the war's effects, and as long as they continued to believe that hunger, inflation, inconvenience, and personal tragedy were the fault of enemies whose defeat meant the end of those things, the passions of war could continue to be directed in ways that authorities intended.

Troops coming home from the front were a potential source of complaint and dissent.[44] Their mail was surveyed for seditious or inappropriate sentiments,

---

42 *MNN*, "Neujahr 1917," December 31, 1916. Moltke and Göltz were famous field commanders who both died in 1916. Helmuth von Moltke was the nephew of the legendary architect of victory in the Wars of Unification and served Chief of thc General Staff at the beginning of the war. He was swiftly replaced after suffering emotional distress as the German offensive in France bogged down. Field Marshal Kolmar von der Göltz was a hero of the Belgian campaign who later led Turkish forces that defeated the British invasion of Mesopotamia. He died in Baghdad.

43 *MNN*, "Zum Neuen Jahr." December 31, 1917. NB: The "Bavarian Statesman" here referenced was Georg von Hertling, a superannuated Center Party leader and politically trustworthy figure who joined the now regular rotation of Chancellors in the tug-of-war between parliament and the military.

44 See Anne Lipp's excellent "Friedenssehnsucht und Durchhaltbereitschaft. Wahrnehmungen und Erfahrungen deutscher Soldaten im Ersten Weltkrieg," *Archiv für Sozialgeschichte* 36 (1996): 281.

but when they returned home on furlough, such surveillance was impossible. Accordingly, returning soldiers were issued a pamphlet urging them to help keep spirits up upon their return home. The pamphlet, which featured an image of an eagle swooping down on a nest of snakes, offered advice like:

1. As you have held on at the front, now hold on when you are home on leave. Don't grumble about the low food supplies…
2. Your speech should not worsen the spirit of the Homeland, but improve it.
3. Hold your tongue! Stick with the truth. Don't relate what you have heard, but what you actually know to have taken place.[45]

Clearly military authorities feared that soldiers would connect the increasingly grim supply problems at the fronts with the similarly deteriorating situation at home. As wartime propaganda relied on the idea that soldiers were fighting for a better life for those at home, the implication that the conditions of the war were beginning to profoundly affect the home fronts was not one that authorities wished to confront. Soldiers were explicitly barred from taking part in politics, and in 1917 the War Ministry forbade members of political groups or parties from advertising to soldiers on active duty.[46] This proved all but unenforceable, and it is clear that at the same time, the army became deeply politicized, though not necessarily in the way that anyone imagined. The existence of such orders at this late stage of the war indicated the deepening fear among authorities of the possibly decisive influence of soldiers on the home front and *vice versa*. The failure of such orders illustrated the limits of military authority in wartime.

Hans Bonenberg of Kempten, serving in a reserve Mortar Battalion in Munich and a Social Democrat, regularly attended meetings of a radical new political party at the *Goldenen Anker* bar, which became much more interesting to authorities later. The Independent Social Democratic Party (USPD), was a result of a split in the Social Democrats (SPD) over issues like the party's support for war loans and support for the Russian Revolutionaries. The USPD across Germany was comprised of a small group of parliamentarians and an umbrella of splinter groups from SPD (now the Majority Social Democrats or MSPD) formations.[47] Military and civilian authorities tried to keep a close watch on the USPD, fearing that they were the vanguard of a revolution.

Far from being a secretive clique of revolutionaries, the *Goldenen Anker* circle took out an advertisement in the *Münchener Post*. Their discussion evenings, where they read and discussed items like the latest speeches of Trotsky, were well attended by soldiers, students, and others, including such future political figures as the young Ernst Toller, and (though Bromberg did not mention him in

45 "Merkblatt für Fronturlauber in der Heimat." I b.A.K. 1724. BHStA IV. Document is undated, but is in a folder holding documents related to "Stimmung in der Heimat, 1917–18.

46 Order issued December 27, 1917. I b.A.k. 1937. BHStA IV.

47 Chickering, 159.

his interrogation) the future Prime Minister of Bavaria Kurt Eisner.[48] By the time Bromberg was interrogated by Bavarian Army Intelligence in February 1918, the discussions of socialism over beer had transformed into something altogether more alarming. This case, while small and isolated, pointed to something of a disconnect between the intentions of the Army to keep its personnel from engaging in politics and its ability to enforce even obvious public violations of those orders.

Since the governments at the state, national, and local levels had taken such a direct role in and responsibility for food supply issues, propaganda urging citizens to hold on was keenly interested in presenting the idea that the government knew the answer to declining conditions. The problem with this was that it directly implicated the state in failure, since the food problem had reached a level by 1917 in which only dramatic victory could hope to alleviate the supply problem. A postcard called "To the Memory of Wartime, Anno Domini 1917" featured anthropomorphic food products like butter, cheese, and bacon, ration coupons, and the legend "If we persevere and are loyal to [Imperial Chancellor Thebold von] Bethmann-Hollweg's teachings, we can see off the Hunger Devil."[49] By 1917, neither Bethmann-Hollweg nor any of his colleagues could do much about hunger, and this vast gulf between promise and result became all the more clear to the German population. Talk of victory turned to talk of endurance as even the good news in 1917, a year of defensive victories in the West, dramatic triumphs in the East and the crushing of the Italian army did not seem to bring Germany any closer to ultimate victory. "The order of the hour," wrote the *Münchener Neueste Nachrichten*, "is 'hold on.'"[50]

Against an increasingly bleak existence, authorities faced the problem of keeping public enthusiasm for the war high enough to withstand the pressures of material deprivation. What emerged was a rhetoric of sacrifice that stressed the need to hold on until the war could be brought to a conclusion. The corollary to this demand, both stated and unstated, was that an end to the conflict would result in a tangible improvement in the lives of ordinary citizens. "A day is coming," promised the *Münchener Neueste Nachrichten* at Easter 1917, "a day of gold after an Easter of iron."[51] While much of the rhetoric still stressed the possibility of victory, after 1917 the discourse of holding on effectively decoupled victory from reciprocity. This crucial shift in tone had profound implications for the postwar world, in which a population could insist that it had done its part and even in the wakc of defeat asserted claims for rewards promised for their loyalty and suffering.

Popular entertainment also mobilized in the service of the war effort. In April 1917, for instance, those planning to go the cinema were able to see "East Prussia and Her Hindenburg" at the *Licht-Schauspielhaus* or "Vienna at War" at the

48 "Niederschrift über die Vernehmung des Pioniers Hans Bomberg." February 13, 1918. I b.A.K. 1371, BHStA IV.

49 "Zur Erinnerung an die Kriegszeit Anno Domini 1917." ZS 221, StdAM.

50 "Unser tägliches Brot." April 8, 1917.

51 "Unser tägliches Brot." *MNN*, April 8, 1917, 5.

Fern Andra. The *Sendlingertor Lichtspiele* showed a version of Henrik Ibsen's *Tere Vijan* (presumably Victor Sjolstrom's film of the same year). Audiences probably did not need much encouragement to see parallels between their situation and Ibsen's poem about a Norwegian fishing community struggling to survive in the face of the blockading British navy during the Napoleonic Wars.[52]

War also took an inescapably prominent place in the other forms of consumer culture, which generally served to contrast "normal" life with wartime existence with the goal of demonstrating that consumption could put right the juxtaposition. According to their advertisements, "A man can clean up, shave, and brush his teeth just like he did in peacetime," if he used Tangosol shaving products. A furniture dealer took out an advertisement seeking new retail space but only after the war ended. Some advertisers found commercial utility in the unprecedented death toll of the war. Advertisements for the less-than-subtly named book "Death" asked "Is there an afterlife? What becomes of our dead? Will we see them again?" This normalization of the war experience, which George Mosse has elsewhere called "the process of trivialization," served to make the war a part of everyday life. Even if one could not easily accept the war as a glorious and ennobling crusade, then at least it could be channeled into a banal and manageable inconvenience.[53]

On September 15, 1917, somewhere on the Western Front, a 22-year-old infantryman named Karl Schwörer died in a gas attack. His grieving family took out a death notice in the *Münchener Neueste Nachrichten* a few weeks later, commemorating their son's "heroic death for the Fatherland." His was just one of several columns of such notices, which appeared daily and followed the grim pattern of a vast and costly war.[54]

Anyone perusing the daily newspaper at the same time could also find a series of curious personal ads, taken by the war's victims, in the hopes of finding mates who might have also suffered loss as a result of the conflict. "G.G.," a 30-year-old mechanic, sought "to get to know a young woman for the purpose of marriage." In a description all too familiar to those who might be searching the ads, G.G. described himself as "war wounded in good health. Amputee."[55]

As we have seen above and in much of the scholarly literature on German society during the First World War, public debate over the war was dominated by debates over consumption, profiteering, and the manifest unfairness of life in a highly but unevenly mobilized society. At the same time, it is worth keeping in mind that there was an equally omnipresent discussion of death and suffering. This public grieving had strongly integrative effects within civil society in Munich. Loss was something that one experienced both privately and publicly, since it was such a common occurrence in the war years. Grieving families could pay tribute to their

52 Advertisements in *MNN*, April 28, 1917.

53 George Mosse, *Fallen Soldiers: Reshaping the Memory of the World Wars* (New York: Oxford University Press, 1990), 156.

54 *MNN*, October 2, 1917.

55 *MNN*, November 3, 1917.

lost loved ones in the pages of the local newspaper, while a shorthand of injury fostered a sense of common feeling among men who had fought and women who, presumably, had been robbed of their romantic opportunities by the same conflict.

The self-mobilization of Bavarian society was suffused and catalyzed with language of loss and mourning. Death and maiming at the front, like the common suffering on the home front, built communities in wartime. The arch-nationalist Munich publisher J.F. Lehmann produced 12,000 copies of his pamphlet "Germany's Future with a Good Peace or a Bad One" for the army. When he enjoined his readers to "see that only a complete victory can secure their future, that every rotten peace is a betrayal of the blood of our sons, who have given their lives for their country's honor and its future" he was not speaking abstractly. His own son, Arnold, was killed in battle in 1917.[56]

One can also see in this propaganda attempts to overcome Germany's pervasive local and provincial divisions, a problem especially acute in states like Bavaria that possessed considerable elements of self-rule. Posters urging Bavarians to contribute to the 9th War Bond, for instance, were printed in Bavarian blue and white and illustrated with typical Bavarian mountain farm scenes, yet carried texts which made it absolutely clear that breaking England's stranglehold on Germany's commerce and food supply was an imperial issue.[57]

War bonds, or *Kriegsanleihe*, were an integral aspect of the financing of the war and part of the foundation of the crumbling edifice of the German war economy. The staggering expenditures of the war, along with limited opportunities for foreign borrowing and an overall reluctance to raise taxes, created a climate in which domestic debt issues became the only means to sustain the war. Such short-term borrowing proved dangerously inflationary, a situation not helped by the profusion of agencies that were essentially empowered to print their own money.[58] The war bond drives brought together banks, government agencies, and consumers in a network of public and quasi-public financing on which much of the German war effort rested.

War bond drives were not just economic necessities, they were moments at which the state propaganda apparatus functioned at its greatest intensity. They were, or attempted to be, public celebrations of patriotism and national feeling.

---

56 Pamphlet. "Deutschlands Zukunft, bei einem guten und bei einem schlechten Frieden," (Munich: Lehmann, 1917) BhstA IV, 1724.

57 See poster "9th Kriegsanleihe" Zeitgeschichtliche Sammlung 220, StdAM.

58 Chickering, 105–7. Germany was not the only combatant nation to rely heavily on domestic borrowing. The fact that Germany lost the war meant that not only did Germany not gain the industrial resources that war planners hoped for, but also that the new government had a much more difficult time refinancing the debt by converting short-term obligations to longer term instruments. It is also too often forgotten that most of the combatant nations suffered wartime inflation to some degree or another, including the United States, despite that nation's late entry into the conflict. Without recognizing this fact, it is impossible to fully understand the economic mobilizations of the Second World War, which tried to draw lessons from the First.

One of the problems here was that "patriotism" in the Bavarian context was a potentially difficult issue. Many of the conservatives who might be expected to be supportive of mobilizing efforts were Bavarian patriots as much, or sometimes more, than they were German patriots. Such regional, national, and sometime sub-regional loyalties could and did co-exist within communities and individuals, but the continuation of Bavarian particularism colored the already vertiginous landscape of cultural mobilization in Munich. The problem of Bavarian goods being internally exported to northern Germany and allegations of preferential treatment for North German cities became increasingly pervasive as wartime economic conditions worsened.

In April 1917, during efforts to promote the 6th War Bond, the war hero and future mayor of Kempten Dr. Otto Merkt addressed a crowd at the *Löwenbräukeller*, where he regaled them with stories about his service in Flanders.

> We have done our duty and gone out as soldiers. The soil of Germany is free of the enemy. I was out there. I watched and was full of admiration for their struggle and their endurance. I saw young men storming the enemy's machine guns not once but two or three times, 'till half were gone with the words "With God for King and Fatherland" on their lips.[59]

Similar propaganda from the same period took a very different approach, evoking the national instead of the regional and revealing some of the limitations of the German imperial mobilization. One important symbol of the national mobilization was the taciturn figure of Field Marshall Paul Ludwig Hans von Beneckendorff und von Hindenburg, the hero of the early battles in the East and since 1916, Chief of Staff and virtual ruler of Germany. Hindenburg was not just a military figure but came to symbolize the national struggle of the war years. Giant wooden figures of the "icon of German militarism" appeared in cities and towns, and subscribers paid to drive nails into the figure in tribute to his reputation as a man of iron.[60] As Susanne Brandt has argued, the rituals associated with the figure of Hindenburg served to demonstrate and reinforce social cohesion at a time when the fabric of the social order seemed under pressure from war and deprivation.[61]

The creation of a Hindenburg cult was also a recognition of a problem in the mobilization of symbols in German political culture: in a relatively new and still culturally divided nation, symbols intended to unite could also be divisive. An excellent example of this is the figure of Martin Luther, celebrated during the 400th anniversary of his first public split with Rome in 1917. While historians

59 Typescript of speech in ZS 220, StdAM.

60 William J. Astore and Dennis E. Showalter, *Hindenburg: Icon of German Militarism* (Washington: Potomac Books, 2005), 75.

61 Susanne Brandt, "Nagelfiguren: Nailing Patriotism in Germany, 1914–18" in Nicolas J. Saunders, *Matters of Conflict: Material Culture, Memory, and the First World War* (London: Routledge, 2004), 62–3.

have pointed to the *Lutherfeier* as a means of showing and promoting German unity, such celebrations had little resonance in Catholic parts of the country like Southern Bavaria.[62]

In contrast to Luther, Hindenburg seemed to be a safe rallying point for national unity, a sentiment expressed most openly at the *Hindenburgfeier* on the Field Marshall's birthday, October 2, 1917. This celebration of the German nation was held at the *Königsplatz*, an open space bordered by the Greek revival splendors of the Philhellene King Ludwig I. The ceremony, held at night by torch and electric lights, seems to have drawn a considerable crowd, estimated to be 80,000–100,000. The procession was typical of official demonstrations of the time, led by schoolgirls in white with flowers and including musicians, folk dancers, soldiers with banners, and representatives of civic organizations. The centerpiece of the procession was a large ceremonial shield with the inscription "Hindenburg 1847–1917" followed by a list of "his" victories (Tannenburg, Masurian Lakes, Czernowitz, Riga, etc.).

The master of ceremonies for the evening was the aged Field Marshal Crown Prince Leopold of Bavaria, who emerged from retirement to take a series of commands in the East and who, like the King, fought against Prussia in the Seven Weeks War. The Crown Prince did not emphasize victory but endurance. "But we must hold on, so that our nation becomes a fortress.... We can do no better for our enemies than to become cowards and meekly submit." This mass celebration of the birthday of Germany's man of hour closed with a singing of the nationalist hymn "*Wacht am Rhein*."[63] While the popularity of such spectacles cannot be denied, it is difficult to assess how effective they were in promoting the kind of nationalist sentiment for which they were designed. This was a thoroughly Bavarian spectacle, with a Wittelsbach prince paying homage to a Prussian General, a Prussian Kaiser, and a Bavarian King in a setting that symbolized better than just about any other the grandeur of the nineteenth-century Bavarian monarchy. While events like the *Hindenburgfeier* certainly had the potential to evoke German nationalism, it did so through a framework of alternative and complimentary loyalties that ultimately proved both persistent and problematic for the imperial mobilization program.

The symbol of Hindenburg was not just an abstract representation of the national will. The imperial government, increasingly dominated by the Army High Command (OHL), used Hindenburg's popularity in an effort to deal with the manpower crises of total war. The Hindenburg Program of 1916–17 attempted to put a legal framework around the spiritual mobilization of German society by rationalizing and compelling the nationalization of facets of the German workforce that had previously managed to remain outside the mobilizing process.[64] The program, which further blurred the boundaries of civilian control in late Imperial society, gave military bureaucrats, particularly the able technocrat General

62 See, for instance, Chickering, 127, and Audoin-Rouzeau and Becker, 117.

63 "Die Hindenburg-Feier auf dem Königsplatz." *MNN*, October 3, 1917.

64 Chickering, 76–7.

Wilhelm Groener of the newly created *Kriegsamt* (War Office), extraordinary power to manage labor markets.

For Groener and the *Kriegsamt*, the greatest threats to the war effort were those parts of the labor movement who had not come along willingly with the mobilization and those who were growing tired of the deprivations and restrictions of wartime. In an open letter to armaments workers, Groener thundered:

> In the west at Arras, on the Aisne, and in Champagne our brothers in grey stand amidst the fiercest and bloodiest combat in the history of the world. Our army needs weapons and ammunition! Have you not read Hindenburg's letter? "A guilt beyond forgiveness upon those who celebrate at home instead of working. Our men in grey bleed for your sins. The worst of our enemies live among us – the cowards and even worse – those who call for strikes. These must be branded before the people as traitors to the Fatherland and to the army.[65]

Authorities at all levels cultivated a vision of a German people united against enemies foreign and domestic. The language of the "fortress," echoing Kaiser's 1914 proclamation of the *Burgfrieden* highlights the imaginary construction of a nation in arms, encircled by it enemies.[66] By 1917, the resonance of these appeals appears to have changed. While the original connotation drew from the language of encirclement and imminent threat that helped propel Germany to war, by 1917, observers of the civil truce could not help but notice the increasing resemblance to a walled town starved by its besiegers and unable to compel them to abandon the siege.[67] By the time of the harsh winter of 1917, the bold rhetoric of the civil truce was still very much in evidence but increasingly mocked in the streets and satirized by those who had ceased to believe in it.

Perhaps the most convincing proof of this pervasiveness of such atavistic, communitarian propaganda was that the emerging rhetoric of dissent, which fused anti-war, anti-monarchist, and eventually anti-system ideas into the torrent of upheaval that burst forth in 1918, consciously mimicked it both in style and language. In mid-1917, a crude satirical broadsheet called "The New Profession of Faith" circulated widely among workers in Munich and soldiers at the front. This attack on ration administrators, profiteering farmers, and the ubiquity of turnips ended with "I believe in the sacred war, a united society of profiteers, the

---

65 "An die Rüstungsarbeiter!" Berlin, April 17, 1917. MKr 17306. BHStA IV.

66 The term *Burgfrieden*, or "Peace of the Fortress," referred to the civil truce that theoretically existed between all parties within a walled community in a time of siege, to be lifted when the danger had passed. In the context of the First World War, it refers to the assumption of unprecedented power by the state, which received the approval the *Reichstag* on August 4, 1914.

67 A good brief discussion of the "unspoken assumptions" and the German decision for war can be found in Richard Hamilton and Holger Herwig, *Decisions for War, 1914–1917* (Cambridge: Cambridge University Press, 2004), 73–81.

fellowship of hoarders, the raising of taxes, the cutting of meat rations and an eternal persistence of bread ration cards. Amen."[68] While such sentiments were far from universal, they indicated a growing incredulity toward official propaganda.

The greatest problem with the cultural mobilization of the German population was that the effort eventually reached its explanatory limits. "Holding on" was no longer sufficient as the basic requirements of life became more and more difficult to obtain. There was no moment at which wartime domestic consensus shattered, but as the last full year of the war began, significant cracks began to show in the mobilization of German society, fissures that in early 1918 opened too widely to be concealed.

The Limits of Consensus: Dissent and the January Strikes

On the morning of July 12, 1917, Joseph Raimann awoke to find a crudely printed broadsheet slid under his front door just east of the Isar on Grillparzerstrasse. He took it to the police. The same day, the poster appeared across the eastern neighborhoods, including the garrison of the Royal Regiment of Infantry. "Women, Workers, Soldiers! The war will go on and on until you stand up and join together, and with all your strength and any means available advance the cause of Bread, Freedom, and Peace. In this struggle against war and mass murder, all methods are allowed. No bread without peace! No peace without revolution!"[69] This connection, explicit and implicit, between peace and food became a remarkably durable theme in political protests during the rest of the war and the immediate postwar years. This emerging anti-war rhetoric had at its heart a rejection of the twin notions of the justification of sacrifice in the name of national good and the claims by regime authorities and loyal media sources that sacrifices were fair and equitable.

Attempts by authorities to actually limit the content and scope of information available to the citizenry were problematic for a number of reasons. First was the sheer amount of political material available, sometimes locally produced and sometimes manufactured elsewhere in Germany or abroad. In October 1918, for instance, the I Corps Command issued a list of pamphlets to be confiscated on sight. Some of the titles were more or less identical to titles used in conventional propaganda, like "Alsatians and Lorrainers!," "German Soldiers!," "German Women!," or "German Comrades in Arms!" Others were explicitly oppositional or antiwar, like "Comrades," "Help from America," "You Impoverished People of Germany," or "Germany in the Bonds of Prussia," the last of which was printed in New York by the Association of Friends of German Democracy.[70]

68 "Das neue Glaubensbekenntnis" Anon. No date, but mid-1917. MKr, 251, BhstA IV.

69 Broadsheet "Frauen, Arbeiter, Soldaten." I Armee-Korps, 1902, BHStA IV.

70 Letter from Stellv. Generalkommandos I.b.A.K. to various police and postal surveillance authorities, October 15, 1918. I A.K, 1895, BHtA IV. Other banned pamphlets,

It might well have been difficult to survey and limit the content of political pamphlets, but it is also apparent that the authorities were unable to control even the public appearance of foreign newspapers in the city, some of which were clearly oriented well away from the propaganda lines of the Bavarian and German authorities. In mid-1918, as the German offensives in the West faltered and fell back, educated Bavarians could still go to a handful of bookshops and purchase, among other newspapers, *The Times*, the *Manchester Guardian*, the *New York Times*, *Figaro*, *Le Journal*, and *L'Humanité*. Switzerland was apparently the source of these publications, which were displayed openly in at least four Munich booksellers.[71]

These reports suggest the limits of censorship, even at a time of national mobilization and significant consensus. Even in 1918, it was still possible to acquire, openly and sometimes legally, alternative and possibly hostile viewpoints on the war. The international dimension of this trade in propaganda was clearly of vital importance, as was the element of political choice. Clearly anyone who perused a copy of a pamphlet called "To the German Socialist Proletariat" or chose to read or purchase *The Times* was at some level rejecting the propaganda apparatus of the wartime state.

In other cases, censorship seemed arbitrary and capricious. In 1917, the press office of the local command confiscated a series of prints contracted from a printer in Munich by a Swiss firm in Bern. Images of Samson pulling down the Philistine temple, the French Revolution, "Workers and Capitalism," or "The Earthquake" may have appeared too much like revolutionary propaganda, but they left the printer in a compromised position vis-à-vis their Swiss client.[72]

In other cases, the connection between foreign powers and propaganda was entirely explicit. By 1917, Allied planes occasionally penetrated Bavarian airspace, dropping, among other things, print propaganda. The French were heavily involved in distributing antiwar material across the border. In June 1917 police were warned to be on the lookout for recently dropped leaflets that threatened to "agitate Bavaria against Prussia and to put forth that Prussia alone is responsible [for the war]."[73] A year before, an apoplectic note passed between members of the I Bavarian Army Corps command pointing out that the French were using cartoons from *Simplicissimus* that voiced complaints about the food situation in Germany in fliers dropped over German lines.[74]

---

like "The Merry Widow," had no apparent political connotation and can be assumed to have been dangerously allegorical.

71 Report dated June 21, 1918 in I b.A.K. 1910, BHStA IV.

72 Letter from Brend'amour, Simhart Co. to Firma Franco-Swiss, Bern. May 16, 1917. I b.A.K., 1895, BHStA IV.

73 Letter from K. Staatsministerium des Innern to K. Regierungen, Kammern des Innern. June 16, 1917. I b.A.K. 1895. BHStA IV.

74 Note attached to flier. I b.A.K. 1895. BHStA IV.

Dissent was not necessarily anti-war or anti-government, but it was clearly anti-system in that it tended to criticize elements of mobilization by claiming that it was manifestly unfair. Dissenters claimed that the mechanics of mobilization favored one group over another, and that some groups by malfeasance or neglect, were allowed to profit from the misery of others. Jews were one of the most frequently identified of these enemies of mobilization. Munich's Jewish community frequently found itself a target of criticism as the supposed beneficiary of the largesse of wartime. The logic of anti-Jewish "fairness" rhetoric stemmed from the melding of traditional anti-Semitic tropes of secrecy, clannishness, and behind-the-scenes dealings with the inability of Bavarians to grasp what seemed to be an increasing reality: what once was commonly available was now expensive or utterly unavailable. Since it was inconceivable that consumer goods had simply vanished, such reasoning went, someone must have intercepted them and profited from their scarcity. Typical of this line of thinking was a piece of doggerel that began to appear in factories in Augsburg and Munich in 1917 and titled, initially, "The Jew in the World War."

> Everything that the Army can use
> Food, drinks, clothes, smokes
> Boots, swords, and guns
> And a whole lot more
> Barbed wire and hand grenades
> Canned meat and marmalade
> Horses, pigs, oxen, and beef
> And all the things that one can imagine
> Have to go through the Jews' hands
> And running these dens of thieves
> Are the big-time Jews (*Judenbuben*)[75]

While the language of this poem (which in full took up two very densely printed columns of type) explicitly refers to the needs of the military, clearly the complaints were also phrased in terms of consumer society. Invoking the needs of the Army was a more effective way to castigate the Jews as traitors who, in the poem's refrain "weren't in the trenches." While the importance of anti-Jewish sentiment in mobilizing street demonstrations grew, the actual Jewish population of Munich was at the same time in significant decline, falling in 15 years from 11,000 to 10,000 and from about 2 percent of the city's population to less than 1.5 percent.[76] This juxtaposition between the physical absence of Jews and their reported importance made them ideal targets for those who sought convenient targets for resentments

75 Poster found September 1919. I b.A.K. 1895, BHStA IV. We will see an alternative version of this poem in a later chapter.

76 Baruch Z. Ophir and Falk Weisemann, *Die jüdischen Gemeinden in Bayern, 1918–1945: Geschichte und Zerstörung* (Munich: Oldenbourg, 1979), 33.

that could not be directed at the government. These criticisms of Jews and Jewish influence had lasting effects on the political culture of the city. In the wake of the war this scapegoating took the form of physical violence against Jews and Jewish property as Jews remained a central symbol to critics of the ways in which demobilization was being carried out.

Since 1915, there had been occasional demonstrations in the center of Munich concerned with food provision and the ever-escalating price of coal. Authorities were not particularly concerned with these outbursts. It may well be that police did not concern themselves overmuch because such demonstrations were sporadic or because they were almost entirely composed of women. Like the chaotic scene that ensued outside Bronberger's at the beginning of the chapter, many of these demonstrations were spontaneous, though there were small assemblies at strategic locations like *Marienplatz* with some regularity. Women also played a role in inspiring workplace unrest, like the "unknown female" whose complaints about the food situation inspired a brief strike by about 15 male and female employees at the Kustermann coal depot on May 1, 1917.[77] Women's demonstrations took on a much larger role in the mind of authorities later on.

Women were certainly the explicit targets of anti-war propaganda. Given their new and singular role in war industries, agitation directed toward workers in general could and was sometimes directed at female laborers. One of the curious things about female propaganda was that it tended to appeal to a perceived feeling of commonality between women of the warring countries. This appeal to women *as women*, rather than as part of the international community of workers, was a departure from much of the more common anti-war agitation.[78] One anonymous poster found in the city in September 1918 asked:

> How much longer do you want this war to go on? You play your role in this, working for the government and munitions factories. Have you not had enough of this ceaseless hunger and deprivation, or do you have more sons, brothers and lovers to give? Every grenade … costs the enemy as many lives as it does us, makes women into widows, parents childless, and takes fiancés from their would-be-brides.[79]

It was the issue of strikes that created the greatest opportunities for conflicts between authorities and civil society. Like Manchester, Munich's particular place as a center of the armaments industry generated special sensitivities among military authorities to any strike agitation, real or perceived. As material conditions

77 Report of Schutzmann Georg Kiefer to K. Polizeidirektion München. May 2, 1917. I b.A.K. 1372. BHStA IV.

78 This perception continued to mark political appeals to women in the postwar republic. See Julia Sneeringer, "The Political Mobilization of Women in Weimar Germany, 1918–1932" (PhD diss., University of Pennsylvania, 1995), 16.

79 Poster found September 25, 1918. I b.A.K., 1895. BHStA IV.

deteriorated, labor issues came to center on the perceived power of workers to leverage their skills against the mounting economic crisis.

Where Munich and Manchester differed strongly was in the methods of mediation. Crucially, in Manchester the institutions of organized labor clung to the notion of reciprocity, convincing their members to see the benefits of operating within the sometimes strained legal frameworks of the wartime system. Strikers in Munich increasingly rejected the labor mediation tools available in wartime, precisely because they represented the same system that was currently failing to provide basic standards of living. When 80 workers at the building firm Wayss und Freytag walked off the job in September 1917, they demanded cost of living raises that might allow them to keep up with inflation. Significantly, the strikers refused to negotiate with the labor committees established to keep the peace in the workplace, preferring to establish their own representative committee.[80]

For labor organizations, the growing assertiveness and independence of industrial workers posed a significant challenge. Just as authorities appealed to Bavarians to remain loyal to king and country, organized labor appealed to workers to continue to operate within the system. The local branch of the metal workers union wrote to members in 1917 that they were aware of the twin problems of food and wages and that "your interests are in good hands. The workplace representatives in the armaments industry have recently discussed a drastic adjustment of the wage question."[81] Clearly the unions were concerned that matters might well slip out of their hands and wanted their membership to understand that even without legal recourse, they could still effectively represent their membership.

By the middle of 1917, military authorities were convinced that labor trouble was already bad and only going to get worse. Groener wrote from the *Kriegsamt* to regional commanders in July that "Unrest is becoming more substantial and more dangerous. Its simultaneity and ubiquity confirm my prediction that they are being planned and used for political purposes.... <u>You can look forward to more unrest this month and early next month</u>." Groener blamed the newly formed USPD, who he claimed, was trying to curry favor with Lenin.[82] At the same time, the Foreign Ministry warned the Bavarian government that the situation in Russia was going to inspire Social Democrats in Germany to "demonstrations against the war and anti-monarchist gatherings." The end result of such agitation would be "to weaken the strength of our resistance and give the war the character of struggle against the ruling system in Germany."[83]

Part of this newly energized concern among authorities was the result of events in Russia, which were being closely if not always accurately followed by the OHL

80 "Wochenmeldung über Arbeiterbewegung vom 10–17/9.1917." MKr 251. BHStA IV.

81 "Werte Kollegen und Kolleginnin." Undated, but 1917. MKr 251, BHStA IV.

82 Letter dated July 14, 1917. MKr 251, BHStA IV. Underlining in original.

83 Letter from Auswärtiges Amt (Zimmerman) to k.b. Staatsministerium des Innern. April 6, 1917. I b.A.K. 1373 BHStA IV.

and to a lesser extent by ordinary citizens. Reporting on the Russian Revolutions of 1917 was sporadic, particularly in places where connections to Russia had been broken by three years of war. Germans were in something of a bind when it came to the most radical variants of Russian revolutionary thought. At one level, it was clear that the Bolsheviks wanted Russia out of the war as quickly as possible, a task that many in war weary Germany would welcome. For many who followed these events in the *Münchener Neueste Nachrichten*, Bolshevism meant peace.[84] However, it was equally clear that such radical strains could be destabilizing if they permeated westward into Germany. The OHL believed that this danger was real while Bavarian authorities took a somewhat more measured tone.

The Bavarian government's response to rumors of labor agitation was, at least privately, more nuanced than Groener's public pronouncements of April 1917. In a letter from the Minister of War to the Army Command, von Hellingrath urged that a clear differentiation be made "between strike agitators and workers ensnared in the strikes."[85] This suggests an approach more consonant with traditional Bavarian methods of labor dispute resolution, which emphasized compromise and conciliation rather than the sort of possibly violent confrontation urged by the OHL and *Kriegsamt*.

The critical moment in the developing struggle between labor and authorities was the January Strike of 1918, which represented the most significant breach of the domestic consensus during the war years in Munich. The reasons for the strikes were various and complicated. Strike leaders hoped to send a clear message that labor peace would hereafter need to be explicitly linked with a program of political and constitutional reform, while others were frustrated at a perceived lack of progress in the byzantine peace negotiations with the Russian government.[86]

January 1918 witnessed a collapse, albeit temporary, of reciprocity. Ordinary people tired of escalating prices and diminishing supplies while state propaganda, before so effective, wore thin. Alternative visions of social order, which had been largely silenced during the national mobilization, now made their way back into prominent places in public discourse. The January Strikes allowed these voices to be heard in the streets, and they proved extraordinarily difficult to silence in the months to come. The January Strikes laid the groundwork for the political crisis of the last year of the war in Munich and they provided some of the momentum that allowed the coup of November 1918 and its successors. The confused reaction of authorities to the strikes, which combined ruthlessness and passivity and reflected the traditions of Bavarian labor conflict management, only served to remind the

84 Manuela Siegl, "Aspekte einer Rezeptionsgeschichte der Russische Oktoberrevolution und der Bolschewismusbegriffs in Münchner Quellen von November 1917 bis Mai 1919" (Magister Artium: LMU, 1990), 20–22.

85 Letter from von Hellingrath to K. stellv. Gen. Kdo. July 6, 1917. MKr 251, BHStA IV. Underlining in original.

86 Bauer and Piper, 250.

citizenry of the government's increasingly precarious position and the growing limits of both its power and its political will.

The Strikes of January 1918 were not limited to Munich but rather one part of a nationwide collapse of consensus that demonstrated the enormous discontent of industrial workers. The Strikes also highlighted the new organizing capabilities of the USPD, which by official estimates had about 15,000 members in Munich in 1918.[87] In Berlin, at the heart of the Strikes, more than 400,000 workers were involved, and the Strikes soon spread throughout Germany's industrial regions.[88] They were above all a sign that the methods and structures for keeping the labor peace in Germany had lost their efficacy and that events in the streets could now play an important role in shaping policy at the highest levels.

From January 28 until February 8, about 8,000 Munich workers laid down tools, in an action which mirrored others across Bavaria and the Reich. The Strike stopped work at a number of strategic facilities in Munich, notably the Krupp works in Freimann and the BMW plant in the north of the city. They also brought to the fore Kurt Eisner, the Jewish, Prussian-born writer and USPD agitator, who the police had previously known primarily as the organizer of a leftist discussion group at the *Goldenen Anker* bar. Eisner was a curious figure, a writer of socialist fairy tales and a journalist who had cut his teeth in the SPD milieus of Berlin and Nürnberg before coming to Munich a few years earlier. He had joined the more radical USPD at their founding in 1917, after becoming dissatisfied with the SPD over their continued support for the war effort. Eisner cut a distinctive profile with his famously unruly shock of grey hair and permanently unkempt appearance. He proved to be an exceptionally good agitator, capable of stirring intense passions in his listeners when allowed to speak freely. Suddenly, in the last days of January, the restrictions seemed to fall away, and people like Eisner emerged to fill the void.[89]

On Thursday, January 31, 160 workers building new a plant at the Krupp gunworks walked off the job, joined in a demonstration by workers from the main plant. The relatively large security detail that guarded the plants, 1 officer, 2 NCOs, and 45 troops, clearly expected attacks or sabotage, but neither were in the offing. The strikers managed to seriously limit production over the weekend before

87 "Wochenstimmungsbericht." July 17, 1918. RWGrKdo 4, 347, BHStA IV. I have no way of verifying this estimate, but if it is correct this is a considerable number for a party whose activism was essentially underground. Even if it is not correct, the perception that the party was this strong is in itself significant.

88 Chickering, 160.

89 Eisner is one of the most fascinating and controversial figures to emerge from the Munich milieu of the First World War, and until recently he has lacked a comprehensive scholarly biography. His legacy remains extraordinarily contentious within Bavaria as both an example of dangerous and "alien" radicalism and at the same time the intellectual wellspring of the Bavarian self-conception as a "*Freistaat*." Two good studies of Eisner are Franz Schade, *Kurt Eisner und die bayerische Sozialdemokratie* (Hannover: Verlag für Literatur und Zeitgeschichte, 1961) and the more recent biography by Bernhard Grau, *Kurt Eisner, 1867–1919: eine Biographie* (Munich: C.H. Beck, 2001).

coming back to work on Monday, though the officer-in-charge was convinced that many of the workers used the time off to go out into the country to gather food.[90]

At the Strike's political locus, the Schwabinger Beer Hall, the presence of USPD agitators and large numbers of workers changed the dynamic of protest movements in Bavaria. The Strikes were explicitly tied to the increasingly popular desire for an end to the war and not necessarily the victorious end that played a role in the maintenance of the domestic political consensus. For Eisner, who helped represent the USPD in negotiations with labor unions to organize the strike, the demonstrations were clearly about peace, which he passionately believed was not possible with the current regime[91] As he explained to a crowd at the *Kolosseumsbierhalle* several days before, "The time has come that the German people need to choose for themselves – we hear so much about the self-determination – Poland, Lithuania, Kurland. We must first have this right in our own country!" Shortly thereafter, a young policeman named Georg Rauh attempted to interrupt the speaker, and for his pains was shouted down with cries of "We want to hear the truth! Speak on!"[92]

The strikers at the *Schwabinger* heard speeches that explicitly referred to the coming demobilization of German society and to the emerging crisis of reciprocity. Metal workers assembled on January 29, along with a number of women and soldiers in uniform, heard *Landtag* deputy Franz Schmid speak on "The Transition Economy Between War and Peace." Schmid reminded his listeners that 10 million workers served in uniform and that they would need jobs when they returned. It could not have been lost on his audience, particularly the women, that many of those returning soldiers would demand their old jobs back and would probably not be content to see female labor filling their place.[93] Two days later, at the height of the strike, Eisner addressed the same hall and proclaimed, to the horror of the two policemen watching and the evident delight of the crowd, "The military is going with us!"[94]

Women played an inescapably prominent role in political developments. By 1918, there were about 70,000 workers employed in war-related industries in the zone of the I Bavarian Army Corps, of whom roughly 25,000 were female. At BMW, for example, women made up about 10 percent of the workforce.[95]

90 "Wochenbericht," written by Olt. Lyman, dated January 4, 1918, but February 4 was the correct date. Iluft 148, BHStA IV.

91 Grau, 333.

92 "Betreff: Versammlung der unabhängigen sozialdemokratischen Partei München in den Kolosseumsbierhallen am 27.1.1918." Stellv. GenKdo I 1372. BhstA IV.

93 Report from Sicherheitskommissar Simon Herold to K. Polizeidirecktion. "Metallarbeiterversammlung in der Schwabinger-Brauerei." January 29, 1918.

94 Transcription of Schutzmann Kopp's report. January 31, 1918. I b.A.K. 1372. BHStA IV.

95 SJFB, 169 and "Inspektion des Ingenieurkorps." 1.4.1918. Archiv des BMW AG, File 1918.

One of the most radical speeches the first night of the Strike was, according to a police agent at the meeting, a female worker "of Russian appearance" who spoke "very passionately" about the role of women in the proletariat and the need to make common cause between the Russian and German proletariats.[96]

Authorities moved swiftly to try to limit the damage caused by the Strikes. They swiftly arrested Eisner and many of his associates, who spent most of the rest of the war in prison. Still, the very public demonstrations of the last week of January spread quickly through the city. The main Strike action centered around the *Schwabinger* hall swiftly spawned other satellite strikes across Munich. A partial list of firms affected by the strike included the Otto-Werke machine tool and airplane factory, the *Bayerische Flugzeugwerke*, several cigarette concerns, a number of furniture makers, and the large *Rapp-Motorenwerke*. Of the 7,800 workers affected by the Strikes, Military Intelligence estimated that about half were women or juveniles. Some of factories remained closed until February 2 as workers held out for the demands that brought them together a few days earlier.[97]

The same day, a crowd of about 2,000 assembled at the *Theresienwiese*, led by figures like the student radical Ernst Toller. One observer recorded that the speakers issued demands that included the release of political prisoners (a list that now included Eisner), the democratization of the government, press freedom, and equitable distribution of food. The same observer found, somewhat hopefully, that "the majority of the crowd is in favor of the resumption of work."[98] While the workers did return to the factories the next day, the damage was done. Large sections of the population had taken to the streets to reject the state's efforts to mobilize them for war. Even the rhetoric of 1917, which emphasized holding in place of the expectation of victory, no longer held much appeal among Munich's critical skilled workers.

This collapse of confidence stemmed directly from the evident failures of mobilization. Because the state strived so hard to assert its claim as the sole authority in wartime, it took the blame when that mobilization could not deliver on its promises. Even in January 1918, when victory still appeared possible, much of the public had simply lost confidence in the ability of the state to abide by its reciprocal obligations. Conversations about the end of war, in public and private, became all the more frequent as the limits of mobilization and mobilized society grew ever clearer.

---

96 "Betreff: Versammlung der unabhängigen sozialdemokratischen Partei München in den Kolosseumsbierhallen am 27.1.1918." Stellv. GenKdo I 1372. BhstA IV.

97 "Wochenbericht … 27 Januar mit 2 Februar." Stellv. GenKdo I 1372. BhstA IV.

98 Ibid.

Planning for the End: Thinking about Demobilization in Munich

Planning for the eventual end of the war went on in public and private even as the mobilization efforts proceeded. As Richard Bessel has ably described, planning at the national level began in 1916 and intensified during the following two years, an effort dominated by concern for an orderly return of the millions in uniform and an economic transition that would not create widespread unemployment and industrial dislocation.[99] Demobilization planning, as we have seen previously, was a common task of civilian and military leadership during the war. It was a frustrating and difficult task during the dark days of war, not least because no one knew when the war might end or under what circumstances. German/Bavarian planners, like their allied and enemy counterparts, confronted a set of assumptions and constraints that were broadly similar.

The biggest problem with demobilization planning, at least the part of it directed from Berlin through the War Office, was that it was (sensibly) predicated on the idea that Germany would emerge from the war victorious. If planners had doubts about the scope of that victory, there was in the very least no public or private suggestion that Germany would suffer the kind of defeat that eventually befell it.

Planning for post-conflict military demobilization began in late 1916 and continued until the end of the war. In general, planning became more focused and specific as it moved from national authorities down to regional or corps commands. Much like mobilization, demobilization was supposed to be largely the responsibility of corps commanders, and early guidance stressed the autonomy of corps commands and "special formations" like Bavaria, Saxony, and Württemberg.[100] Within a few months, planners in the *Kriegsamt* projected that the complete demobilization of the German army after the war would take about four months and that local and regional bureaucracies should take steps to begin serious planning for such an eventuality. In Bavaria, an informal group of officials from the relevant ministries met regularly by early 1918 under the auspices of the Bavarian War Ministry.[101]

The military demobilization of the Bavarian Army was to begin before troops actually crossed back into Bavaria. Most units were to turn in their arms at depots between Metz and Saarlouis, with most units at least passing through the great depot at Metz. After, they would move by rail to demobilization camps in northern Bavaria, including large facilities at Nürnberg and Ingolstadt.[102]

---

99 Richard Bessel, *Germany After the First World War* (Oxford: Clarendon, 1993), 49–68.

100 "Bestimmung für die Demobilmachung des Deutschen Heeres." August, 1916. MKr 1754, BHstA IV.

101 "Niederschrift über die Besprechung in KB Kriegsministerium an 19. April 1918." MKr 1757, BHstA IV.

102 The military demobilization plans, which went through almost daily revisions, can be found in Stellv. Generalkommando, I. Armee-Korps 53. BHStA IV.

Planners recognized that the disarmament of the troops and their confinement to camps had to be accomplished swiftly in order to transition to the third phase of military demobilization, the orderly homecoming of demobilized troops. It is interesting to note that the generally agreed upon order for the conversion of troops back to civilian life was very similar to the scheme then being drawn up by British planners. By the middle of 1918, the Bavarian General Staff concluded that the first soldiers to be demobilized were to be specialists whose presence in the peacetime economy would stimulate job creation. These would be followed by those whose expertise would help organize and direct the economy (including civil servants), and finally different grades of demobilization based on the likelihood that the soldier would find work upon leaving the Army. This would encourage soldiers to get in touch with their old employers and, it was hoped, ensure a smooth transition back to civilian life.[103] While, as we will see, British personnel demobilization plans had to be revised in the face of discontent at the slow pace of transition, planners in Munich and Berlin faced the potentially dangerous problem of having to scrap many of their plans after their armies experienced defeat in 1918.

Even when scenarios that did not explicitly refer to a victorious conclusion to war were considered, no thought was given to the idea that the monarchy, its subordinate monarchies, and the institution of the military might all be swept away. In July 1917, for instance, the Imperial War Ministry's Demobilization staff sent their opposite numbers in Munich a projection of the postwar armaments requirements of the German army. In the first three to four years after the war, Berlin estimated, the Bavarian Army would require about 600,000 new rifles, while Prussia would need about 5.4 million.[104] Clearly, such projections depended on such formations continuing to exist in something resembling the contemporary arrangement.

While this appears in hindsight to have been a monumental error, it must be remembered that until Fall 1918, the German Army was in a strong enough position to suggest at least a negotiated peace that would leave Germany with considerable possessions in the East and some kind of accommodation in the West. For this reason, the mechanisms for managing demobilization vanished in the face of defeat. Since so much of the planning for the demobilization of the Bavarian Army changed when that defeat became evident, I will discuss the evolving legal and bureaucratic frameworks of demobilization in more detail in Chapter 5. This is not to say that there were not important continuities between wartime planning and postwar reality. The Bavarian *Demobilmachungskommissar* was the Social Democrat Martin Segitz, who would attempt to carry through the return of the troops and their reintegration into Bavarian society even after the government that he represented collapsed at the end of the war.

It is, however, worth discussing some of the visions of demobilization circulating in Munich in the last years of the war, as they have a direct bearing on the creation

103 This formula is repeated a number of times. See, for example, "Arbeitsvermittlung bei der Demobilmachung," September 1918, MKr 1759, BHStA IV.

104 "Verteilung." MKr Berlin, July 27, 1917. MKr 4466. BHStA IV.

of postwar expectations in the city. The expectation of victory and its rewards were vital to the creation and maintenance of wartime consensus. Discussions of what would happen when the war concluded changed dramatically as the war dragged on and any ending to the conflict promised relief from the deprivation of wartime. A 1916 pamphlet, for instance, stressed that "the German people have given in the course of this war so much evidence of their faithful loyalty to the Fatherland and so many sacrifices, that they can expect that after the successful end of the war government protection from any new difficulties that are within its power to prevent."[105] A local representative for a shop owners' association was even more explicit in his expectation that the end of the war should mark the beginning of effective demobilization in his trade. "We cannot lose sight of the basis of our previous economic system. These monopolistic and state-socialist tendencies … must be confronted with decisiveness and energy."[106]

Discussions of demobilization within Bavaria were well underway by early 1917, when the Ministry of War prepared a report on its expectations for postwar reordering of public life. The report strongly supports Bessel's larger contention that the primary concern of demobilization planners was maintaining order in the immediate postwar period. "The possibility of unrest during or after the demobilization is quite real, particularly given the persistent shortage of food." The report further recommended strict, though undefined, measures to prevent outbreaks of public disorder.[107]

The key to the imagined successful demobilization of German society was to be the economy. Economic demobilization rested upon the continuation of social programs for the provision of consumer goods and the reintegration of returning troops into the labor market. The principal national body for coordinating the economic demobilization of strategic materials, the *Reichskommissarat für Übergangswirtschaft*, was formed in August 1916, and unfortunately most of its records were destroyed by bombing in 1945.

Military planners in May 1917 identified 15 vital questions concerning economic demobilization. Recognizing the growing crisis of confidence among consumer society and the economic necessities of the postwar transition, the majority of the proposed measures, and almost all of the most important, had to do with reintroducing consumer goods markets with all possible speed. At the top of the list was food, followed by the loosening of agricultural controls, the building trade, transportation (most notably trains), and heating supplies like coal and wood.[108] At a meeting on September 14, 1918, as the German army

105 Pamphlet. "Wenn der Friede kommt." Deutschnationaler Handlungshilfen Verband. Kriegswirtschaftamt 268, StdAM.

106 Speech by Max Weisnmann, Zentralverbandes des Deutschen Grosshandels, Gruppe Sudbayern, E.V. February 8, 1917. Handelskammer München, Kriegswirtschaftamt 268. StdAM.

107 Letter from MKr (Frh. von Speidel). May 5, 1917. MKr 18262, BHStA IV.

108 Ibid.

continued its collapse in the West, a meeting chaired by Segitz in Munich heard the *Demobilimachungskommissar* urge the assembled regional leaders to make sure that the "the regulated flow of materials, the coal provisions provided through employment agencies, and all such provisions of welfare should not be interrupted" by the potential end of the war.[109]

This concern for the quality of quotidian existence was mirrored in the public rhetoric of Munich officials, who stressed that the developments of wartime would bring prosperity when the war ended. *Stadtbaurat* Dr. Gräffel, speaking on "The Further Development of Munich After the War" stressed that Munich had changed before, from "a city of wine to the world's best known city of beer." Invoking the city's self-image as a place of conciliation and moderation, he claimed it was "a peculiarity of Munich that its people can live with one another and not be the worse off for it, as in the present heightened growth of industry."[110]

A report by the Army Command in October 1918 addressed in starkly realistic terms the mood in the streets of Munich. "The improvement of the public mood is overwhelmingly dependent on material factors – the food question, the housing question, profiteering, etc." The author noted that the "hurrah patriotism" of the past was gone. "There will be no more celebratory send-offs of troops going into the field." What the author did not, and probably could not bring himself to write, was that the careful instantiation of public morale that kept the German war effort together for years had worn down against the hard realities of a failed effort to prosecute total war.[111]

In 1969, a store owner on Effnerstrasse named Dr. Robert Wohlmuth recorded his memories of those days toward the end of the war, when he was a young reserve Lieutenant of Pioneers, stationed at the *Ausstellungspark* and ill with the influenza that would soon sweep through Europe with a fury more deadly than the war. Wohlmuth was then 23 and had been in the Bavarian army since 1914. In his account we can clearly see the profound weariness that had set in after four years of war and death. Even a half-century and another World War after the fact, Wohlmuth's account rings true:

> We forgot all about the "Great Victory"... The people were so thoroughly worn down by hunger and dissatisfaction that any resistance they had was simply broken. The wish at the front and at home was just "Let's be done with it."[112]

109 "Die Demobilmachung des bayerischen Heeres." MAA, September 14, 1918. PrASlg 3131. BhStA V.

110 "Beitrage zur Weiterentwicklung Münchens nach dem Krieg." *MNN*, April 29, 1917, 1.

111 Letter from Stellv Generalkommando I b.A.K. to K. bayer. Kriegsministerium, October 7, 1918. I b.A.K. 1724. BHStA IV.

112 Document in ZS 441. StdAM.

By late Fall, it was clear that the war would not and could not continue as it had. Even after the breakdown of the army in the West and the accompanying collapse of morale, military planners still could not bring themselves to discuss defeat. Instead, they began to consider the possibility of an armistice, a temporary cessation of hostilities. It is striking that, despite this obfuscation, they were increasingly convinced that an agreement to end the fighting would be permanent. There was simply no more will or capacity to wage war. On October 18, Chief of Staff von Hellingrath wrote to commanders in the field that an armistice was likely and that their "first priority during the armistice is … to bolster the spirit and morale of the men." In an ominous sign of the impending collapse of the painstaking plans for an orderly demobilization, von Hellingrath also advised that, because fathers and older reservists "will be a positive influence in rural areas," they should be furloughed as quickly as possible.[113] The most senior officer in the Bavarian Army sensed, as many around him did, that the coming days were going to unpredictable and that maintaining control of the Army would be critical in determining the outcome.

Before the deluge, which would sweep away the Bavarian and German monarchs in early November 1918 there was a pause, a moment in which it seems to have been clear to thinking Germans that the war was lost. Members of the Munich Chamber of Commerce, meeting on October 31, 1918, considered the likely course of events that would follow the by then almost inevitable cessation of hostilities. The speakers that night emphasized again the need for unity and evoked again the rhetoric of common sacrifice. The Chairman, Josef Pschorr, scion of the brewing family, opened the meeting by reminding his compatriots that both classes would need to work together for the common German fatherland in the "difficult times of the coming peacetime economy."

There was an unmistakable tone of sadness and loss in the room that night. Many of those present had lost businesses while others had lost sons and brothers. Of the just over 2 million Germans who fell in the war, about 13,000 had been from Munich.[114] Across Bavaria, more than 170,000 had been killed, about 65 percent of whom were between 20 and 29 years old.[115] The communities of mourning grew larger with each passing day, and the end that was so clearly in sight promised none of the bounties of victory that had seemed so close even a few months before. Delegate Fränkel suggested that all "fatherland-minded Germans" should consider the question "Must this immeasurable sacrifice in blood and treasure, after a display of our armed might more glorious than anything in the history of the world come to such a bitter end?"[116]

113 Letter of October 18, 1918. MKr 1753, BHStA IV.

114 Chickering, 195, and Bauer and Piper, 243.

115 SJFB, 50.

116 Minutes of the Handelskammer München, October 31, 1918. Kriegswirtschaftamt, 268, StdAM.

The bitter end in the Fall of 1918 brought to a conclusion a period of mobilization and remobilization that transformed the city of Munich and its inhabitants. Like demobilization, mobilization is not a normative process. Mobilization within the German empire was and was perceived to be highly state-directed. The state and its constituent entities claimed from the earliest days of the conflict that it and it alone knew how to manage the war effort on the front and at home. While this was very different from the far less centralized and less intrusive mobilization strategy pursued in Britain, both produced highly mobilized societies at war by 1917.

As late as the early months of 1918, it appeared very likely that Germany and her allies might emerge from the war victorious. The defeat that cleared the path for the upheavals of 1918–19 in Germany was by no means preordained or evident to observers. Before the twinned experiences of defeat and victory limited the options available to authorities and civil society in Britain and Germany, the different strategies of mobilization played an important role in shaping wartime political culture and in turn the events that followed the end of the conflict.

The crowd that assembled in front of Bronberger waited in the cold for a few grams of sugar. They were not protestors, in large part because they had little expectation that protest would have done any good. The rules of wartime society, with its ration books, substitute foods, and ostensibly stringent regulations on public discourse, simply broke down. The imperial government in distant Berlin and the Bavarian government just a few short blocks away told the people in that crowd for three years that their sacrifices could and would be rewarded then failed to provide for even the most basic needs.

When demonstrators in Manchester took their grievances to city authorities, they did so with some expectation that they might compel those officials to alter policy on material issues. Those who took to the streets in Munich had no such expectations, in large part because they confronted a state that claimed to be the sole legitimate arbiter of wartime life. The strikers of January 1918 openly questioned the legitimacy of that authority and the institutions that tried to instantiate it. The process that began in the snow in front of Bronberger, and in hundreds of places like it, found its clearest articulation in the muddied and sometimes bloody days that followed.

SECTION II
"The Man Afterwards Changed Completely:" Demobilizations, Homecomings, and Transformations

In his influential study of the round of peacemaking that followed the Armistice, John Maynard Keynes captured some of the extraordinary dislocation and ambivalence being felt more and more among both victors and vanquished in the first year of peacetime. Keynes wrote that he "cannot disinterest himself from the unfolding of the great historical drama of these days which will destroy great institutions, but may also create a new world."[1] This juxtaposition of anxiety and hope was perhaps the characteristic emotion of the year after the Armistice as the visions of the future discussed and debated during the years of war encountered the realities and limitations of the period that followed.

Munich and Manchester diverged in significant ways in the year after the end of the war. As the magnitude of the defeat instantiated itself on the German home front, the tensions of the war years burst forth into civil strife and violence. Munich experienced the collapse of the monarchy, the rise of a brief but radical experiment in revolutionary government, and the suppression of that regime by force of arms. Even in revolution-haunted Germany, Munich seemed to be an exception.

Manchester, on the other hand, transitioned into the postwar period largely without massive social upheaval. Soldiers and sailors returned home, the wartime economy began to show signs of reverting to peaceful production, and the slow recovery of postwar society seemed to nudge the English northwest back toward normalcy. If perhaps these trends were not as quick as one might have hoped, they were nonetheless evident in the months after the war.

In the previous chapters, I have argued that wartime political culture in Munich and Manchester was shaped by similar sets of pressures, but within the context of different national, local, and regional strategies of mobilization. As European states and societies demobilized at the end of the conflict, those differing mobilization strategies had important consequences in the postwar world as defeated and victorious states sought to manage the demands of postwar transition. Britain and Germany took very different paths to the highly mobilized societies of 1917 and 1918. After November 11, those differences created different sets of options for postwar demobilization.

---

1 John Maynard Keynes, *The Economic Consequences of the Peace* (New York: Harcourt, Brace, and Howe, 1920), 8.

At the heart of the demobilization crisis lay the dramatic juxtaposition of expectation and outcome. The rhetoric of the war years firmly established the obligatory function of the reciprocal relationship between the state and society. In victorious and defeated states, populations emerged from the war convinced that the state owed them some tangible reward for their loyal service. In Britain and Germany, like the rest of former combatants, this created enormous expectations that demobilizing states did not meet. While this budding crisis existed across former combatant societies, the reasons for it and the outcomes that emerged from it were quite different.

In Britain, the wartime reliance on a sometimes uneasy partnership between the state and private enterprise now yielded a situation in which much of the impetus for rebuilding a peacetime economy rested with the private sector. In the Northwest, the slow economic recovery after the end of the war sharply limited that recovery effort, creating an unemployment and underemployment crisis. At the same time, millions of men under arms chaffed at long and seemingly capricious delays to their return to civilian life. The result was an overwhelming sense that the government was capable of solving these related problems, but that it was not willing to do so. As elements within civil society pursued redress of their grievances, they did so by attempting to convince a state that they believed would respond to sorts of pressures that proved workable during the war.

In Germany, on the other hand, the beginning of demobilization seemed to highlight the manifest inability of the state to live up to the obligations of wartime that had not been mitigated by defeat. The state's wartime claim to near total authority over domestic affairs left its postwar successor with the insoluble problems of achieving continuity in demobilization policy while undergoing the sometimes violent transformation. Just as the wartime state lost legitimacy when it failed to live up to its obligations, the postwar state lost ground to the political margins when it failed to effectively manage the challenges of demobilization.

The year after the Armistice saw the beginning of the complex processes through which authority, which concentrated at the national level during wartime, devolved back to regional/local authorities. While reversing the wartime flow of power, this trend tended to exacerbate conflicts over bureaucratic responsibility and revealed the limits of the duplication of responsibility that resulted from mobilization. Each of these chapters considers four aspects of the immediate postwar period; postwar political transitions, the return of the troops, economic demobilization, and political radicalism. Each of these postwar transformations drew from wartime political culture. In particular, the rhetoric of reciprocity informed the actions of authorities and civil society, catalyzing a postwar situation already fraught with instability and limiting the willingness and ability of all sides to compromise.

For Bavarians, 1919 was not just a year of violence and political chaos. For most Munich residents, the year was spent coping with far more quotidian concerns like food, housing, and employment. The political violence for which Munich is justly remembered was, after all, brief and localized. While it left important legacies in the city and far beyond its borders, it is too simplistic to consider the city simply as a site of violent contestation. Many of the institutions that dealt with the practicalities of demobilization retained an astonishing degree of administrative continuity throughout that turbulent year, a measure of how important successive governments considered the practical challenges of restoring peacetime social order.

If social upheaval did not happen at nearly the same level in Manchester, that outcome was by no means clear at the time. For many reasonable Mancunians, the year after the war seemed to hold the real danger of revolutionary violence. Just because these visions did not come to pass does not mean that they were not seriously held at the time. These fears were compounded when the postwar economic recovery proved to be illusory at best. As local industries struggled to transform to meet the needs of the postwar world, a society in transition seethed at the bewildering pace of change after November 11.

Participants in the first rounds of postwar elections drew explicitly from the war experience. Postwar political parties claimed legitimacy based on their willingness and ability to right the real or perceived injustices of the war years and to embark on the reform programs that had been the hallmark of wartime debates over the postwar future. While the postwar elections in Munich and Manchester were held under very different circumstances, the efficacy of those appeals was evident in the bitterness of the campaigns and the decisiveness of the results.

The physical demobilization of the armed forces, which began in earnest in the immediate aftermath of the conclusion of hostilities, was also similar in important ways. Despite the self-demobilization the Imperial German Army, the return of troops to urban areas, their provision while awaiting return home, and the need to maintain some sort of order throughout the process led to close coordination between returning units and local officials. In Manchester, returning military personnel expected speedy demobilization and, when they discovered a halting and sclerotic process, organized to demand their rights.

Just as similar wartime demands for production drove economic mobilization, the war's termination presented analogous challenges for postwar governments in victorious and defeated states. The dual imperatives of resuming consumer production while minimizing unemployment meant that the often uncomfortable partnership between the state and private sectors had to continue, even when the nature of the state was very much in flux. Since consumption was a crucial point of contestation during the war, the inability of postwar economies to generate sufficient consumer products within a short time revealed fundamental weaknesses in the recovery effort. In both cities, this shortfall combined with unemployment to generate grievances in postwar civil society that combined continuities from wartime with the possibilities of protest now allowed with the lifting of wartime restrictions.

Finally, the story of postwar political radicalization took distinct but related paths in these two cities. In Munich, postwar violence created and reinforced myriad constellations of leftists, conservatives, and a growing but still protean "new right" movement that sought a third way between the political poles.

The violent legacies of that evolving conflict, which resulted in assassinations, street violence, and the grim events of early May, helped to set Munich's course in the interwar period. Manchester experienced nothing like this level of violence. At the same time, postwar conditions bred considerable discontent and gave those advocating radical solutions the problems of urban life a critical entrepôt into English politics. While the profusion of radical political responses that defined the interwar years were by no means established or clear in the immediate aftermath of the First World War, the crisis of reciprocity helped to set the conditions in which such solutions seemed appropriate, possible, or thinkable.

The postwar transition in the industrial north of England was neither easy nor uncontested. A population that had been told it would enjoy the fruits of victory grew rapidly disappointed when it became clear that such rewards were not going to be fast in coming or indeed that material conditions might well be worse in the short term. Yet even as dissent grew more visible in the wake of wartime restrictions, it was channeled and limited by the legacies of wartime mobilization. While extremist visions of social change grew in number and volume, they proved to have relatively little traction within civil society. The wartime experience proved for many ordinary Mancunians that the most effective way to advocate for reciprocity was to do so within the boundaries of existing institutions.

In Munich, the defeat of 1918 and the failure of the state to effectively manage the home front at war produced powerful incentives to create institutions outside of or opposed to the state. Wartime demonstrations, emboldened by successive catastrophes at home and on the front lines, turned into threats to the wartime state. As authority collapsed, Bavarians faced an array of new formations, some of them armed, which claimed the mantle of political legitimacy. These new institutions, ranging from alternative governments to militias and radical political formations, based their claims to legitimacy on their willingness and ability to fulfill the expectations of reciprocity and to manage the process of demobilization.

Chapter 4

"The Fabric of Europe and the World was Being Remade:" The Armistice and After in Manchester

The war was over. On November 11, 1918, the city of Manchester celebrated the end of more than four years of bitter and brutal conflict. A day in which hundreds of thousands of Mancunians cheered, reflected, and grieved alone or in small groups merged into a night of joyous and raucous festivities across the city, the country, and swaths of exhausted Europe. Accounts of the day focused on the sounds of the Armistice; a woman shouting joyously on a tram, two men dressed in black crying together, the tugs at Salford Quays riotously sounding their horns, and women workers in Salford's factories leading the singing of "God Save the King." After dark, the workers who spontaneously took the afternoon off mixed in the streets with soldiers and sailors eager to celebrate the return of peace.[1]

The public outpouring of November 11, and in the days to come, were just a preview of a year in which street demonstrations were common and rarely celebratory. Even as celebrations of the Armistice continued, there was evidence of disquiet over the unseemly haste of the government's call for postwar elections. The tensions of wartime did not diminish with the end of hostilities. Instead, they took on new life as labor and social unrest stemming from the great changes of the war years resulted in a cluster of strikes and labor actions that involved considerably higher numbers of workers than even the prewar strike waves.[2] One contemporary publication referred to this period following the end of the war "the year of demonstrations."[3]

Contemporaries saw this time as one of momentous change. In a 1946 tribute to C.P. Scott, the legendary editor of the *Manchester Guardian* who guided the paper from a regional giant to a prominent place in the national press, one former editor remembered 1919 as a time when "the fabric of Europe and of the world was being remade."[4] But how would this new world come about? Whose interests

---

1 Accounts from *Manchester Evening News* (*MEN*), November 11, 12, 1918.

2 David Gilbert, "Industrial Protest, 1900–39," in *An Atlas of Industrial Protest in Britain, 1750–1990*, ed. Andrew Charlesworth, et al. (London: Macmillan, 1996), 130.

3 Co-Operative Press Agency, *The People's Year Book, 1922* (Manchester Co-Operative Wholesale Society Press, 1922), 255.

4 D. Mitrany, Unpublished volume of tributes to C.P. Scott. October 26, 1946. Manchester Archives F920 5 S84.

would dominate in the society to come? These questions loomed large over discussions of rebuilding British society in the wake of the war. The propaganda of wartime ostensibly promised a postwar society that would not simply replicate prewar conditions but would allow those whose voices had been marginalized to gain influence commensurate with their wartime sacrifice. As the celebrations of November gave way to a more sober reckoning, conflicts that wartime had only imperfectly kept at a simmer threatened to boil again. Circumstances, some of them peculiar to the industrial economy of the Northwest, began to circumscribe the promise of a new and just society and popular resentments carried over into the streets.

How do we understand the gap between the hopeful celebrations of November and the labor unrest of the next year? How did the improvised mobilization of British society affect efforts to demobilize society at the end of the war? How did different groups experience this process of demobilization?

The answers had everything to with the specific legacies of Britain's mobilization strategy. The obligations owed to those who served, men and women, were clear and very much at the forefront of public discussion of the war. Any effort to assert political legitimacy in the postwar period, including the elections held just months after the Armistice, centered on the claims of political parties that they would and could ensure fair and equitable treatment for those whose efforts contributed to victory. At the same time, conditions on the ground all but precluded a smooth transition from wartime to postwar. The massive task of physical demobilization and a weak domestic economy in the Northwest created structural impediments to transition just as the rhetoric of reward and sacrifice reached their apogee in the wake of November's victory. The private–public partnership that sustained Britain's wartime mobilization now faced the task of managing demobilization. When this challenge proved overwhelming, the British state appeared uncaring and vacillating, unwilling to fulfill the obligations it assumed in wartime. This perceived unwillingness lay at the heart of public disquiet in the year after the Armistice. It circumscribed the limits of dissent within a framework of loyal opposition and limited the appeal of radical solutions and their advocates. At the same time, the experience of victory created enormous expectations and sharpened popular disappointment when those expectations went unmet.

The end of the war generated a boom period of about 18 months in Britain, during which wartime production and wages remained high, along with consumer demand. It was, however, a highly artificial situation and the government was keenly aware that it was going to end when the economy settled into a postwar pace. It also did not extend to the Northwest, where the combination of a changed market for cotton goods and the slow resumption of coal production created serious impediments to recovery.

The fact of the postwar boom meant far less to people on the ground in Manchester as did the perceived and real inequalities of the emerging postwar system, the continuance of wartime regulations, and the terrible practical problems of reintegrating a labor force that had endured a series of profound dislocations over five years. Britain's government was thinking very hard about creating a stable and viable postwar economic order, but it often did not appear that way in the factories, streets, and demobilization camps. This difference of perception helped to turn 1919 into a year fraught with peril and uncertainty. C.P. Scott wrote to an associate in October that he feared "the biggest industrial war in our history."[5]

"The Peace," wrote a local historian in 1940, "brought no real feeling of confidence to the city. There were numerous strikes among the industrial workers ... and the industrial disturbances were complicated by the persistence of political unrest."[6] One observer, writing in 1920, was much more specific in his condemnation of government inaction and barely concealed anxiety about the future.

> No statesman had the vision to see or raised his voice to point out that before the final coming of peace there must be delay and uncertainty, but that from the moment of the cessation of fighting reaction must begin.... A state of unpreparedness, lack of leadership, and the example of state extravagance were to lead up to the "land fit for heroes to live in." The actual result was that, after the first days of holiday, the Parliamentary Election, and a brief period of reaction, Labour began, *with added factors*, to resume the claims and movements suspended by the war.[7]

The theme of government inaction and apathy was a common one. President Wilson's friend and plenipotentiary Colonel House wrote to Scott in March 1919 that "I have long since given up hope of having the kind of peace the world desires. It is a question now of getting the best that we can, or stopping the machinery and running the risk of chaos.... The so-called governing classes seem to me to be completely asleep and it is nearly impossible to wake them."[8] The memoirs of Mancunian social reformer and Lord Mayor E.D. Simon blamed the attitudes of wartime for the vacuum of postwar leadership:

> Those who tried during the Great War of 1914–18, whether in England or America or France or Germany, to discuss a policy for the situation which must follow the war were constantly told that such a discussion would prevent us from concentrating our whole minds on the attainment of victory. In consequence,

5 C.P. Scott to L.T. Hobhouse. October 1, 1919. C.P. Scott Papers, Manchester Guardian Archive, John Rylands Library, 132/287.

6 Arthur Redford, *The History of Local Government in Manchester*, vol. 3 (London: Longmans, Green, and Co., 1940), 222.

7 Lord George Askwith, *Industrial Problems and Disputes* (London: John Murray, 1920), 467.

8 Letter from C.M. House to C.P. Scott. March 10, 1919. C.P. Scott Papers, Manchester Guardian Archive, John Rylands Library, 335/87.

> when victory came, the statesmen of Versailles were without thought or plan, and their victory brought mankind nothing but disaster and disillusion.[9]

The postwar experience for many Britons whose lives had been upended in some way by the war was one of dashed expectations and an increasing feeling of bitterness toward the war they had come through. As the American journalist Arthur Gleason, who took an intense interest in the coal and cotton industries of Lancashire, wrote:

> Memories of the Brotherhood of the Trenches fail to content the demoralized Tommy with the England to which he returns. By the guerrilla warfare of sectional strikes and one-day stoppages, by the mass warfare of great strikes, and by the steady wear and wastage of slack work, petty obstructions, and passive resistance, the workers pick and nibble and dynamite the system to pieces.[10]

The appeal to fairness and a just reward for the sacrifices of wartime played a critical role in the first political contest of the postwar period in Britain. As wartime political restrictions gave way, old debates over the country's future resumed with a new vitriol expressed through this language of reciprocity. In areas like Manchester, debates over the nation's future began in the immediate aftermath of November's uncertain victory.

The Khaki Election in Manchester

With the guns on the Western Front barely silent, the wartime government called a general election for December. Despite well-founded criticism that Lloyd-George was taking advantage of the victory to increase his margin in Parliament, his government, a Coalition dominated by Liberals and Bonar Law's Conservatives, was determined to test its political fortunes at the ballot box. The government felt confident they could achieve a comfortable victory against Liberals still loyal to Herbert Asquith, whom Lloyd-George forced out of Downing Street in 1916, and against the Labour opposition.[11] The presence of so many soldiers in uniform led some to call this a "Khaki Election," while others termed it the "Coupon Election" after the slips of paper given to candidates supported by the Coalition.

Coming as it did a month after the Armistice, many voters saw the election as a continuation of the war and considered the impact of the results on the

9 Graham Wallas "Introduction" in E.D. Simon. *A City Council from Within* (London: Longmans, 1926), XIV.

10 Arthur Gleason, *What the Workers Want: A Study of British Labour* (London: George Allen and Unwin, 1920), 249–50.

11 Alfred Havighurst, *Britain in Transition* (Chicago: University of Chicago Press, 1985), 147–9.

process of demobilization. In endorsing the Coalition, the *Manchester Evening News* reminded readers, with a notable degree of selective memory, that Britain's workers had stood by the government's war effort:

> They stand by it now, and say to the Government "Complete the task. Make a good job of it." To turn out the Coalition now will be tantamount to a vote of censure on their work, and a want of confidence in their ability to turn chaos into order.[12]

This connection between the just-completed war and the upcoming election was mirrored, if negatively, in the appeal of the Labour party. Joseph Hallsworth, then a leader of the Amalgamated Union of Co-operative Employees, ran unsuccessfully on the Labour ticket for a seat in Stretford in the postwar election. In a letter to prospective voters, he laid out an ambitious vision of postwar Britain based on rewarding workers for their war service:

> The task of the new Parliament will be concerned not only with the Peace Terms, but with the Reconstruction of our entire Social Order. The Labour Party, in whose name I appeal for your support, desires the work of Reconstruction to be undertaken not from the point of view of profit making, not in the interests of a small class, but for the physical, moral and intellectual well-being and enjoyment of the nation as a whole.[13]

Hallsworth's program called for, among other things, Home Rule for Ireland, the devolution of power to Scotland and Wales, and the nationalization of capital industries. It was demobilization that formed the core of the appeal. Trade Union rights "abrogated in the public interest" should be immediately restored. He called for "full provision for the probably large number of civilian workers whom the dislocation of industry following upon the cessation of hostilities will throw out of employment." Labour appealed directly to soldiers and sailors, arguing that "the experience of past wars shows a shameful treatment of those who have been called to face death and disaster, and if this is not to be repeated, the soldiers and sailors can look with confidence only to the Labour Party – the party of their own class, which has already made their cause its special care."[14]

In the electoral struggle between the Coalition and its opposition, the issue of who was best prepared to "reconstruct" British society in the wake of the war was the one most commonly evoked in late 1918. The government's clumsy call

---

12 "Labour and Coalition: What the Working Man is Thinking," *MEN*, November 19, 1918.

13 Letter "to the electors in Stretford". December, 1918. Sir Joseph Hallsworth Papers, Manchester Archives. M547/1/1–4. Hallsworth went on to serve in a variety of labor and government posts, including as a board member of the ILO. He was knighted in 1946.

14 Ibid.

for early elections did not help matters by making it appear (not without some justification) that it was calling early elections because it feared that postwar dislocation would alienate voters. Ultimately, the election appeared to be a referendum on the government's handling of the war and on the changes in British society over the previous four years. This focus on reconstruction was evident in the campaign song of Wright Robinson, the politician and labor organizer who we last saw as an opponent of conscription during the war. The slight, boyish Robinson campaigned for Labour with a jingle that focused on rebuilding the postwar world and addressing the practical problems of urban life that had been marginalized during the war:

> If you want the children's friend
> That's WRIGHT ROBINSON
> If you want the world to mend
> That's WRIGHT ROBINSON
> He'll give us more work, and he'll give us more pay
> He'll give us houses, and give us more play,
> So Sisters and Brothers ask Fathers and Mothers,
> To VOTE for WRIGHT ROBINSON.[15]

One of the most obvious differences between the parliamentary elections of 1918 and any that came before it was the inclusion of women among the voters. Appeals to women as voters, and for women as candidates, tended to reference either (or both) the supposedly ingrained tendency of women to heal the spiritual problems of society or to their special competencies as the witnesses to, and victims of, wartime shortages and consumer problems. While the importance of women voters was evident, it was equally critical that women came to be included in the widening circles of war participants, so they, too, could claim the mantle of wartime sacrifice.

The Co-operative Society, in one of its increasingly radical-sounding appeals, suggested that women could play an essential role in defeating "the grand conspiracy to foist an arbitrary plutocratic government upon the people in the name of unity and reconstruction."

> Although women have not had the vote in the past, they have not been blind to what had been going on. And particularly they have been keen to note the progress of profiteering. While their brothers, husbands and sons have been away fighting, they have had to fend for themselves, and they know better than men how prices have soared, and how hard it has been to make ends meet. And they will want to have a reckoning with somebody. *And how else will that somebody be but the Government, which having permitted the profiteering, now comes forward and asks to be returned to power again so that it can reconstruct*

15 Campaign pamphlet. Papers of Wright Robinson. Manchester Archives, M/284/1.

> *the war-shattered fabric of society on the same old lines of capitalist domination and profit!*[16]

The Khaki Election was, unsurprisingly, a resounding victory for the wartime coalition, which won 520 out of 707 seats. The election was also a clear win for the "Man Who Won the War," as the Asquith Liberals suffered ignominious defeat. The results of the Khaki election concealed as much as they revealed about the future of national politics. Labour faced a number of humiliating defeats in which senior leaders lost their seats. The party, however, did surprisingly well, winning 22 percent of the popular vote and consolidating its role as an opposition party.[17] For the Coalition Liberals, it was to be the last of their great electoral triumphs. In places like Manchester, the Liberals began to lose their place as one of the dominant parties in British politics.

In Manchester, the election mirrored some of the broader trends in postwar British politics. The precipitous decline of the Liberals cleared the battlefield for a contest between Labour and the Conservatives. Labour's "steady but unspectacular rise" in Manchester survived the Coalition juggernaut in 1918.[18] J.R. Clynes was returned unopposed in Miles Platting, while Ben Tillett easily survived a Liberal challenge in the vital North Salford division, and John Hodge won a three-way contest in Gorton with an independent candidate and a Socialist. In the other ten divisions, Coalition candidates won fairly resounding victories.[19] The Alternative Service Guild, a conscientious objector (CO) group that had been active in the city, proclaimed somewhat wishfully that "in a number of cases, candidates who were entirely CO in their sympathy secured second places in three-cornered contests with war men in third places."[20] Still, it was hard to conceal the apparent scale of the coalition's parliamentary victory.

The 1918 parliamentary elections set the tone for much of what was to come in Mancunian and British politics. While Labour did better than expected, it was by no means clear at the time that they could continue to function as a meaningful opposition party. It was all too easy to believe that the wartime government had enough inertia to carry itself over the considerable fissures that developed between the partners on economic and social issues. Why had Labour come through intact? One convincing explanation for this changing constellation of local and national politics is that state intervention during the war made voters more aware of labor issues and, consequently, more willing to look to the Labour Party for redress of

---

16 "An Appeal to Women. Some Pertinent Facts," *The Co-operative News*. December 7, 1918. Italics in original.

17 Havighurst, 149.

18 Alan Kidd, *Manchester* (Edinburgh: Edinburgh University Press, 2002), 207.

19 *Handbook of the City of Manchester*. 1918, 553–5.

20 "News of the Guild." Newsletter. January, 1919. Papers of Wright Robinson, Manchester Archives, M/284/3.

grievances once the war was over.[21] Labour's message of social equality found literally tens of thousands of listeners as troops began to make their way back to Manchester in the months after the election.

"The Army Takes Some Getting Away From:" The Return of the Troops

The British state and civil society faced an enormous challenge in the physical demobilization of the armed forces. At the end of 1918, Britain had an army of about 3.84 million, a Navy of about 407,000, and a 290,000 man Air Force.[22] Like some of their continental allies (and enemies), these troops were distributed all over the globe. The Manchester Regiment, with whom many, though by no means all, locals served, had battalions in England, France, Italy, Mesopotamia, and Egypt. The Regiment, which swelled to 53 battalions, suffered about 45,000 total casualties, of whom 14,122 had been killed, 1,121 of them in the hard-hit 2nd Battalion.[23]

The homecoming of hundreds of thousands of British troops was a tremendous enterprise, not just for the already overtaxed supply system, but for the towns and cities that benefited (and sometimes suffered) from four years of close proximity to the soldiers, their wages, and the massive infrastructure needed to keep armies in the field. France was also celebrating a victory in those months, and despite the divisions which would later emerge between the two governments over war aims, there seems to have been a great deal of good feeling between French communities and British soldiers at the end of the war. "Big camps have sprung up in our vicinity and the British base has become, so to speak, a part of the Havre community; our streets are enlivered [*sic*] by your presence, and when you leave we shall miss you as we should old friends," wrote M. Morand, Le Havre's mayor, to the commander of the 2nd Battalion of the Manchesters in 1919. Morand stressed the bonds forged over the years of wartime:

> Now, after Germany's military collapse, when she is trying to rise from her knees, we must remain close Allies, standing shoulder to shoulder, hand in hand. Nothing will shake our union and we shall always hold to President Poincare's address to King George V, summing up on these words: "Together we have

21 Tony Adams, "Labour Vanguard, Tory Bastion, or the Triumph of New Liberalism? Manchester Politics 1900–1914 in Comparative Perspective," *Manchester Region History Review* XIV (2001): 35.

22 Martin Pugh, *State and Society: A Social and Political History of Great Britain, 1870–1997* (London: Arnold, 1999), 167.

23 *The Manchester Regiment*. Official History. Manchester Regiment Archive, Tameside Local Studies Library. MR#/26/129. 334–5.

suffered, together, we have fought and we have vanquished; we are united forever."[24]

The system through which troops returned from active service emerged from the compromises between the military and the Ministry of Reconstruction. At least initially, the planning of military demobilization fell to Edwin Montague's Committee on the Demobilisation of the Army within the Ministry. Montague and his superiors operated under the assumption that the most likely result of overly hasty demobilization would be widespread and catastrophic unemployment. As one of Ministry's widely-distributed pamphlets described the task, Montague's mandate was "Demobilisation and Restoration: how to get men back as quickly as possible from their war-stations in the Army or in industry to their old niches in civil life, and how to release employers, workmen, and others from controls and restrictions imposed upon them for the duration of the war." The Ministry saw its mission as the restoration of "the social situation as it existed at the beginning of the war."[25] Practically, this act of putting the genie back in the bottle was impossible, and it is surprising that the bureaucrats charged with planning and implementing demobilization on the ground took as long as they did to realize this.

Much like the plans first developed in Berlin, the initial scheme for the physical demobilization of the armed forces called for a tiered draw-down of forces driven by the needs of the transition economy. Briefly, the first to be released were "demobilisers," who performed tasks in civilian life that would speed the demobilization of others, followed by "pivotal men" who could provide employment for others. After these groups came "slip men," who could provide proof that civilian employment awaited them.[26] This category, so-called because of the coveted slips of paper that sped their process, caused more resentment than any other aspect of the physical demobilization plan.

Second Lieutenant Frank Broady of the 3rd Battalion of the Manchester Regiment was an example of this second group. Broady was still recovering from wounds received in late October when he got a letter from the Ministry of Labour, indicating that his old employers in the Manchester City Rates Department had offered him his old job back at "prewar situation." By the end of December, Lt. Broady was well on the way home to the job he would hold until his retirement.[27]

Gunner Herbert Williams was also fortunate enough to be considered indispensable by his former employers, the lead works of Baxendale and Co.

24 Letter from Morand to HQ, 2nd Battalion, Manchester Regiment. May 1919. Manchester Regiment Archive, Tameside Local Studies Library. MR1/27/2/44.

25 Pamphlet: "Reconstruction Problems I: The Aims of Reconstruction." 1919, 3. NA NUM 5/45/2643.2/4.

26 Stephen Richards Graubard, "Military Demobilization in Great Britain Following the First World War," *Journal of Modern History* 19, no. 4 (December 1947), 298.

27 Letter from Lt. Col. J. Franklin-Smith, Ministry of Labour to Lt. Frank Broady. December 20, 1918. From the collection of Duncan Broady.

After Baxendale contacted the Employment Exchange in Manchester, Gunner Williams received the necessary forms for an expedited demobilization. He returned to his career as a salesman, retiring in 1947.[28] These two cases illustrated above all the continued *ad hoc* nature of war and postwar planning. The situation was much the same as it had been in wartime, with multiple bureaucracies working toward the same ends and significant potential for conflict between national and local institutions. For those who had employers at home who were interested in tracking them down, the process worked fairly well. For those who did not, things were considerably more difficult.

For the rest of the troops, demobilization was a frustrating and drawn-out process. The key to speeding demobilization was the ability to secure employment at home, favoring those who had not served long and still had contact with their previous employers.[29] For those who could not, demobilization was often a baffling experience of moving from camp to camp. Priority for demobilization was based on a complicated point system related to length of service. This created a curious situation in which both long-serving soldiers and those who entered service late in the conflict were disadvantaged in different ways. Those who had been in uniform for longer periods felt, not without justification, that they were less likely to have access to their old jobs. Those who entered service late in the war and who were not "slip men" found themselves in a frustrating period of delay while they accumulated priority. As a result, they feared that their jobs would already be filled when they finally made good their exit from the ranks.

One old soldier named Barker, who enlisted in 1916 at the age of 40 and served with the 23rd Manchesters, spent much of 1918 and 1919 trying to avoid going back to France before he was demobilized. Following a hospital stay in Ripon, he was bounced from base to base, spending time in, respectively, Grimsby, Cleethorpes, Waltham (where he did "light jobs, amusing myself in the canteens, joining the "jugs" playing Crown and Anchor, watching and sometimes playing pontoon in tents, with the lads, singing army songs with gusto, and in fact trying my best to be a social animal") before being sent to Cromer, Woolwich, and finally Aldershot where he was demobilized.[30]

Archibald "Arch" English, a Londoner who spent the last year of the war recovering from wounds at a hospital in Stockport, became more frustrated as the Fall and early Winter wore on. "Every morning we wait for the mail to come, and when it does, the inevitable disappointment," he wrote to his family in January, "There will be trouble with the fellows if something isn't done soon." A few days later, shortly before his ticket arrived, he added "Hoping to have been

28 Files related to Herbert Williams. Manchester Archives M444/1/2/1–15.

29 Gerard DeGroot, *Blighty: British Society in the Era of the Great War* (London: Longman, 1996), 255.

30 G. Barker, *Agony's Anguish* (Manchester: Alf Eva, 1931), Unpaginated.

away and settled long before this – but the Army takes some getting away from, I can tell you!"[31]

Soldiers and sailors on their way home received pamphlets from the Ministry of Reconstruction explaining their options. The news was not good. Promising a time of "considerable difficulty," the Ministry suggested that the experience of return would likely include some period of unemployment.[32] Soldiers and sailors who chose to remain in the forces could earn bonuses of up to £50. The rest received month-long furloughs and unemployment insurance for up to 12 weeks during the year following their formal demobilization. For men, the base unemployment donation was 24s., while for women it was only 20s.[33] Otherwise, the demobilized were urged to contact their local employment exchanges as quickly as possible and hope for the best. For millions of Britons, return from wartime service meant an uncertain future.

During the first few months of 1919, the demobilized soldier was ubiquitous, not only on the streets and in the railroad stations, but as a popular culture icon. Just as advertisers had taken advantage of wartime shortages and the imagined heroism of the men at the front, they now gladly appropriated images of anxious homecomings and the orderly transition back to civilian life. "Jack's coming home tonight," one woman remarked to another on a crowded tram in one advertisement. "Let's give him a warm welcome with Rowntree's Elect Cocoa." Postwar optimism, still riding a tentative wave in February, inspired fond hopes that shortages were coming to an end and that the return of the soldiers meant that the restraints on consumer society would soon be lifted. Less tangibly, the return of the troops seemed to offer some measure of normalcy to a population that had lived through four anxious years of war. The return of the soldier appeared to be a literal manifestation of the anticipated demobilization of society.

Lewis's Limited Men's Outfitters, one of the most celebrated old Manchester merchants, promised to facilitate "The Change from Clothes O'War to the Clothes O'Peace." A demobilized man who "left Heaton Park with his sand-bag at 9.30. Arrived home at 10.30 p.m. A joyous homecoming – some supper – then to bed at midnight" might in fifteen minutes buy a new suit at Lewis's the next day. "The man afterwards changed completely … called upon his employer the same morning, and reported for duty. He was a pivotal man, urgently needed, and he had finished with khaki."[34] These "pivotal men," like Herbert Williams and Frank Broady, were to be the vanguard of postwar society. The fact that they were unabashedly men, returning to a country and city in which women had managed

31 Undated letters in the file of Arch English, IWMA 97/10/1.

32 Pamphlet "Guide to Work and Benefits for Soldiers and War-Service Workers." Ministry of Reconstruction, 1918, 3.

33 Ibid., 6.

34 Advertisements in *MEN*. February 25, 1919, February 12, 1919, and February 7, 1919.

just fine, and sometimes remarkably well, in their absence was just one of the conflicts that emerged from these homecomings.

The act of demobilization and the resulting homecomings inspired intense optimism and even a burgeoning nostalgia for the very recent past. Soldiers were reminded of the debt that society owed them and of the sacrifices that they made during wartime. While it is very easy to view such messages with cynicism in hindsight, there was clearly a palpable sense of communal feeling attached to the post-victory demobilization. Even formal hierarchical relationships like those between officers and enlisted men acquired at least a patina of common sacrifice and struggle as the troops began to come home. Some of this rhetoric even came close to sounding politically radical. As they passed through the depots on their way home, the men of the 6th Manchesters received letters from their commander, Colonel Robertson, wishing them "every prosperity and happiness. You have helped to win a Great War. The fruits of Victory are yours. *See to it that no one takes them from you.*"[35]

Major General A. Solly-Flood echoed this strikingly communitarian sentiment in a letter to his troops from the 42nd (East Lancashire) Division, to which part of the Manchester Regiment belonged. He encouraged his men to begin a veterans' group to "keep alive old memories and old friendships, and lend a hand to those amongst us who may be in need, in the same spirit of mutual helpfulness which has inspired us in the past.[36] By December 1918, the 42nd moved from Hautmont, where they ended the war, to Charleroi, where they spent Christmas. Evidently, some officers and men were discharged early, while the remainder of the division stayed in France until late March. The Manchester battalions finally reached home on March 31. Upon arrival, they paraded to the regimental depot on Burlington Street "amidst a tremendous and enthusiastic concourse of people."[37]

This feeling of camaraderie and the resulting goodwill among soldiers and the population at large was by no means universal, and when it ceased to soothe over problems, the results could be spectacular. Hints of trouble began in Manchester less than a month after the Armistice. Ellis Smith remembered later that his "return home coincided with the beginning of bitter industrial strife which lasted for many years."[38] The number of soldiers arriving in the transit camps in England were painfully few, and even fewer were able to secure quick demobilization and a passage home. By early December, the *Manchester Evening News* suggested that

35 Letter from Col. Robertson. Files of Pvt. Percy Hilton. Manchester Regiment Archive, Tameside Local Studies Library. MR2/17/60. [Italics mine.]

36 Letter from Maj. Gen. A. Solly-Flood. Undated. Manchester Regiment Archive, Tameside Local Studies Library. MR3/12/2/25.

37 Captain S.J. Wilson, *The Seventh Manchesters* (Manchester: The University Press, 1920), 142–3.

38 "Reminisces." Compiled from United Patternworkers' Association Newsletters. Bound volume, possibly a retirement gift. Manchester Archives.

the machinery of demobilization had "broken down."[39] Not only were the soldiers unhappy with the slow pace of demobilization, but employers and loved ones expressed strong misgivings about the pace of events.

> If the employers and relatives of soldiers yield to their rising impatience and allow their personal interests to override the national interests, which the army still has to safeguard, they are liable to do their country a grave injury ... The patriotism which has buoyed up the "Home Front" for four years must not dissolve in percipient irritation. It must hold out yet awhile and trust a little further to the discretion of the authorities.[40]

The Soldiers' Strikes of 1919 are deeply contested ground in British historiography. For some radical historians, they marked a turning point that did not turn toward revolution and a moment in which the lack of an organized Left opposition in Britain prevented any real attempt at change from organizing.[41] Even more cautious historians have imbued the strikes with significance far exceeding what the weight of evidence will bear. Clearly, there was significant sympathy for the Russian revolutionaries in Britain and Manchester, but the strikes in early 1919 were the product of disquiet over demobilization conditions.[42] Protesters only turned to the Russian example later, largely after they had returned home.

Protests began in Folkestone, among troops being sent back to France at the end of a leave, on January 4, 1919. They spread quickly in England and in France and briefly looked like they might paralyze the armed forces. Ironically, the protests were spurred in part by conservative newspapers like the *Daily Mail* and *Daily Express*, which competed with each other for distribution among the troops and had every reason to highlight the problems with the demobilization of the forces.[43]

It was difficult to keep news of unrest among the troops concealed from those on the home front, though the censors helped matters. The news of trouble at the Folkestone camp and in France was greeted with apprehension at home, though lack of details made it difficult for the press to fully explicate the protestor's demands. "Demobilisation is a huge business in which the human element is prominent,"

---

39 "Demoralised Demobilisation," *MEN*, December 10, 1918.

40 "Demobilisation – Appeal to Employers and Relatives," *MEN*, December 11, 1918.

41 See, for instance Chanie Rosenberg, *1919: Britain on the Brink of a Revolution* (London: Bookmarks, 1987)

42 Andrew Rothstein, *The Soldiers' Strikes of 1919* (London: Macmillan, 1980), esp. 105. Aside from some infelicitous language, Rothstein's book remains a definitive account of the strikes.

43 Ibid., 31.

concluded a *Manchester Evening News* editorial on January 9, "and unless it is managed with discretion and with kindliness no end of trouble is in store."[44]

These troubles reached Manchester just a few days later. As the transit camps at Heaton Park and Altrincham swelled, and facing rumors of unrest, military authorities reacted clumsily, canceling leave for soldiers, some of whom were probably just miles from home. On January 9, 500 soldiers went on strike at Heaton Park, demanding better food and reinstatement of leave.[45] A few days later, 250 soldiers at Altrincham staged a demonstration demanding reduced duty hours and more rapid return to civilian life. Significantly, the Heaton Park demonstrators won a number of concessions. The Altricham strikers, whose demands were beyond the remit of camp authorities, had no such luck, and the demonstration broke up after a few hours in the chilly January air.

The Soldiers' Strikes, not only in Manchester but all over Britain, served to highlight the growing dissatisfaction of troops and probably helped to accelerate the process of physical demobilization, if only by convincing military authorities that any problems that might be engendered by releasing troops too quickly paled in comparison to the potential for trouble if the troops were too long delayed. As they did during the war, authorities proved willing to work with dissenters who stayed within the bounds of reciprocity. While the Soldiers' Strikes point to the limits of demobilization, they also suggest that the flexible wartime relationship that sustained mobilization survived the end of the war. Under the direction of Winston Churchill, demobilization sped up considerably in the wake of the strikes. In just over two months, nearly 80 percent of enlisted men eligible for demobilization were released and sent home.[46] The strikers achieved many of their immediate goals.

The home front seems to have been generally well informed about the demobilization protests, particularly when they occurred in England. Still, there was considerable anxiety as to the protestors' goals and ideological orientation. On February 9, the Manchester art historian and teacher John E. Pythian wrote home to his wife from a demobilization camp near Lille, where he was giving lectures on the art of Venice to about 250 (presumably restless) British officers. "It looks now as if I should be home sooner than I suspected. The Fifth Army is being demobilised so quickly that there is not very much to be done now.... I hear plenty of interesting things here, to be talked about when I get home. There are many things, of course, that we do not hear of in England."[47]

When the soldiers and sailors did reach home again, they faced a new set of challenges. One of the most pressing was securing employment at a decent wage. The mechanisms for providing jobs for the demobilized, like so much of British postwar planning, was an *ad hoc* affair, leaving many veterans embittered.

---

44 "Demobilisation Troubles," *MEN*, January 6, 1919.

45 Rothstein uses the figure of 600. Rothstein, 61.

46 DeGroot, 257.

47 Letter from J.E. to Ada Pythian. Manchester Archives M270/10.

The same tensions that troubled the waters of the demobilization camps now moved into the growing lines at Manchester's employment exchanges.

The Economy: Demobilizing and Building Again

The principal difficulties in reconstructing the economy were rebalancing consumer needs and avoiding flooding the employment market with demobilized troops and those whose war work was at an end. Many of the institutions established to manage the war economy continued to work for years after the end of hostilities to try to keep this balance. In the Manchester area, where so much of the economy was export-driven and required recovery elsewhere as well, the task seemed positively Sysiphean. Added to this was the general attitude among national authorities that the recovery should be based on the restoration of private enterprise.[48] The result was, almost inevitably, a situation in which those most directly affected by demobilization planning came to believe that their needs were not being looked after with appropriate sensitivity and that their sacrifice would be met with indifference.

This challenge was recognized by none other than Field Marshal Douglas Haig, who came to Manchester in March to accept the freedom of the city. Haig, whose postwar career was dedicated to securing the rights of veterans, reminded the crowd of the debts owed to Britain's servicemen:

> none of us [can] afford to forget, and I last of all, the obligations that the great war has left in the present and for the future. It must be long years before these obligations are discharged. So long as there remains in our midst a single man blinded, crippled, or disabled in that great struggle for our national freedom, our obligation to help and care for him will remain. As yet we have scarcely shouldered our burden; a burden that to my mind should be regarded as almost, if not absolutely, as a religious duty. (*Cheers*) … the whole problem of the ex-service officer and man, whether fit or disabled, has not yet been completely solved, and will not be solved so long as a single case of hardship remains.[49]

---

48 Debates over the economic demobilization of Britain after the First World War began not long after and produced a number of highly-politicized arguments. R.H. Tawney's classic essay from the Second World War Era, "The Abolition of Economic Controls, 1918–1921," *Economic History Review*, 13 (1943): 1–30 argued that capitalist interests exercised too much control over the process of economic demobilization. Peter K. Cline's more nuanced argument in "Reopening the Case of the Lloyd George Coalition and the Postwar Economic Transition, 1918–1919," *Journal of British Studies*, 10 (1970): 162–75 suggested that the "capitalist" influence on demobilization planning proved far less united than Tawney allowed.

49 Proceedings of the Manchester City Council, 1919, 244.

The local Area Armaments Output Committee, whose work during the war had helped guide industrial efforts in the Northwest, was typical of this conflict of means and expectations. Nearly a year after the end of the war, the Committee met in Birmingham, where they set priorities for what they called "Reconstruction." Sensibly, they committed to taking steps to ramp up coal production and generally to divert raw materials back into the peacetime economy as expeditiously as possible. Most important, they judged, was the issue of employment. "The first essential in Reconstruction is that the people of the country should be maintained in employment, and no rigid financial question should be allowed to stand in the way of this."[50] The problem was that they expected the private sector to take up the slack immediately. "On no account," the report read, "should the people be pauperised by being maintained in unemployment by the wide provision of out-of-work pay."[51]

Despite promises and plans to the contrary, the economic demobilization that followed the end of hostilities proved to be contentious, and the cessation of war revealed some difficult truths for industry in Greater Manchester. Contracts for war work, which terminated at the cessation of hostilities, began to be cut off almost immediately. By January, total value of cancelled contracts in the Manchester area was greater than any other regional center and nearly twice the value of those canceled in the Southeast Midlands, the second hardest hit region.[52]

The cotton industry was particularly hard hit and would continue to decline from its prewar global position of importance as other centers of cotton production emerged. Having been sustained by promises that work would pick up again once exports picked up in the wake of the war, cotton operators found themselves out of work and factories idle just as the first wave of returning soldiers arrived. In Burnley, reports indicated that more than 20 plants had ceased production completely, and a third of ex-soldiers were unable to find work "although when they joined the Army they were promised reinstatement to their former positions." The problem was that there simply was not enough work to go around. "Burnley's manufactures mostly go overseas, and until the export trade is set going again Burnley has no hope of an industrial recovery. The war work ended with the Armistice."[53]

The end of war work affected industries haltingly, unevenly, and in ways that provoked outrage among workers. On December 7, munitions workers thought to have been from the Belsize Motor Works organized a series of small protests in factories across the city against decontrol. The protests never grew to the level that organizers had hoped and there were evidently a number of scuffles with uniformed soldiers at some of the affected plants. While protestors complained that police had failed to protect them from assaults by soldiers, the Ministry of Munitions

50 Report of the Special Meeting of the No. 4 Area Executive Committee." November 4, 1919. Manchester Archives MSf 623.4 M1.

51 Ibid.

52 "Munitions Council Daily Report," January 9, 1919. NA MUN 4/3413.

53 "Hard Times at Burnley," *The Times*, March 21, 1919.

took the occasion to announce that, in light of the end of the war, Christmas and New Year would once again be holidays for munitions workers.[54]

The government realized the full extent of the economic crisis in the region in the first months of 1919. While the local economy was diverse, much of its prewar growth rested on the strength of the textile industry and the need for complementary manufacturing. When war work ended, textiles were not ready to pick up the considerable slack. The Area Armaments Committee reported in March that the local textile manufacturers had about a month of war work remaining and an "enormous stock" of goods in storage for which there were no customers, no shipping capacity, and often, no labor. This affected other area industries, including bleachers, dyers, chemical manufacturers, machinists, and printers.[55] Heavy industries were equally affected by the end of war work. Machinists, fabricators, and engine makers now petitioned the Committee for any sort of available work to replace lost contracts. A.V. Roe tried to convert from metal working to manufacturing furniture, but had little initial success. Armstrong, Whitworth and Co. in Openshaw, which had done well during the war manufacturing armor plate and gun mountings, now found itself with poor prospects in peacetime, "this plant being in the main too heavy for private orders."[56]

With this transition came dramatic and deep job cuts that transformed the local employment landscape. When the war ended, 22,701 men and 17,721 women worked in the National Filling Factories in the Manchester Area. Within a few weeks about 12 percent of the men and 71 percent of the women lost their jobs. The Aintree Number Two Plant went from 11,600 workers to 500 before its conversion into an ordnance depot in March. The National Aircraft Factory shed more than 50 percent of its workers, male and female, by January 10.[57] Other firms survived by reverting to prewar production or converting their plants entirely. Bamford and Co. of Stockport shifted from producing 18lb. shells to building marine propellers for the Admiralty. The Trafford Park Tractor Assembly had an easier task, modifying its military tractor engines for civilian use. A far more inventive solution came from the tinsmiths of Thomas Fildes in Ancoats. They began coppering and adding three legs to their canister fuses and marketing them as ornaments. "Similar action might be taken with advantage by other firms when possible," suggested the Munitions Council.[58]

Decontrol had a variety of interesting legal and administrative consequences. Restriction on the movement of labor posed a challenge, particularly for skilled workers whose labor in the postwar economy was particularly valuable.

54 "Munitions Council Daily Report," December 12, 1919. NA MUN 4/3412.

55 "No. 2 Area Report." March, 1919. NA NUM 4/6701.

56 "Area No. 2 List of Large Firms Requiring Work." April 16, 1919. NA NUM 4/6701.

57 Munitions Council Daily Reports of November 26, 1918, January 6, 1919, and March 3, 1919. NA MUN 4/3413.

58 "Munitions Council Daily Report." December 20, 1918. NA MUN 4/3413.

Harry Bingham sued the packing plant where he had been an employee for 29 years (beginning at age 13 and working alongside his father) after receiving a better offer from a competitor. In the end, the local Munitions Tribunal found that there was no compelling reason to force Bingham to remain, and he was given his leaving certificate. On the other hand, wartime regulations could actually help workers avoid or mitigate the effects of layoffs. In 1919 and 1920, the bulk of the Munition Tribunal's work seems to have been hearing cases of workers who claimed job protection under the Munitions Control Act. The ship painter Hiram Mathers sued a Salford firm in January, claiming that he specialized in camouflage painting and therefore should be considered a munitions worker and could not be laid off without notice or payment. While his employers argued that Mathers' service was actually repair work, the Tribunal found for Mathers and he received £5 in compensation.[59]

While the cotton industry had an easier time re-tooling for peacetime production, its economic and labor situations were no less perilous. Many of the cotton operatives that were working walked off the job for several days in June of 1919 in what turned out to be one of the largest labor actions of the year. More than 450,000 put down tools for more than a week.[60] Some of the reactions to the cotton strike reflected the divisive impact of the war as the lines between the employed, however marginal their employment, and the unemployed became clearer. "It is all very well for those who during the war received big wages and bonuses to now agitate for still more money with shorter hours," wrote "Stop It" in the *Manchester Evening News*, "but what about those who have done their bit and come back to no work and no prospects … to help them combat the ever-rising prices, followed now by rents, rates, etc.?"[61]

By February, the managers of the Gilbert Gilkes and Co. textile mills in Burnley were at their wits' end. The widely-foreseen resumption of cotton goods exports seemed no closer to fruition, and even if it had their labor situation was getting worse instead of better. The firm's "pivotal men" had not been released from the army, while hundreds of former employees who had not been so designated were making their way back to Burnley following demobilization. Gilkes had neither demand nor labor, and the result was an idle plant and jobless workers.[62] A Munitions Council report on unemployment in April 1918 presented the grimmest possible portrait of the stinging impact of the end of war in the Northwest. The report ranked communities by category. If prospects across the country were not good, they were disastrous in the Northwest. Among those communities receiving

59 Munitions Tribunal Appeals for Manchester District in NA LAB 2/552/MT125/6.

60 David Butler and Jennie Freemen. *British Political Facts*. 3rd edn (London: Macmillan, 1969), 217.

61 Letter in *MEN*. June 11, 1919.

62 Munitions Council Daily Report, February 10, 1919, NA MUN 4/3413.

the worst possible rating were Manchester, Bolton, Burnley, Preston, Rochdale, Stockport, Bury, Ashton-under-Lyme, Staleybridge, and St. Helens.[63]

Much of the impetus for retraining and placing veterans came from the private sector. The YMCA set up a Discharged Soldiers' Employment Bureau in early 1918. The YMCA Bureau took a special interest in placing disabled veterans, whose placements and training were obviously fraught with considerable difficulty. In their first three months, they received 839 disabled petitioners, of whom 114 were more than 50 percent disabled. Interestingly, the largest group of those claiming more than a 50 percent disability were "head and nerves" cases, followed by those missing arms and legs. The YMCA was able to place about 65 percent of those who registered with them, but 30 percent of those placed left within a brief period, giving them a fairly modest success rate of 45 percent.[64]

The Employment Exchanges attempted to help bridge these gaps by encouraging employers to reserve at least 5 percent of employment slots for disabled veterans. Correspondence with the Exchange in Manchester indicates that at least in the early postwar period, these pledges were sometimes but not often met. The Co-operative Society, for instance, employed 9 disabled veterans out of 248 employees (50 of them female) at their distribution center in Ardwick, 18 out of 258 in other distribution centers in the city, and 2 out of 33 at the coal depot, where presumably the physical nature of the work made it difficult to find places for the disabled.[65] The rhetoric of bureaucrats about finding employment for those physically damaged by the war did not square up with the reality, in which local officials could only cajole and plead with employers and lacked any effective oversight or regulatory capacity.

Once the troops were home, there were a number of potential pitfalls to their successful resumption of their old jobs or training for new ones. It was difficult for men who had spent in some cases years in service, earning positions of command and living in disciplined, hierarchical systems to return to jobs in which they would be expected to be employees in the civilian world. A constable from Manchester alluded to this problem when he wrote to the Chief Constable from France, where he was serving with the Connaught Rangers. "Upon leaving the Army with the Hon. Rank of Lieutenant, or Captain, and having regard to my qualifications and service, what rank I would receive on rejoining and continuing to serve in that force?"[66]

Returning troops sometimes found the attitudes of civilians supercilious and condescending, as appears to have been the case with a horticultural training

---

63 "State of Unemployment in Connection with the Placing of Contracts." April 8, 1919. NA MUN 4/3414.

64 Letter from Winifred Giles, Manchester YMCA to A.B. Woodhouse. September 23, 1918. Manchester Archives. M138 / Box 68.

65 Letter from General Board, Manchester and Salford Equitable Co-operative Society to Employment Exchange. October 27, 1919. Manchester Archives M473/1/1/23.

66 Letter from M. Byrne, 5th Battalion, Connaught Rangers, to Chief Constable, December 9, 1918. Watch Committee Minutes, Greater Manchester Police Archive. 78/35.

program in Carrington in which a group of disabled veterans were forbidden to smoke, gamble, or drink, and were required to be in "barracks" at 10:00 p.m. A group of Labour councilors brought this to the attention of the City Council in January, protesting "the perpetuation of Army conditions, and objected to this moral overseeship where grown men who had served their country were concerned."[67]

For many returning veterans, finding employment of any sort proved difficult. Unemployment in Manchester increased dramatically through the first half of 1919, peaking at more than 59,000 in May.[68] One ex-soldier, under the pen name "1914 Contemptible," wrote to the *Manchester Evening News* to complain that he had been trying to find a job since returning in March, and asked for "more consideration by employers for the men who saved England."[69] Attempts by veterans to organize into cohesive groups to protest against unemployment, while clearly beginning, were not particularly well-developed in mid-1919, and much of the impetus for protest seems to have come from informal gatherings of ex-servicemen.

The inherent conservatism of the veteran's movements sometimes dovetailed with the sometimes crushing weight of bureaucracy to blunt all but the most symbolic and ultimately futile acts of protest. Veterans' groups believed that they were entitled to rewards for their service. Their actions were mitigated by an expectation that all concerned naturally agreed with their position and that any behavior or rhetoric that smacked of extremism would cost them the credibility that they assumed as veterans. Typical of these tendencies was a disastrous attempt to march on London in the Fall of 1919.

In late August, a group of ex-servicemen, evidently without any formal organization, began to organize a march from Manchester to London to demand higher unemployment compensation. At one point, it appeared that there would be around 6,000 marchers, a number that surely would have clogged up the roads of the north of England and attracted a great deal of attention.[70] While it would certainly have been difficult to actually get all 6,000 together for a march, the Ministry of Labour managed in one fell swoop to eviscerate what enthusiasm did exist by warning prospective marchers that they would almost surely miss their required weekly registration that allowed them to claim unemployment, and, therefore, would forfeit their benefits.

Whether this announcement was calculated or simply informative is unclear, but what is clear is that initial enthusiasm all but expired at this point. On September 15, when the march began in Albert Square, organizers estimated that they would number 500. A total of 28 men showed up, though the crowd of several hundred fellow veterans was on hand to cheer them on. The marcher's statement, presented

67 "Maintaining the Army Atmosphere," Unpaginated clipping from the *Manchester Guardian*, January 7, 1919. Papers of Lord and Lady Simon, Manchester Archives M/14/4/1.

68 "Unemployment," *MEN*, May 7, 1919.

69 Letter in *MEN*, May 10, 1919.

70 "Ex-Service Men March to London," *The Times*, August 22, 1919.

to the Lord Mayor, reflected many of the problems and attitudes of the first year of peace:

> We, the unemployed Ex-Service Men of Manchester, having patiently waited for the government to move in the matter or providing work for men whose sacrifices have saved the country, and seeing the apathy of the Government have decided to bring our case before the public and the Government.... We need work, not doles, the right to live in the land we have saved.[71]

The marchers reached London fifteen days later, where they met with officials from the Ministry of Labour. The meetings were inconclusive and, in a final indignity, the marchers, who had little desire to walk back to Manchester, asked the Ministry for financial assistance to get home.[72] The march, and its failure, is symptomatic of the levels of resentment and the restrictions on their effective airing.

Importantly, the rhetoric of war service both implicitly and explicitly excluded women, who just months before had been considered part of the national community of reconstruction. The changing economy, legal restrictions on women like the Pre-War Practices Act of 1919 and the growing stigma attached to working women accused of taking jobs from returning men combined to drive about 750,000 women out of the workplace in 1919.[73] A letter in the *Manchester Evening News* just after the Armistice mocked "pampered" munitions workers, male and female, who failed to realize that "the golden days would suddenly end, and that there would be a big change for them when they were no longer required."[74]

The issue of unemployment was a very public and divisive one in the immediate postwar period. The new sense of assertiveness among those who had come through the war emerges clearly even from otherwise formulaic and dry reports of council and committee meetings. Typical was a *Manchester Guardian* report of a Manchester Council meeting that apparently was all but broken up by an angry delegation of unemployed tacitly backed by the Labour members of the council who "savoured an excess of zeal, but they were perhaps the outcome of unfamiliarity with the ordinary forms of procedure." The Mayor reported on a meeting with another group of unemployed men in language that was in itself extraordinarily bloodless, but that also conveyed the atmosphere of mutual threats and recriminations:

> [the unemployed delegation] had made a statement that they would not be responsible for anything that might happen if they remained hungry. He told them that such threats were foolish (*hear, hear*) and that they were not likely to assist him as Lord Mayor in getting adequate measures of relief. All his

71 "Work, Not Doles," *The Times*, September 15, 1919.

72 "Sir R. Horne and Ex-Service Men," *The Times*, September 30, 1919.

73 DeGroot, 262–3.

74 Letter in *MEN*, December 6, 1918.

> sympathies were with those men in their difficult circumstances, and what he told them was for their own good, because he knew that if they carried out their threats all the injured would be on one side.[75]

The police department was a site in which some of these conflicts could be most acute. There were strong incentives to seek employment elsewhere. As the Committee on the Police Service (better known as the Desborough Commission) found in a 1919 survey, married urban constables in England earned £3 8s 3d a month, versus average expenses of £3 13s.[76] One alternative which promised to replicate the experiences of wartime while taking advantage of training and experience as constables was in increasingly dangerous Ireland. One recruiting poster for the Royal Irish Constabulary (RIC) probably spent some time on a police station wall. Clearly designed to induce men who longed for more excitement than rousting drunks in Piccadilly, the RIC promised "A Man's Job. Do you want it? An open-air Life in the RIC. ESCORTS and PATROLS. A life not without difficulty and danger, but a FULL-SIZED MAN'S JOB!" Furthermore, as someone noted in pencil, the normal height requirement of 5' 7" was lowered to 5' 6" for veterans.[77]

Manchester's constabulary was also involved in one of the most spectacular episodes of labor unrest in postwar Britain, the Metropolitan Police Strike of 1918. While the strike, which seemed to threaten the very bedrock of the social order in London, did not spread to Manchester, it arguably started there. Scotland Yard was convinced that union organizers from London were recruiting members in Manchester. After a Mancunian constable provided them with union correspondence supplied by Constable Tommy Thiel, the would-be organizer was dismissed from the Metropolitan Police. This action directly precipitated the strike, which brought London to a virtual halt for several days.[78] The next year, fears of a national police strike nearly came to pass, particularly in Liverpool and the Merseyside area, where more than half the force briefly walked off the job.

The constabulary, not just in Manchester but across Britain, found itself in an awkward position in terms of organizing. Most constables saw themselves as being working class, and in their role as observers of labor activity, they seem to have held deeply ambivalent feelings toward the principle of organization. Their employers seem to have been surprised by the sudden postwar desire of police to organize.

75 Clipping from the *Manchester Guardian* "Manchester Council: Labour Presses its Case," December 4, 1919. Papers of Lord and Lady Simon. Manchester Archives M/14/4/1.

76 Committee of the Police Services, *Report of the Committee on the Police Service* (London: HM Stationary Office, 1920), 26.

77 RIC recruitment poster. General Orders 1921/62. Greater Manchester Police Archive.

78 Eric Hewitt, *A History of Policing in Manchester* (Didsbury: E.J. Morton, 1979), 22.

The City Council discussed the issue at the height of the national fear of a police strike. The Council's reaction was marked by hesitation and decidedly mixed signals. In May, the Council rejected the notion of a police union, sending letters to all precincts indicating that any striking constables would be dismissed without pension, accompanied by copies of the Common's debates on the subject. Labor agitation among the police force, the report asserted, was "partly due to outside influences and partly due to genuine grievances…. While the police are not a military force they are not an industrial body, and cannot be organised along industrial lines."[79] While it is unclear how politicized the striking police forces really were, it is obvious that the government recognized at the time that reforms were needed.[80] The Desborough Commission, while late, was a significant step in that direction.

1919 was also the occasion of the anniversary of one of the pivotal moments in the history of the English labor movement. A hundred years before, yeoman cavalry from nearby Cheshire broke up a demonstration at Peter's Fields, killing at least 11 among the crowd that had assembled to hear reform speakers. The incident earned the sobriquet "Peterloo" and was a reference point for English labor activists.[81] For the Left, particularly the ILP, the anniversary was a portentous symbol and an opportunity to rally the faithful. There were a number of marches in the city as the August 16 anniversary approached. The largest of these, at Free Trade Hall, featured Philip Snowden, while another crowd marched down Oxford Street from Albert Square to Platt Fields. Mrs. Annot Robinson, who rose to prominence in the food and conscientious objection demonstrations of the previous two years, addressed the crowd at Platt Fields, leading at least one observer to note how much politics had changed in the past few years. "The Centenary of Peterloo," cried one headline, "And a Woman Now Addresses the Crowd!"[82] Clearly, the violent suppression of the Peter's Fields demonstration was an important symbol of the progress, or lack of it, in English industrial society.

The symbolic value of Peterloo was particularly potent given the comparability of the postwar situations. The organizers of 1919 stressed that those who demonstrated in 1819 faced a similar set of issues related to the end of the Napoleonic Wars and the postwar disillusionment of an earlier age. "To-day the working classes are again confronted with the same war-impoverished England," proclaimed the *Labour Leader*, "All the conditions which followed Waterloo are

79 Memorandum from City Council. "Threatened Strike of Police." May 31, 1919. Manchester Police Archive, 79/110.

80 Ron Bean, "Police Unrest, Unionization, and the 1919 Strike in Liverpool," *Journal of Contemporary History*, 15 (1980): 644.

81 D. Read, *Peterloo: The Massacre and Its Background* (Manchester: Manchester University Press, 1958). In 1819, Peter's Fields were at the edge of the city. By 1919 they were at the heart Manchester, just a few hundred yards from Town Hall.

82 Paper unknown. Clipping from collection of Mr. and Mrs. B. Caldicott. Manchester Archives, MISC/718/67.

again present – with one striking difference. The people who marched to Peterloo were weaponless in every way. We are not." While the weapon referred to here was the power of the vote, this language was intentionally menacing and the possibility of violent reaction quite real. The appeal of the Peterloo celebrants was based on this comparison across the century. Organizers made sure to explicitly evoke and hold up for comparison the material circumstances of the postwar England of 1819 and 1919.

> For the men of Peterloo, as for us, the tawdry patriotism of the Great War, the gilt and glamour of military pomp had quickly faded. The glory of Waterloo was drowning miserably in 1819, in the watery porridge bowls of a poverty stricken people "the scanty meal of oatmeal and water their only meal in the twenty-four hours.[83]

The potential for serious labor and social unrest certainly existed in the months following the end of hostilities. The task of managing that potential fell in large part to local authorities, who with sometimes only vague direction from London tried to walk a line between an orderly transition to peacetime and the demands of an assertive and increasingly organized working population. In 1919, local bureaucracies and labor groups tried to find accommodation, and this search helped to shape the course of the city's postwar history.

It is not surprising that political organizations with a clear message of social and economic justice attracted considerable attention and public interest during this period. Given the rising tide of grievances within this discourse of social justice, one can also see the potential for such appeals to take on progressively more radical overtones. One of the organizations that radicalized in the last years of the war and the early postwar period was the Co-Operative Society. The Society's critiques of economic mobilization and its subsequent labor troubles won it considerable publicity during the war. It also participated the government's consultative process on wartime social concerns. As discussed in Chapter 2, the Co-operatives played a role in wartime planning and consulted with the government on issues of housing reform. From its complex of offices, factories, and warehouses near the city center, the Co-Operative Society had quietly become an economic force in the city. In the wake of the war they hoped to turn their economic clout into political power. This transition brought them into conflict with local authorities and, in turn, provided valuable publicity for the movement.

In 1913, there were roughly 15,000 members of the society in Greater Manchester. During the war this number rose to 21,400.[84] In the immediate postwar period, this number seems to have dipped a little before returning to roughly the

83 J.H. Hudson, "Peterloo: The Baptismal Hour of the Labour Movement. What We Owe to the Manchester Martyrs," *Labour Leader*, August 14, 1919.

84 Peter Gurney, "The Politics of Public Space in Manchester, 1896–1919," *Manchester Region History Review* XI (1997): 19.

same point in 1920. Nationally, local Co-operative Societies began to seriously examine the possibility of nominating candidates for national and local office and Greater Manchester, where the movement was headquartered, was no exception. In Summer 1919, the local General Board reported a membership of 19,786, a number which they felt made them "a suitable [constituency] in which to nominate a Co-operative candidate."[85]

The Co-Operative Societies across Britain not only expanded during the war, they also became considerably more politically radical. Co-operators before the war were socially progressive, but the pinch of wartime shortages and the unwillingness of local food committees to work with Co-operators pushed the movement toward the margins of political life.[86] Just before the war ended, the Manchester and Salford Society's board discussed its political agenda for the postwar world. Their discussions looked very much like those of leftist parties like the ILP. These included widespread nationalization of industry, the capping of interest, "the abolition of slums," and the establishment of a state bank to prevent profit-making during the rebuilding of British society "so that the works of reconstruction, and other matter for the well being of the people, may be carried out at a minimum of expense … by the use of public assets and credit."[87]

The high water mark of the Co-operative Movement in Manchester came in July 1919, when bureaucratic bungling handed them a propaganda victory and vastly increased their public presence in the city. At issue was a planned demonstration at Platt Fields, on the southern edge of the city. For reasons that were unclear even to the participants, the City Council declined the group permission to hold a march on the Fields, but the Parks Committee had already given them permission to use the site. The Council was faced with the disagreeable task of overruling one of its own committees or incurring the wrath of some of its most powerful constituents.

Local businesses and trade organizations sent letters to the city protesting the planned demonstration. Letter writers opposed the Co-operative protest for several reasons. The first had to do with the supposed radicalism of the movement. Robert Walker, the General Secretary of the National Trader's Defence League, reminded the Council that a local Co-operative leader had declared, "I make no secret of the fact that we are out to absolutely do away with the private individual in trade and production." Another local business owner called the demonstration "propaganda work," but his chief complaint was more commercial in nature. The Co-operative Movement was, after all, a thriving and vertically integrated business as well as

85 Letter from General Board, Manchester and Salford Equitable Co-operative Society to National Co-operative Representation Committee. June 5, 1919. Manchester Archives. M473/1/1/23.

86 Gurney, 19.

87 List of resolutions for quarterly meeting. September 5, 1918. General Board of the Manchester and Salford Equitable Co-operative Society. Manchester Archives M473/1/1/23.

political reform program. "The parks," complained James Scott, "are intended for the recreation and restful enjoyment of the public, not for the battle-ground of trade interests, and we do not see how similar advantages can reasonably be withheld from other business houses if granted to one section of the community."[88] This uncertainty as to whether the Co-operative Movement was primarily political or commercial had clearly not been satisfactorily resolved since the dual nature of the movement had left it open to criticism of its labor practices during the war.

Photographs of the demonstration itself showed an orderly crowd led by a brass band from the Co-operative Tobacco Warehouse as it moved down Oxford Road. The march and demonstration were a reflection of the growing relationship between the Co-operative Movement and the Labour Party, which ran in coalition during municipal elections in the early 1920s. Speakers appear to have divided between Co-operators, Labour Party representatives, and officials from the Trades and Labour Council. Speakers reiterated the Movement's commitment to "a new social order founded upon equity and justice." One Councilor proclaimed, evidently with tongue in cheek, that he was "delighted to take part in [this] manifestation of rebellion" and mocked the Government's wartime claims that the workers were "the watchdogs of civilization, that they were the backbone of the Empire."[89] The demonstration proved highly embarrassing for the Council, who responded to complaints from local businesses by pledging to prosecute the Co-operative Society for illegal use of the park. Despite this, the Council took no action and compounded its initial folly.[90]

Within wider calls for a reform of postwar British society along more equitable lines, there was a growing and increasingly impatient radical strain suggested by the attitude of the Co-operative Movement. This was not the story of the development of an English revolutionary consciousness, but it did represent earnest attempts by political radicals to channel discontent over the conditions of demobilization into a coherent political program. For local authorities, any hint of the melding of local labor grievances with a formal revolutionary ideology was a serious threat. Wartime fears of social upheaval could now be twinned with anxieties about revolution from the East, and the result was a continuation of the politicization of social and economic protest that marked the war years.

Radicals, Bolsheviks, and Workers

Two months after the Armistice, as the worst of the postwar layoffs were in full swing, the Munitions Council became convinced that the ranks of labor had been infiltrated by Communists. There was "considerable trouble" among the workers at Grossley's Motors and in the aircraft factories at Gorse Mill and Shaw.

88 Letters in Manchester City Council Proceedings, 1918–19, vol. 1, 319–22.

89 "Co-operators Assert their Civic Rights," *The Co-operative News*, July 12, 1919.

90 Gurney, 20.

Despite the fact that the workers at these plants faced the near certainty of deep job cuts, the council saw the hidden hands of Bolshevism behind the disturbances. One Grossley's worker, "an Italian, said to have resided in Berlin for many years" was arrested, fined, and recommended for deportation as an undesirable alien.[91]

One of the mainstays of the radical vision of a new Britain was a passionate program of worker education that was intended to channel the discontent of the postwar period into an ideologically coherent concept of revolutionary social change. Members of the multitudes of leftist parties and groups like the ILP and the Plebs League appeared in the streets of working class with the earnest desire to mobilize workers. Typically, this involved formal courses of instruction in History and Political Theory. An umbrella group called the Lancashire and Cheshire League for Independent Working Class Education offered one such program. The League hoped to use "Lancashire's vast treasury of history" to explain "the struggles and sufferings of the toiling masses" and intended to help the workers "organize and to act as fit helpmates of the Clyde and other advanced areas." Classes were to last a week each, with lectures in different halls each night on topics like "The Industrial Revolution and Political Reaction," "The Manchester Man and the Liverpool Gentleman," and "The Apostasy of the Trade Union Leaders."[92]

The appeal of such courses to people who had been working, or not working, all day was limited, but the impetus for political radicalization was certainly present in the neighborhoods that these groups were canvassing. Robert Roberts remembers a sudden profusion of books and newspapers in homes in his Salford neighborhood, a trend he attributed to "the new awareness that men brought back from the war."[93] Notwithstanding any new interest in literacy, Salford was not especially welcoming to working class educators:

> I recall a course which opened with fanfare and fifty-four students in a room over a bar at the local trades club, to study (under a man with a large red beard) the 'first nine chapters of *Das Kapital*.' After a month only three of us remained, and one was a girl whose father (standing guard at the bar below) insisted on her attendance.

Roberts concluded that in the end, workers "wanted not even the first nine chapters" of Marxist doctrine.... But the government believed otherwise."[94] As with the Co-operative Movement, people like Roberts do not appear to have been drawn to the radical Left as a programmatic solution to the problems of capitalism. Instead, it

91 "Munitions Council Daily Report," January 3, 1919. NA MUN 4/3414.

92 "Syllabus of Lectures on Industrial History." Lancashire and Cheshire League for Independent Working Class Education, Session 1919–1920. Pamphlet Collection, Working Class Movement Library, F34/3.

93 Robert Roberts, *The Classic Slum: Salford Life in the First Quarter of the Century* (Manchester: Manchester University Press, 1971), 185.

94 Ibid., 178.

was because in the era of wartime restrictions on formal politics and the politically staid coalition period that succeeded it, the radicals were able to at least suggest solutions to the pragmatic grievances of postwar society. The most successful inducement for the radical Left were the reported reforms going on in Russia.

If most of the working-class citizens of Manchester had little interest in the epic sweep of *Das Kapital* or the formulations of well-meaning ILP organizers, there was nonetheless an intense interest in events in Eastern Europe. Discussions of Russia, and Britain's role in the Russian Revolution, were an important part of political discourse in Manchester in the year after the war. The extraordinary concerns on the part of authorities about "Bolshevism" dovetailed with this public discourse and helped to radicalize the political conversation by casting those who discussed the revolution in positive terms as dangerous enemies of the state. At the same time, there was widespread support among working-class constituencies for some of the more attractive rhetorical features of revolutionary socialism, and radical discourses on equality and social justice found adherents among those who emerged from the war with hopes for a more just society to follow. As one historian of the relationship between the Labour Party and the Soviet Union wryly observed, "Sympathy gave birth to enthusiasm which acted as an antidote to doubt."[95]

Since the collapse of the Czarist regime, which as we have seen was widely hailed in the city, particularly among Russian émigrés, the Revolutionary governments held a certain fascination for working-class organizers. While this affection was not held equally among the workers whom these organizers tried to rally, it is clear that references to events in Russia were a touchstone of political discourse in the wake of the war. In the face of postwar national and local governments that seemed slow and halting in their reactions to demands for economic and political opportunities, post-Czarist governments in Russia seemed to embody the same generalized principles being discussed in public forums in Manchester. Wright Robinson, certainly no dangerous political radical, helped to distribute a pamphlet asserting that Russians now enjoyed:

1. Immediate amnesty for political and religious offenses.
2. Freedom of speech, press, association, and labour organization, with freedom to strike.
3. Abolition of all social, religious, and national distinction.
4. Universal suffrage.[96]

Not coincidentally, these were the same broad demands of both the mainstream and radical Left in Britain at the time. The sympathy felt for the Russian revolutionary regime had far less to do with the particulars of the government in

95 Bill Jones, *The Russia Complex: The British Labour Party and the Soviet Union* (Manchester: Manchester University Press, 1977), 6.

96 Pamphlet "Russia's Charter of Freedom." Papers of Wright Robinson, Manchester Archives, M/284/7.

St. Petersburg and Moscow than it did with projecting the demands and desires of the postwar population of the industrial north of England onto the template of the new regime in Russia. The revolutionaries in St. Petersburg were safely ensconced far away and could be used as sympathetic figures for concerns much closer to home.

One of the most visible manifestations of this sympathy was the success of the "Hands Off Russia" movement, which later fought a series of industrial battles with the national government over intervention in Russia and support for the anti-Bolshevik White cause. Droylsden native and future Communist Party of Great Britain leader Harry Pollitt was one of the most visible organizers of the movement, and Manchester was one of the centers of its public activities. Pollitt had gone to work as a boilermaker at 12 and had been an ILP member since he was a teenager.[97] A divisive figure in English labor history because of his later unapologetic Stalinism, he remembered later that he:

> was not concerned as to whether or not the Russian Revolution had caused bloodshed, been violent and the rest of it. I had lived my life in Lancashire, had read and seen what kind-hearted British bosses had done to the Lancashire working classes. I knew about Peterloo.[98]

Pollitt crossed the country speaking at public meetings like one in London in January that was attended by more than 350 people. Speakers condemned those who believed reports of any "real disorder in Russia." Pollitt's later claim that such disorder had not bothered him seems to belie his earlier denials. One speaker inveighed that it was a "red letter day in working class history, marking another step towards the smash up of the vile capitalist system."[99]

A few days later, Pollitt's organization sponsored a similar meeting in Manchester's Free Trade Hall, addressed by, among others, Annott Robinson of the ILP. The language at the Manchester meeting was similarly intemperate, though also mitigated by a curious sense of civility. The rally began, for instance, with a 30-minute organ recital before the crowd settled in to hear resolutions condemning British support for "old reactionary gangs" in Russia.

> We are living in revolutionary times. The Russian Revolution holds out great hopes for the workers of all lands. No nation can escape its vibrations; no Government can stem the flowing tide of Socialism. Any moment the call may come to the stalwarts of that cause in this district to "spring to your places, Pioneers." The Council's aim is to effect the consolidation of Socialist and Industrialist forces

97 John Mahon, *Harry Pollitt: A Biography* (London: Lawrence and Wishart, 1976) 12.

98 Ibid., 55.

99 Report "The Hands Off Russia Conference." Harry Pollitt papers, Labour History Archive, CP/IND/POLL/1/6.

> in the Manchester District as shall make for a united effort towards the greater aim – the establishment of a Co-operative Commonwealth.[100]

Later in the year, just as concern about a possible cotton strike reached its peak, committee speaker Robert Williams told a crowd of cotton workers that "If the workers had the right to strike to help another union to secure better conditions, how much more would they be prepared to assist those who were striking for socialism and the world for the workers? Bolshevism [is] only socialism with the courage of its convictions."[101]

Concerns about Bolshevism could dovetail with simple public order concerns, and it was sometimes unclear whether Manchester's police were more interested in pursuing the former or the latter. One Sergeant King, for instance, came across a Russian immigrant named Michael Cobven along St. Peter's Street in early March. Cobven was haranguing a crowd "against monied men." When King asked Cobven to move along, the Russian relocated to the square nearby and started again, drawing another crowd. When King again approached, Cobven called him a "money man servant of the Corporation," which resulted in his arrest for disturbing the peace. Sergeant King later described Cobven as "a rabid Bolshevik [who] had been living in lodging houses up and down the country, preaching a mixture of Socialism and religion among the working men he came into contact with." The "rabid Bolshevik," when questioned, pleaded that he had never heard the term before.[102]

In all likelihood, the minor incident between Sergeant King and Michael Cobven at St. Peter's Square was little more than an encounter between the constabulary and an economically marginal and possibly deranged immigrant wanderer. Cobven, who did not have proper papers and faced deportation, was in all likelihood no more a Bolshevik than Sergeant King. In the political atmosphere of the time it was simply easy to class a broad spectrum of divergent views as "Bolshevik." For authorities as well as dissenters, the image of the Bolshevik became far more important and relevant than any coherent political program or activity that might reasonably be called such.

The Times characteristically took an even more truculent attitude toward "dangerous political aliens" operating in Britain, including a "Russian Jew who has recently been particularly active in Manchester." These agitators, identified as mostly "Jews and Russians … are to be dealt with in their turn."[103] This inflammatory language, laced with national and ethnic stereotypes, reinforced prewar and wartime images of political radicalism as inherently foreign in origin

100 "Hands Off Russia Demonstration," Manchester Free Trade Hall. Pamphlet Collection, Working Class Movement Library, F26/12.

101 "British Intervention in Russia: A Manchester Protest," *The Times*, June 23, 1919.

102 "A Rabid Bolshevik," *MEN*, March 10, 1919.

103 "Bolshevists in England," *The Times*, February 15, 1919.

and certainly did little to alleviate lingering tensions between immigrant groups in postwar Manchester.

Given this climate, it was remarkable that there was still middle ground for negotiation and possible compromise. In June, the British Empire Producers Association organized a meeting with employees and labor leaders in Manchester, ostensibly to combat Bolshevism in the cotton trade. The brief meeting's consensus was that the only effective way to combat political radicalism was to "improve[e] workplace tensions" and stop blaming workers for arguing for reform.[104] This spirit of dialogue and compromise was drowned out shortly thereafter by the outbreak of the cotton strike.

The concerns of demobilized soldiers had powerful friends in the opposition, who hoped to draw political capital from their appeals to returning troops. The ILP, meeting at Huddersfield in 1919, condemned the terms of the peace as insufficiently revolutionary. Philip Snowden, a former MP from Blackburn who had lost his seat in the Khaki Election, attacked the peace from the Chair. "The governing classes appear to be living in the realm of pre-war conditions and ideas.... The war has hastened the break-up of the capitalist system, and the only solution of the Labour and Social Problem is the establishment of the Socialist Commonwealth."[105]

The conference passed, by acclaim, a "Soldiers' Charter" that addressed many of the grievances then being expressed in the streets. Broadly, the charter addressed perceived unfairness in the pension scheme and the tensions inherent in a system that tried to compensate unemployed veterans while endeavoring to get them back to work. The ILP also proposed to give more power to local Pensions Committees in an effort to move the wheels of bureaucracy faster and to provide "the fullest possible measure of civil and political liberty" to those still in the armed services. This provision, and one that called for an end to the perceived harshness of courts martial, suggests that the ILP was tapping into fears among soldiers and veterans that military authorities would severely punish any repeat of the demobilization strikes.[106]

Another of the city's postwar problems, one that would descend into sporadic but significant violence in the coming years, was the Irish issue. Manchester's sizable Irish community, which was divided politically yet avoided much of the violence that affected the Irish community in Liverpool, experienced a remarkable political transformation in the wake of the war. Manchester had been the site of a number of Free State meetings during and just after the war. The Irish Self-Determination League held its first meeting at Free Trade Hall in mid-1919. Yet, by the early 1920s, Manchester's Irish community came sharply around to support Sinn Fein and the Republicans.[107] Given the politically charged atmosphere at the time, the city surprisingly allowed the annual "Manchester Martyrs" procession,

104 "Fighting Bolshevism," *The Times*, June 5, 1919.

105 *Report of the Annual Conference*. Independent Labour Party. 1919, 36.

106 Ibid., 90.

107 Michael Herbert, *The Wearing of the Green: A Political History of the Irish in Manchester* (London: Irish in Britain Representation Group, 2001), 94.

a parade in November that celebrated the 1865 execution by hanging of three men who might have been involved in the rescue of several Fenian prisoners in Manchester in which a constable was killed. The local chapter of the Loyal Orange Order protested the granting of a permit:

> I see by the press reports that the reason you would not prohibit the "Manchester Martyrs" procession is that it is a customary procession and has been held for many years. We are quite aware of this fact and we should have protested against it being held this last five years only for the great crisis that this City has been going through during the progress of this terrible war.[108]

The variety of radical strains of thought in the city in the year after the war caused no end of concern among authorities, and events in the future only served to worsen those worries. Yet, the violence of revolutionary ideology remained rhetorical. There was still room for compromise and concession, and the future of Manchester's industrial identity hinged on finding that space while limiting the appeal of violence in the years to come.

The spirit of 1919 was a sharp corrective to the relative optimism of the previous year, when a series of disastrous military setbacks had swiftly been replaced by victory and the chance to impose a victor's peace. The battle over the peace dividend revolved around the question of reward for the sacrifices of wartime. *The Times* commented early in the year strike activity threatened to paralyze the postwar industrial order because of "circumstances arising from the necessary interval between war and reconstruction." Strikers, in their view, did not understand the complexities involved in this transition and were walking away from work because:

> They believe that by this means they will secure the better conditions they are demanding, and which represent the limit of their present quarrel with their employers, the Government, and "capitalism." *They have been told by their leaders that they are justifiably entitled to no less.*[109]

Workers in Manchester in 1919 did not need labor leaders to tell them to feel justifiably entitled to tangible reward. This language drew from their wartime experiences and the frustrations of an unevenly paced demobilization and a halting process of reconstruction that was never clearly articulated by local or national authorities. If 1919 was a year of demonstrations in Manchester, it was so in large part because of the unevenness of demobilization. Elements of the physical, economic, and bureaucratic demobilization of the nation and city remained in place in some areas of life, while their disappearance in others created at least

108 Letter from William Hewitt, Secry. LOOE, to Chief Constable. November 18, 1919. Greater Manchester Police Archives. Box 80 (no document number).

109 "Rebel Strike Leaders," *The Times*, February 1, 1919. [Italics mine.]

the perception of unfairness, injustice, and lack of forethought. At the same time, attitudes toward those who took to the streets in protest were inconsistent and often served to radicalize an already precarious situation by tarring protestors with the brush of radicalism.

The events of 1919 highlighted the limits of the demobilization process. While the mobilization of British society was largely improvised as a result of the government's desire to minimally disrupt economic and social life, it is difficult to see how a better organized mobilization might have significantly smoothed the transition in 1919. The effort of demobilization proved vast and dizzyingly complex. The largest problem in the relationship between authorities and civil society was the manifest unfairness of the process, which seemed to reward and punish capriciously. The rhetoric of war service seemed to offer a vision of equality, even if that vision was strained by the problematic inclusion or exclusion of women. Successive demobilization schemes seemed to offer nothing but inequality, followed in some cases by what appeared to be the collapse of any sort of planning whatsoever. Local authorities tried to mediate between a national government seeking the most painless way out and a population that demanded, in the name of their own sacrifices, that they be compensated for their service.

In Manchester, the structural weaknesses in the export economy made this all the more difficult as jobs seemed to be vanishing at precisely the same time that wartime industry employment declined, and tens of thousands of veterans returned. This nightmarish triangle appeared to men and women who had given so much during the war as another example of government indifference and inefficiency. At the same time, large sections of the working class remained committed to expressing their grievances within the system, further muddying the waters. The perceived commonalities of war service did not produce a less divided electorate or civil society.

In the years to come, these divisions became clearer as organizations dedicated to remembering the war and it veterans coalesced, along with formal political groups that tried to give an official voice to the more radical forms of discontent. If 1919 was not the year of disaster that some in Manchester predicted it would be, it was certainly evidence that the benefits of peace were not apparent to all and that the process of demobilization did not end with the return of the troops or the cessation of wartime bureaucracies. The demobilization of Manchester, and of English society, proved far more complex and perilous than anticipated and still had a long course to run.

If demobilization in the English Northwest proved troubled, it at least had the sometimes dubious benefit of political continuity. In Germany, the twinned experiences of defeat and revolution added new imperatives to the quest for social stability. Protesters and dissenters in England largely confined themselves to seeking ways to force the system to respond to their needs and demands. In Germany, the same pressures helped to produce loud, strident, and sometimes violent calls to punish the wartime state for its failures by destroying it altogether.

Chapter 5
"We Don't Want Gratitude, We Want Our Rights:" Demobilization, Violence, and Politics in Munich, 1919

On October 9, 1919, the Munich chapter of the National Federation of War Wounded met in a large hall in the north of the city. A series of chapter officers and speakers addressed the crowd, attacking the postwar republic for its failure to take care of the wounded. While the organization, promised one of the presenters, would remain "politically neutral," he castigated the government for providing plenty of hollow words but little that would be of tangible assistance to the most visible human reminders of the years of war. Since 1914, the speaker said, "we have been told, 'the thanks of the Fatherland are yours.' We don't want gratitude. We want our rights."[1]

If the language of reciprocity and the claims of civil society on the rewards promised by the wartime state were limited to the war's winners, such a speech would have been impossible. The wounded veterans of that October night had lived through a year that brought tumult, violence, and political upheaval to their city and their country. The wartime government, the Bavarian monarchy, and the German Empire all fell, replaced by a regime that proved to be highly unstable. Still, these veterans insisted that the successors of the wartime state abide by the promises and compromises that allowed and sustained mobilization. In 1919, a series of governments came and went, each claiming the mantle of legitimacy and then failing to deal with the multiple crisis of postwar society.

In a paradoxical way, the experience of defeat and unrest did not diminish the claims of wartime reciprocity, but multiplied them. Successive administrations came to power in Munich during that dangerous year with the promise that they and only they could resolve the manifest and evident problems of postwar conversion. As in Britain, the assertion of political legitimacy in the year following the end of the war rested on the task of managing the complex transition in an equitable way. Also like in Britain, the specific conditions under which the war ended made accomplishing this virtually impossible.

1 "Bezirksversammlung Schwabing des Reichsbundes der Kriegsbeschädigten ..." October 9, 1919. RwGrKdo 4, 452, BHStA IV.

However, the postwar instability in Bavaria and more broadly in Germany, along with the specific ways in which German society mobilized during wartime, produced important differences between these two examples that move far beyond the gap between victory and defeat. Because these successive governments badly needed popular support, they repeatedly insisted upon and emphasized their *willingness* to take up the reciprocal obligations left by their wartime predecessors. For the ordinary Münchner/in, this constantly reinforced the juxtaposition between expectation and outcome and led to the conclusion that the regimes which claimed power in the postwar vacuum were *unable* to live up to the obligations that they so loudly promised to fulfill. As a result, public confidence in the postwar political constellation proved weak, further aggravating an already tenuous domestic stability.

While it is easy to characterize Munich's year-long interregnum as one of extraordinary violence and chaos, it was also a fertile period of political discourse, discussion, and debate after four years of legal constraints on formal politics. At the same time that some of the most famous and violent events in the city's history took place, there were also direct mayoral elections in which many women were allowed to vote and the construction and ratification of a strikingly liberal Bavarian constitution, albeit by a parliament that had fled its capital in the face of renewed political upheaval. Wartime restrictions halted the progress of reform in Bavarian politics. When the war ended, a variety of competing reformist programs asserted themselves once more.

Within the course of less than a year, a string of governments attempted to deal with the lingering problems of war and the present difficulties of demobilization. Even the most radical variant of the Munich experiments, the brief and misbegotten Munich Soviet of Spring 1919, found itself constrained by the awesome task of reorienting society after years of war. To this extent, this series of political upheavals represented the realization of visions of a postwar society that were expressed in the streets of Munich during the long years of war. As different visions of Munich's future emerged from Germany's experience of defeat and revolution in 1918, competing claims of political legitimacy came to rest on different visions of postwar society and the debts owed to those who had sacrificed during the war.

The literature on Munich's political struggles in 1918 and 1919 is vast, reflecting the turbulent historiography of this crucial period in modern German history and the bitter and divisive legacies of Munich's role in what was to come. Until the 1960s, most studies of the political chaos in Germany in 1918 focused on Berlin. Cold War historians in the divided Germany and in the English-speaking world struggled to contextualize the influence of international communism in Munich's postwar politics. There were several principal debates within the historiography. Some, particularly East German historians like Hans Beyer, emphasized the role of the "Council's Republic" (*Räterepublik*) as a forerunner of working-class political consciousness.[2] Others focused their attention on the putschist and later

2 Hans Beyer, *Die Revolution in Bayern, 1918/19* (Berlin: VEB Deutscher Verlag der Wissenschaften, 1982).

quasi-constitutional Eisner regime and its successors, while marginalizing the brief *Räterepublik* as an ill-conceived endgame or as an example of the subversive power of international communism.[3]

More recent post-Cold War histories of the period have tried to strike a balance between these needlessly polarized visions. One significant problem with much of the historiography has been that it has marginalized the people of Munich, treating them as pawns responding to the actions of small cliques of radicals. There is also a pronounced tendency to treat the period of unrest as a discrete phenomenon, rather than to weave it into the complex narrative of the history of the city, the region, and indeed of Europe at the time.[4] Martin Geyer's work has done much to challenge this orthodoxy, though I would argue that more needs to be done to determine the sources of legitimacy sought by the various factions in postwar Munich.[5]

One of the reasons for the enduring fascination with the events in Munich in 1919 was that they were separated by only four years from the Beer Hall Putsch of 1923, an event which brought national attention to the cohort of conservatives, monarchists, and extremists who gathered in Munich after 1920. More obviously, historians have connected the political chaos of Munich's postwar period with the extraordinary rise of Adolf Hitler and what would become the National Socialist German Workers' Party (NSDAP). While the "No Eisner, No Hitler" historiography is powerful and the connections between the two clearly present, it is also highly teleological. One of the most striking things about the period is the pervasive sense that in the aftermath of the war any outcome was possible. It was only later that the constraints of the lost war, particularly in the economy, became inescapably evident.

The events of 1919 in Munich have to be seen in the context of the postwar period, a time in which all sides made political claims based on war service and sacrifice. This occurred mostly for pragmatic reasons, as the demands of the demobilization of urban society had their own peculiar logic and imperatives.

---

3 Karl Bosl, ed., *Bayern in Umbruch* (Munich: Oldenbourg, 1969); Hans Fenske, *Konservatismus und Rechtsradikalismus in Bayern nach 1918* (Bad Homburg: Verlag Gehlen, 1969); Richard Grunberger, *Red Rising in Bavaria* (New York: St. Martins, 1973); Heinrich Hillmayr, *Roter und Weisser Terror in Bayern nach 1918* (Munich: Nusser Verlag, 1974); Friedrich Hitzer, *Der Mord im Hofbräuhaus* (Frankfurt a.M.: Röderberg-Verlag, 1981); David Clay Large, *Where Ghosts Walked* (New York: Norton, 1997); Alan Mitchell, *Revolution in Bavaria* (Princeton: Princeton University Press, 1965); John Raatjes, "The Role of Communism during the Munich Revolutionary Period, Nov. 1918–May 1919" (PhD diss., University of Illinois, 1958).

4 Ralf Höller, *Der Anfang, der ein Ende war. Die Revolution in Bayern, 1918/19* (Berlin: Aufbau, 1999). Eliza Ablovatski has explored the process of counter-revolutionary terror and remembrance in her dissertation "Cleansing the Red Nest: Counterrevolution and White Terror in Munich and Budapest, 1919" (PhD diss, Columbia University, 2005).

5 Martin Geyer, "Formen der Radikalisierung in der Münchener Revolution, 1918/19," in *Revolutionäres Potential in Europa am Ende des Ersten Weltkrieges*, ed. Helmut Konrad and Karin M. Schmidlechner (Vienna: Böhlau Verlag, 1991), 64.

Even the brief Soviet experiment, which self-consciously asserted a break with the past, grappled with the momentum of the demobilization effort. The execution of demobilization in the early postwar period existed in the context of a fluid and unpredictable physical demobilization of the German armed forces along with a concurrent economic transformation and a bureaucratic demobilization that only sometimes followed the logic of political events.

Alan Mitchell, in what has become the standard blow-by-blow account of Munich's postwar crisis, suggests that the SPD and its leadership was bent upon "reform rather than revolution."[6] This is not entirely fair, since the Majority Social Democrats' public proclamations represented a particular vision of how to manage the coming social dislocation of demobilization. It was a vision of a new Bavaria and a new Germany but one conditioned on the careful management of demobilization and rewards for wartime sacrifice. Any vision of the political future that had any currency in the streets of Munich in the early days of November might be called "revolutionary," to the extent that the term has little explanatory value. There was simply no way that any political platform could not advocate sweeping changes, the outstanding question was to what extent those changes altered or did not alter the perceived social realities of the war years.

The end of the war in Germany, while surprising for a population that had every reason to be optimistic a year before, was not the complete shock that it is often portrayed as being. After the Army in the West crumbled in August, the question became essentially one of determining the nature of the government that would end the war. The military dictatorship that had more or less run the country for more than a year backed away in the earnest hope that someone else would shoulder the burden of defeat. By the end of September, when Max von Baden replaced the Bavarian Hertling as Chancellor, the end was clearly approaching. As the Allied armies opened unbridgeable gaps in the German lines, her allies quit the war or disintegrated.[7] The war's October endgame, in which combatant governments tacked for advantage as the offensive continued, was clearly directed toward a cessation of hostilities.

This military collapse was mirrored domestically by increasingly visible and violent discontent. While the events in Munich had special and important characteristics not seen elsewhere, they were no way unique within Germany. Munich's population was keenly aware of and influenced by events elsewhere in the country. At the end of October, a group of soldiers and industrial workers in Stuttgart formed a provisional Workers' and Soldiers' Council that all but shut down the city's industries. On November 4, 1918, in the face of orders to sail against the British fleet, sailors in Kiel mutinied against their officers and formed Sailors'

---

6 Mitchell, 81.

7 A lively description of these events, carefully woven into the context of evolving military activity, can be found in David Stevenson, *Cataclysm: The First World War as Political Tragedy* (New York: Basic Books, 2004), 379–406.

Councils.[8] The self-demobilization of the armed forces of the German Empire was well under way by the beginning of November and it is unsurprising that Munich experienced a similar set of processes. When the Chamber of Commerce in Munich met to consider the "bitter end," it was an ending whose conditions were becoming clearer with each passing day.

Voters and Plotters: The November Days in Munich

The last days of the First World War in Munich were a chaotic scene, out of which eventually emerged a fragile republic. The end of the Bavarian monarchy was a surprise for many, but the coup that forced the monarchs from power emerged from political debates that were percolating in the streets of Munich in the weeks and months before. The government that seized power on November 7 immediately assumed responsibility for the demobilization of both the Bavarian Army and Bavarian society. This was a monumental task, but one for which those who took power believed they were well suited.

The coup of November 7 began several days earlier with a series of demonstrations in the center of the city. Ostensibly, much of this public activity had to do with an election that was never to be – a *Landtag* by-election scheduled for mid-November to replace the ailing SPD leader Georg von Vollmar. Among the candidates was Kurt Eisner for the USPD, released from prison in October in part because authorities thought that Eisner might be far less dangerous as part of the formal political process than he had been on the fringes.[9] Also in the early days of November, the Bavarian government announced a further series of electoral reforms that they hoped would placate SPD and USPD supporters. As it turned out, protesters already emboldened by the assertive strikes in January saw these concessions as opportunities to press harder for their demands.

On November 3, Eisner gave a public address to supporters on the *Theresienwiese* in which he seemed less concerned about stumping for votes than he was about positioning himself and his party for the days to come. August Fass, a policeman in attendance, admitted that listening to the crowd, largely composed of soldiers, NCOs, and wounded veterans, provided little clarity. Interestingly, his report was much more concerned with the crowd's reaction than with the scope of Eisner's speech. "Every hour brings more rumor. One minute it's 'The Kaiser is going' (something like: 'The bastard oughtta go!'). The next it's 'He's not going.

8 Georg Köglmeier, *Die zentralen Rätegremien in Bayern, 1918/19* (Munich: C.H. Beck, 2001), 30 and Hans Mommsen, *The Rise and Fall of Weimar Democracy*, trans. Elborg Forster and Larry Eugene Jones (Chapel Hill: University of North Carolina Press, 1996), 18.

9 Bernhard Grau, *Kurt Eisner, 1867–1919: eine Biographie* (Munich: C.H. Beck, 2001), 344.

He's the defender of the *Reich*.' Most of what the soldiers were shouting I couldn't understand."[10]

By the next day, there was enough reason for concern that the I Army Corps contacted the Munich police to warn them that there were likely to be significant demonstrations by soldiers in the city during the coming days. More ominously, the report suggests that the police should be the "front rank" in the maintenance of order and security to avoid the possibility of bodies of soldiers confronting each other in the streets.[11] The local army command had clearly lost its faith in the loyalty of its own troops and in their willingness to continue to serve under orders.

On the night of November 5, Eisner arrived at the *Hackerkeller* to give an electoral address. In one of those incidents that has passed into legend surrounding Eisner, he reportedly entered through a side entrance to find an all-but empty hall, only to be told by a doubtlessly annoyed waitress that the crowd, and her paying customers, were too numerous for the hall and now awaited Eisner on the nearby *Theresienwiese* in the shadow of the giant female statue *Bavaria*.[12] A police report suggests that about 1,000 people attempted to enter the hall, which had a legal limit of 400.[13]

The *Theresienwiese* was a swirl of demonstrators, speakers, and interested bystanders that cold evening, with even the police observers apparently unable to determine who was speaking or what causes they represented. There is no question that the language being employed by the speakers was far more radical than what authorities would allow if they could do anything about it. Speakers applauded the formation of Sailors' Councils in Kiel and Workers' and Soldiers' Councils in Stuttgart who represented soldiers and a population "that had been lied to for 50 months." While Eisner, at least in the hearing of the informant who reported on the event, counseled calm, others around him were not so inclined. "Down with Wilhelm! Down with the Dairy Farmer."[14]

On November 6, the prominent SPD politician Erhard Auer addressed a large gathering at the *Franziskanerkeller* as part of his campaign for Vollmar's seat. One observer estimated a crowd of about 1,100, with nearly half of those assembled women or men in uniform. Auer's address is remarkable in the context in which it was given. At a time when the national government was engaged in peace negotiations and the war was evidently about to end, this was clearly Auer's hour. The SPD in Bavaria were on the verge of the kind of opportunity they had awaited for decades, and Auer, a 44-year-old merchant from Niederbayern who had come

10 Letter from August Fass, Sicherheitskommissar, to I.A.K. November 3, 1918. I Armee-Korps, 1371. BHStA IV.

11 "*Betreff: Unruhen*," November 4, 1918. I Armee-Korps, 1371. BHStA IV.

12 Mitchell, 89.

13 Letter from Bezirkskommissar Micheler to Polizeidirektion. November 6, 1918. I Armee-Korps, 1371. BHStA IV.

14 Ibid.

to the SPD via the more radical Farmer's League (*Bauernbund*) movement, was poised to be a political force.[15]

His speech reflected the sort of caution and hesitancy that hampered the mobilizing potential of the SPD in a time when audacity like that displayed by the crowd who heard Eisner the previous night seemed to be the chief criterion for political effectiveness. Among the nine conditions Auer laid out for a successful transition to peace were acceptance of the Allies' peace conditions, the abdication of the Kaiser, rights of grievance for soldiers, the defense of the constitution by the Army, and the development of measures to ensure "order, security, and calm" during the homecoming of demobilized troops. "We want," Auer assured his audience "to be a free and happy people, not to be the running-dogs and slaves of the Entente."[16] While this lacked the rhetorical fire of Eisner, it was still a heady attack on the wartime government of the Empire, the military whose ham-handed management of the war had alienated so much of the population, and the plans for demobilization and the rebuilding of Germany.

Perhaps more interesting than Auer's address was the discussion that followed. While his speech had emphasized loyalty to the institutions of King and Kaiser, his conversation with a group of soldiers and civilians (at least one of whom was evidently a police informant) apparently revealed the extent to which the SPD leader realized that winning demobilized soldiers to his side would be critical in the days to come. The soldiers who had come to hear Auer appear to have been divided in their intentions but broadly sympathetic to the idea of dramatic action. While some argued that in the name of social solidarity "the chasm between officers and men must be overcome," others were scornful of the possibility of officers playing a constructive role in the reformation of postwar German society. One soldier pointed to a recent article in the *Münchener Post* claiming that 18 train cars full of loot taken from Belgium sat on a siding in Würzburg. Given the supposed shortage of railroad stock, "can anyone still respect officers who would do such a thing?"[17]

The next day, the two divergent Socialist parties held a joint demonstration on the *Theresienwiese* that, before it was over, literally altered the course of Munich's history. It is obvious in hindsight that the MSPD seriously miscalculated in cooperating with the USPD in this demonstration, since it only served to highlight the relative dynamism of the splinter party. Still, as we have seen, the two parties

15 This important and ultimately rather tragic figure, who eventually died while his nursing home was being evacuated to escape the Red Army in 1945, is little studied. See Michael Lotterschmid and Hartmut Mehringer, "Erhard Auer: Ein königlich-bayerischer Sozialdemokrat und Republikaner wider Willen," in *Freistaat! Die Anfänge des Demokratischen Bayern, 1918/19*, ed. Friedrich Weckerlein (Munich: Piper, 1994), 106–24.

16 Letter from Probst, Sicherheitskommissar, 16th Bezirk, to I Army Corps Command. November 7, 1918. I Armee-Korps 1371. BHStA IV.

17 Ibid.

had a great deal in common in those chaotic November days, so the collaboration that looks so strange in retrospect makes altogether more sense within its context. If USPD supporters were more inclined to explicitly demand a Republic, as one apparently shouted at Auer's *Fransizkanerkeller* speech, this difference seems to have been largely semantic by early November.

Whatever the goals of the organizers going into the demonstration, the results seem to have been a surprise for virtually all of the participants. A large crowd of workers, military personnel, and some number of spectators there to see what promised to be quite a show split into two marches, with one led by Auer and another by Eisner, *Bauernbund* radical Ludwig Gandorfer, and Eisner's trusted aide and companion Felix Fechenbach. The second of these columns moved through the city, gathering momentum as it became apparent that the military was largely unable or unwilling to resist what was now clearly about to happen. Within a few hours, the crowd was the de facto master of the city and arguably of Bavaria.[18] The recently imprisoned Kurt Eisner now had a grip, however tenuous, on Munich.

Soldiers feature prominently in accounts of the coup by two of its most famous literary observers, Thomas Mann and Oskar Maria von Graf, and it was support, or at least lack of opposition, from the barracks, which allowed the coup to be carried off more or less bloodlessly. Graf remembered moments of tension outside the Maximillian II barracks, when it was by no means certain that the soldiers would come over, followed by the soldiers tossing aside their weapons, cries of "Its over! Revolution! We march!," and the incongruous sight of an alpine soldier launching into a traditional mountain dance.[19]

The Bavarian royal family, taken by surprise by the coup, were warned by aides on the night of November 7 that their safety could no longer be guaranteed. In the dark of night, with the queen ailing, the monarchs fled the city toward the safety of Austria. While the influence of the Wittelsbach family would again play a role in Bavarian politics, the durable but anachronistic Bavarian monarchy passed from history in the face of the hostile crowd.[20] Two days later, after a series of concessions to Germany's labor unions failed to stem the apparent tide of discontent, the Kaiser, now without the support of the General Staff upon whom he had relied, abdicated.[21] For Bavarians, this was an extraordinary set of developments. In two days, they lost two monarchs and witnessed or heard reports of two republics being declared, ostensibly in their names. It is little wonder that even those providing the news were confused by the swirl of events.

Readers of the *Amersee Post*, available along the shores of one of the lovely lakes south of the city, got a sense of the chaos and almost unbelievable upheaval as

18 Mitchell, 94–6.

19 Quoted in Friedrich Prinz, *Die Geschichte Bayerns* (Munich: Piper, 2001), 442.

20 The flight of the monarchs is covered in more detail in Mitchell, Large, and Prinz.

21 Roger Chickering. *Imperial Germany and the Great War, 1914–1918* (Cambridge: Cambridge University Press, 1998), 188.

their paper was reduced to elementary sentences. "Ebert is Chancellor. Prince Max has departed. General Headquarters has recognized the authority of the Councils. Württemberg is a Republic. Every hour more news of the almost bloodless accession of the Revolution. Munich is quiet."[22] Remarkably, Munich was quiet for several months thereafter. While its new rulers tried to manage a fractious government by consensus, the terms under which civil society demobilized in the first days of peace developed in the barracks, factories, and streets of the city. While the bloodless coup of November eventually turned to bloodshed, this development should not obscure events taking place below the surface of formal political life.

The new Bavarian republic existed in a state of permanent threat to its existence. The crisis of the Eisner administration, which could best be described as a rapid polarization of both the Right and the Left away from the new Bavarian Minister President, was to have fatal consequences for the new government and its leader. Eisner, facing a threat from the radical Councils' movement, which held considerable authority in the barracks, opted for a course of caution, adopting the mantle of traditionally moderate Bavarian socialism. His foreign adventures, in which he fumblingly tried to forge a separate peace for Bavaria and made some spectacularly ill-judged remarks about German POWs rebuilding France, reflected his more radical bent but did little credit to him or his government.

The Republic tried hard to recruit returning soldiers into its fold, in large part to keep them out of the hands of the radicals. "Soldiers, Countrymen, Comrades!" read a typical government appeal to the soldiery, signed by most of Eisner's ministers, "The soil that your feet walk on is Bavarian soil! Celebrate with us that it is free. The yoke of despotism is broken, the yoke of your oppressors. The shame of militarism is destroyed!" Where the Councils appealed to the soldiers' supposed instinct for radical revolution, the government adopted an opposite tactic, appealing to what they assumed to be the soldiers' desire to return to a *status quo ante* as soon as possible.

> Each man must feel the catastrophe of the collapse.... We must now find a way to a happier future. Work and Peace is the motto of the hour. Our fearful women and children will bless us if we now tread the path of peace.[23]

For the regime's opponents on the Right, which included monarchists, significant portions of the army, and the anti-Semitic movement led by members of the nascent Thule Society, Eisner's socialism and Jewishness were a threat, and they tarred his explicitly moderate program with the invective of revolution. "Bavarians, Awake!" read one broadside found on Munich's streets during those tumultuous days. "Away with Jewish tyranny! Down with Bolshevism!"

---

22 Clipping from *Amersee Post*. Undated. FlSlg 993. BHStA V. Friedrich Ebert was the SPD General Secretary who was, at least nominally, the head of the Republic.

23 Poster, "Soldaten, Landsleute, Kameraden," Poster collection. Captured German Documents Collection. (CGD) National Archives II.

> Do the Bavarian people want to allow themselves to continue to be terrorized by these foreign and conscience-less agitators? Should Bavaria be transformed into a Jewish-Bolshevik wasteland, in which this scum has control? The majority of our *Volk* want calm and order. Only these revolutionary Jews want Anarchy![24]

The new administration was keenly aware of the difficulties that it would face in demobilizing Bavaria, a duty referred to in one of its early proclamations as "one of the most important tasks" of the new regime.[25] To do so, the administration would need to convince the Bavarian bureaucracy to continue in their tasks. The bureaucratic mobilization of German society that facilitated the war effort did not disappear in the political vacuum of the postwar period. In many cases, the bureaucratic transition was jarringly easy. For months, bureaucrats in Munich used the same stationary they had before, simply drawing a line through the world "royal" on their letterhead. Bureaucrats were expected to function in much the same way they had before, a task certainly complicated by the experience of defeat and the self-demobilization of the German army. In mid-January, for instance, the War Ministry in Berlin contacted their counterparts in Munich with regards to the difficulties being experienced across the country in disarming returning troops. They suggested that the Bavarian government "take all necessary measures to take possession of rifles, pistols, machine guns, and munitions from returning and demobilized troops and deposit them in the nearest available Artillery depot."[26]

Even the institutional framework for managing the demobilization effort remained remarkably consistent through this tumultuous period. *Staatskommissar* for Demobilization, Martin Segitz, went back to work almost immediately after the coup, organizing local committees, publicly pledging to manage an orderly transition, and urging calm.[27] A flurry of orders went out from Munich to units that remained intact, demarcating lines of march and depots into which they were expected to deposit weapons. The expectation seems to have been that the Army was spontaneously demobilizing itself, and no assumptions could be made about the willingness of troops to listen to their officers.[28]

Landtag elections in mid-January provided the first opportunity for Munich's voters to stake a political position in the postwar world. For the parties, this presented an opportunity to claim themselves as the legitimate heirs of the pre-revolution government and to try to reverse some of the opprobrium surrounding

---

24 Poster, "Bayernvolk, erwache!" CGD, NARA.

25 Draft proclamation "An das bayerische Volk." November 15, 1918. MA 988, BHStA II.

26 Letter from War Minstry (von Wrisberg and Göhre) to Bavarian War Ministry. January 14, 1919. MKr 4466, BHStA IV.

27 See for example his "Bekanntmachung an die Zeitungen." November 12, 1918. MA 988, BHStA II.

28 See for instance "Merkblatt für das Verhalten der Truppe auf dem Marsch." November 27, 1918, signed by Gen. der Infantrie von Quast. ZS 218. StdAM.

the rather unseemly transfer of power at the end of the war. Political advertising for the election centered on these claims of legitimate right to authority, derived in large part from wartime service. The SPD, in an advertisement for its list and leader Erhard Auer, appealed directly to the service of women on the home front:

> When you go on January 19 to decide the fate of the German people, think about the horrors you have lived through during four years of war.... Think about the terrible hours you spent crowded together in long lines, in storms and in cold, in poor clothes and bad shoes in front of a grocer waiting for your tiny rations, most of which were of low quality anyway.[29]

This type of appeal, which stressed material conditions and suffering outdoors, drew an implicit comparison to appeals made to returning soldiers. It compared the "service" of ill-outfitted women in the rain and cold with similar experiences had by millions of men who had fought in the trenches or on the Eastern Front. Such images resonated with a population that had spent long hours over several years waiting for scarce foodstuffs.

The January *Landtag* elections provide perhaps the best example of how opaque the political situation in Munich had become. The USPD, whose representatives were the most visible symbols and motivators of the November coup, was soundly thrashed in the first postwar elections. Statewide, the electoral map seemed to refute the changes that had supposedly taken place in wartime and looked very much like the emerging prewar order. Across Bavaria, the SPD and BVP dominated, with the USPD winning outright only in a few heavily industrialized Franconian districts like Hof. In Munich, with 359,743 voters, the SPD was the clear winner with nearly 45 percent of the vote, followed by the BVP with 23 percent and the DVP with 18 percent. The USPD, whose leader was the acting Prime Minister, polled slightly over 10 percent. As Eisner scrambled and largely failed to form a coalition state government with other leftist parties, the optimism of November turned into a protracted political struggle.[30] Eisner, commented his colleague, the poet Gustav Landauer, was "the most cursed man in Germany."[31]

The end of the war only served to widen the gap between expectations, fueled by wartime propaganda promising rewards for the sacrifices of the population, and a set of postwar outcomes in which the state and local government proved manifestly unable to deliver on any of those promises. Military authorities, concerned about the impact of economic turmoil on working-class politics, assumed that workers were attracted to the Bolshevik revolutionary model. One report on an USPD section meeting that summer claimed that the speaker told his audience that it was their duty "to play a role in securing and expanding the

29 "Frauen, denkt daran!" F80/1919, BHStA V.

30 SJFB, 579 and Mitchell, 215–21.

31 Large, 90.

Russian Soviet Republic."[32] Such assumptions guided the actions of authorities throughout this period, even when there was little evidence that they were valid. Events on the ground proved far more complicated.

The crisis of the Eisner administration reached a new phase on February 21, 1919, as Eisner left his office to tender his resignation. Waiting for him on *Promenadestrasse* was a young nobleman, Count Anton Arco-Valley, who fired several shots into Eisner. The Prime Minister died almost immediately, while Eisner's bodyguards shot and wounded the assassin. Exactly why Arco-Valley killed Eisner is unclear. One possible explanation was that Arco was seeking to expunge his shame following his rejection for membership in the anti-Semitic Thule Society. The Society, which was becoming more important in local affairs, had evidently discovered that Arco had Jewish ancestors.[33] Whatever the reason, the killing of Eisner swiftly spiraled out of control as a gunman burst into Parliament and shot Erhard Auer along with several bystanders. The gunmen presumably targeted Auer because of suspicions that he had played some part in Eisner's murder. The SPD leader survived the shooting, though two others in the hall did not. The rhetorical violence of the *putschist* administration moved swiftly into a period of physical violence.

Eisner in death acquired much of the popular appeal that he so critically lacked in his last weeks of life. His funeral was a magnificent affair, complete with tolling church bells, a grand procession, and threats of vengeful violence from the councils whose relationship with the late Prime Minister apparently improved when he was physically no longer present.[34] The outstanding question in Bavarian politics became: who could seize upon the legacy of Eisner? Of course, this meant establishing what his legacy was and finding some way to implement it.

The Eisner administration's singular failure to acquire much more than enemies in its four months in office reflected the crisis of legitimacy in postwar Munich. It failed to garner popular support because of the continued decline in material conditions and because of its stance toward the war and the war's aftermath. For its erstwhile supporters on the Left, the break with the war and wartime government was not complete enough, while what efforts Eisner made to distance his administration from the royal and imperial wartime governments were clumsy and proved unacceptable to critics from the center and right.

Eisner's death did not immediately bring about the kind of violence that many feared in the last days of February. His former Culture Minister, the SPD politician Johannes Hoffman, took Eisner's place as Prime Minister and tried to calm some of the swirling political winds. Attempts to find a middle ground in March failed because of the increasing power of the Councils. By early April, the conflict

32 "Donnerstag, 7.8.1919, Bezirk Siegestor…" RwGrKdo 4, 455. BHStA IV.

33 Hermann Wilhelm, *Dichter, Denker, Fememörder: Rechtsradikalismus und Antisemitismus in München von der Jahrhundertwende bis 1921* (Berlin: Transit Buchverlag, 1989), 62.

34 Mitchell, 276.

between the government and the councils reached a crisis point. The city of Munich was poised to enter the most perilous phase of its postwar demobilization.

At the heart of this unrest were the unresolved issues of Council authority that had been such a prominent element of the Eisner regime's vision of demobilization. Contrary to traditional portrayals of the Councils as revolutionary cliques who hijacked the government in Munich, they were an integral and integrated element of postwar Bavarian society. Council power was an inescapable reality of Bavarian life in the wake of the war. Between the Soldiers', Workers', and Peasants' Councils, there were 6,000–7,000 council formations across the *Land*.[35] One recent historian of the movement has suggested that the importance of the Councils after Eisner's assassination was tied to the general radicalization of political language in Munich that followed Eisner's death and the March revolution in Hungary along with the ability of the Councils to proclaim themselves willing and able to tackle worsening economic conditions.[36]

On April 7, the Central Council proclaimed a Councils' Republic, a tactic that seemed to have the support of much of the Munich garrison. The Hoffman government and the *Landtag* took flight to Bamberg and a series of complicated and opaque maneuvers began behind the scenes to work out a successful power distribution scheme in Munich. It was this April government that seemed to confirm stereotypes about Munich's attraction for artists and dreamers. The Finance Minister believed in an arcane system of floating currencies and the erstwhile Foreign Minister was a well-meaning, if deranged, figure who sent cryptic telegrams to the Pope and Lenin before being dismissed.

Despite attempts by Hoffman to restore order, which resulted in a pitched battle between security forces and the newly proclaimed Red Army in the center of the city, the self-proclaimed Munich Soviet Republic, then under the playwright Ernst Toller, survived. It could not, however, solve its leadership problems, and another coup on April 13 brought to power a cadre of Communists led by Eugen Leviné. This succession of revolutionary regimes took a series of precipitous steps toward communalization, notably raiding banks to confiscate anything of value therein. They also prepared for what they knew was to come, an impending invasion by forces loyal to the Bavarian government in exile and backed by the national government, which had by now grown tired of regional radical movements and was increasingly in the position to take armed measures against them. While the Bavarian government in Bamberg had nominal responsibility for the operation, the force that moved on Munich in early May was a hasty assemblage of militias and Free Corps formations from Bavaria and neighboring states under the authority of Reich War Minister Gustav Noske. While the assault was nominally directed from Berlin and under the command of the Prussian General Arnold von Möhl, many of the troops involved came from local militias and Free Corps adventurers like the Munich-born Franz Ritter von Epp.

35 Mitchell, 146.

36 Köglmeier, 317.

The final offensive against Munich took place over the first few days of May and was highlighted by brutal excesses on both sides. Forces inside Munich took a number of hostages, murdering ten of them on the eve of the invasion. The invading army, ostensibly aware of the hostage murder, was little inclined to show mercy after they were done brushing aside the Red Army outside the city. A group of priests was executed for violating curfew, and a number of political figures who had played a prominent role in the events since November were arrested or liquidated. Gustav Landauer, whose political role had primarily been as an advocate of pacifism, was among those beaten and killed.

The Chamber of Commerce, in its assessment of the Soviet's actions, blamed this "rule by lunacy" for "wanting not to bring healing to the already sick body" of Munich's postwar economy, "but to the contrary trying to induce its death."[37] The Munich garrison, which was largely demobilized in May, played an ambivalent role in these developments with considerable numbers of troops openly supporting the revolutionary Councils' Red Army, while others tried where possible to gauge the shifting winds before committing.[38]

The events of late April and early May highlighted the fragmentation of power in postwar Bavaria. At the same time the Soviet was crushed, the parliament in Bamberg began to discuss a new constitution, which would integrate Bavaria into the new German republic. The resulting constitution, ratified in August, was either a triumph of the liberal tendencies in Bavarian politics or the capitulation of Bavarian autonomy forced upon the state by its own political chaos.[39] In either case, the legacies of the brief experience of civil unrest in the Bavarian capital took years to fully manifest themselves. The radicals of April represented a brief and ultimately failed attempt to demobilize German society by effectively rejecting its past and declaring a new period in its history. They failed in both because they had difficulty turning this vision into a coherent program of action and because the structures of authority, even in the painful process of demobilization, were simply too well organized and entrenched to be dislodged so easily. The task remained for the restored government of May to carry out the demobilization while coping with the legacy of the Spring of 1919.

Munich held municipal elections in June of 1919, less than two months after the violent collapse of the Munich Soviet. The elections, which were a fascinating and important event in their own right, were dominated by discussion of the postwar transition. The rival parties, citing both the unrest of the previous months and the experience of war, based their competing claims on the restoration and maintenance

37 "Die Zerstörung des Wirtschaftslebens Münchens durch die Kommunistenwirtschaft, 8. bis 30. April 1919" Handelskammer München. Handelsministerium, 15463, BHStA II.

38 See, for instance, Ian Kershaw's difficulties in determining Adolf Hitler's activities and whereabouts during these critical days. Ian Kershaw, *Hitler, 1889–1936: Hubris* (New York: Norton, 1998), 116–21.

39 Prinz, 445, and D.R. Dorondo, *Bavaria and German Federalism* (New York: St. Martin's, 1992), 1–11.

of order and on the rebuilding of German society. Like the postwar elections in Britain, the core of each party's appeal rested on the idea of reciprocity; that citizens who served the state during the war now deserved to be compensated for their sacrifices. Just as the Eisner government based its narrow mandate on its willingness to rescue Munich and Bavaria from the disaster of war, these postwar parties based their claims on the promise to resolve the crises of the transition to peace.

The BVP, one of the traditional middle-class parties in Bavaria, spoke out strongly that the interests of society would best be served by returning power to their constituents; who they presumed to be the retailers and small business people who had been hit particularly hard by wartime regulations:

> After 4 ½ years of war and its unhappy outcome the Empire, Nation, and community are politically and economically broken down. A rescue is only possible through the immediate commencement of construction in all communities. New building must be fundamental for effective communities.... The provision of food and the granting of credit must take into account the needs of small business and artisans. We want no part in socialization experiments that run counter to the existence of small businesses.[40]

The SPD passed out election leaflets bearing messages like "Mother, protect your children, so that they never again have to die for a king, and vote for Eduard Schmid", "Social Democracy fights grocery profiteers, usurers, and wage controllers. Vote Johannes Timm", or "We crippled, war wounded, and war widows will only be protected by Social Democracy, so we are voting for Karl Schmidt."[41] The USPD also sought to claim the mantle of the war in their appeal to the electorate that summer. Interestingly, they did so by appealing to the interests of the lower-middle-class groups that usually voted for the established parties, rather than the working-class constituency that the USPD hoped would be its backbone. "During the war and then the Revolution," proclaimed one USPD flyer from the period, "the representatives of all of the parties betrayed and trod on the interests of the productive classes of limited means (*schaffenden minderbemittelten Klassen*); serving only their capitalist interests."[42]

The greatest difference between this and the last municipal election in 1914 was the expansion of the voter rolls, which included the granting of franchise to women 21 and older. The number of eligible voters rose from about 47,000 to 358,000, and the expanded voting pool was capable of producing some surprising results. Astonishingly enough given their debacle in the January elections, the USPD was the biggest winner in the municipal elections, with about 32 percent of the vote. The BVP ran close behind, followed by the SPD and the liberal DDP. For the SPD, this was a stunning reversal, having shed about 18 percent of their

---

40 BVP poster "Münchener! Wähler! Wählerinnen!" FlSlg 58/1919. BHStA V.

41 Election leaflets found in F80/1919 BHStA V.

42 USPD flyer. June 1919. RwGroKdo 4, BHStA IV.

vote from the *Landtag* elections in January.[43] The USPD now controlled 16 of 50 seats on the city council. Female candidates did moderately well, despite being consistently ranked low on party lists. Female candidates from across the spectrum of parties made up 10 percent of the new Council.[44]

The only bright spot for the SPD came in the mayoral race. Munich now had its first popularly elected mayor, the Eduard Schmid, who we last saw as one of the SPD's rationing experts in the early days of the wartime food crisis. Schmid, while widely popular, also had a number of political antagonists on the Left. The USPD's newspaper, the *Neue Zeitung*, declared him "a spiritual author of the May Days in Munich who has the bloody suppression of Munich's workers on his conscience."[45] This attack on Schmid suggests another set of problems with which authorities had to contend; finding some way to compromise on a new security apparatus in a city in which the control of armed formations had several times in just a year determined the course of a contest for political power.

The collapse of the Munich Soviet brought to an end the tumultuous phase of Munich's demobilization crisis. It did not, however, ease the tensions caused by those events. As formal politics resumed, the dual legacies of the defeat of 1918 and the chaos of 1919 became the touchstones of political discourse. Despite the wide-ranging visions of the parties and interest groups that contended for power in the year after the war, each based its appeal on its willingness to justly and fairly compensate the population for the trials and losses of the war years.

At the same time, each successive administration faced the very real problems of managing that transition. Two of the most visible challenges were the return of the troops and the restoration of the consumer economy. Despite real differences in the political orientation of Munich's governments in 1919, each faced these pragmatic issues with serious structural limitations. The solutions they sought demonstrate a remarkable degree of continuity through this period of apparent dramatic rupture. Victorious or defeated, Europeans faced the common challenges of bringing troops home and transforming economies geared toward war production. In both of these cases, public expectations ran high and postwar governments knew that they had much to lose if they failed to fulfill wartime visions of a better life to come.

The Return of the Troops

In the final days of the war, the increasingly isolated leadership of the German Empire's armed forces issued a series of communiqués to units in the field, emphasizing the need for order and a peaceful return to the homeland. Since a significant proportion

43 Richard Bauer, *Geschichte Münchens*. (Munich: C.H. Beck, 2005), 348.

44 Reinhard Bauer and Ernst Piper, *München: Die Geschichte einer Stadt* (Munich: Piper, 1993), 272–3.

45 Elisabeth Angermair, *Eduard Schmid (1861–1933): Ein Sozialdemokratischer Bürgermeister in schwerer Zeit* (Munich: Stadtarchiv München, 2001), 58.

of Germany's combat strength was on foreign soil, this promised to be an especially difficult withdrawal. On November 10, one of Hindenburg's last messages before the Armistice stressed that the Army High Command "does not wish to unleash a new bloodbath or a civil war" and warned against crime and plundering.[46] This message clearly conveyed that the OHL understood that the defeated army would likely find its own way back to Germany.

The physical demobilization of the Bavarian Army on the Western Front, as with much of Germany's armed forces, combined the fruits of years of dedicated staff work with the improvisation that came from the suddenness of defeat. To a remarkable degree, soldiers returned from the front in orderly columns. The breakdown in cohesion that many feared came only later.[47] There was considerable confusion but little of the violence against civilians that had been feared. Reports indicate that some units "demobilized themselves," while others "disbanded in the field."[48] Gradually, the War Ministry in Munich gained a more comprehensive picture of where their units actually were and how they were planning to make it back home. A telegram from Heidelburg on November 18 indicated that large numbers of Bavarian troops had crossed the Rhine by train and seemed to be making good progress. The 82nd Landwehr Brigade, marching through the Saarland, was not so lucky. A telegram from both the commander and the Soldiers' Council of one of the battalions reported that troops were "uneasy and embittered."[49]

The means through which this orderly self-demobilization was to happen was the institution of the Soldiers' Council. Despite the potential threat that the radical councils posed to the new government in Munich, the Administration believed that they were a necessary component of a successful and peaceful demobilization. Eisner clearly placed a great deal of importance in the support of the Councils and had addressed them on the night of the coup. He made it clear at that point that the Councils would be an important part of the transition but that he did not see them as a permanent part of the rebuilt German society.[50] As early as November 15, orders went out under the signature of the new Minister for Military Affairs that soldiers were to organize themselves in unit-level councils that would provide order and discipline in an army that was rapidly falling apart.[51] The Soldiers' Councils, like their Worker and Peasant counterparts, were to fill the void in authority during the period of demobilization.

These were not questions of merely bureaucratic interest. While the political uncertainties of postwar Germany began to coalesce, troops were streaming

---

46 Copy in MKr 1753, BHStA IV.

47 Donald S. Stephenson, "*Frontschweine* and Revolution: The Role of Front-Line Soldiers in the German Revolution of 1918." (PhD diss., University of Kansas, 1997).

48 Reports of January 30, 1919 in MKr 1761, BHStA IV.

49 Telegrams in MKr 1759, BHStA IV.

50 Köglmeier, 50.

51 "An die Armee des Volksstaates Bayern!" November 15, 1918. FlSlg 1716. BHStA V.

homeward, looking for trains, and seeking food and shelter along the way. In early December, there were more an estimated 20,123 men in uniform in the city, ranging in unit size from a small telephone detachment to the 5,200 well-armed men of the 1st Field Artillery Regiment. The city's Welfare Committee for Homecoming Troops, which earnestly but unsuccessfully planned a giant welcome parade to have been held on November 18, took charge of making the soldiers feel welcome in the city. The nineteen distinct formations arrived with widely varying levels of provisions. While some seem to have been self-sufficient, others had to be fed at municipal expense.[52] Significantly, there was little or no effort to coordinate the accommodation of returning troops with the notional commanders of the units, suggesting, at least by omission, that planners believed that the Councils were the most effective advocates for the soldiers.

If matters seemed confused in the West, the return of troops from the East was chaotic, sometimes violent, and uncertain. General Kress von Kressenstein, scion of a great Bavarian military family and overall German commander in the Caucasus, tried to keep Munich informed of efforts to get Bavarian troops onto ships bound for Germany. As late as August, several small Bavarian units were at sea on the steamships *Reshid Pasha* and *Akdenis*.[53]

In East-Central Europe, things were more confused still. At the time of the Armistice, a Bavarian cavalry division, three infantry regiments, and a host of smaller formations sat scattered across a front running from the Baltic to the southern Ukraine.[54] With the Russian Civil War continuing to escalate, armed formations roamed freely across the region. Some were evidently large or brave enough to directly attack retreating German units. The commander of the 15th Infantry Brigade was killed on January 11 in a fight against unknown enemies at Berdichev, while "bandits" at Rovno killed two officers, eleven men, and wounded twenty others of the Ulan Brigade.[55]

In an extraordinary step, the Eisner government sent a diplomatic mission to the Eastern Front with the expressed goal of negotiating the peaceful withdrawal of Bavarian and non-Bavarian troops from the region. The mission, which carried on a series of tense negotiations with Lithuanian and Polish officials, faced the delicate task of keeping German troops from becoming involved in disputes between rival nationalists or with the Bolshevik armies. While a number of German military officials appear to have favored confronting the Bolsheviks, others feared losing the support of Soldiers' Councils if they did so.[56] All sides realized that

52 The surviving records of the committee are in StaMu BuR 729/2.

53 Kressenstein letter of December 12, 1918 and reports from the region in MKr 1762, BHStA IV.

54 "Rückführung der bayerischen Truppen aus dem Osten" Undated, but December 1918. BA-R, 706, Vertreter der Reichsregierung in Bialystock, 1.

55 Telegram of January 20 in MKr 1761, BHStA IV.

56 Telegram of February 10, 1919 BA-R, 706, Vertreter der Reichsregierung in Bialystock, 1.

the continued presence of German troops made a difficult situation worse. On February 5, delegations of Polish and German soldiers and civilians worked out a compromise document allowing German troops to return home unhindered across the still-hazy demarcation line between Poland and Ukraine.[57]

One of the most important and potentially difficult tasks in the physical demobilization of the Army in Bavaria was the stunning profusion of weapons left behind and in some cases all but unguarded by the defeated armed forces. When the Ministry of War attempted in January to get a count of available weapons at various depots in the Munich area, the count was maddeningly imprecise. What they could account for suggested that any force strong enough to control the depots would be a formidable one indeed. There were, for example, more than 350,000 rounds of ammunition of various calibers seized from the enemy armies in local caches.[58] The Army command had serious doubts about the loyalty of their own troops and by the Fall, there was evidence of large-scale weapons smuggling out of the city's barracks. This seems to have been particularly notable at the *Türkenkaserne*, from which the command believed the Communist Party (KPD) was able to reliably obtain rifles, machine guns, and ammunition.[59] For months after the collapse of the Soviet, often-contradictory reports and rumors of massive stockpiles of arms left over from the self-styled "Red Army" fueled fears of an insurgency and increased the anxieties of already concerned security officials.[60]

Despite these challenges, the first phase of the physical demobilization of the Bavarian Army, the return of the troops, took place much more smoothly than any reasonable observer imagined it would. Much of this was good fortune and the evidently fervent desire on the part of most soldiers to simply find a way to return home. Still, successive governments took reasonably proactive measures to ensure that troops returned swiftly and without undue hindrance.

Perhaps the most pressing manifestation of this issue faced by the new government was negotiating the transition between the Bavarian Army and the new *Reichswehr* into which the Bavarian force was to be melded. Ironically, one of the most delicate, complex, and ultimately intractable problems faced by the new government in the process of demobilization was the issue of remobilization. When the Republic decided in early 1919 to fashion a transitional army, it did so knowing that whatever permanent peace emerged from postwar negotiations, it would leave Germany with limited capacity to defend itself. However, the profusion of armed militias throughout the country, which were now enforcing Council rule in cities like Bremen, was a cause of deep concern for the national

57 "Artikel der Vereinbarung" February 5, 1919 in ibid.

58 List dated January 16, 1919. MKr 4466. BHStA IV.

59 See reports on "*Waffenschmuggel an KPD Mitglieder aus der Türkenkaserne*" October 29 and 31, 1919. RwGrKdo 4, 246. BHStA IV.

60 For example, the reports of 30,000 rifles hidden in Grosshadern recorded in "Sammelmeldung der 5. Bataillone und Zentrale." Wehrregiment München. June 15, 1919. RwGrKdo 4, 177. BHStA IV.

government. The Bavarian army, like other sub-national formations, would vanish in this transition.[61] In its place rose a compromise formation, the Bavarian *Reichswehr*, based on the national law of March 6 but only promulgated in Bavaria on May 10 after the government finally secured Munich.

The new Bavarian *Reichswehr* was "under the command of the government of the Bavaria, [but] in time of war under the authority of the national President." The framers were clearly aware of the regional sensitivities of Bavarians and the possibly destabilizing results if the new formation appeared to be a Prussian cat's paw. Soldiers pledged "my whole strength to the defense of the German Reich and Bavaria at any time and in any place."[62]

The remobilization process was driven simultaneously from below and above, resulting in claims that were variously antagonistic to each other, complementary or competing. While the *Reichswehr* reorganization required coordination between the national and *Land* governments, the attempted consolidation of the militia movement emerged from civil society and while expressing support for the state, also represented a potentially dangerous alternative source of power and legitimacy. Munich's experience with the Councils and the self-styled Red Army of the Spring Soviet was a cautionary lesson for the government.

This uncomfortable transformation was not eased by the sense that the Army was perhaps the final manifestation of Bavarian autonomy. Wartime protests over the centralizing tendencies of Berlin and the loss of local control were fresh in the minds of observers in 1919. At a time when power seemed to be shifting back to local and regional governments, the *Reichswehr* went in the other direction. Particularly for Eisner, whose November coup intended to decouple Bavaria from the catastrophic endgame of the empire, the possibility of transferring control of the Army to the republic proved particularly galling.

Regardless of the notional autonomy of Eisner's administration within the postwar Republic, the *Reichswehr* issue could not be ducked. The new model *Reichswehr* angered any number of Bavarian sensibilities. For militias like the ones that had taken the city from the Red Army and the new citizen militia formations (about which more below), it seemed likely to take away or at least co-opt their growing authority. For the Left, it seemed to be a calculated ploy to create a force capable of crushing their new assertiveness. The fact that both of these suspicions were true did not help matters. For all concerned, this seemed to be another example of North German cultural and political imperialism, which following the economic resentments of the war years and the heady days of Eisner's visions of Bavarian autonomy was particularly anathema.

Recruiting posters for the new *Reichswehr* attempted to allay these sentiments. One early effort appealed to Bavarians "of all classes" to enlist, suggesting that "The *Reichswehr* in Bavaria is not a Prussian formation, rather it sits under the

61 Mommsen, 39–41.

62 HAA Bayern, *Verordnungsblatt des Heeresabwicklungsamtes Bayern*, No. 1 (Munich: HAA Bayern, 1919), 442–3.

command of the constitutional government of Bavaria, providing peace and order in our Bavarian fatherland." At the same time, the leaflet promised that there would be "no place for reactionary militarism" in the new formation.[63] Another recruiting poster from the period pledged what must have seemed an exceptional liberal organizational and disciplinary scheme for recruits. Doubtless as a concession to the popularity of the Councils' Movement, deputies would serve as liaisons between officers and men. Discipline would be conducted "in a democratic manner," and there were unheard of opportunities for qualified men and NCOs to rise to officer's rank.[64]

This delicate balance between demobilization and remobilization was perhaps most apparent and most difficult in the case of the Bavarian *Einwohnerwehr*, or citizen militia. Its founders drew from the then-pervasive fear of disorder and unrest, emerging from both within and outside the borders of Bavaria. Led by veterans like Rudolf Kanzler and Georg Escherich, the movement set up a headquarters in the Ring Hotel in Munich and within a few months had 200,000 members all over Bavaria.

What is perhaps most interesting about the *Einwohnerwehr* was its political heterogeneity. Units represented a variety of parties and opinions, excluding only the furthest left-leaning political groups brought together by unease over security and the fear of further revolution.[65] As the organization's founding documents indicated, it was intended as an "instrument of prevention against violence," with no explicit indication of which of the spiraling profusion of violent entities it intended to stop.[66] The *Einwohnerwehr* presented considerable difficulties for authorities who tried to use them as a way to circumvent restrictions on the size of Germany's armed forces. While they represented order, it was a particular kind of order. During their few years in existence, it became clear that this vision often conflicted with that of municipal and regional authorities. An early *Einwohnerwehr* recruiting poster captures this tension. Around a stark image of the iconic *Frauenkirche* in flames and citizens fleeing in terror through the streets, the poster asks "Are you for Order and Peace? Then why have you not yet joined the *Einwohnerwehr*?" While it does not explicitly say so, it is clear that the purpose of the militia is to guard against order's enemies within the city, rather than to protect it from external forces. "If city, family, and livelihood are to be protected from the aftermath of violence, every individual, including you, needs to join the *Einwohnerwehr*."[67]

63 "Die Reichswehr in Bayern." Undated, but handwritten date February 14, 1919. ZS 428. StdAM.

64 "Auflkärung" Undated, but spring or summer 1919. ZS 428. StdAM.

65 The best work on the *Einwohnerwehr* remains David Clay Large, *The Politics of Law and Order: A History of the Bavarian Einwohnerwehr, 1918–21* (Philadelphia: American Philosophical Society, 1980), 23–31.

66 "Vorlaufige Bestimmungen über die Errichtung einer Einwohnerwehr f.d. Stadt München," BA-MA PH 3/14.

67 "Sind Sie nicht für Ordnung u.Sicherheit?" Undated poster in ZS 443, StdAM.

The postwar Bavarian governments were in agreement about the need to integrate existing troop formations effectively into the new army. Returning soldiers found themselves part of an extensive campaign of propaganda designed to accomplish several things. First, it was clearly geared toward reminding troops of their loyalty to the military as an institution, rather than to the form of government they served when they put on their uniforms for the first time. If the institution of the Army remained loyal to the successor regimes, so should the troops. Second, the propaganda campaign was designed to encourage troops to see their new mission as the prevention of disorder and the maintenance of state authority. This meant an increasingly explicit anti-Communist program and helped ensure that those leading the education courses would be only the most dogmatic and sometimes extreme anti-Marxists available. This pairing of grudging republicanism and anti-communism was uneasy at best, and the selection of instructors and instruction material suggests just how little enthusiasm there was among those in the military in Bavaria for the new postwar order.

Troops returning to Bavaria received a booklet called "Questions and Answers: A Small Guide for Soldiers of the *Reichswehr*." The booklet stressed that the Army would not try to reinstall the monarchy but that the people of Germany should decide their form of government and that the police alone were not able to fight the kind of disorder that now threatened Germany:

> Question: Are there now so many bad elements (*Gesindel*) out there in the cities that they might pose a threat to the state itself?
> Answer: The bloody fighting in Germany's cities has proven this to be true. In cities with 500,000 residents there are at least 20,000 whores, pimps, laid-off convicts, opportunist criminals, and recalcitrant Spartacists who don't fight from "Idealism" for a belief system, but as thieves for their personal gain.[68]

Particularly after the events of Spring 1919 in Munich, many within the military began to call for more significant efforts to reeducate troops. An undated report, apparently written within a few weeks of the collapse of the Soviet, suggests some of the uncertainties and anxieties of those carrying out the demobilization within the military.

> A new age has begun. The *Volk* have abandoned the old Militarism. The current situation does not permit the military to vanish. Anyone who has any sense of vision has to see this, particularly after the events of the past few weeks. We need a solid cohort (*eine gute Truppe*), a new cohort in form but one that emerges from the proud traditions of the Bavarian Army.[69]

68 "Frage und Antworten: Lesebuchlein für den Reichswehrsoldaten" Published Würzburg, 1919. RwGrKdo 4, 149. BHStA IV.

69 "Bildung der bay. Reichswehr." RwGrKdo 4, 309. BHStA IV.

Education was to be the key to molding this new core for the army in Bavaria. Accordingly, von Möhl's *Gruppenkommando 4* brought together local academics, self-proclaimed experts in politics and economics, and particularly bright members of units stationed in the area. The reeducation of returning troops in and around Munich became the task of the intelligence and propaganda unit of the Bavarian *Reichswehr*. The job went to Captain Karl Mayr, who assembled a group of young soldiers to deliver instruction to their comrades in arms.

Captain Mayr's cohort of instructors has been the subject of a disproportionate amount of scholarly interest because it included a young NCO named Adolf Hitler, who would later act as Mayr's "Jewish expert" and corresponded with other educators about Jewish affairs.[70] That one of the educators went on to a meteoric political career should not overshadow the significance of what the propaganda courses were trying to achieve or the considerable weight that military authorities placed on this program as a means of combating disorder in the ranks.

There was considerable anxiety, some of it well-founded, about the political condition of the troops in camps like *Lager* Lechfeld. Karl Graf von Bothmer, a leading anti-Semitic writer and at the time an associate of Dietrich Eckart and the nationalist publication *Auf Gut Deutsch*, was one of the educators sent to Lechfeld to provide political education. Bothmer wrote that the troops were living in "a swirl of public opinion" and that they seemed to come from a wide range of political persuasions. Simple anti-Bolshevik propaganda, wrote Bothmer, was not likely to be effective. Instead he suggested a rigorous program of historical, national-economic, and political education reinforced by discussion.[71]

Courses seem to have been a mix of earnest efforts to give troops a quick education and an equally important opportunity to give them something to do aside from remaining in their barracks waiting to go home. The propaganda officers seem to have figured out that many soldiers would not be amenable to sitting for long periods listening to academic discussions of politics and economics. A typical class was one offered at the Regina-Palast Hotel on June 2, to the men of the I Battalion, I Bavarian *Schützenregiment*. The event began with an address from their commander, followed by a folk music concert and a brief lecture on German songs and ballads. Only then did an academic (unnamed) deliver a 25-minute lecture on "Spiritually Overcoming Bolshevism." Following that was a discussion, a break for dinner, and the evening's entertainment, which consisted of a one-act play and comedy.[72]

For their part the soldiers in the courses seem to have understood the message they were to take away from the exchange. Hitler's lectures at Lechfeld were

---

70 Kershaw, 121–5.

71 "Erfahrungen um Beobachtungen gesammelt bei den Aufklärungskursen des Gruppenkommandos IV" June 25, 1919. RwGrKdo IV, 307, BHStA IV.

72 "Propagandatätigkeit bei den Truppen." June 2, 1919. RwGrKdo 4, 149, BHStA IV.

blatantly anti-Semitic, and they seem to have struck a chord with his listeners.[73] An Infantryman named Karl praised "Herr Beischlag (sic) and also Herr Hittler (sic) … who through well-informed and easy to understand speeches brought the crowd to a right and zealous spirit."[74] The integration of blatantly anti-Semitic ideas into the propaganda courses, the *de facto* promotion of these ideas by the *Reichswehr*, and the evidently warm welcome that they received in the demobilization camps suggest some of the tensions that the new Bavarian government had to contend with in the early days of the Weimar Republic and the antagonisms felt by many ordinary Bavarians as they imagined a world after the war.

Demobilizing the Economy

While there was no *Oktoberfest* in 1919, the *Theresienwiese* did see a smaller Fall Festival (*Herbstfest*). While the substitute festival did feature a traditional shooting contest, continuing food shortages meant that some staple items, namely pork sausage, chicken, and roast ox were unavailable.[75] As the program for the shooting contest makes clear, the connection between the festival and the process of demobilization was quite clear to its participants:

> After an involuntary five-year break we can begin our beloved shooting sports again. A great opening shoot marks the beginning of our festival and this beginning will be an honor to our dear brothers in shooting who have thankfully come home from the POW camps and the field…. And so, a hearty *Grüss Gott*! Let's forget the troubles of this new age and with no heavy hearts let the bullets fly![76]

The troubles of this new age ultimately threatened to outweigh the government's very real successes at bringing soldiers home from the field. Far more difficult to manage was what those troops faced when they arrived home again. The German war economy, the result of a series of compromises and delayed decisions, faced a new set of challenges after the war. Now, as thousands of workers returned from their time in uniform, the situation was bound to worsen before it might improve.

In January, more than 52,000 workers, male and female, were registered as unemployed at the city's labor exchanges.[77] Inflation and scarcity created a crisis in consumer society. According to government estimates, the price of a half-kilo of flour had risen 400 percent since 1914, a cup of coffee by 990 percent, and men's

---

73 Kershaw, 124.

74 Letter from Inf. Karl. August 24, 1919. RwGrKdo 4, 309 BHStA IV. Rudolf Beyschlag was the commander of the detail sent to conduct the course at Lechfeld.

75 *175 Jahre Oktoberfest* (Munich: Bruckmann, 1985), 82.

76 "Offizielle-Festzeitung zum Heimkehr-Krieger Schiessen…" ZS 218, StdAM.

77 Richard Bessel, *Germany After the First World War* (Oxford: Clarendon, 1993), 157.

shoes by a staggering 1180 percent. Actual wages for adult male workers, on the other hand, were up by only about 40 percent.[78]

This represented a precipitous decline in real wages, and consumers were angered by what they saw as government inaction. The war was over, reasoned many, so why did prices remain so high? In July, reports on consumer attitudes revealed deep resentments at the apparent unfairness of the postwar economy. Rumors spread that in Frankfurt, closer to the French border, goods from France and England were easy and inexpensive to obtain. Consumers were particularly angry about the beer and milk markets, where they perceived producers getting rich from their economic misery, consistently raising prices in any political conditions.[79]

Work for any wage proved difficult to find during the transition from wartime to peacetime economy. Defeat or victory mattered far less here than the economic realities of postwar conversion. While Britain and Germany took very different paths to economic mobilization, both faced the stark reality of unemployment and sometimes unsuccessful industrial conversion in the wake of the war. Germany faced the added problem of restrictions on arms production imposed at Versailles, which hastened the mandated conversion of armaments facilities. But even before the treaty, the wartime industrial transformation of Munich staggered under the blows of rapid decontrol.

In December 1918, BMW released 3,400 workers. By January, a month that saw the total number of unemployed citywide reach 45,000, they employed only 260. Across the city, the new industries that transformed the local economy during the war now fed its unemployment lines. The Bavarian Cannon Works laid off all of their more than 3,000 workers between November and January, while the Goeggl and Sons Metal Works let all 1,200 of its workers go.[80]

For Munich's female workers, the dislocation caused by demobilization was acute. Women were pushed out of work relatively quickly upon the return of the troops. At Pmf Dachau, female workers were let go at a much higher rate than their male co-workers. Of the 2,400 adult males employed in mid-1918, almost 1,000 still had their jobs a year later. By contrast, of nearly 3,000 adult women workers in 1918, just 480 remained the next year. In Munich's municipal kitchens, which had been a key component of the city's strategy for food provision during the hard years of war, 108 female employees were let go in the summer of 1919 to make way for male veterans.[81] While there were far fewer female registered unemployed

78 SJFB, 601, 305.

79 "Stimmungsbericht." July 8, 1919. RwGrKdo 4, 347. BHStA IV.

80 Gabrielle Sperl, *Wirtschaft und Staat in Bayern, 1914–1924* (Berlin: Haude & Spener, 1996), 310.

81 Sieglinde Reif, "Hunger, Wohnungsnot, Arbeitslosigkeit, <Demobilmachung>: Folgen des Ersten Weltkrieges in München." In *Zwischen den Fronten: Münchner Frauen in Krieg und Frieden, 1900–1950*, ed. Sybille Krafft (Munich: Buchendorf, 1995), 115.

than male, women in Munich were proportionally more likely to be and remain unemployed, as they were across Germany during the period of demobilization.[82]

The great works at Pmf Dachau, built to provide munitions for the war effort, were largely unable to come to grips with the challenge of conversion to peacetime, particularly as it became clear that Germany would not be permitted to rebuild her armed strength. The plant, which had almost 5,400 workers at its height, was reduced to about 1,400 by Fall 1919. While the workers' council urged the Bavarian government to consider keeping the plant open to aid in the dismantling of existing stocks of munitions, it was clear that Pmf Dachau could not continue to operate in postwar conditions. The works, now renamed the *Deutsche Werke AG*, converted to the production of wood products for industrial and commercial use. Efforts to sell machinery from the plant proved far more complex than expected as peace terms imposed strict limits on equipment designed for the arms industry. When the Kempe-Werk of Nürnberg offered to buy an extractor, management responded that the device was "registered as a specialized munitions machine and we have to destroy it. Transporting it intact is not permitted."[83]

The city's perpetual housing crisis was also exacerbated by the war as new home construction came to an effective halt. In the year before the outbreak of war, 703 new dwellings had been built. In 1916, there were only 23.[84] The problem, as a contemporary observer wrote, was that "the entirety of industry worked directly or indirectly for the war effort."[85] One of the results was chronic overcrowding in low-cost housing stock. The Pension Oberpollinger, with 44 beds, housed 524 people by April 1919.[86]

The *Wohnungsamt*, just a year old when the war ended, swung into action in late 1918. Its activities during a chaotic and uncertain period, while purely stop-gap in nature, can probably be counted as one of the few success stories of the demobilization effort. At least temporarily, they managed to keep thousands under a roof of some sort. By December 1918, housing officials proposed a radical program of temporary building, quartering in private houses, and use of public buildings to house the homeless or returning troops. By April 1919, according to official reports, 4,125 dwellings of various types had been requisitioned, built, or converted. By far the largest part of this was the quartering of demobilized soldiers

---

82 Richard Bessel, "Unemployment and Demobilization in Germany after the First World War," in *The German Unemployed*, eds Richard Evans and Dick Geary (New York: St. Martins, 1997).

83 Documents related to its conversion in Feldzeugmeisterei 1864, BHStA IV.

84 Reinhard Bauer and Ernst Piper, 270. Caroline Festa. "Als BMW noch in den Kinderschuhen steckte: die schwierigen Anfänge eines Symbols der deutschen Autoindustrie" (Thesis: Universite de Nice Sophia-Antipolis, UFR Lettres, 2001), 82.

85 Kurt Königsberger, "Die wirtschaftliche Demobilmachung in Bayern während der Zeit vom November 1918 bis Mai 1919," *Zeitschrift des bayerischen statistischen Landesamts*, 52 (1920), 197.

86 "Bericht über die Tätigkeit des Münchener Wohnungsamtes…" April 1, 1919. Wohnungsamt 83a, Sta Mu.

in private housing. About 2,200 soldiers had been so quartered, though "passive resistance" by the population was overcome only through significant increases in payments made to homeowners.

Existing barracks like the *Schwere Reiterkaserne* were converted for civilian use, while three new barracks complexes were built. The collapse of the Bavarian monarchy freed some space as well, with the lovely Nymphenburg palace divided into 39 separate living spaces.[87] While these efforts did not alleviate all of the population's housing worries, they were a rare example of a bureaucratic institution navigating successfully between successive governments before and after the war.

The political and social upheavals in Munich and across Germany seriously impeded efforts at substantive housing reform in the immediate postwar period. A serious municipal building program began after 1924, following the end of the "Great Inflation." A series of housing blocks, built in no small part thanks to the energy of municipal officials like Karl Preis, helped to transform the cityscape once again. Areas like Neuhausen and Harras witnessed the building of self-sustaining communities of homes and businesses.[88] This development closely followed the rebuilding and restructuring of Munich's industrial capacity.

Aside from the necessary re-tooling in the wake of the war, there were other impediments to keeping the fires of industry burning. Years of blockade, internal chaos, the end of reliable shipments from Bohemia, and the loss of the coal fields of Eastern France that had been a fond dream of national and Bavarian expansionists deprived industry of critical raw materials. Even those industrial concerns that wanted to continue working were desperately short of raw materials. Königsberger estimated that demand, 6–8 million tons of coal per year for Bavaria "right of the Rhine," was about 3 times the available supply in 1918–19.[89] The Bavarian industrial economy was in rapid transition and strangling itself at the same time.

The result was pervasive unemployment and underemployment. As successive governments tried, and largely failed, to deal with the structural and circumstantial problems of economic demobilization, angry voices emerged from the streets and beer halls of the city, demanding more effective action. These increasingly radical visions of social transformation, which often conflicted, played a crucial role in shaping the future of the city.

---

87 Ibid.

88 Landeshauptstadt München. *München wie geplant: Die Entwicklung der Stadt von 1158 bis 2008* (Munich: Landeshauptstadt München, 2007), 90–93.

89 Königsberger, 202.

Politics, Radicalism, and Everyday Life in Munich

For the anti-Semitic Right, demobilization offered opportunities to tie Jewish influence in with broader concerns about the future of German society. In much the same way that traditional anti-Semitic tropes bolstered accusations of profiteering and cowardice during the war and images of Eisner and the Soviet as agents of Jewish power, Jews could be connected with the problems of postwar German and Bavarian society. Posters displayed by the local chapter of the *Deutschvölkische Schutz-und Trutzbund* (German League for Defense and Defiance) in September illustrate this point well. One, addressed to workers, asked when during their "decades' long struggle against capitalism and the exploitation of your labor" they had ever seen a Jew among them, particularly in their work at the front for the protection of their fellows.[90]

Another such appeal, addressed specifically to "Our Brothers and Comrades who are now coming home" accused Jews of "setting German racial comrades against one another, making brother the enemy of brother, all so they can make ever more of their sordid money." To do so, Germany's Jews had of course supported the Revolution as another means of weakening "the already broken Fatherland."[91] This was neither the first nor the last time when Jewish influence would be, in the same breath, associated with both unrestrained capitalism and the revolutionary Socialists who had made and sustained the various revolutionary movements.

Increasingly, the voices of radical anti-Semitic and anti-Republican thought were drawn together in the miasma of Munich politics. The most famous example was the Thule Society (*Thule Gesellschaft*), an organization whose reputation, largely based on its illustrious membership, is today well in excess of what it deserved. Founded during the last months of the war by a conman with a keen sense of self-promotion who went by the *nom de guerre* of Freiherr von Sebottendorff, by the middle of 1919, it had 250 members in Munich among about 4,000 in Bavaria. Among these were such later luminaries at Rudolf Hess, Dietrich Eckhart, and Anton Drexler. The Society represented a variety of opinions, including the *völkisch* racial nationalism that would later come to distinguish the new Right in Munich.[92]

For the moment, however, the Society was most important because its adherents were among those managing the militia movement. The Society attracted some of the best-known Bavarian nationalists, like the publisher Julius Lehmann, many of whom were later early supporters of Nazism. The society in its early days was an uneasy amalgam of ideas, from the racial nationalism of its slogan ("Remember that you are a German! Keep your blood pure!") to the Catholic nationalism of the "Break from Rome and Break with Berlin" advocates. With its membership bound together by opposition to the postwar order and a fearsome anti-Semitism, the Thule Society reflected the growing self-confidence of the Right in Munich.

90 Poster in RwGrKdo 4, 183. BHStA IV.

91 "Den Heimkehrenden Brüdern und Kameraden" RwGrKdo 4, 183. BHStA IV.

92 Wilhelm, 41–4.

Such sentiments were by no means confined to an anti-Semitic fringe. An intelligence officer serving in Munich reported in August on a train voyage to Lindau during which his fellow passengers talked openly about their feelings toward Bavaria's Jewish inhabitants. One passenger asserted that the "Jewish scum" bore most of the responsibility for the war and the republic that followed it. "One worker suggested that it would have been better if the government forces on May 1 had shot the Jews…. These people proclaimed a pogrom was just as certain as the revolution was."[93]

Groups across the political spectrum held large public demonstrations that sought to promote their platforms and demonstrate their ability to mobilize their constituencies. This created significant problems for authorities who sought to maintain public order while allowing some degree of freedom for assembly. Municipal authorities tended to allow wider latitude to rightist groups. These conflicts proved most acute when they dealt with commemorations or memorials to Eisner, the end of the war, or the political upheavals of early 1919.

Establishing a pattern that was to last for years to come, the USPD and KPD were particularly vocal advocates of celebrating the anniversary of the November coup. For their political opponents, celebrations of November seemed only to celebrate defeat and humiliation. Making matters worse, November 7 fell on a Friday in 1919, and any public commemoration seemed likely to shut down the city on a business day. "In the interests of thc building of our economy," workers were forbidden by order of the *Stadtkommandant*, and later ally of the *Einwohnerwehr*, Gen. Major Arnold von Möhl to take the day off. Also banned were outdoor celebrations, gatherings at cemeteries, and processions. Posters distributed in the city for the occasion reminded citizens that appearing in public in uniform and the printing of political material without the written authorization of a political party were expressly forbidden.[94] As a compromise, the leftist parties agreed to hold their celebrations on November 8. The celebrations were for the most part peaceful, though not without controversy. When the socialist paper *Der Kampf* described Hindenburg and Ludendorff as "incompetent," their offices were attacked by unknown assailants several days later.[95]

Demonstrations were not solely a tactic of the organized Left in Munich. Patriotic demonstrations of various sorts, similar to the ones organized during the war drew large crowds in 1919. This was particularly true in the immediate aftermath of the city's "liberation," when anti-communist and pro-law and order sentiments drew middle-class residents to such demonstrations. Municipal officials, including the Mayor, held a concert in the Odeon Theater on July 11 "to greet the

93 Copies of both versions in RwGrKdo 4, 352. BHStA IV.

94 "Bekanntmachung betreff Revolutionsfeiern." November 2, 1919. RwGrKdo 4, 40, BHStA IV

95 Günther Gerstenberg, *Freiheit: Sozialdemokratische Selbstschutz in München der zwanziger und frühen dreiziger Jahre* (Munich: Ulenspiegel, 1997), 38–9.

homeward-bound troops."[96] A typical patriotic demonstration in July saw a crowd waving imperial flags gathered at the *Feldhernhalle* for a patriotic concert. "Of course," an observer noted, there was a counter-demonstration comprised mostly of students who sang the *Internationale* in an effort to drown out the "Watch on the Rhine."[97]

In a political climate in which police or military intelligence attempted to compile reports on any meeting or demonstration with political overtones, even the feverish imagination of city and military officials otherwise keen to find signs of political radicalism could not manage to find political discussion everywhere. An agent patrolling for signs of discontent in July found no political discussion in the charity kitchen attached to the *Arbeitsamt*. In the bar at the *zur Bayerischen Krone*, there was precious little political conversation but rather, "a flourishing trade in cigarettes, trinkets, gold watches, and other sundries."[98] This was evidently not enough to allay concerns about the kind of politics being discussed there because a month later the *Stadtkommandant* issued a list of bars forbidden to troops that included the *zur Bayerischen Krone*. This could not have been welcome news to the owners, as reports indicated that up to 75 percent of the bar's customers were in uniform.[99] Agents seeking to gauge political opinion in Munich often had far more luck finding politics discussed at Munich's many beer halls and guest houses.

The changing electoral fortunes of the major political parties were reflected in the behavior and attitudes of their local constituencies and at meetings where the parties debated and disseminated their platforms. Surveillance reports from USPD meetings in the Westend neighborhood after the mid-year elections reveal much about the concerns of party affiliates and the importance that party members placed on the legacies of the war and demobilization. Like all of the major parties, the USPD was an amalgam of neighborhood organizations, which for the most part met in bars and cafes across the city to hear speakers and debate. In times of crisis or when opposing parties felt inclined to do so, such meetings could often descend into physical or rhetorical violence. Bars were associated with parties, so supporters were relatively easy to find.

In the Westend districts (there were two USPD organizations, I and II, in Westend) meetings were usually held at the *Tirolerhof* or *Drei Hirsche*. The messages conveyed at these meetings were consistent and had the effect of reinforcing the party's message among the local faithful. For USPD members, the greatest threat to their position was the remilitarization of German society, which in Munich was represented by the *Einwohnerwehr* movement. The USPD was one of the few large parties (the KPD being the other) not represented in the

96 "Das Dankfest." ZS 218, StdAM.

97 "Nationale Kundgebung auf dem Standkonzert in der Feldhernhalle." June 26, 1919. RwGrKdo 4, 347, BHStA IV.

98 "Stimmungsbericht." June 24, 1919. RwGrKdo 4, 347, BHStA IV.

99 "Wirtschaftverbot für Militärpersonnel RwGrKdo 4." July 23, 1919. RwGrKdo 4, 20. BHStA IV.

Einwohnerwehr, and it was not difficult to see why. After the disaster of May, the spectrum of militias seemed an enormous threat to the USPD's political survival. There was also a less tangible reason for the USPD's intense distrust of militias. As Feuchtwanger pointed out, the violent experiences of May left personal memories sharply at odds with the official portrayal of Munich's "liberation" in May.

> Troops called 'Special Volunteers,' temporarily put into uniform and responsible to no-body, had shot down at sight countless men, women, and children. The Government pretended to ignore the fact, but victims' relatives had not forgotten it, and men who were naturally peaceable were still burning for revenge and battle.[100]

The party of Eisner was in disarray for the first half of 1919, its supporters increasingly marginalized in the constellation of political power in Munich. The USPD's fortunes changed dramatically, however, after the municipal elections. One military intelligence report on the outcome of the municipal elections suggested that the USPD's membership was expected to react noisily to the outcome of the vote. "The USPD comported itself well.... At all of the polling places in the western part of the city the situation was the same – they were confident of their victory."[101]

At a meeting in July, a speaker named Hierl told a crowd of about 150 at the *Tirolerhof* that there were four enemies of socialism: capitalism, red-tapeism (*Burokratismus*), militarism, and clericalism. Though socialists had a duty to teach young Germans to avoid all of these, the worst was militarism:

One could argue that we as teachers have nothing to do with [militarism], but this would be wrong.... Consider a formation of soldiers in steel helmets or trooping through the streets on horseback. The strongest impression that they leave will be on the young people who watch them pass.[102]

While this critique of the continued militarization of German society was clearly aimed at the paramilitary formations that played a role in the crushing of the Munich Soviet in May, it also avoided pointing to specific groups, probably because in the election season it was unwise to risk alienating potential voters whose loyalties might lie somewhere along the spectrum of political identities that made up the militia formations. By the end of the year, however, the USPD's attention had fallen on the *Einwohnerwehr* issue. Calling it a "circumvention of the peace accord," a speaker at the anniversary celebration in November asked:

---

100 Lion Feuchtwanger, *Success*, trans. Willa Muir and Edwin Muir (New York: Viking, 1930), 439.

101 "Betreff: Beobachtung Westend I und II," June 16, 1919. RwGrKdo 4 451, BHStA IV.

102 Report on meeting of USP Section Westend II, July 17, 1919. RwGrKdo 4, 459. BHStA Iv.

> Is the Entente aware that before the war Bavaria had 80,000 men under arms and that after the war it could have only 20,000 more – yet now we count 400,000 men in uniform? ... The organization of the *Einwohnerwehr* is against the Entente. What does the Entente imagine that it is going to do about this? (applause)[103]

The victorious powers were aware of the *Einwohnerwehr*, and shortly thereafter they began to take more and more aggressive steps to force the Bavarian government to abandon the militia.[104] In a report written at the end of the year, a military intelligence officer concluded that while the *Einwohnerwehr* situation remained very much in flux, the public seemed much better disposed toward the *Reichswehr* after their "well disciplined and controlled manner" during the disputes over the celebration of the anniversary of the end of the war.[105]

If the attitude of the population toward the *Reichswehr* was improving, as the author of that report clearly hoped it was, then there were also clear signs that the citizens of Munich transferred their grievances toward the government readily from the Royal/Imperial state to the sequence of successor regimes. At the heart of these resentments was the sense that the war had created manifest inequalities that demobilization had failed to rectify. In May, a report from the headquarters of the Prussian commander of the "liberation" suggested the emphatic nature of some of these complaints.

> The feeling among the out-of-work is very much against the Hoffman regime. They find it a great injustice that they were the first to have their benefits cut.... According to them, they have plenty of weapons. Where these can be found is not forthcoming. They assume everyone is a police spy.[106]

In the streets of Munich, the population readily linked the continued downward spiral of the economy with the war and the limits of demobilization. The economic crises of the war years seemed to be worsening, and for those who had served in some capacity this seemed all the more unfair.

This language of rights and privileges based on war service was one of the most important and effective rhetorical devices available to civil society in the

---

103 "Versammlung der USP Section Schwabing-Ost," November 12, 1919. RwGrKdo 4, 451, BHStA IV.

104 Early evidence of concerns about the power of the *Einwohnerwehr* among Allied officials can be found in the May, 1920 report "Compte-Rendu des Opérations de Controle pour la Périod du Ier au 7 Mai." Prepared by Col. Moreigne, District de Munich. RwGrKdo 4, 187. BHStA IV.

105 "Bericht über die innenpolitische Lage, Anfang December 1919." December 9, 1919. RwGrKdo 4, 289. BHStA IV.

106 "Stimmungsbericht." Kdo v. Oven. May 31, 1919. Initialed by Maj. Prager, RwGrKdo 4, 347. BHStA IV.

postwar period. It became entrenched in political discourse by the end of the war. As authorities and civil society negotiated the terms under which German society would rebuild, it was heard more often.

In Munich, 1919 saw the rise and fall of a series of governments, each promising to fix the unjust and inequitable legacies of mobilization. They faced a population that imbibed years of promises that life would improve once the war ended. Defeat did not save postwar governments from living up to wartime obligations because civil society believed that the promises made to them did not depend on victory. As "normal" life resumed after the chaos of 1919, the postwar order confronted the same challenges of economic, physical, and bureaucratic demobilization that effected states across Europe. In Munich and Bavaria, demobilization reflected the complexities and inefficiencies of wartime mobilization. For them, and for people across Europe, the next years proved crucial as governments and civil societies negotiated the terms of a world beyond the war.

SECTION III
"The Dregs of this Bitter Chalice:" Crisis and the End of Demobilization, 1920–21

The English writer and politician Norman Angell was one of the most famous members of that remarkable pre-1914 cohort of optimistic antiwar intellectuals. For Angell, and many like him, the events of four years of war seemed to undo many of the hopeful assumptions upon which they had based their fundamental ideas and appeals. In 1921, he published *The Fruits of Victory*, a sardonically-titled re-assessment of his famously confident masterpiece *The Great Illusion* of 1911:

> The real 'economic argument' against war does not consist in the presentation of a balance sheet showing so much cost and destruction and so much gain. The real argument consists in the fact that war, and still more the ideas out of which it arises, produce ultimately an unworkable society.[1]

Much as Angell and those who followed him were wrong about the economic impossibility of war, they were wrong about the ultimate consequences of armed conflict. European societies became workable again in the years after 1918. They did so through a process of negotiation, confrontation, and sometimes conflict. This restoration of workability lay at the heart of the project of demobilization, a period during which Europeans and their governments transitioned from war to postwar.

Just as it is difficult to assign a beginning to the demobilization of European societies, it is equally problematic to define precisely when the period of demobilization ended. Since the legacies of the First World War shaped and informed politics in Europe for decades after the end of the armed conflict in 1918, it seems perverse to suggest that demobilization "ended" at a definite point during the postwar period. Yet clearly the intense stresses of demobilization eased, or were transformed, in the years after the war. This section considers how the period of demobilization transitioned into a period that can be definitively called "postwar."

In previous sections, we have considered the similar sets of debates ongoing in victorious Manchester and defeated Munich. As civil society and authorities negotiated over the course of demobilization, pragmatic concerns over the postwar

---

1 Norman Angell, *The Fruits of Victory* (New York: Century, 1921), 59.

transition became suffused with the language of social revolution, radicalizing those debates and fostering a real and perceived danger of renewed social violence.

At the same time, the dismantling of wartime institutions and the culture of wartime proceeded, however unevenly, across the former combatant states. By the early 1920s, the last regulations and institutions designed to bolster the war effort were dismantled or fell into disuse. While Europeans by no means forgot about the war, its regimen no longer defined everyday life in the way that it had for six years. Life in wartime ceased to be everyday life across much of the continent.

In both of these cities, the end of the demobilization period was marked by crises that both drew from preexisting ruptures in wartime society and shaped the political future of the cities, their regions, and their respective national polities. Most importantly, the crises of 1920 and 1921 had profoundly different effects on the political culture of the two cities. This divergence marked a moment of real transition, even if this was by no means clear at the time.

The crises of 1920–21 reinforced the importance of wartime mobilization strategies in the postwar world and the ensuing debates over sacrifice and reciprocity. Instruments of wartime mobilization and control continued to function into the early 1920s, strengthening the linkages that many saw between the war years and their aftermath. The decisions taken during wartime continued to shape the range of possibilities in the postwar world and to frame the ways in which ordinary Europeans thought about their relationship with their governments and each other.

Both cities witnessed significant unrest during this period, with episodic but terrifying outbreaks of real and rhetorical violence. The war continued to function as the primary legitimating element for political claims of all kinds. In both cities, dissenters characterized the postwar domestic settlement as a failure and continued to demand that their respective states provide the rewards promised during the years of war. The way in which dissenters framed those demands, however, varied widely. In Manchester, the state and local institutions continued to be seen as an instrument through which reform could be possible if authorities could be convinced of the necessity to do so. In Munich, those same institutions came to be widely viewed as an impediment to real substantive reform. This continuation of the bitter and sometimes violent disputes of the previous years served to further delegitimize the postwar order and, just as important, to legitimize radical alternatives on the right and left.

In Manchester, the crisis appeared in the Spring of 1921, when a set of forces converged and convinced many observers that the fragile social peace after the war was unraveling. A surge in labor militancy threatened to culminate in a massive coordinated strike originating in lingering debates over decontrol from the last years of the war. At the same time, Manchester played host to a violent outgrowth of the Irish Civil War. When this new war came to Manchester, public response drew on related fears of criminality and moral decay that emerged from 1914–18. These two simultaneous events had a profound effect on public opinion with important consequences for the city's future.

For Manchester's powerful and assertive community of organized dissenters, this dual-headed crisis was a disaster. The presence of very real violence, however low-intensity, resulted in widespread rejection of violence as a means to achieve political and social goals more broadly. When combined with the inherent conservatism of many of the dissenting groups within Mancunian society, the crisis of 1921 significantly reduced the political space available to radical variants of reform.

In Munich the crisis began earlier, at the beginning of 1920. A military coup in Berlin had significant repercussions in southern Germany as a band of conservative military adventurers seized power in Munich. They claimed political legitimacy based on their willingness and ability to right the wrongs of demobilization and to restore the order that many felt had vanished in the wake of 1918. The weeks before the coup had been marked by a surge in street protests, so the plotters had every reason to believe that their appeal would fall on fertile ground.

Aside from the change of government, the events of March 1920 had two long-term effects on Munich's political culture. First, it seemed to legitimize the use or threat of armed intervention to achieve political gains. Second, and just as pernicious, the coup opened wide political space for different variants of radical social and political thought.

This section explores this important period of transition as the last wartime controls were lifted, durable postwar political arrangements came into existence, and the war itself began to recede into memory. The culture of war persisted, but shifted to a battle over how the conflict would be commemorated and the ownership of those memories. Just as the war shaped the range of possible outcomes in the period immediately following the end of hostilities, the crises of 1920–21 helped to establish the range of possible outcomes in the years and decades after the end of the war and the institutions that helped to make it possible.

Chapter 6

Ordeal by Peace: Manchester, 1920–21

The largest May Day 1920 celebration in Manchester had all of the hallmarks of popular demonstrations in postwar industrial England. It was, above all, a family affair, with sports, games, food, and the crowning of a May Queen on Ardwick Green. Despite the fact that it was organized by the loose coalition of Trades Councils, Socialists, Co-operators, and Labour that emerged from the war two years before, there was little outward sign of the sort of revolutionary specter that had preyed on the minds of city and national authorities. "The bulk of the people," wrote the *Manchester Evening News*, "have shown common sense as usual. The wild men, though noisier than ever, did not get their way."[1]

The political business of the day got underway after the demonstrators marched from Ardwick to Belle Vue Gardens, the amusement park that during the war served as a production facility for armaments. Representatives of a number of groups addressed the audience, including a speaker from the National Union of Ex-Servicemen. The topics of the day centered around the slowing postwar economy and the growing problems of unemployment and underemployment. The *Manchester Evening News* acidly commented that:

> High wages alone are not enough. Accompanying them ought to be honest work, the equivalent of the money which is paid. We fear however that this form of service has lost some of its old-time popularity. After the upheaval of the war perhaps this was inevitable.[2]

The most radical voice that day came from Harry Webb, who addressed the audience as "Comrades and Fellow Bolsheviks." This salutation was immediately picked up by the local press and cited as an example of the movement's growing radicalism. The Co-Operative Society in their capacity as organizers of the event later publicly disavowed Webb, calling his remarks "totally opposed to the principles of the Co-operative Movement."[3]

---

1 "The Labour Problem." *Manchester Evening News* (*MEN*), May 3, 1920. Information about the demonstration from program for "May Day Demonstration and Gala" Collection of Mr. and Mrs. B. Caldicott, Manchester Archives, MISC/718/68.

2 Ibid.

3 "Against Extremists," *MEN*, May 10, 1920. This may be the same Harry Webb who later served with George Orwell in Spain, as recounted in *Homage to Catalonia*.

The best-known of the speakers that May Day was J.R. Clynes, elected in 1920 as the Parliamentary Chairman of the Labour Party. Clynes was born to a mill-working family in Oldham and had established himself as a voice of moderation and conciliation within the party and beyond. During the war, he succeeded Lord Rhondda as Food Controller, and the growing strength of Labour in Parliament seemed to suggest that he was a likely future Prime Minister.[4] It was surprising then that the reception Clynes received was far more hostile than what might be expected for a successful native son. Clynes would quickly regret accepting the invitation as large sections of the crowd turned on him audibly.

Clynes found himself roundly booed by two critical constituencies, radical organized labor and the Irish. When he rose to address the crowds at Belle Vue, the "wild men" managed to make enough noise that he was unable to continue with his speech. Shortly thereafter, Clynes found himself among a crowd of Irish Mancunians, most of whom were female, who assailed in a "lively and unsympathetic" manner the policies of Clynes and other Labour moderates on the Irish issue.[5] Labour continued to support Home Rule but was not yet prepared to support independence for Ireland. Six months after this, facing pressure from Irish constituents in Britain and mounting violence in Ireland, the party had a change of heart on the issue and ended its opposition to independence.[6]

J.R. Clynes's experience with the Manchester electorate on May Day nicely encapsulated the political fortunes of the city in the years following 1919. The issue of unemployment continued to occupy the forefront of debates about Britain's political and industrial future. At the same time, the problems in Ireland took on new and dangerous dimensions as Home Rule and the civil war across the Irish Sea spilled over into episodic but sometimes deadly violence in Manchester and other English cities. At the same time, ordinary Mancunians tried to assess the results of the war two years on. While much of the physical, bureaucratic, and economic demobilization was either completed or well underway, the cultural aspects of the demobilization struggles had only begun.

During these years, when the danger of red revolution seemed to be receding, questions remained about what the workers of Lancashire and Cheshire had sacrificed to gain. For the increasingly organized veterans' movement, the government's unwillingness to grant the concessions they sought seemed to call into question the legitimacy of the demobilization project. While their protests generally remained within the boundaries of loyalty, authorities feared the potential for radicalization. The growth of radical movements within organized labor and within Manchester's Irish community exacerbated these fears. In 1921, both of these forces mobilized for a confrontation with the postwar government.

4 This was not to be. Clynes was replaced as Chairman by Ramsay McDonald after MacDonald, who lost his seat in 1918, was re-elected in the 1922 General Election.

5 "Mr Clynes and the Irish," *MEN*, May 4, 1920.

6 Michael Herbert, *The Wearing of the Green: A Political History of the Irish in Manchester*. (London: Irish in Britain Representation Group, 2001), 100.

The results only confirmed the trends that shaped Britain's wartime mobilization and demobilization.

In his 1940 *History of Local Government in Manchester*, Arthur Redford summarized these years as a time when "the glamour of 'Reconstruction' was wearing thin, but the problems of reconstruction remained urgent and were now seen to be more complicated than had at first been realized…. The ordeal by war was over for the time being, but the ordeal by peace was only just beginning."[7] Clearly the ordeal by peace proved much less destructive than its predecessor, yet for many contemporary observers, this was by no means clear at the time.

While the demobilization of British society was deeply flawed in the eyes of many ordinary Britons, by 1920 the fears of imminent violence largely diminished even as formal institutions of dissent like the Communist Party of Great Britain emerged from the inchoate discontent of the immediate postwar period. Still, the strike wave that followed the end of the war showed no sign of abating, gradually becoming more of a quotidian nuisance than a harbinger of red revolution.

The revolutionary moment, it seemed, had passed without major incident. What were the boundaries of this ordeal that kept it from expanding into violence or large-scale civic disturbance? Why did the most drastic threat of labor actions during this period, the Triple Alliance strike of April 1921, dissipate without effect?

The answers are twofold. First, dissenting groups in postwar Britain never rallied around a common cause and were bitterly divided across a spectrum from constitutional to revolutionary.[8] For reasons already discussed, organized dissenters faced tremendous pressure to state their demands within a loyal and system-supporting framework, marginalizing the truly radical groups within. Second, the Irish issue was critical in Manchester and other cities with significant immigrant populations. This was not a revolutionary situation, but rather was part of the broader nationalities question in Europe during the postwar period. It should be considered an issue of civic order, along with the perceived crime wave in postwar Britain. While there was certainly overlap between these variants, their interests tended to diverge rather than intersect.

The less-than-welcoming crowd that greeted J.R. Clynes on May Day is a great example of this divergence. During 1920–21, the extent to which a "revolutionary situation" existed in Manchester or the country as a whole in the wake of the war depended entirely on the perspective of the observer. While there was clearly

7 Arthur Redford, *The History of Local Government in Manchester*, vol. 3 (London: Longmans, Green, and Co., 1940), 223.

8 A very good analysis of these divisions can be found in Chris Wrigley, "The State and the Challenge of Labor in Britain, 1917–20" in Chris Wrigley, ed. *The Challenges of Labour: Central and Western Europe, 1917–20* (London: Routledge, 1993), 263. See also Paul Ward's fascinating study of the relationship between loyalty and labor in Britain *Red Flag and Union Jack: Englishness, Patriotism, and the British Left, 1881–1924* (Woodbridge and Rochester: Royal Historical Society and the Boydell Press, 1998).

a violent faction within the labor movement, it had to contend with a larger contingent that had participated loyally in a more than four-year mobilization and was still determined to press its case for rewards. In this way, the demobilization crisis actually hindered the radicalization of the labor movement, by providing a compelling reason to remain within the bounds of loyal opposition.

The problem of order, particularly the violence within the Irish community, was also critical. The Irish crisis in Manchester had two important results. The first is that it represented yet another schism in the already fractious world of labor, particularly since the Irish population in the Northwest represented one of the most consistent sources of Labour voters.[9] The Irish population was divided among itself, and significant numbers of Irish voters were alienated from the Labour Party over Irish affairs. Second, the growing violence of 1920 and 1921 placed a further stigma on "disloyal" activities by other groups, engendering widespread disgust with street violence and terrorism.[10] While discussions of Irish nationalism and violence rarely explicitly invoked the war, it is only by placing this story within the context of debates about loyalty that were instrumental in the demobilization process that we can understand the role played by Irish nationalism in the story of postwar English society.

Unemployment, Morality, and Housing in Manchester

The *Manchester Guardian*, as the threatened Triple Alliance Strike loomed in 1921, captured this sense of impending doom and its perceived origins in the experiences of war and demobilization. The crime wave, problems in Ireland, and labor troubles reminded the editors that:

> We know how, in the main, it has all come about. We had to fight the greatest of wars and we are getting some of the wounds of it now. *Most of us, in all classes, were wounded in purse, wounded in character, wounded in our faith in things we took for granted as true before the war*. We have had darling illusions bled to death and cherished symbols shown up as old rags.[11]

For many contemporaries, the problems of unemployment, the slow pace of housing reform, and the perceived decline in public morality were really one. The war served as the thread that bound all of these crises together. At the heart of

9 Trevor Griffiths, *The Lancashire Working Classes, c. 1880–1930* (Oxford: Clarendon, 2001), 319.

10 This is clearly a morally freighted term that I use advisedly. Contemporary language tended to refer to "incendiarism." As Walter Laqueur helpfully reminds us in his recent *Voices of Terror* (New York: Reed Press, 2004), the term until fairly recently was "a 'value free' strategy that could be used for all kinds of causes." 2.

11 "Before the Dawn?," *Manchester Guardian* (*MG*), April 14, 1921. [Italics mine.]

this pervasive sense of disquiet and disappointment lay the widely held belief that the British state missed its chance to carry out real reform in the wake of the war. While this perception masked important changes then underway, it was nonetheless broadly believed and influenced the reactions of ordinary Mancunians and Britons to demobilization.

The promised postwar boom, as we have seen previously, did not provide a more than transitory sense of relief in Manchester and its surroundings. Aside from the difficulties inherent in converting the region's industries back to a peacetime footing, the nature of the international market had changed. Other centers of cotton production in South Asia and Egypt developed in response to the drop in Lancashire's production during the war. Exports of cotton yarn in 1920 were down about 24 percent by weight from 1913, and the next year the number dipped by roughly the same percentage. Coal exports, another key indicator of the health of the economy in Lancashire and Cheshire, dropped dramatically during the same period, with the 1921 figures only about a quarter of the prewar tonnage.[12] This was part of a general decline of British exports that fell particularly hard on industrial regions like Manchester and its environs.[13]

One of the most dramatic and ultimately important consequences of the general crisis of the postwar economy was widespread unemployment. Britain introduced unemployment insurance with the National Insurance Act of 1911 and demobilization planners were relatively confident that this would ease the transition for military personnel and demobilized workers. Further measures passed in 1920 made the majority of workers eligible, but by that time, the scale of unemployment surpassed even the most pessimistic projections of the new Act's parliamentary champions. Alfred Havighurst characterized the Act, which by July 1921 was supporting more than 2,000,000 workers (roughly 22 percent of the total), as "a mass of piecemeal legislation."[14] This lamentably typical arrangement, in which well-meaning but conflicting bureaucracies doled out aid to a confused and increasingly irritated population, reminded many of the war years and inspired some degree of nostalgia for the clarity of purpose of 1914–18. In addition, contemporaries connected the problems of unemployment with the perceived crisis of morality in postwar Britain. Remedies for the former, it seemed to observers, would have a salutary effect on the latter.

Relief plans for the unemployed, however well intended, ran into difficulties as they transferred the burdens of unemployment into a kind of institutionalized underemployment. As it had during the war years, the private sector was expected

12 Co-operative Press Agency, *The People's Year Book, 1922* (Manchester: Co-Operative Wholesale Society, 1992), 323.

13 Alfred Havighurst, *Britain in Transition* (Chicago: University of Chicago Press, 1985), 159. As Havighurst and others note, Britain's economic woes in the early 1920s were not general. Farmers, for instance, did somewhat better after the war than before. Debates continue as to whether Britain's decline was absolute or relative.

14 Havighurst, 169–70, 160.

to act as the primary engine of economic recovery. In the Northwest, were industrial transition after 1918 proved exceptionally difficult, such hopes often came to little.

While Labour Exchanges made up the bulk of relief efforts, government hiring schemes that favored veterans proved to be inefficient and resulted in wage cutbacks. These cuts, in turn, outraged veterans. Early in his term as Lord Mayor, E.D. Simon visited the Aytoun Street Labour Exchange, which at the time serviced about 16,000 unemployed, of whom 10,000 received their wages through the exchange. On both Thursday and Friday, 5,000 unemployed lined up to receive their wages. The rest were paid by their unions. The Lord Mayor was impressed by the orderliness of the sizable crowd, which required just two policemen to supervise it.

While Simon claimed to be happy with the work being done by the Labour Exchange, he was undoubtedly less sanguine about the delegation of veterans who awaited him at the exchange, complaining about their wages. Over the past several weeks, the men told the Mayor, their hourly wages for work done for the Corporation had declined from 1s. 5 ½d. per hour to 1s. ¾d. Simon evidently turned the matter over to the City Engineer who was accompanying the visit. When the engineer said that nothing could be done "the men went away disappointed, but without disorder."[15]

Contemporaries readily saw the inextricable connection between the questions of demobilization and unemployment, a linkage most apparent in the figure of the jobless veteran begging or selling small trinkets. One such ex-serviceman (or one who identified himself as such), picked up by police on the streets of Manchester during the postwar period, sold postcards for 2d bearing a "Discharged Soldier's Appeal."

> I have served my country faithfully
> And have given of my best
> In this war for Right and Freedom
> Facing death and worse with jest
>
> Risking life and limb whilst "slackers"
> 'Neath their precious War Badge hide
> Why should they not take their chances
> In the roll of battle's tide?[16]

This language is very similar to that used by dissenters during the last years of the war, drawing upon a reservoir of discontent about the fairness of the war effort while staking in clear terms a claim to loyalty, service, and the obligations of the postwar state. The veteran, both in person and as a symbol, was a powerful reminder

---

15 Clipping from December 7, 1921. Papers of Lord and Lady Simon, Manchester Archives, M/14/4/1.

16 Postcard in the school tour collection, Greater Manchester Police Archive.

of what appeared to be the failure of postwar reconstruction. The veteran's service, in this case literally inscribed onto his body and thus entirely self-evident, acted as a tangible reminder of the evident lack of reciprocity.

The disabled veteran was a particularly potent symbol, both as a signifier of the war's destruction and as a living reminder of the obligations that many felt were owed to those who had suffered because of the war. Joanna Bourke, in her highly original study of masculinity and disability, has pointed to the connection between disablement in dangerous prewar industrial labor conditions and the physical damage done to frontline soldiers at war. Those most grievously affected by the war returned home with uncertain prospects, in competition for jobs with able-bodied veterans, civilians who had not been in uniform, and those disabled by accident or birth defects.[17] As both an icon and an everyday reality, the disabled soldier came to represent the perceived injustice of the demobilization project. While Deborah Cohen has argued that the efforts of the British public saved the government embarrassment over its treatment of the disabled, it is also clear that, in the years of demobilization, those who criticized the project of demobilization could and did readily draw upon the obvious problems of integrating the war's victims into the postwar world.[18] The state, it seemed, was unwilling to live up to its wartime commitments, even to those who most obviously required that support. Not only the disabled, but anyone who served could and did deploy this type of rhetoric.

The problem of veterans now facing unemployment in urban centers drew national attention as benevolent organizations took a more prominent role in relief and veterans' groups consolidated in the postwar period. Field Marshal Haig became one of the most prominent advocates of preferential treatment for veterans. Haig served as the first President of the British Legion, a coalition of smaller veterans' organizations dedicated to advocating for the rights of former combatants while channeling veterans away from radical politics. Haig provoked a round of national patriotic introspection when he claimed in June 1920 that there were more than 200,000 unemployed veterans, of whom more than 10 percent were disabled.

Nearly a year later, Lord Mayor Kay sounded a hollow note of surprise when he claimed that "My attention has been called to the great amount of distress which exists and likely to increase among my fellow citizens, both ex-service men and others, in consequence of the stagnation of trade." He suggested establishing a Lord Mayor's fund to be paid by public subscription in the hope of coordinating various relief efforts under his office.[19] The *Manchester Evening News* suggested that conflicts between unions and management were to blame and that:

---

17 Joanna Bourke, *Dismembering the Male: Men's Bodies, Britain, and the Great War* (Chicago: University of Chicago Press, 1996), 31.

18 Deborah Cohen, *The War Come Home: Disabled Veterans in Britain and Germany, 1914–1939* (Berkeley: University of California Press, 2001), 7.

19 "Unemployed Relief in Manchester," *MG*, April 8, 1921.

> the dominating thought in the consideration of this business should be that but for the sacrifice and the heroism of this noble band of out-of-works and their comrades this island of ours, and all it contains, would now be under the heel of the Hun.[20]

Suggestions for relief of unemployment among veterans came from both government and civil society. Wilson Carlile wrote to the city on behalf of the Church Army, which he founded and led, volunteering its services to raise money and provide jobs for veterans. The Church Army, founded in 1882, was a Church of England-sanctioned evangelical movement that attempted to apply military-style organization to missionary work. Their efforts to become a part of the solution to the problem of unemployment among veterans reflected both a desire for recognition by the government and their need for men with military training in the organization:

> A very large department is dealing with the problem of UNEMPLOYMENT amongst EX-SERVICE MEN. Over 7,000 men have been placed in situations (including a large number of badly disabled men) and in many cases help has been given in the form of clothing, shelter, fares, etc. Help in the latter direction is especially useful as it is outside the scope of most exchanges... Other departments exist for training ex-Service men for trades and able-bodied work in FARM work for EMIGRATION; for providing recreation, etc; for men in the Armies of Occupation on the Rhine and elsewhere; and for escorting relatives of fallen men to visit the graves of their loved ones in France and Belgium.[21]

The Church Army, which had taken an active evangelizing role among British troops during the war, could in the postwar period derive considerable legitimacy from its wartime service. Still, while it purported to represent the interests of veterans (even if only the Christian or Anglican servicemen), it was not strictly speaking a veterans' organization.[22] While there is no record of the success or failure of the Church Army's application to hold such a demonstration, it is fairly clear from the surviving minutes of the Watch Committee that groups which explicitly sought to hold demonstrations that connected unemployment and veterans' issues were often refused, while other civic groups with social concerns were more successful. In July 1921, for instance, Flag Day celebrations by the Manchester, Salford & District Ex-Servicemen's Joint Council and the Jewish National Fund Commission were approved, while applications from the Manchester and District

20 "A National Duty," *MEN*, June 10, 1920.

21 Letter from Wilson Carlile, Secretary, Church Army (London) to Lord Mayor. January, 1920. Greater Manchester Police Archive, General Orders 85/125.

22 For more information on the changing role of civic organizations in the wake of the First World War, see Adam R. Seipp, "A League of Youth: Boy Scouting, Youth, and War, 1907–1925" (MA Thesis, University of North Carolina, 2001).

Central Council of Unemployed Workers' Committees and the Unemployed Ex-Servicemen were turned down for no stated reason.[23]

Part of the problem for veterans was the profusion of such organizations during the last years of the war and the early postwar period. Groups like the National Federation of Discharged and Demobilized Soldiers and Sailors, the National Federation of Discharged and Demobilized Soldiers and Sailors, and the Comrades of the Great War were affiliated with major political parties and maintained fairly moderate aims. On the other hand, some of the veterans' organizations like the National Union of Ex-Servicemen (NUX) were quite radical in orientation. Radical groups had little success organizing in Manchester, but the confusion over which groups should be allowed to demonstrate seems to have emerged from uncertainty over which organizations were above suspicion.[24]

The British Legion began to bring more coherence to this network of veterans' groups, subsuming some rivals and marginalizing others.[25] This national trend is evident in the case of Manchester, where the Legion began to act as the preeminent voice of area veterans. In November 1921, the local branch of the Legion responded to growing frustration with authorities over the manifold failed and failing schemes for unemployment relief by suggesting their own. The Legion, which had conducted similar relief operations before, proposed to open several dining halls to provide cheap meals for men and their families. Costs emerged as an issue, as the unemployed had previously balked at subsidized meals costing as little as 2d. The Legion's proposal called for meals costing from 4–6d and it was unclear how much of a role municipal government was expected to play in underwriting the enterprise. Providing relief of this sort also presented a challenge to the mission of the Legion, since not all of the unemployed were veterans. In their presentation to the Council the Legion claimed that they "while affirming that ex-fighters must always have first claim on their services, are not averse from coming to some arrangement whereby civilian unemployed can be catered for also."[26]

The city did take an active role in attempting to reintegrate returning troops into municipal employment, at one point launching an investigation of this process that provides an interesting glimpse into the opportunities and potential problems of the transformation of the postwar economy. In October 1920, the Corporation demanded reports from various offices detailing the status of veterans in the City's employ. What they found was a snapshot of an ongoing process that was not always smooth or even, but that in the very least achieved its intended goal of providing some sort of work for demobilized troops who wanted it.

---

23 Street Collections Sub-Committee (Watch Committee) minutes. July 14, 1921. Greater Manchester Police Archive, 88/23.

24 Gerard DeGroot, *Blighty: British Society in the Era of the World Wars* (London: Longman, 1996), 266–7.

25 Brian Harding, *Keeping Faith: The History of the Royal British Legion* (London: Leo Cooper, 2001).

26 Clipping from Papers of Lord and Lady Simon. Manchester Archives, M/14/4/1.

About 40 percent of municipal employees in October 1920 were veterans, although some departments clearly intended to inflate their statistics, and thus their compliance, by counting veterans only as a percentage of their male employees. Given that one of the largest problems of the demobilization was the smooth transition from female to male labor, this was disingenuous to say the least. Tramways reported that they had employed 163 women at the outbreak of war and that this number rose to 259 by the Fall of 1920. "During the war a number of women were temporarily engaged to fill positions previously occupied by men," Tramways assured the council. "These positions have in all cases been vacated and the women replaced by men." The rise of female employment in the Gas Department was even more dramatic and durable, growing from 4 in 1914 to 50 in 1920. At the same time, both departments promised that they had re-hired all veterans who wanted their prewar jobs back.[27]

The Paving Department gave by far the most comprehensive answer to the Corporation's questions. During the war, 525 workers served in the military, of whom 58 were killed while a number of others were disabled, remained in the military after the war, or vanished. Paving claimed to have offered employment to the remaining 455 returning workers, all of whom evidently accepted the offer. Two years later, 309 veteran workers remained, while 394 additional veterans had been hired by the department.[28]

One of the most notable features of the rehiring of veterans was the high rate of turnover. Given the nature of the postwar economy, it is striking that so many employees would have voluntarily left secure employment to take their chances in the broader economy. A clue is buried in the response of the Police Department, which reported that 96 veterans had resumed employment, then left again, "the majority expressing themselves as being tired of discipline and restrictions."[29] It is not unreasonable to suppose that after years in uniform, the thought of returning to a position that required another uniform and adherence to another set of regulations might have discouraged returning troops. The Davyhulme Sewage Works saw dramatic turnover among new employees, with 381 of 516 workers hired after November 1918 leaving by late 1920. Sewage claimed, probably somewhat evasively, that they simply did not know how many of these employees were veterans. This lack of enthusiasm for their jobs among sewage workers probably does not need elaborate explanation.

Manchester emerged as one of the symbolic and physical centers of the unemployed movement in England. As conditions in the cotton and coal industries worsened, the region became known for its high rates of unemployment and underemployment. In April 1921, when the Triple Alliance strike was threatening,

27 "Report of Conference on Ex-Service Men and their Employment by the Corporation." October, 1920. *Manchester City Council Proceedings, 1919–20*, vol. 2 (Manchester: City of Manchester). 681.

28 Ibid., 683.

29 Ibid., 687.

there were 131,363 unemployed in Lancashire and Cheshire, a number that showed every sign of increasing before any relief might come.[30] At the same time, unemployment nationwide was growing rapidly as the economy cooled. The number of unemployed veterans rose to at least 500,000 across Britain.[31] In October, the King visited the city, where he dedicated a substantial portion of his public remarks to the region's unemployment problems and particularly to the relationship between unemployment and the war:

> I am sorely troubled by the present widespread unemployment, which is causing so much suffering to so many of my people. It is my sincere hope that the efforts of my Ministers to alleviate present and future unemployment may be successful. I earnestly pray that, by the blessing of Divine Providence, the united efforts of all classes of the community may wipe out the evil effects of the Great War, restore the commercial and productive activity of the Nation, and thus bring employment, well-being, and happiness to all my people.[32]

In 1921, the city hosted the second annual National Conference of the Unemployed Movement. Wal Hannington remembered a march from Gorton Town Hall to the railway stations and "a real feeling of strength and organisation amongst the unemployed."[33] The same month, in his inaugural address as Lord Mayor, E.D. Simon claimed that there were about 40,000 unemployed in the city, or roughly 6 percent of the total population. The Council, the new Lord Mayor asserted, was doing all that it could to provide jobs, despite "ludicrously inadequate" support from the national government.[34]

In addition to the political and economic dimensions of demobilization, observers made explicit connections between the end of the war and a general decline of moral values and respect for the law. These issues hinged on the supposed introduction of young men to the violence of combat and their incomplete reincorporation into the society they had left for the front. The result, worried observers, was an increase in violent crime, dangerous sexuality, and an apparent blurring of gender divisions that threatened the social order.

One particularly poignant case from 1920 concerned John Quinn of Droylsden, accused by his wife of "persistent cruelty" largely stemming from his drinking. Quinn was a disabled soldier on a pension and while he admitted to heavy drinking and treating his wife Mary-Jane poorly, he told the magistrate that "It's the war that has

---

30 "Lancashire and Cheshire Unemployment," *MG*, April 1, 1921.

31 DeGroot, 261.

32 *Manchester City Council Proceedings, 1920–21*. Vol. I (Manchester: City of Manchester, 1921), 559.

33 Wal Hannington, *Unemployed Struggles, 1919–1936* (London: Lawrence and Wishart, 1936), 45.

34 Inaugural Address given on November 10, 1921. Papers of Lord and Lady Simon, Manchester Archives, M/14/4/1.

affected me, not the drink."[35] While the court reporter let this pass without comment, it seems reasonably clear in hindsight that Quinn was one of the millions of Europeans who emerged from the war with psychological trauma, then poorly understood.[36]

Added to the problems of those genuinely physically or emotionally afflicted by the war was the presence of some number of conmen who played on the sympathies of the public. Correspondence between the Manchester police and the Ministry of Pensions suggests that the Ministry was concerned enough about such solicitations to actively investigate those who sought charity as disabled veterans. One such individual, who called himself "W Wilkinson," approached businesses in the city center with a note reading "Kind friend, I have lost my speech and one finger in the war and I keep a wife and one child. Can you please help me by giving 1d or 2d for food? I only get 9/6d pension."[37] The Ministry, which had a keen interest in avoiding suggestions that pensions paid to the most visible victims of wartime trauma were inadequate, concluded that there was no such person on their rolls.[38]

Even if the psychological impact of war on individual combatants was not extensively studied, contemporaries clearly saw the connections between the war and the real or perceived "crime wave" of the postwar period. This was particularly true of sensational crimes like the murders and assaults that were a boon for the inexpensive press of the day. "All great wars have been followed by unrest, discontent, and an epidemic of crime," warned the *Manchester Evening News* in 1920, "and present prevalence of deeds of violence is not unexpected." Its explanation of the rise of violent crime was an ironic mirror of concerns about demobilized soldiers and sailors returning to their old jobs.

> The sacredness of human life is not what it used to be. The able manhood of this country has been taught the art of killing, and practised it for four or five years as part of his daily duty. Criminals who served in the army, some-times with credit and distinction, have returned upon demobilisation to their old avocation, and are disposed to take more risks than in the pre-war days. Many of them possess firearms, know through army training how to use them, and have no scruples about shedding blood to gain their ends.[39]

Concerns about the brutalization of British men returning from the war was widespread. While there does not appear to have been a significant rise in crime

35 "Not Drink, But the War," *MEN*, January 21, 1920.

36 For a good overview of the literature on veterans and PTSD, see Eric Dean, *Shook Over Hell: Post-Traumatic Stress, Vietnam, and the Civil War* (Cambridge: Harvard University Press, 1997).

37 Letter from Ministry of Pensions to Chief Constable's Office. February 18, 1920. Greater Manchester Police Archive, General Orders 1920/18.

38 Cohen, 2.

39 "The Crime Wave," *MEN*, January 21, 1920.

after the war, there were enough spectacular cases, some of which involved soldiers, to create a panic. Britain's modern gun laws have their origin with the 1920 Firearms Bill, which seems to have been a response to fears of an armed and trained citizenry. Furthermore, a series of high-profile riots in cities like Liverpool and Glasgow seemed to indicate a decline in respect for law and order.[40]

A local bank manager remarked that the most effective response to such trained and armed robbers was to arm tellers, a process made more difficult by the continuation of wartime regulations on gun ownership. "We have every confidence that our branch clerks will cope with a dangerous situation well. Many of them are ex-soldiers – resolute young men, with no timidity about them, and with as much knowledge of firearms" as their would-be assailants.[41]

The demobilization of British society brought about, largely through its unevenness, a set of concerns about the moral health of the citizenry, particularly the younger members of society. Early attempts to manage the transition between uniformed service and civil society through charity or the private sector frequently became enmeshed in sometimes ham-handed attempts to mold the moral life of demobilized men. As demobilization proceeded and the unemployment situation worsened, concerns about public morality and unemployment intersected and fostered something of a moral panic. Even dancing, declared the editor of the *Dancing Times*, declined in the postwar years as "Bolshevism has crept into the ballroom."[42]

Discussions about the moral effects of the war even found their way into evolving questions about the relationship between gender and work. In July 1920, a local leader of an unnamed women workers' union commented that men were now applying for jobs as domestic help that had previously been the exclusive domain of women. "The unsettling influence of the Great War is largely responsible for this. Women are now seeking less exacting occupations, because they have become used to more freedom."[43] While this perception of emasculated men seeking traditionally female jobs existed, the reality was somewhat different. Labour Exchanges began to push women back toward domestic work, in large part to further remove them from competition with men for scarce places in industry.[44]

With moral concerns like this in mind, various schemes to deal with the problem of unemployment tended to include provisions for the moral education of the unemployed. These plans sometimes came from city authorities, as when a special committee on unemployment announced the establishment of small shelters for the unemployed during the winter of 1921 in order to give the jobless

40 Jon Lawrence, "Forging a Peaceable Kingdom: War, Violence, and Fear of Brutalization in Post-First World War Britain," *Journal of Modern History* 75 (September 2003): 562–71.

41 "Bank Clerks Arming," *MEN*, January 21, 1920.

42 "Crazy Dancers," *MEN*, May 13, 1920.

43 "The Domesticated Man," *MEN*, July 28, 1920.

44 DeGroot, 263.

a warm place for "reasonable recreation, self-expression, and self-development." Of course, the rules of such centers attempted to facilitate a particular model of self-development:

> No speeches or displayed notices of a political party propagandistic character are allowed in the centers; that gambling and betting are prohibited; and that the rights to use the centers may be forfeited by, and withdrawn from, any men whose conduct is detrimental to the good conduct and best interests of the social centers.[45]

In keeping with the uneven division between public and private sector relief in postwar Britain, such plans did not necessarily emerge only from municipal authorities. At a disastrous 1921 Town Hall conference on the unemployment problem, the YMCA proposed to set up social centers as part of a plan to "make more tolerable the lot of the unemployed in Manchester." These centers were to "improve their minds by means of classes and lectures, and their muscles by organised games." The unemployed at the conference evidently greeted these provisions with noisy derision. The representatives of the British Legion were equally, though more quietly, unimpressed. "We should regard it as the height of presumption" that a private organization would take control of a public project "to the exclusion of other bodies."[46] Of course, the British Legion had less of a problem when the private organization in question was themselves, as they demonstrated with their earlier, and admittedly less tutelary, program for feeding the unemployed. At another gathering of the unemployed at Town Hall that April, attended by nearly 1,500 jobless men, the proposal that "the worker's control of industry was the only solution for the problem of unemployment" carried by acclaim.[47] It was clear that for the mass of workers affected by the slump, existing programs for unemployment relief and job creation proved inadequate.

Just like the earlier transitional job programs that promised structure and moral instruction to returning soldiers and sailors, these attempts to mold the morality of the unemployed ran into stout resistance from those whose spirits were to be saved. In addition, the presence of the British Legion at the YMCA proposal reminds us of the growing power of veterans' groups to speak out in an organized fashion on behalf of ex-Servicemen. These civic organizations had not been nearly as well-organized or active in 1919, and their growing power to mobilize opinion among veterans suggested that they would be a force with which to be reckoned in the future. In any event, clumsy attempts to force moral education on the unemployed did not solve the pressing economic and social problems of demobilization and, in fact, seem to have worsened relations between the unemployed and municipal authorities.

---

45 Clipping from Papers of Lord and Lady Simon, Manchester Archives, M/14/4/1.

46 Clipping from Papers of Lord and Lady Simon. Manchester Archives. M/14/4/1.

47 "Manchester and the Unemployed," *MG*, April 8, 1921.

The failure of authorities to combat unemployment, real or perceived, was mirrored by a similar inability to tackle the problems in the housing industry. The evident and public crisis in urban housing was, if anything, more publicly manifest than any of the other postwar debates. In the most dramatic cases, half-finished shells of buildings provided an all-too-obvious reminder of the limits of reform. For reformers and observers alike, the most galling aspect of this obvious deficiency was the juxtaposition between rhetoric, institutional capacity building, and action. The means to resolve the endemic problem of housing appeared to exist, but the political will did not. Much like the unemployment problem, housing seemed to confirm the unwillingness of the state to act upon its wartime and postwar promises. In reality, there were other factors at work in the persistence of the housing crisis, but it proved an obvious example of government inaction.

At the end of January 1921, thousands of houses sat roofless in Greater Manchester. For fourteen days in the middle of a rainy Northern winter, workers walked away from the Corporation's ten new housing projects, threatening the loss of millions of pounds of materials and labor. The trouble started at the Blackley and Gorton estate, a planned community of more than 2,500 homes. A long-simmering dispute between plumbers and the powerful Heating and Domestic Engineers Joint Industrial Council sparked the walkout as the two unions could not agree as to which had the responsibility for laying hot water pipes to boilers inside the new dwellings. Since roofers could not work before the homes had plumbing, they, too, stood idle across the region.

Finally, on February 8, the Parliamentary Committee of the Trades Union Congress found for the plumbers and work resumed.[48]

Housing represented one of the most contentious and frustrating aspects of the demobilization effort at the local level. In the wake of the war, reformers who had been active for decades saw their moment emerging. Wartime rhetoric about real social transformation dovetailed with visions of slum clearance and affordable housing for residents of Manchester and the rest of industrial England. Perhaps in no other area were expectations so high, so well-intended, or so consistently frustrated. Despite earnest efforts by the national government to plan for and coordinate housing reform with local authorities and private concerns, problems of funding and the persistent effects of decontrol created situations like what happened during those two weeks in the winter of 1921.

Municipal authorities were broadly sympathetic here, since their interest in urban renewal (generally phrased as "the abolition of slums") coincided with the desire of those who had served in the war for the long-promised "homes fit for heroes to live in." Britain's looming postwar housing crisis did not escape the national government, which had studied the problem during the war under the auspices of the Ministry of Reconstruction. The Coalition made an effort to follow up on its promises with the passage of the Addison (Housing and Town Planning)

48 Various clippings and reports related to the incident can be found in TNA LAB 2/791/IR342/4/1921.

Act of 1919, which tried to finance the construction of dwellings through local governments. While the long-term impact of the Addison Act may have been salutary in that it helped shape the development of broader and more inclusive social policy, in the short term it was too little and too late. The public failure of housing reform eventually proved so embarrassing to the government that Addison resigned under pressure.[49]

By the Ministry of Reconstruction's own estimate, England and Wales emerged from the war with a net housing shortage of 300–400,000 homes, plus the large number of dwellings that were unsanitary or otherwise unsuitable for human habitation. If this had been an acute problem before the war, it now "must be solved as early as possible if we are to secure homes for returning soldiers … to prevent industrial employment, to secure adequate employment, and to remove one of the greatest causes of infant mortality and the spread of disease."[50] The solution, suggested the Ministry, should be a partnership between local government, private enterprise, and the state, which would take on the role of funding local improvement plans. It appeared to be an opportunity for reformers, who now possessed a committed ally in the national government and could henceforth assume that their visions of urban renewal would be a priority.

The results were less clear and, despite earnest efforts to provide funding for physical reconstruction, only contributed to the perception that the state was uninterested in living up to its promises. In Manchester, the progressive strain in city government fostered a climate in which some of the most vociferous critics of government inaction on housing came from within the municipal power structure. In August 1920, when Lord Mayor Tom Fox presided at the opening of the Blackley Estate off Victoria Avenue, he castigated the national government for its housing policy.

> If there was one thing at the moment which contributed to the social unrest which was rampant throughout the country, it was that the men who fought and bled for the country had come home again and found they had no homes. No one should wonder, in the circumstances, that there should be social unrest.[51]

At lunch that day, E.D. Simon suggested to Fox that perhaps the wartime command economy would be an effective model for solving the housing shortage. "They ought to introduce the priority system, as they did during the war. It was not popular, but we got the shells we wanted by it, and we would get the houses we wanted by it today.[52]

---

49 Paul Barton Johnson, *Land Fit for Heroes: The Planning of British Reconstruction, 1916–1919* (Chicago: University of Chicago Press, 1968), 495–9 and Havighurst, 169.

50 Pamphlet "Housing in England and Wales," Ministry of Reconstruction, 1918, 15.

51 Clipping in Papers of Lord and Lady Simon, Manchester Archives. M/14/3.

52 Ibid.

Reformer and Lord Mayor E.D. Simon emerged from the war with a radical new vision of Manchester, one that would, if implemented, not only create new housing, but would level much of the already decaying industrial heart of the city. This "new era of city development" would feature 50,000 acres of "either self-contained garden cities or dormitory cities with express transport to the center of Manchester, and [the] transfer to those cities of large portions of the population now forced to live in slums."[53]

Such visions of the urban future were common at the end of the war. We have already seen them expressed by a number of reformers including Clementine Churchill. In practice, the changes being widely discussed were profound, drawing upon the visions of turn-of-the-century urban planners like Ebenezer Howard and Henry George who had seen in the "garden city" concept a way to rationalize and fundamentally humanize urban capitalism by making the ownership of urban land corporate. Simon's vision for a Manchester fed by commuter trains from the suburbs, thus eliminating the slums that had been the enemy of Mancunian social reformers for more than a century, was very much in line with progressive thinking on urbanity in the 1920s.[54]

Given Simon's concern for the social costs of the war, it is clear that the boldness of his vision was integrally tied to his understanding of the postwar period as an unprecedented opportunity for substantive reform. It was also a vision that was doomed from the outset by a lack of funds and of national political will for the kind of dramatic transformation envisioned by reformers like Simon and Fox. The pervasiveness of such understandings of the housing crisis as fundamentally connected to the postwar situation is well illustrated by a conference of building trades unions in Manchester in February 1920. The ostensible reason for the conference was to protest the continued use of dilution in the industry. While the attendees roundly condemned dilution generally, they made significant allowances for the needs of the demobilized. The conference expressed "its intention to abide loyally by the agreement for the training of disabled sailors and soldiers, but regards any further extension of dilution as being unnecessary, impracticable, and economically unsound."[55]

Just as the disabled veteran was the most prominent public symbol of the costs of war, the construction industry and debates over urban reconstruction were the clearest examples of the connections being made between the war and the reconstruction of society. For many, the physical rebuilding of England's cities mirrored the spiritual rebirth of postwar society. While this optimism proved largely misplaced, it was nonetheless a powerful source of political appeal in the postwar years. In the case of Manchester, the vision of urban reformers who sought to abolish the city's legendary slums squared with broader national hopes for the

53 Clipping in Papers of Lord and Lady Simon, Manchester Archives, M/14/6/5.

54 See Lewis Mumford, *The City in History: Its Origins, Its Transformations, and Its Prospects*. (New York: Harcourt, Brace, 1961), 427, 503.

55 "No Dilution in Building," *The Times*, February 7, 1920.

renewal of cities. It created common cause between the city's liberal elite and its increasingly discontented inhabitants and, in doing so, helped inhibit the growth of the kinds of radical political formations that had been the focus of so much fear and anxiety in the postwar period.

While postwar construction in Manchester was slow to start, the city achieved a remarkable level of construction during the next two decades. More than 27,000 council houses were built between the wars in Greater Manchester. As a variety of private and government financing plans developed, the footprint of Manchester expanded significantly. Even if it took decades to achieve the kind of slum clearance that had long been the dream of Mancunian social reformers, interwar developments in housing dramatically changed the city's demographic profile. Eventually, garden city construction like the one in Wythenshawe redefined suburban Manchester.[56] The eventual success of housing schemes in Manchester, however, should not obscure the substantial problems that existed at the end of the war. The shortage of housing proved to be an embarrassing and public manifestation of the limits of demobilization, further contributing to public anxieties over the course of postwar planning.

Unemployment and housing proved intractable in the years after 1918. Wartime promises of a better future and the state's *ad hoc* mobilization strategy during the hard years of war collided to help make it more difficult to solve either of those problems easily or quickly. The apparent juxtaposition between large bureaucracies established to combat looming social problems and the lack of quick progress toward their solution confirmed for many Mancunians and Britons that the postwar state lacked the will to live up to its wartime pledges. These persistent issues might well have led to the sort of real conflict that seemed so ominous in 1919. To understand why they did not, we need to examine the face and contours of the radical challenges to the postwar order in Manchester.

Militancy and Extremism in Manchester

By some standards, labor militancy in Lancashire and Cheshire was at its apogee in 1920 and 1921. Strikes and work stoppages became a part of everyday life, leading many to conclude that industrial society was breaking down under the postwar strain. In the mining communities ringing Manchester and Salford, postwar insecurity generated unprecedented interest in labor organizing. The local branch of the National Union of Miners reached its highest membership in 1920, with a robust 90,000 dues-paying members.[57] From the point of view of those who claimed to represent the political interests of miners and other trades, the problem was that an interest in labor organizing did not necessarily translate

56 Alan Kidd, *Manchester* (Edinburgh: Edinburgh University Press, 2002), 216–21.

57 David Howell, *The Politics of the NUM: A Lancashire View* (Manchester: Manchester University Press, 1989), 3.

into political support for them. Part of what limited the reactions of the political labor movement in the Northwest was the working-class conservatism that made Lancashire such a contentious area before and during the war. At the 1920 annual meeting of the Independent Labour Party in Glasgow, George Benson of Salford castigated his more radical colleagues for seeking to shift the movement toward violence. Benson's frustration with the unwillingness of workers to behave as expected was palpable.

> Were they in favour of armed revolution? Were they in favour of arming the proletariat without exception? Were they in favour of putting rifles into the hands of every Liberal and Tory working man? Did they really suggest that the social revolution was going to be helped by putting rifles and machine guns into the hands of the people who read *John Bull*?[58]

The evolving debate over loyalty and political reliability did not fit neatly into the wartime categories. The St. Paul's Literary Society, distinguished during the war by an earnest if dilettantish conservatism, adopted a different tone in their postwar conversations, at times sounding strikingly progressive in their calls to involve the population in the spiritual reconstruction of the country. In a call to provide education to the urban masses, "Tridentus" reminded his colleagues that:

> We have silently vowed that we refuse to return to pre-war conditions. Very soon that vow will be tested. With knowledge will come sympathy from extremes to extremes. A little knowledge is just as dangerous, as it becomes the tool of prejudice, as is ignorance, perhaps it is far more dangerous in this way and may account for what I call 'mob hysteria.'…. Call anyone a "Bolshevist" and at once the mob howls in derision. Bolshevism is founded upon an idea. Adults must be plucky enough to learn all about this idea and combat it with ideas.[59]

One of the reasons for the apparent surge in radical movements was the self-restraint of the Labour Party as it emerged from the war closer to national power than ever before. Labour's moderates needed to maintain at least the appearance of moderation, which necessitated a conciliatory tone and a frank disavowal of more radical methods. J.R. Clynes, the Labour Parliamentary Chairman whose speech provoked such derision on May Day, wrote that "troubles with our home trades and industries are often provoked too lightly, though much is being done to

---

58 Text of speech in *Report of the Annual Conference*. (London: Independent Labour Party, 1920), 80–81. *John Bull* was a widely popular patriotic serial published by the spectacularly corrupt Horatio Bottomley, distinguished by its vitriolic language and conservatism. Bottomley's postwar career was less successful, spending much of the 1920s in prison for fraud. See Julian Symons, *Horatio Bottomley* (London: Stratus, 2001).

59 Tridentus, "Some Thoughts on Adult Education," in *Odds and Ends*. Manuscript volume. Vol. IXVI. 1920, 125.

guard against them." This was much more a language of political expediency than many in the Labour wards of Manchester expected. "Beneath the troubled surface of industrial disturbances a great deal of substantial word is being done to make these quarrels less likely, though propaganda for the making of new principles of organisation may never end so long as mankind considers that the ideal state has not been reached."[60]

These two trends, the postwar growth of labor unions and attempts by the Labour Party to recast themselves as a party suitable for a more prominent role in national government, created political space for more radical political solutions. The most visible symbol of this new political order was the Communist Party of Great Britain (CPGB), founded in 1920. An organized Communist Party represented the apotheosis of all of the bourgeois anxieties of the postwar years. British communists, *The Times* suggested, were eager to recruit trained soldiers but preferred to "look for the co-operation of ex-Service Men instead of men now serving."[61] The Chief Constable of Manchester instructed his department that "if any soldier or sailor is approached by anyone who attempts to undermine his loyalty or dissuade him from carrying out his duty" then the police were to intervene and arrest the agitators.[62]

Despite all of this attention, the CPGB nationwide had at best a marginal influence on political life, and in Manchester they seem to have been all but invisible. Some histories of political radicalism in Britain have fallen into the trap of following the public statements of organizations like Scotland Yard who generally magnified the threat of the CPGB. In reality, the party never numbered above 3,000 members.[63] While Manchester produced several prominent Communists, including Will Crick from Rusholme, the CPGB never managed to instantiate itself within the local Labour Party or anywhere else.[64] There were so few Communist Party members in Greater Manchester that it is difficult to discern who they were. Most seem to have existed within existing Labour Party formations and were largely unable to stand on their own as a political party.

Part of the problem with the CPGB in Lancashire was that it was all but invisible among the workers who were its intended membership. Even those broadly sympathetic to its causes often found themselves uncertain as to whether protests

60 J.R. Clynes, "Labour in the New Era," *The People's Year Book, 1920*, 25–6.

61 "Sowing the Seeds of Rebellion," *The Times*, December 28, 1920.

62 Order dated April 18, 1921. Greater Manchester Police Archive. General Orders, 1921, 14a.

63 Geoff Eley, *Forging Democracy: The History of the Left in Europe, 1850–2000* (New York: Oxford University Press, 2002), 178. R. Page Arnot, *The Impact of the Russian Revolution in Britain*. (London: Lawrence and Wishart, 1967) or the informative pamphlet by Ruth and Edmund Frow *The Communist Party in Manchester, 1920–26* (Salford: Working Class Movement Library, undated).

64 Robert Garner, "Local Labour Politics in Manchester and Salford and the Communist Question in the 1920s," *Manchester Region History Review*, vol. II, no. 1 (1988): 21.

were being organized by the Communists. Tom Regan, later an Alderman, left a typescript memoir in which he remembered taking part in one of the 1922 Hunger Marches after having been unable to secure work in an engineering works after the war. Despite the fact that years later he professed to be "satisfied that our local cemeteries contained many millions of unspent life due to the enormous number of premature deaths caused by … the Capitalist system" Regan was shocked to discover that the protests in which he took part were organized by the CPGB. "I don't think it would have stopped me," remarked Regan, "if I had known."[65]

This sense that the Communists initially had no real organizing power or clear conception of how to attract members in the industrial cities of England was even evident to Scotland Yard, an organization that normally distinguished itself by overestimating the power of radical political movements in the postwar years. In their 1926 report on the General Strike, Scotland Yard concluded that before the last months of 1921, the Communists "lacked even an elementary knowledge of the psychology of the British people."[66] Two local workmen, Jim Garnet and Danny Mead, echoed this sentiment in their reminisces of the "Struggles of the Lancashire Cotton Workers." The CPGB, in their opinion, was "not blessed with a big and well-informed membership in the cotton areas, but the membership and their sympathisers flung themselves into the ensuing struggles with the utmost enthusiasm."[67]

Even those with whom the Communists might have made common cause, the more radical members of the Labour Party, tended to distance themselves from the rhetoric of the CPGB. The local party enthusiastically complied with the national party's decision to expel Communists. Wright Robinson wrote in his diary in 1921 that he had always been puzzled as to "why Marx appears to have much more power to inspire fanaticism than to stimulate thought."[68] If the local labor movement did not produce the kind of radicalism that the authorities feared it might, there were extremists at work in the city. They emerged from the colonial struggle across the Irish Sea, and their impact on political culture in Manchester is important to our understanding of demobilization.

In the struggle for the political loyalties of Mancunians in the aftermath of the war, one critical element of debates over loyalty and revolutionary consciousness has been largely ignored. The Irish Civil War came to Manchester in dramatic fashion in the postwar period. Manchester became a key organizational center

65 Reminisces of Tom Regan. Manchester Archives MS Q 331 137 R4. Matthias Reiss's forthcoming book on unemployment in interwar Britain carefully explores the hunger march phenomenon, which was one of the most visible methods of unemployed agitation after 1922.

66 "Aspects of the General Strike." May 1926. Greater Manchester Police Archive. Uncataloged item.

67 Jim Garnet and Danny Mead. "The Struggles of the Lancashire Cotton Workers." Self-published. Undated. Working Class Movement Library, General Collection.

68 Garner, 20, 23.

for Nationalist rebels, who carried out a low-level but highly public campaign of violence in the streets of Manchester and its surrounding communities. The city's Irish population, already sharply divided politically, were drawn into wider debates over the future of Britain's rule in Ireland . These conflicts were sharpened by the confusion that marked law enforcement's campaign against potentially violent elements within their community.

The effect of this violence, however brief and episodic, on the development of postwar politics in Manchester was of vital importance, not necessarily for its own sake but for the success or failure of other forms of radical politics. Extra-parliamentary opposition groups like the nascent CPGB were at the same time trying to mobilize potential supporters for illegal or quasi-legal forms of political agitation. However, the widespread disgust at the violence in the streets associated with the Irish Civil War discouraged even those who sympathized with domestic radicals from taking up more aggressive forms of political protest.

Manchester was a leading center of Irish political life in England outside of London. The influential Irish Self-Determination League held its founding conference in the city in 1919. Irish voters played a prominent role in Labour Party branches throughout the region. In addition, by 1920 the city was an unwitting host to an underground network of nationalists dominated by the IRA. The organization operated an arms smuggling operation in the city under the direction of a grocer named Paddy O'Donoghue.[69] As the Civil War worsened in Ireland, the IRA began a violent campaign in England designed to draw attention to the conflict. Their program was an amalgam of audacity and caution; with cells across Britain totaling 400–500 fighters engaging in a campaign of arson and small-scale violence while at the same time under orders from Dublin to avoid almost all kinds of assassination and random violence that might damage the image of the organization abroad.[70]

By late 1920, local authorities were sufficiently concerned to start warning constables of the possibility of reprisal attacks by Irish nationalists on the city in revenge for the increasingly brutal struggle in Ireland.[71] In November, the Irish Office published a set of captured Nationalist documents that purported to detail planned attacks on port facilities in Liverpool and on the Stuart Street power station that supplied much of Manchester's electricity. The council responded by again banning the Manchester Martyrs procession and forcing the cancellation of a Self-Determination League meeting. "Manchester has been ever tolerant," declared *The Times*, but these threats "roused a feeling of intense anger."[72]

---

69 Herbert, 105.

70 Peter Hart, *The IRA at War, 1916–1923* (Oxford: Oxford University Press, 2003), 141–78.

71 See, for instance orders from Chief Constable to Superintendents, December 23, 1920. Greater Manchester Police Archive, General Orders, 1920, 314.

72 "The Manchester Plot," *The Times*, November 27, 1920.

February 1921 saw several violent incidents, most spectacularly on the night of February 12, when small bands of arsonists set nearly simultaneous fires at the Union Acid Company, a local druggist, Premier Waterproof and Rubber Company, and Smith and Forrest oil and tar distillery. At the last of these, the raiders opened fire on a night watchman, who described them as Irishmen one of whom bore "a strong resemblance to ... Edward Carson."[73] A few days later, a constable patrolling Oxford Road, along with an Inspector who happened to be in the area, were attacked by a group of Irishmen in a melee that eventually drew in a tram driver on the side of the officers.[74] Throughout the rest of April and March, the city watched in grim fascination as a series of incendiary attacks and brazen robberies brought the reality of the Civil War across the Irish Sea home to Manchester.

In early April, this struggle culminated in a series of early morning attacks on cleaners and hotels in the center of the city. That night the police raided an Irish club in Hulme. The raid ended with an exchange of gunfire in which several inhabitants were wounded and one was killed. By the end of the weekend, a number of IRA members in Manchester were in custody, including O'Donoghue.[75] The raids, according to the Chief Constable "struck at the centre of the Sinn Fein organization in Manchester.... The proof that the action of the Manchester Police was effective is in the fact that in Manchester and East Lancashire the activities of the Sinn Fein movement were scotched."[76]

At their trial, 16 of the 19 accused were convicted and given sentences of 5 to 15 years of penal servitude. The city petitioned the Treasury for help with the costs of the proceedings, totaling about £4,500. The report suggests how seriously local officials took the incidents of the previous year. The Lord Mayor carefully enumerated the defendant's crimes against the city and the nation, including:

> storage of explosive substances, firearms, paraffin oil, and seditious literature, the use of firearms to shoot at police officers with intent to kill or maim, the setting fire to and attempting to set fire to certain goods and premises, the practising of rifle firing and military training[77]

The conspirators, the report went on, were members of a "treasonable combination called Sinn Fein or the Irish Republican Army," bent on trying to:

---

73 Report on "Incediarism in Manchester on Saturday evening, the twelfth February, 1921." Detective Office. Greater Manchester Police Archive. General Orders, 1921, 354. Needless to say Carson, one of the most prominent leaders of the Ulster Unionist movement, had nothing to do with the incident.

74 Incident Report. February 17, 1921. Chief Constable's Office. Greater Manchester Police Archive. 86/4.

75 Herbert, 111.

76 Chief Constable's report and recommendations for police awards. Greater Manchester Police Archives. 88/40.

77 Report of September 1921. Greater Manchester Police Archives. 88/66.

> … depose his Majesty from the style or honour of the Imperial Crown of the United Kingdom and to overthrow the power of the King in Ireland and to levy war against His Majesty within the United Kingdom in order by force and constraint to compel his Majesty to change his measures.[78]

As Peter Hart has pointed out in his excellent book on the IRA, the Manchester cell proved to be undone more by its own lack of competence and cohesion than by the ruthless efficiency of the local constabulary.[79] The IRA's incendiary campaign in Manchester, while not particularly destructive or deadly, has to be seen within its context. It reached its apogee at the same time that postwar industrial Britain faced its most potentially destabilizing labor dispute – the abortive Triple Alliance Strike of April 1921. This connection was not lost on observers, who saw in the IRA's activity another manifestation of the dangers facing British society after the war. Even the *Manchester Guardian*, which was broadly sympathetic to many of the concerns then being expressed in the streets, saw a link that April between the headlines "General Strike on Friday, Revolver Fight in Hulme, Rioters at Work in Scotland, …. No Profits to Pool, Irish Rebels Active." It was enough "to make a man of melancholic complexion."[80]

Ironically, the presence of actual armed political movements in the Northwest may have helped to delegitimize other radical variants in the broader spectrum of politics in Lancashire and Cheshire. The violent revolutionary menace that conservatives saw in groups like the CPGB did, in fact, exist but not in the form in which those conservatives imagined it would. Part of the reason that radical leftists tried hard to disassociate themselves from any hint of armed revolutionary struggle was that not to do so ran the risk of being associated with the very real presence of anti-state paramilitaries emerging from the Irish Civil War. The Irish problem served as a firebreak in postwar political geography, limiting the effectiveness of rhetorical violence by presenting the very real possibility of physical violence. The linkages between the IRA's campaign in England in 1920–21 and the evolving labor problems that culminated in the Triple Alliance episode in April are not wholly clear, but it is evident that the presence of armed and potentially lethal political groups cast a pall over the other set of potentially destabilizing events taking place simultaneously in England's mines.

The failed Triple Alliance Strike of 1921, which ended with a humiliating collapse of trade union unity that came to be called "Black Friday," was in many ways a direct result of the uneven demobilization of British society. The Triple Alliance, a coalition of unions whose very name evoked fear of a massive shutdown of British industry, originated in prewar efforts to link labor organizing across industries. In 1921, the affiliated unions threatened to strike in support of

78 Ibid.

79 Hart, 171.

80 "Before the Dawn?," *MG*, April 14, 1921.

mine workers. The strike failed to materialize when the unions fell out among themselves, but Britain came very close to a major industrial action.

The roots of the strike lay in surviving wartime industrial controls. For many in the union movement, wartime regulations proved an unexpected boon as price and wage controls forced the kind of stability and living standards that prewar union activists had sought fruitlessly. In 1920, the state still controlled a number of key industries, including mining, shipping, railroads, and food production. The problem was that wartime controls bound industry, and with it the government, to prices even when those prices fluctuated broadly as the postwar economy settled. In the coal industry, the government beat a precipitous retreat in March 1921, abandoning control months ahead of schedule.

Miners feared that decontrol was the beginning of a broader assault on trade union rights and on the social controls of the war years. The Miners' Federation launched a series of strikes in the face of pay cuts, and the Railwaymen and Transport Workers' unions threatened to strike as well. The miners' demands included relatively far-reaching steps like the pooling of industry profits and the maintenance of wages that had until recently been subsidized by the state. Conditions looked ripe for the closest thing to a general strike seen so far in postwar Britain.[81]

As with previous strike actions, paramilitary civil defense organizations came into being to deal with expected service disruptions and public order problems. In the mining districts, these Defense Forces performed the delicate task of escorting those who continued working to their posts. These paramilitaries, raised in early April to combat possible unrest, grew to about 70,000 in ten days before disbanding.[82] Many of those who volunteered, lured in large part by pay equivalent to active duty army wages, were veterans. In the coal communities around Manchester, there were grim scenes as Defense Forces comprised largely of striking miners who needed the wages to feed their families escorted workers to the pits.[83]

In many ways, the labor unrest of previous years left Manchester much better prepared than it might have been. Civilian volunteers had performed civil and commercial services during previous strikes, volunteer militias were prepared to keep order, and coal stocks were ready to absorb at least a temporary halt in

81 The best book on the subject of decontrol generally, and on the Triple Alliance, is still Susan Armitage, *The Politics of Decontrol of Industry: Britain and the United States* (London: Weidenfeld & Nicholson, 1969). See also Peter Clarke, *Hope and Glory: Britain, 1900–2000* (London: Penguin, 1996), 109.; W. Hamish Fraser, *A History of British Trade Unionism* (Houndmills: Macmillan, 1999), 152–3; Duncan Tanner, "The Politics of the Labour Movement, 1900–1939." in Chris Wrigley, ed. *A Companion to Early Twentieth-Century Britain* (Malden: Blackwell, 2003), 42–3.

82 Ralph Desmarais. "The British Government's Strikebreaking Organization and Black Friday," *Journal of Contemporary History*, vol. 6, no. 2 (1971): 125.

83 "Miners Joining the Defense Forces," *MG*, April 13, 1921.

production. The population was at least ostensibly prepared for an extended labor battle, provided that it remained peaceful. The Alliance, for its part, was intent on demonstrating that its actions would not seek violence and actually adhered to previous affirmations of loyalty. Its manifesto, issued days before the proposed strike, emphasized that "We resent that suggestion made in Government quarters that the miner's fight is a political one. We are not proclaiming a revolution. We are standing shoulder to shoulder for fundamental trade union rights."[84]

For some observers, the looming strike was very much a product of the same postwar situation that had disrupted economic life across the continent. The *Manchester Guardian* proclaimed early in that gloomy April that:

> May Day of this year of grace may prove to be a day of fate… Yet here it is, and unless steps are promptly taken to avert or break its force we may soon find ourselves in the presence of an economic tragedy comparable in its effects on the life of Europe to the war of which it is a legacy. The Coal Strike and its settlement are, after all, matters within our own control, and if we do not by hook or crook, find a way out consistent with the national safety we shall have ourselves to blame.[85]

What actually transpired on Black Friday is still a matter of some contention. None of the leaders of the unions involved seem to have been particularly interested in carrying out a mass industrial action, and the divided leaderships proved pliant when confronted with government negotiators. Throughout the week, rumors flew that one of the unions was secretly negotiating with the government. Since no union wanted to be left out of a potential deal, the leadership stopped trusting each other. Sensing weakness on the part of the miners, the other unions backed away from their show of solidarity, and the threatened strike disappeared within hours of its anticipated beginning on April 15. With the end of solidarity went any realistic hope of achieving the miners' proposed pooling of profits.[86] For the Miners' Federation, Black Friday proved a comprehensive defeat, one that further weakened the already struggling industry. Coal in England began its long and precipitous decline as both owners and miners suffered.[87]

The "betrayal" of the workers by their unions has since become an article of faith among historians of unionism in Britain. "It was like the Somme," concluded Peter Clarke later, with the union leaders playing the role of Haig. "The miners were left stranded on the barbed wire, bitter and bloody but unbowed."[88] A frustrated observer at the time bitterly noted that:

---

84 "The Alliance Manifesto," *MG*, April 14, 1921.

85 "May 1," *MG*, April 12, 1921.

86 Fraser, 153.

87 Armitage, 154–5.

88 Clarke, 107.

> It is generally recognised that victory of a very far-reaching kind was actually within the grip of the Labour Movement on April 15, 1921, and that on that day the Movement suffered a defeat of which all the subsequent defeats have been the natural and logical consequences.[89]

The collapse of the Triple Alliance strike was a watershed for the labor movement in Britain. Collective action lost much of its threat as the collapse of the strike highlighted the real differences between various unions. It also represented a critical moment in the history of demobilization after the First World War, as it was effectively the last time that groups within British civil society tried to influence the course of demobilization and mitigate its impact. As the battle over decontrol ended with a whimper rather than a bang, so too did much of the public debate over demobilization. Within a year, the political constellation that produced these circumstances came to an end with the collapse of the Coalition.

Britain's postwar demobilization crisis drew to a close with the collapse on Black Friday. Most wartime regulations had been lifted, the Army had retreated to peacetime troop levels, and the immediate postwar economic upturn had reversed itself. After Black Friday, the mobilizing power of organized labor weakened dramatically, emerging five years later with the General Strike of 1926. The tensions left behind by the war were far from resolved, but the extraordinary period in which the national government, local authorities, and civil society debated the terms of demobilization was at an end.

The years 1920–21 marked a turn in the history of the First World War in British society. The coalition that carried Britain through the long years of war finally collapsed the next Fall with the withdrawal of the Conservatives. The end of the Coalition was a vital marker of the arrival of a new era in British politics. Domestic policy would now be more concerned with the legacies of the postwar settlement than with those of the war itself.

Why did extreme variants of dissent largely fail in Greater Manchester? The city suffered disproportionately in the period after the war, beginning a decline that heralded the slow death of industrial Manchester. Some of the most politically active and mobilized unions in the country had constituencies in the area, and the region had been the heartland of British supporters of the revolutionary regime in Russia. Was it the durable conservatism of the Lancashire working classes? Was revolution simply not British? Were the workers of Lancashire betrayed by their ambitious union bosses and would-be political representatives?

While all of these may have been factors, a synthetic approach to the political culture of Manchester at the end of the First World War reveals how limited was the space in which radical politics could operate. As they had been in 1919, those most directly affected by demobilization were overwhelmingly determined to present their grievances within a framework of loyalty. With few exceptions, protests

89 Gerald Gould, *The Lesson of Black Friday: A Note on Trade Union Structure* (London: Labour Publishing Company, 1921), 7.

erupted over pragmatic issues and called for reforms of existing programs like unemployment insurance or the continuation of wartime government controls.

The role of municipal government was particularly important in this case. Local authorities felt pressed between the demands of civil society and the confused and largely improvised response of the national government. The city's political elite was convinced, just as large swaths of civil society was, that the end of the war presented unprecedented opportunities for reform. While protestors and municipal authorities did not always agree on the best course of action, a dialog between the two survived, which cultivated the rhetorics of loyalty through which protestors phrased their petitions. Critically, protesters believed that the institutions of reciprocity existed and, if persuaded to, authorities could negotiate positive outcomes. This sentiment provided a significant disincentive to support more radical variants of dissent which withdrew from the formal and informal reciprocity of the postwar years.

One of the most remarkable after-effects of the war was this continued recognition of common citizenship and common purpose, despite tangible and important differences over crucial and complex issues. This sense of commonality was only catalyzed by the presence of the closest thing to a revolution that England saw in the postwar years; the violent civil conflict in Ireland and the expansion of that struggle into urban Britain. At almost precisely the same time that groups like the CPGB were recruiting in Manchester, there was a genuine fear of foreign influence and political violence in the streets. The violence that authorities had feared since before the end of the war came not from Russian-inspired domestic political radicals but as an outgrowth of an increasingly disastrous occupation policy across the narrow sea from the Northwest. As the demobilization of British society moved forward, however unevenly, there was a nearby and ever-present example of the costs of political violence.

Slowly and haltingly, the war began to recede into the past. The mobilization of 1914–18 and the slow and uneven demobilization of the immediate aftermath gradually transformed into a quotidian postwar reality. The battles over how to commemorate the war and its participants, however, had only just begun.

In March 1920, the Manchester Art Gallery hosted part of the exhibition of "The Nation's War Paintings," a collection of war art by young artists like Paul Nash and Wyndham Lewis. While British avant-garde representations of the war have not generally received the same renown as their German contemporaries like Otto Dix or Georg Grosz, the art displayed in this exhibition captured what one critic has called "disfigurement of national self-image" engendered by the war. In a nation and a city where real physical disfigurement was an all-too-common site, the broken bodies and shattered landscapes of the war artists was both shocking and strangely familiar to contemporary observers.[90]

---

90 Sue Malvern, *Modern Art, Britain, and the Great War: Witnessing, Testimony, and Remembrance* (New Haven: Yale University Press, 2004), 93.

For those who had themselves returned from the front, the experience of seeing these early representations of the war could be jarring. A young ex-soldier trying to "escape from the commonplaces of city life for a few moments" stepped into the gallery during a busy work-day. He left disgusted, convinced that he and his comrades had been made to look "like clowns." He had gone, he wrote, to feel himself "back into the environment of the hateful Salient, to the men and horses straining at the guns, to feel the tenseness of zero hour, to experience again the thrill of battle – possibly the fear. Nothing like it."[91]

His experience was one that must have been all too common in those postwar years. Millions of young men returned home to a nation, and a city, that imperfectly understood what had happened to them, that was eager to move on with life, and that lacked the excitement and energy that they, looking back, remembered from 1914–18. For veterans, women, activists, and bureaucrats, the years surrounding the end of the war had been marked by extraordinary transition, bitter battles, and differing visions of postwar society. Just as the veteran in the museum had been unable to see his own memories expressed in the representations of war there, many who had been through that conflict now wondered if their visions of the future would ever compare with the reality of a demobilized world.

91 "Heroes Made to Look Like Clowns," *MEN*, March 22, 1920.

Chapter 7
Scapegoats for a Lost War: The Crisis of Demobilization in Munich, 1920–21

"The prevailing political currents are reaching a climax, which will soon reach a point where they must explode." The officer who typed out these words somewhere in the Ministry of War building on *Leopoldstrasse* during the second day of 1920 was every bit as anxious as the opening lines of his report seemed to suggest. The deep divisions in the city, the anonymous officer wrote, reminded him of the early days of the previous February. The suggestion was clear; there was outward calm but violence in the air. "Dark clouds are appearing in the skies, heralding dangerous threats to our Fatherland. Whoever would forecast the future must see the coming unrest that will stem from our miserable economic situation."[1]

The anxieties of one intelligence officer trying to summarize the confused political situation on a cold day in mid-winter interest us today because of what they tell us about the palpable sense of paranoia that suffused political life in Bavaria's capital in 1920. The city had been through a year of violence, turmoil, and chronic insecurity, which followed years of war, shortage, and escalating internal conflict. Clearly for this officer, and for many in the city who thought like him, 1919 was a benchmark for disaster, and they would do anything in their power to keep such events from happening again.

The waves of crisis that crested and broke in Munich in 1919 barely subsided when events outside Bavaria's borders brought new intensity to the city's fractious politics. When 1920 began, Munich was the base of a revivified, electorally successful moderate leftist Bavarian government. By the end of that year, the city was well on its way to establishing itself as a European center for counter-revolutionary incendiarism. The novelist Lion Feuchtwanger lamented the pernicious effects of those who came to take advantage of the city's new relaxed attitude toward extremism: "In former times the beautiful, comfortable, well-beloved city had attracted the best brains in the Empire. How was it that all these had left now, and that all the lazy and the vicious, who could not find a home in

1 "Allgemeiner Stimmungsbericht." January 2, 1920. RWGrKdo 4, 347, BHStA IV. Note: The author dated the document January 2, 1919. Aside from context, the error is clear from the collection stamp used by the *Nachrichtenabteilung*.

the Empire or anywhere else, rushed, as if magically drawn, to Munich?"[2] What he failed to capture in this extraordinary passage, though he did in the rest of the novel, was that it was not outside agitators who defined the political life of the city, but the people of Munich.

The war lay at the heart of these debates over the city's future. As we have seen, the language of reciprocity survived the experience of defeat and the chaos of 1919. Despite these experiences, which Bavarians of different political opinions thought of in very different ways, a near consensus remained that the obligations of wartime persisted. As normal life resumed after the upheavals of the previous year, expectations rose that some of those rewards would be forthcoming. When they were not, political groups of the Left and Right searched for targets to blame.

In marked contrast to the experience in Manchester, the debates over demobilization in Munich had a zero-sum calculus. The rhetoric of common citizenship, which played a critical role in wartime mobilization and which survived in the consensus-driven politics of postwar Manchester, collapsed completely in Munich. The lesson of 1919, and of 1920–21, was that the power to affect successful demobilization could not be negotiated but had to be seized. The resulting legitimation of extra-legal politics drew from the widely held belief that previous administrations had been unable to successfully meet the challenges of demobilizing German and Bavarian society. The resulting bifurcation of interests not only served to further destabilize local and regional politics, but also catalyzed a political language of accusation, innuendo, and threat.

Discussion of the war suffused the language of politics with the same vivid intensity that marked the epochal events of the year before. An important change was evident, however, in the forces at work in the fractious politics of the streets. For the Left, particularly those who had pursued the most radical agendas in 1919, the war had been an opportunity. The events of 1917 and the collapse of domestic consensus was a rallying point. For the city's fractious but growing Right, the war had been a disaster, and the tumult that followed had swept away treasured institutions like the monarchies and the army. The triumph, however transitory, of the Left was proof of the pernicious effects of the war and of the disastrous legacies of demobilization.

For many on the Left and the Right, anti-foreign and anti-Semitic language became increasingly prominent, adding to the vehemence of political rhetoric. This type of language acted as a code through which people and parties could question the legitimacy of their government. What took place was an example of what Helmut Walser Smith has termed "process," the convergence of ideas and circumstances that create historically specific forms of anti-Semitic discourse.[3] In the case of Munich, it was all but impossible to separate political language from

2 Lion Feuchtwanger, *Success*, trans. Willa Muir and Edwin Muir (New York: Viking Press, 1930), 28.

3 Helmut Walser Smith, *The Butcher's Tale: Murder and Anti-Semitism in a German Town* (New York: Norton, 2002), 22.

anti-Semitism. As memories of the lost war, the troubled postwar transition, and the powerful pull of nostalgia played upon preexisting ideas, images of foreigners and Jews became potent signifiers in the battle for the symbolic landscape of Munich's political life.

The multiple crises in Munich during the years after 1918 emerged from the very real problems of demobilizing a highly mobilized society at the end of a long war. Ordinary people took to the streets to demand help with the everyday problems of consumer society in crisis. Their political representatives appealed to them with the claim that only they could rectify the inequities of demobilization. As the nameless intelligence officer commented: "When the Fatherland is in such profound danger, it is the duty of all Germans, whether Right or Left, to find a healthy middle ground in order to secure the soil of our new Fatherland."[4]

Consumer Politics in the Streets, 1920

The political crises of early 1920, both in Bavaria and in the wider Republic, revealed just how impossible such unity had become. The crises of March proceeded the way that they did in Munich in large part due to concerns that remained from the early postwar period. Foremost was a tendency on the part of authorities to equate any kind of disorder, actual or potential, with the threat of revolution. The police, led by men like Ernst Pöhner and Wilhelm Frick, had little tolerance for leftists of any stripe.[5] Memories of the coup of November 1918 were fresh in the public mind, along with the equally frightening memory of the radical insurgency of the previous Spring. An army intelligence report on Carnival celebrations in February reported that some carnival troupes were shouting slogans like "Up with Eisner – Up with Toller!" The agent reported that one reveler declared his wish that "the Entente occupy Germany and completely disarm her, so that Bolshevism can have an easier time of it." The agent, placing a great deal of faith in the probably less-than-sober political conversations of carnival, concluded that "they put their greatest hope in Russia."[6]

This anxiety about domestic radicalism dovetailed with concerns about the course of events beyond Germany's borders. In February, as concerns grew over worsening tensions between Poland and Russia, the police received a report from the border police post outside Salzburg titled "The Bolshevik Western Offensive." The report detailed concerns about the potential collapse of White resistance and

4 "Allgemeiner Stimmungsbericht." January 2, 1920. RWGrKdo 4, 347, BHStA IV.

5 An oft-repeated and possibly apocryphal story has a concerned citizen coming to see Pöhner and breathlessly reporting: "There are political murder gangs out there!" The bemused *Polizeipräsident* responded coolly: "Indeed, but too few." See Wilhelm Hermann, *Dichter, Denker, Fememörder: Rechtsradikalismus und Antisemitismus in München von der Jahrhundertwende bis 1921* (Berlin: Transit Buchverlag, 1989), 131.

6 Meldung. February 18, 1920. RWGrKdo 4, 347. BHStA IV.

the emergence of Soviet formations among Austrians who had previously been POWs in the East.[7] Given the fluid and often violent situation in the mountainous border region, authorities in Munich were keenly concerned about events in Austria and viewed any sign of communist activity in Tyrol with great alarm.

Second, and equally important, were the unresolved problems of shortages and price increases remaining from the war. Despite the lifting of the Allied blockade and the easing of food regulations, shortages remained and prices skyrocketed. Coal supplies in the city remained at less than two-thirds of prewar levels, while the number of long-term unemployed nearly doubled in the first six months of 1921.[8] Again, these problems were exacerbated by conflicts over regional autonomy and tensions remaining from the war between Munich and its rural hinterland. On a trip to the Chiemsee in January, one army agent found, in addition to a "widespread … fanatical hatred of Jews," an equally virulent loathing of "profiteers and hoarders." This seemed to be especially bitterly felt by those engaged in the leather industry, an important part of the rural economy in the Alpine uplands of Oberbayern. "If all our leather stayed here in Bavaria, then all our animals could go toward making shoes. Apparently, though, the *Saupreussen* (damned Prussians) need it all."[9]

A third issue that helped shape the responses to the problems of early 1920 was widespread concern about immigration. These anxieties, which often took on virulently anti-Semitic language, were widespread and crossed class and political boundaries.[10] They were also frequently cast in terms related to the war and its aftermath. In early March the border police Commissar in Passau, on the Austrian border in Niederbayern, wrote to Pöhner expressing his fear that:

> The flood of East European Jewish scum that is overrunning Germany and the insertion of these human parasites among the German *Volk* represents not just a moral danger, but a threat to the healing of the German people and the rebuilding of Germany.[11]

The *Münchener Zeitung*, in an article in late February called "30,000 Foreigners in Munich!" decried the city's lack of affordable housing and food, which affected women, children, and men who had "given five years of their lives for their country."

7 "Betreff: Anmarsch des Bolshewismus gegen Westen." Grenzepolizeistelle Salzburg (author's name illegible) to Polizedirektion München. February 4, 1920. MInn 71732. BHtSA IV.

8 Bayer. Statistisches Landesamt, *Statistisches Jahrbuch für den Freistaat Bayern, 1921* (Munich: J. Lindauersche Universitäts-Buchhandlung, 1921), 253, 212. After SJFB.

9 "Stimmungsbericht aus der Landbevolkerung am Chiemsee." January 7, 1920. RWGrKdo 4, 347, BHtSA IV.

10 The connection between shifting German national identity, border security, and immigration is discussed in Annemarie Sammartino, "Migration and Crisis in Germany, 1914–1922." PhD diss., University of Michigan, 2004.

11 Letter from Grenzpolizeikommisar Passau (Ibel) to Polizeidirektion München. March 8, 1920. StaMu 4118.

"In the same Munich there are 30,000 aliens who gorge themselves at full tables. Not a day goes by without meat. And the portions – because price doesn't matter to them – are large, even including thirds and fourths if seconds aren't enough." Engaging in some possibly specious mathematics, the paper concluded that, without the influx of foreign mouths, Munich's citizens could have "a quarter pound more meat per day than before. Is the Minister of the Interior aware of this?"[12]

A confidential report from an officer in the local *Reichswehr* command two months earlier predicted that the declining effectiveness of leftist radicals did not necessarily indicate that the situation in Munich was any less dangerous, in no small part because of the agitation of right-wing anti-Semites and the worsening economic situation.[13] Police and military archives suggest that anti-Semitic agitation was on the rise in Munich. There were rumors that Jews were receiving special shipments of scarce flour and sugar, and posters began appearing on Jewish-owned shop windows. Sometimes agitators did not stop at affixing inflammatory messages, and there were a number of acts of vandalism. These rumors of preferential treatment acquired enough currency that the Jewish cultural organization in the city took out an advertisement in the *Neue Zeitung* to deny that there was any special arrangement.[14]

Such rumors exacerbated already existing tensions in the city, and right-wing groups became much more active in late February and early March. In late February, a tiny political fringe group called the German Worker's Party (DAP) and its best speaker, the young demobilized soldier and former instructor for the propaganda course Adolf Hitler, proclaimed its program at a beer-hall meeting. By early March, groups like the *Schutz-und Trutzbund* were meeting almost nightly in large halls like the *Löwenbraükeller*. Reports of meetings rarely contained reliable estimates of the size of the crowd, and often two reporters would provide widely varied estimates. The *Schutz-und Trutzbund* was one of the most widely recognized organizations of its type, and early in 1920 their meetings often drew more than 5,000 people.[15] Membership in the local *Bund* chapter grew quickly, more than doubling in the early months of 1920 until it numbered about 4,000 active members.[16] Their meetings were known for caustic and inflammatory rhetoric. Speakers complained about "foreigners" consuming more than their share of precious foodstuffs. The local *Bund* membership were particularly aggrieved by commemorations of the putschists of 1918. One speaker complained that

12 *Münchener Zeitung*. February 27, 1920. Unpaginated clipping in StaMu 4118.

13 "Bericht über die innenpolitische Lage" written in early December, 1919, by Major Prager. RwGrKdo 4, 289, BHStA IV.

14 "Erklärung," *Neue Zeitung*, March 3, 1920.

15 See, for example, the estimate of 6–7,000 at a gathering in the *Kindlkeller* on January 7. "Versammlung des Schutz-und Trutzbundes am 7.1.20" RWGrKdo 4, 288, BHStA IV.

16 Martin Geyer, *Verkehrte Welt: Revolution, Inflation, und Moderne in München* (Göttingen: Vandenhoeck und Rupprecht, 1998), 281.

"If they are permitted to have a memorial for Kurt Eisner [the anniversary of whose death had transpired on February 21], we should be allowed to commemorate the Kaiser!"[17] *Bund* agitators universally condemned the force that they felt was more or less responsible for this state of affairs: Munich's Jews. "The workers have not been properly educated about the Jews. Bolshevism is nothing but Jewish tyranny, and the workers there are nothing more than slaves of the Jews."[18]

These issues emerged on the streets for two days in early March, as large crowds (the agreed figure was about 2,000) assembled to hear anti-Semitic speakers. The gatherings centered around *Lenbachplatz*, between the city's medieval heart and the train station. All observers noted the presence of significant numbers of *Reichswehr* troops and officers among the crowd, some of whom took an active part in distributing literature. Police were on hand to keep order, prompting the familiar cry of "*Judenschutztruppe*" (Jew-protection corps) from the crowd. Speakers repeated allegations of sugar and flour hoarding, as well as returning to Munich's housing shortage. "One should not forget," warned one agitator, "that our terrible housing crisis has been worsened by the arrival of East Galician Jews, which our government has supported, and that because of this our worthy warriors, who have finally come home, find themselves homeless."[19]

One group distributed literature "demanding" that the city's Jews give ill-gotten flour and sugar to local hospitals, that the government end all immigration by Jews, and that any Jew who had immigrated since November 1, 1918 be sent back to their place of origin.[20] Like most meetings of its type, some had come to shout the speakers down. One observer saw an onlooker, described as "a worker" trying to argue with one of the speakers, telling the crowd that this was "just agitation and an attempt to use the Jews as a scapegoat for a lost war."[21]

One group of indeterminate size broke off from the main body and, led by a group of soldiers carrying a black-white-and-red flag, headed for the *Feldherrnhalle*. Outside the former residence of the Bavarian monarchy, they attacked "the Republic and the Jews," called for the restoration of the Wittelsbach monarchy ("*Hoch Rupprecht*!"), sang patriotic songs like the *Wacht am Rhein*, and harangued police units that set up machine guns along the narrow streets between *Odeonsplatz* and *Marienplatz*.[22] The *Feldhernnhalle* demonstration was quite different from the one at *Lenbachplatz* from which it emerged. It appears to

17 "Stimmungsbericht aus deutschvölkischen Kreisen." March 11, 1920. RWGrKdo 4, 204, BhstA IV.

18 Ibid.

19 "Strassendemonstrationen gegen die Juden." March 7, 1920. RWGrKdo 4, 204, BhstA IV. There seems to have been some debate as to the number of participants. One correspondent suggested 700–800, while Major Prager penciled in a figure of 1500–2000.

20 Ibid.

21 "Stimmungsbericht aus Arbeiterkreisen zur antisemitischen Kundgebung am Lenbachplatz am 7. ds. Mts." RWGrKdo 4, 204, BhstA IV.

22 "Meldung." March 8, 1920. RWGrKdo 4, 204, BHStA IV.

have been dominated by soldiers and expressed the bifurcated face of Bavarian nationalism at the time. As the varying fortunes of traditional Bavarian particularist parties in elections the previous year had demonstrated, it was difficult to rally significant support for expressions of purely Bavarian restorationism. However, if it was done in the German context, as it was here, monarchism could recover some of its emotional resonance. What is abundantly clear in both cases was that the war and its outcomes lay at the heart of the grievances of the protestors. Protest leaders were able to seize upon older mistrust of socialism, liberalism, and Jews to direct protests against the new Bavarian government.

Initial reports indicated that the mass of workers, whom authorities tended to view in largely collective terms, were not sympathetic to the anti-Semites. Authorities tried to explain the relationship between Jews, workers, and politics in convoluted terms that evoked the complexities of German–Jewish identity in the interwar period. One typically obtuse example was a report from March 8, in which an agent claimed that workers at a local *Arbeitsamt* felt that the anti-Semitic movement was just a "way to use workers to bring about reactionary goals." However, since "there are a lot of Jews among the capitalists, so in that sense the workers are the enemies of the Jews. They have nothing against the Jewish religion however." In any case, this group of workers believed "the day of reckoning is not long off, when the Bolsheviks will settle with the Poles. They'll be at Germany's border by May, and the *Reichswehr* won't be able to stop them."[23]

At the same time as the anti-Semitic demonstrations in the center of the city, police began to find flyers calling for a large demonstration of women and children for March 11. Organizers took great pains to make it clear that the protest was apolitical and was driven only by a desire to end food shortages and escalating prices. "Think of your children's future!" admonished the flyers. "To prevent bloodshed, men should stay at home or go to work. If they still have any honor left, they will not shoot at unarmed women and innocent children. Bring your children with you! It doesn't matter what your politics are when all of us are hungry!"[24] It is unclear who was responsible for the posters. The organization and printing of such a campaign suggests that a formal political group planned the event, but they did so without claiming responsibility. In any case, the planned demonstration quickly became a popular event.

The police were swift to intervene, banning any such demonstration under the public order laws promulgated late the previous year. Within a day of the banning order, posters appeared in central Munich taunting the police. "A German police chief threatens starving women and children with rifles. Our future looks bright indeed."[25] Rumors of violent plans among the protesters fueled the suspicions of

23 "Stimmungsbericht aus dem Arbeitsamt." March 8, 1920. RWGrKdo 4, 347. BHStA IV.

24 Poster "Frauen und Kinder." Polizeidirektion 4316. StaMu.

25 See "Bekanntmachung" of March 10, 1920 and Poster found "in der Nähe der alten Schiessstatte" in Polizeidirektion 4316, StaMu.

authorities. Reportedly, food store owners in the central city were warned that they would be targets of mob actions. A shop owner on Sonnenstrasse reported being warned "You are going to be cleaned out [*richtig ausgeplundert*]."[26]

Intelligence on the intentions of the demonstrators took on two wholly different forms. While one type stressed the pragmatic nature of the protester's demands, another emphasized the revolutionary "Bolshevik" nature of the protests. "If the reactionaries can demonstrate, then the workers can too." The government can't end profiteering, because they are profiteers too. Bolshevism will put an end to all that."[27] The government's instinctive fear of the radical Left led figures like Police Chief Ernst Pöhner to look for Bolshevism in any major act of disorder. These assumptions are borne out in descriptions of the demonstration, which look as hard as possible for any evidence, no matter how slim, of discernable communist influence. "Obviously," wrote one observer, "the demonstration was planned by radical groups."[28] Events on the ground proved somewhat different.

On the morning of Thursday March 11, one of the largest and best-organized protests of the postwar years got underway at the festival grounds of the *Theresienwiese*. A crowd of women and children, estimated to have been about 4,000 at its peak, marched north toward *Marienplatz*. Under a banner proclaiming "We are starving," the crowd brushed past police under orders to stop the march. As they marched past the shops whose owners felt threatened by the crowd, demonstrators could not have failed to see in the windows prices for foodstuffs that simply defied belief, signs that certainly reinforced the protesters claim that something was deeply wrong. Since the beginning of the war, the price of rice had risen more than 18 times. Peas cost more than 10 times prewar levels, while potatoes, perhaps the staple food of the region's workers, cost more than 20 times what they had before the war began.[29] For the crowd, these numbers must have seemed absolutely astonishing, and it is little wonder that they wanted solutions in place of explanations.

The women and children of March 11 were concerned not with revolution but with food. "The feeling among the women was highly agitated. They bombarded officials, particularly the police, with insults. They also demanded strikes until rations were raised."[30] Police, both mounted and on foot, kept their distance from the demonstrators but maintained a significant presence throughout the day. While groups of women and a few men considered the next step, children shouted insults and threw snowballs at police. One report indicates that the demonstrators moved off from *Theresienwiese* just after two in the afternoon, reaching the area around

26 "Meldung," March 11, 1920. RWGrKdo 4, 172, BHStA IV.

27 "Stimmungsbericht aus dem Arbeitsamt." March 11, 1920. RWGrKdo 4, 172. BhstA IV.

28 "Betreff: Demonstration vom 11.3.20." RWGrKdo 4, 172, BHStA IV.

29 SJFB, 259–60.

30 "Stimmungsbericht zur Demonstration am 11.3.1920." RWGrKdo 4, 172, BhstA IV.

Marienplatz by 2:45. The crowd was mostly women and children but with some number of "young adolescents, unemployed, and disreputable characters."[31] Street cars ground to a halt as the crowd filled the square. Proceedings remained largely peaceful, although there were incidents in which police and demonstrators got into shoving matches as demonstrators hurled insults at authorities. Police, taking no chances, set up two light machine gun positions at *Marienplatz* as the crowd blocked access to Theatinerstrasse just to the west of the city hall.

The crowd, united in their desire for increased rations, held a variety of opinions as to exactly who was to blame for their plight. They blamed the regime for high prices, but it is clear from the extensive reports filed on the event that, contrary to the expected response of "the workers," they were quite ready to blame Jews for their plight. A postal employee argued that, while "the SPD city council should be hanged, because they bear most of the blame, the Jews also play a part in this wheat flour business."[32] One group of demonstrators broke off and went into the *Cafe Deutsches Theater* to harass Jewish customers. One observer, perhaps seeking a ready answer, attributed this to "a detectable aftereffect of the last anti-Semitic demonstration."[33] Adding to the confusion, there were SPD agitators in the crowd, encouraging people to come to a public meeting the next day at the *Löwenbraükeller*.

By 4:00, the demonstration was all but over. A smaller crowd had assembled at *Sendlinger Tor*, but even they had disbursed. Munich's most significant postwar food demonstration ended peacefully, without any of the looting or violence that authorities feared. It is difficult to reconstruct from contemporary records just what the crowd was hoping to accomplish that day, save a general agreement that rations were too low. If reports are to be believed, then the SPD actively participated in the demonstration, despite the fact that many in the crowd blamed the SPD administration for the food situation.

This suggests two interesting possibilities. First, it was entirely possible that the demonstration was closer to achieving its aim of being a non-political event than authorities initially gave it credit. People from across the political spectrum had indeed taken part, as organizers had hoped, and they represented a multiplicity of formal political affiliations. Second, it is also possible that police reports were quite simply incorrect. Given the context, the former is more likely. The food crisis, tied integrally with the results of the war, reached almost all levels of society and created a consensus of suffering that formal politics could not hope to replicate.

---

31 "Meldung über die Demonstration am 11.3.20, 2.05 Uhr." RWGrKdo 4, 172, BHStA IV. This author very much doubts the time estimates in this report. It is difficult to believe that a large group could have walked that considerable distance in such a short time. This seems to suggest that this particular report was assembled based on information provided by those who had witnessed the event.

32 "Stimmungsbericht zur Demonstration am 11.3.1920." RWGrKdo 4, 172, BhstA IV.

33 Ibid.

Munich's Jews were targets because they could be made to represent the entire spectrum of crisis. The sizable community of unassimilated or barely assimilated immigrant Jews represented postwar immigration and the menace of eastern Bolshevism. Those Jews already in Munich represented the violence and ultimate failure of postwar governments in the city, along with all of the stereotypes of Jewish behavior that the protestors carried with them into the streets.

The end results of the *Frauendemonstration* were and remain unclear. Some observers compared the demonstrations with those of November 1918, in which the radicalization of food protests led to the collapse of the Bavarian and German monarchies. "The worse things get," warned the *Augsburger Postzeitung*, "the greater the crisis becomes. We risk slipping into a vicious cycle."[34] The events of the demonstration, and the extraordinarily overwrought reaction of authorities suggests that this interpretation was not far from the truth. The continued politicization of the food question, a holdover from the war years, reveals the fundamental weakness of postwar reconstruction efforts.

The willingness of some protestors to blame Jews for their plight further indicates the pervasiveness of nativist, exclusionary ideas in the city's political culture. Again, it is far too simplistic to imagine that anti-Semitism was merely a tool of the Right, but it is interesting that in the public airing of grievances, all sides were willing to use the image of the Jew as a symbol of the enemy, be that the city ration administrators, predatory capitalists, or lurking Bolsheviks. A poster of the period effectively illustrates this extraordinary malleability of the image of the Jew in Munich's political culture. The poem is a variant of the anti-Semitic doggerel that circulated in the city during the last year of the war, and its persistence suggests that its distributors found that the message was all too effective:

> Who financed the world war?
> But wasn't in the trenches!
> Who are the labor leaders?
> But shun physical work!
> Who says "we have to economize?"
> But lives more grandly than ever!
> Who opposes the death penalty for profiteers and hoarders?
> But allows thousands of striking workers to be shot?
> It is the Jew! And he has the help of Jewish Finance capitalism[35]

---

34 "Ruhig Blut!" *Augsburger Postzeitung*. March 13, 1920. Clipping in StaMu 4316.

35 Poster found in ZS 187, StaMu. The remarkable claim that Jews "w(eren't) in the trenches" refers to the curious and unpleasant incident in 1916 when the army "investigated" the supposed absence of Jews among German troops. The fact that an investigation took place fueled popular images of Jews as shirkers, despite the fact that Jews were, if anything,

It is all but impossible to fit anonymous attacks like this into a conventional framework of "Right" and "Left." Within a few lines of screed, Munich's Jews stood accused of being revolutionary socialists, wire-pulling reactionaries, and capitalist grandees. What emerged from these muddled sources is that the anxieties of postwar political culture needed symbolic outlets upon which a range of neuroses could be projected. This search for a scapegoat suggested that the crisis of reciprocity was far more potent a molder of political identity than any sense of formal political affiliation.

A Change of Course: Turmoil and Radicalism in Munich

The catalyst for dramatic political change was the Kapp Putsch of early 1920, during which a small band of military adventurers briefly overthrew the new Republic and installed a stillborn military dictatorship. The collapse of the Bavarian government in the face of the putsch was preceded by several weeks of increasingly vocal public agitation against local and national authorities in Munich. The Kapp Putsch precipitated the collapse of the Hoffman government on March 14th and the forming of a new government under the monarchist Gustav Ritter von Kahr, a shift that one Bavarian historian has called a "date of destiny."[36] While this was a vital moment in the city's modern history, it did not happen in a vacuum. In order to understand the transition from a socialist government to a conservative regime, we must place it within the context of events happening in the streets of Bavaria's capital.

The Kapp Putsch was one of the most dramatic of the political spasms of the early Weimar Republic. Following a month in which Germany lost territory to Denmark in a plebiscite in Schleswig and Allied troops seized control of parts of Silesia, a group of disaffected soldiers under a right-wing civil servant named Wolfgang Kapp seized control of the national government in Berlin on March 13. Even with parts of the military and almost all of the Germany's heavy industrial behind it, the new government was mortally stricken from the outset. Almost immediately, the Social Democrats began to organize a general strike against the putschist regime. The military clique suffered from what one historian has called "dilettantism" and lacked the political skills or the will to enforce their self-awarded mandate.[37]

statistically over-represented in the field. See Roger Chickering, *Imperial Germany and the Great War, 1914–1918* (Cambridge: Cambridge University Press, 1998), 130.

36 Friedrich Prinz, *Die Geschichte Bayerns* (Munich: Piper, 2001), 455.

37 See Hans Mommsen, *The Rise and Fall of Weimar Democracy* (Chapel Hill: University of North Carolina Press, 1996), 83. A more detailed account of the internal workings of the coup can be found in Heinrich August Winkler, *Weimar, 1918–1933: Die Geschichte der ersten deutschen Demokratie* (Munich: C.H. Beck, 1993), 121–38. For an account of the putsch in Munich, see Adam R. Seipp, "Scapegoats for a Lost War:

The coup, which collapsed after four days, revealed how few real defenders the new republic had among political elites and how weak the bonds of civil–military relations were in the new Germany. The repercussions of the failed coup were immediate and severe. Aside from the collapse of the government, it helped to inspire the large and bloody leftist uprising in the Ruhr industrial belt days later. This led to the occupation of parts of western Germany by the French. Curiously, historians have devoted considerable attention to the events in Berlin and Stuttgart (where the Bauer government fled), but relatively little to the reaction to the putsch in the provinces.

At a national level, many observers connected the events in Berlin with the problems of demobilization. The SPD leadership's call for a general strike, issued as the coup was in flux, claimed that "The *Freikorps* members who fear disbandment want to install reactionaries in high government positions. We refuse to buckle under to this military pressure. We did not make the revolution so as once again to legitimize the bloody *Freikorps* regiments. We will not sign a pact with the Baltic criminals."[38] The political crisis of March 1920 provided a fascinating glimpse into the ways in which the concerns of the postwar settlement manifested themselves in the streets of Munich.

The morning of the coup, flyers appeared in the city printed by the local *Einwohnerwehr* and undersigned by Captain Kuehner. The militia members were "called upon by the *Staatskommissar* to uphold peace and order, to protect families, house, and home from plundering and lawlessness. Without political affiliation, the *Einwohnerwehr* will not take part in violent putsch activity."[39] In the face of a general strike, a stance against "plundering and lawlessness" seems to have been shorthand for supporting the putsch. The *Einwohnerwehr* leadership had their own ideas about how to use the chaos in Berlin to their advantage in Munich, and these plans required calm in the streets.

Initial reports on the reaction of the population at large reveal another surprising reversal. After several weeks of reports indicating that large sections of the working class would welcome the coming of Russian troops, an intelligence officer wrote on the day of the putsch that "the majority think well overall of the new Berlin regime. It is about time that someone did something about the Jew-economy (*Judenwirtschaft*) that has been in place since 1914 and that we settled accounts with this band of bloodsuckers and profiteers."[40] This assessment was probably far more wrong than it was right. Only a very narrow section of the population actually supported the putsch on its own merits. What this does suggest, however, is the level of disaffection that was widely felt against anything identified with the

---

Demobilisation, the Kapp Putsch, and the Politics of the Streets in Munich, 1919–20," *War and Society* 25, no. 1 (May 2006): 55–76.

38 Anton Kaes, Martin Jay, and Edward Dimendberg, eds, *The Weimar Republic Sourcebook* (Berkley: University of California Press, 1994), 16.

39 Poster "Die Einwohnerwehr." March 13, 1920. ZS 428, StAM.

40 "Stimmungsbericht." March 14, 1920. RWGrKdo 4, 347, BHStA IV.

postwar reconstruction of the nation. Again anti-Semitism appeared in the popular political vocabulary as a way to contextualize dissatisfaction with the status quo without actually suggesting any form of government that might be more effective at managing Germany's postwar crisis.

The local SPD began in earnest to call for a general strike against events unfolding both in Munich and across Germany. Claiming that "an armed minority has trampled the constitution into dust," the labor movement and its key political ally made a last desperate effort to stave off disaster.[41] An industrial committee in Munich published a call to resist the putsch, which it blamed on "the Prussian *Junker* caste, the people responsible for the war and for bringing misfortune down upon the heads of the German people." The *Betriebsräte* mocked the law and order pretensions of the putschists:

> They promise the people freedom, order, and the end of the command economy. Their freedom means that everyone not among the ten thousand of the upper crust will be left without rights and muzzled. Their order means ten and twelve-hour days for the workers. Their end to the command economy means a jump in food prices and the most insane prices for bread, potatoes, and meat, the most important staples of working people.[42]

Across Germany, the general strike was generally quite effective. Not only did it highlight how little support the putschists could count upon, but it also prevented the Bauer government, which had fled to Stuttgart, from making any sort of deal with the Kapp regime for fear of alienating workers.[43] The experience in Bavaria, however, was somewhat different. While strikers were able to shut down some the more important industrial concerns in and around Munich, the strike never became general. As the *Polizeidirektion* crowed on March 16, "All industries vital to life are at work. Unscrupulous agitators are provoking city dwellers by telling them that the farmers have called for a sympathy strike. To this point – thank God – this news is untrue."[44]

In Munich, the Hoffman government immediately came under intense pressure from the "forces of order," here represented by Escherich's *Einwohnerwehr* and the local *Reichswehr* commander, Arnold von Möhl. On March 14, Hoffman stepped down, along with his entire government.[45] The collapse of the SPD regime cleared the way for the ascendancy of the *Einwohnerwehr*'s chosen candidate,

41 "Mitteilungsblatt der Generalstreikleitung." March 15, 1920. ZS 441, StaMu.

42 Erwin Könnemann and Gerhard Scholze, eds. *Der Kapp-Lüttwitz-Ludendorff Putsch: Dokumente*. (Munich: Olzog, 2002), 930.

43 Winkler, 126.

44 Poster "Kein Generalstreik!" ZS 441. StaMu.

45 It is still not entirely clear what the plotters hoped to achieve by pressuring Hoffman. Clearly they sought his resignation, but it is reasonable to suppose that they hoped to at least keep some of the cabinet intact to avoid the appearance of a coup.

the conservative monarchist and former wartime Prime Minister of Oberbayern Dr. Gustav Ritter von Kahr. The *Landtag*, including the SPD, assented to the new arrangement two days later.[46] It remains difficult to assess exactly what transpired in this dramatic power shift. Prinz suggests that the SDP made a "terrible mistake" in approving of the constitutional coup, while Geyer indicates, probably correctly, that this was part of the broader trend toward a less effective and unified Left in Munich.[47] In either case, the repercussions were immediate and severe. Nowhere was this clearer than in the city's right-wing circles, already emboldened by the success of their recent demonstrations and now enjoying the tacit support of the political leadership at the regional and national level.

For more traditional Bavarian conservatives, the new government was a much needed friend after nearly two years in the wilderness, a constitution that was written largely without their input, and a wartime political arrangement that stifled their activism. Particularly for the BVP, who backed von Kahr and had recently ended an alliance with the Center over the BVP's support for a more federalist arrangement in Germany, these were bright days indeed.[48] The Bavarian federalists were much more able to generate smoke than heat, and their lack of any real enthusiastic support, coupled with the recovery of the national government, effectively rendered them a spent force. The real winners of March 1920 were those on the steadily widening fringes of the Right in Bavaria.

For groups of the radical Right, the Kapp Putsch was not simply a counter-revolution but a revolution of its own. During and just after the putsch, rightist groups generated considerable amounts of propaganda material, hastily sketching out their visions of what the new regime would mean for Germany. The amount of material that seems to have been printed as the coup was collapsing suggests how badly its supporters misjudged the political winds. The *Ortsgruppe München des deutschvölkishen Schutz-und Trutzbundes* (German Ethnic League of Defense and Defiance – Munich Chapter) saw the putsch as a way to reverse Germany's stark decline since the end of the war:

> Germany has lost the war, and England and America need no longer fear her as a competitor on the world market. But the destruction of the German economy has done great damage not just to Europe, but the whole world. It is therefore in

46 There is surprisingly little written about the transfer of power between the two governments. The most detailed description of these events can be found in Karl Schwend, *Bayern zwischen Monarchie und Diktatur* (Munich, 1954), 143–50. A good summary appears in Prinz, 455–6. Biographical information about von Kahr appears in Schwend, 579.

47 Prinz, 456; Geyer, 91.

48 D.R. Dorondo, *Bavaria and German Federalism: Reich to Republic, 1918–33, 1945–49* (New York: St. Martin's Press, 1992), 9–11 and Werner Gabriel Zimmerman, *Bayern und das Reich 1918–1923. Der bayerische Föderalismus zwischen Revolution und Reaktion* (Munich: R. Plfaum, 1953).

> the interests of England and America to support the rebuilding of the German economy only to the point where it will not be a serious competitor on the world market.... Therefore, we must support any new and nationally-minded regime. The Kapp regime is ready to take action on food, raw materials, and monetary policy.[49]

This connection between the putsch and the nascent hopes of groups like the *Schutz-und Trutzbund* for the future of German society was more explicit in a contemporary pamphlet called "What Do We Demand of the New Regime?" This eight-point program reflects the increasingly shrill and violent language of organizations like the league. Three of the proposals called for restrictions on German and foreign Jews, while four demanded increased use of the death penalty for various crimes. These included "immediate execution" for "profiteers in foodstuffs and raw materials markets" and anyone who supports "Bolshevism as a political remedy for us Germans." Aside from what we have seen to be the increasingly common call for an end to Jewish immigration, the League demanded the "breaking of Jewish influence" in commerce and the press, to ensure "the end of agitation pitting German against German and the classes against one another."[50]

Taken together, these two programmatic documents demonstrate how seriously one of the most important right-wing groups in postwar Germany saw the events in Berlin. This was more than a simple putsch; it was a serious attempt to remake German society and correct the wrongs brought about by the war. Even for an organization as militant and anti-Semitic as the *Schutz-und Trutzbund*, this was fairly heady rhetoric. The fact that the documents did not get to press until after the coup had collapsed says much about how flimsy the edifice upon which the group built its program for Germany's future was.

As the putsch unraveled in Berlin, the strike's leadership in Munich met with government representatives. On March 17, strike leader Gustav Schiefer met with von Kahr and Frick. While the strikers issued a series of demands, they were of decidedly moderate scope, and probably suggest more the weakness of the strike than its potential to seriously disrupt the political process. Essentially, the strikers wanted the government to uphold its constitutional duties and to release political prisoners (apparently without regard for political affiliation). Tellingly, two of the demands had to do with changing the postwar military order. The first was a pledge to finally dissolve the controversial volunteer formations like the *Einwohnerwehr*, the second was a rather less specific call for a reorganization of units in the "army of workers."[51]

If the striking workers were concerned about the domination of the Republic's Army by the Right, events validated their concerns before their leaders even left

49 Flyer. "Das deutschen Volkes Schicksalstunde, England und Amerika." March 18, 1920. ZS 26, StAM.

50 Pamphlet "Was fordern wir von der neuen Regierung?" ZS 26, StAM.

51 Meeting notes, March 17, 1920, found in MA 99515, BHStA II.

the building. As the meeting went on, the strikers' precarious position became even clearer. Schiefer was called away and returned some time later, probably in a state of considerable agitation, to report that troops assumed to be in Herrsching were in fact making their way toward the center of the city. "If you don't do something," Schiefer told those assembled, "there is likely going to be a bloodbath."[52] The von Kahr regime, however, did not want a repeat of the disaster of May 1919. Von Kahr himself was far too cautious for that. He preferred to pursue a policy of conciliation, at least in the near term, which won the new government some much needed breathing space in potentially turbulent times.

The new regime in Munich was swift to distance itself from the events that had provided the impetus for its constitutional coup. Von Kahr publicly condemned anti-constitutional violence in a speech applauded by the *Gewerkschaftsverein München*, which hoped that the new government would take measures to "finally turn the Army into a useful tool of a democratic and social Republic."[53] Speaking before the *Landtag* on March 18, von Kahr returned to the now familiar theme of the need for sober leadership in the ongoing period of postwar transition. "The government will do everything that it can to uphold the peace and work for the interests of everyone who devote themselves to working for our people, protecting us from peril, and the ruthless struggle against dangerous enemies, greedy profiteers, and exploitation."[54]

The new regime's appeal stemmed from this palpable sense that only a strong centralizing government could stem the tides of disorder and control the violent elements in society that had launched the putsch in Berlin. The irony here was that without the putsch, the Hoffman government might still be in power. This law and order platform, however logically flawed, that won the von Kahr government much needed support in its early days had long-term consequences in Munich and Bavaria.

The results of the putsch took some time to fully reveal themselves but were, nonetheless, profound. In Bavaria, the failure of the labor movement to mold a general strike boded badly for the future of the organized Left in the state. The law enforcement community was still not entirely confident that they had won the day. One police officer wrote at the end of the month that for the Left, the strike "was considered a success.... We have to consider that any future political conflict will lead to a strike. The coming strikes will be ever more organized and because of that increasingly dangerous."[55] Ironically, as the labor movement was losing ground as a political force they were gaining mobilizing power in the factories.

52 Ibid.

53 "Nachrichtenblatt des Gewirkschaftvereins München." March 19, 1920. Polizeidirektion München 6662. Sta.Mu.

54 Text in ZS 441. StaMu.

55 Letter from Inspekteur von Seisser, staatl. Polizeiwehr to M.Inn. March 27, 1920. RwGrKdo 4, 34, BHStA IV.

According to government statistics, there were 82 strikes in *Oberbayern* in 1921, up from 21 the year before.[56]

The danger, however, came not from the parties of the left but from the parties and organizations of the Right, for whom a new day was dawning in Munich. The most successful of these groups drew their rhetoric from the palpable sense of injustice and dislocation that nurtured political radicalism in those dangerous postwar years.

As many historians of the period have noted, the Kapp Putsch made the Right an effective, though still divided national force and destabilized the already dizzying political constellation of the Weimar party system.[57] Perhaps most important for Munich, the Right had successfully challenged the state's new constitution. As the trickle of rightist thinkers who came to Munich seeking refuge turned into a flood of what one historian described as "military officials who wanted to alter their defeat in the world war, counter-revolutionaries, Kapp Putschists, the holdouts of Czarism, and agents of international Nationalisms on secret missions."[58]

The symbolic Chief of the evolving self-styled "General Staff of the Counter-Revolution" was Erich Ludendorff, one of the most enduring symbols of Germany's lost war and the protean "stab-in-the-back" myth that served to vindicate the Imperial army from the taint of defeat.[59] It is important to remember that within this loose coalition of right-wing forces there were differences over their sometimes competing visions of Germany's future. This was particularly true with regard to confessional and monarchist issues, where the traditional Catholicism within Bavarian identity mixed uneasily with newer ideas of neo-pagan authoritarianism.[60] Within this coalition, the Ludendorff circle formed an enduring counterweight to the fragile coalitions that sustained the new republic.[61]

The new government moved quickly to associate itself with the war and those who had served. In September, the city staged a veterans' parade, ostensibly to honor the fallen. What transpired more closely resembled a celebration of the new order than an apolitical day of remembrance. Sources estimate that about 20,000 people took part in the parade, which made its way from the *Hofgarten* to the *Frauenkirche*, where the Archbishop of Munich-Freising celebrated Mass.

56 SJFB (1921), 222.

57 Detlev Peukert, *The Weimar Republic*, trans. Richard Deveson (New York: Hill and Wang, 1992), 70.

58 Günther Gerstenberg, *Freiheit: Sozialdemokratische Selbstschutz in München der zwanziger and frühen dreiziger Jahre* (Munich: Ulenspiegle, 1997), 44.

59 Bruno Thoss, *Der Ludendorff-Kreis, 1919–1923. München als Zentrum der Mitteleuropäischen Gegenrevolution zwischen Revolution und Hitler-Putsch* (Munich: Neue Schriftenreihe des Stadtarchives München, 1978), 351.

60 The Thule Society, for instance, began to date their correspondence according a calendar of their own devising that supposedly represented a more "Germanic" dating system.

61 Franz Uhle-Wettler, *Erich Ludendorff in seiner Zeit* (Berg: Verlagsgesellschaft Berg, 1996), 386–9.

The procession then moved across the Isar to the *Friedensengel* (Angel of Peace), the golden statue erected for the twentieth anniversary of the Franco-Prussian War. The day's symbolic leader was Franz Ritter von Epp, who received a generally warm ovation from the crowd. Epp was one of the most visible personalities associated with the suppression of the Munich Soviet the year before, and his militia had been a swaggering presence in the hyper-militarized atmosphere of the city after the May days. His place in the march was a clear bellwether of the new order in Munich.

Veterans participating in the event were heard to remark that the message should be clear to anyone from the Entente Disarmament commission who might be watching that Bavarian veterans stood together. Reports suggest that there had been some critical voices, chiefly from leftist newspapers. The presence of Epp was also a source of some disquiet. For many, Epp was a symbol of the worst excesses of the previous Spring, and his participation detracted from the temporary aura of good feelings. One man was heard to remark "There goes Epp, the guy who slaughters workers." (*Does is' da Epp, da Arbeiterfresser*).[62] Epp's leadership on that day, however symbolic, was yet another reminder of the violent days of the year before and of the growing confidence among conservatives.

Still, honoring veterans was one of the few subjects upon which wide segments of the population could agree. The campaign to erect a memorial to the war dead in Munich illustrates this attempt to find common ground. The Warriors Association (*Kriegerbund*), emboldened by the success of the memorial parade, began a concerted campaign to build such a memorial.[63] "All inhabitants of the city, without regard for station or confession, political conviction or ideology (*Weltanschaaung)*, age or gender, without exception owe a debt of memory to those who fell."[64] Not for the first or the last time, we see an interest group attempt to base their appeal on the idea that differences of opinion and situation could only be overcome by recapturing the imagined unity of the war years. This phenomenon could be seen even more directly in the dramatic story of the militia movement in Bavaria, and its most important member, the *Einwohnerwehr*.

For the *Einwohnerwehr* in Bavaria, the chaos following the Kapp interlude was an unmitigated blessing. The militia, which we first encountered in the wreckage of the summer of 1919, had become one of the most important political forces in Bavaria. After the void in authority the year before, the *Einwohnerwehr* emerged

---

62 "Stimmungsbericht über die Krieger-Trauerfeier am Sonntag, den 12.9.20." RWGrKdo 4, 347, BHStA IV.

63 A memorial was built in 1926 in a recess in front of then War Museum near the Hofgarten. The Museum was heavily damaged during the Second World War, and left as a standing memorial until the 1990s, when in a controversial move the Bavarian government repaired and expanded the building to convert it into the office of the Bavarian Prime Minister.

64 Poster "Aufruf zur Errichtung eines Kriegerdenkmals in München." FlSg 993, BHStA V.

as one of the most active militia formations in Germany. It remained a coalition of autonomous militias that took on a range of tasks from law enforcement to policing the chaotic and violent Austrian border region. With the ascendancy of von Kahr, who owed a great debt to Escherich for providing the threat of force in March, the *Einwohnerwehr* entered a period of dramatic growth, expanding from about 290,000 members across Bavaria to about 360,000 a year later. Of these, about 30,000 were in Munich. What was really interesting about the militia was that it effectively mirrored wider developments in regional politics, reflecting more the efficacy of the "*Ruhe und Ordnung*" message than any party political loyalty. As one historian of the movement has pointed out, membership in the *Einwohnerwehr* ranged from radical Right militias like the notorious *Freikorps Oberland* to formations like the *Republikanische Schutztruppe München* that were ostensibly socialist.[65]

While the *Einwohnerwehr* benefited tangibly from this new arrangement, it also sowed the seeds of its own destruction. The public presence of an armed and organized militia almost certainly contravened the disarmament clauses of the peace settlement. The Allies, particularly the French, lodged repeated protests against the existence of paramilitaries like the Bavarian *Einwohnerwehr*, which were solemnly disregarded or given nominal attention.[66] In September, the militia celebrated its successes of the previous year with a massive shooting festival and gathering at the *Theresienwiese* in Munich. Von Kahr, along with familiar militia leaders like Kuehner and Escherich, spoke during the nearly week-long event.[67]

This convention was the most public display of paramilitary power and impunity in the postwar period and represented the high-water mark of *Einwohnerwehr* political activism.[68] Its success was not without cost to the militia and its backers. The enthusiastic participation of some the senior political figures in Bavaria made it very difficult for the government to deny its support of the movement. Allied observers decried the relationship between the government and the militias, causing a crisis in the Bavarian government the next year that ended with the resignation of the von Kahr government. In May, 1921, the *Einwohnerwehr*, increasingly without the support they once enjoyed in the halls of government and under intense scrutiny from the Allied Disarmament Commission, dissolved itself.

The existence of an organization like the *Einwohnerwehr* highlighted the potency of widespread anxiety over the terms of demobilization to bring people

65 The best work on the EW remains David Clay Large, *The Politics of Law and Order: A History of the Bavarian Einwohnerwehr, 1918–21* (Philadelphia: American Philosophical Society, 1980), 31, 45.

66 See, for instance, the poster "Regierung und Einwohnerwehr." April 11, 1920. ZS 433, StaMu. An example of the planned use of *Einwohnerwehr* formations in case of civic unrest can be found in "Massnahmen zur Lebensmittelversorgung bei Eintritt des Bürgerabwehrstreiks" undated, but prob. March, 1921. RWGrKdo 4, 34, BHStA IV.

67 Program found in ZS 428, StaMu.

68 Large, 44 and Geyer, 123.

together from across the political spectrum. The success of such a militia formation, however transitory, would not have been possible without three important developments. The first was a large pool of men, many of them middle-class conservatives, who had received military training and in many cases had combat experience. Secondly, such movements point to the efficacy of the law and order political platform following the chaos of the immediate postwar period. Finally, and perhaps most amorphous of the three, was the marked brutalization of politics and political language. If these were to be violent times, then organizations committed to the management of violence were all the more necessary.

Nowhere was this brutalization more evident than in the growing ranks of the *völkisch* Right in Munich, a movement then made of a welter of some fifteen tiny competing groups and the much larger *Schutz-und Trutzbund*.[69] We have already seen the reaction of such groups to the Kapp Putsch, which suggested important parts of the protean ideology that they came to espouse. They are worth considering again, however, in light of the importance that one of them, then called the German Workers' Party and soon renamed the National Socialist German Workers' Party (NSDAP), later took on in the history of the city, the region, the nation, and the world.

As Hitler's most recent and comprehensive biographer has pointed out, we still know very little about the early history of what became the National Socialist German Workers' Party.[70] In its early days, it appears to have been comprised of a small band of racial nationalists and conservative academics, most of whom cut a fairly poor figure in the rough-and-tumble world of beer-hall politics. Its leaders were Karl Harrer, a member of *Thule-Gesellschaft*, and locksmith named Anton Drexler. When the young Adolf Hitler joined the party in the Fall of 1919, it consisted of a few members, a very small treasury, and very little in the way of practical prospects for getting their message out or new members in.

The famous Nazi Party Program, proclaimed at the *Hofbräuhaus* on February 24, 1920, has been extensively debated and written about as an early programmatic document spelling out in rather lurid detail the fantasies of the small group of men (probably Anton Drexler, Gottfried Feder, and Adolf Hitler) who composed it.[71] What is most remarkable about the document is that rather than simply encapsulating the program of the *völkisch* block in Munich, it mirrored many of the opinions expressed in public by a wide range of groups in the city during this period, employing some of the same language heard repeatedly in the "mood reports" of the postwar period. If there is anything surprising in this 25-point program, it is how neatly the demands fit into the broader political culture of the community in which the document was presented.

---

69 Ian Kershaw, *Hitler 1889–1936: Hubris*, vol. 1, *Hitler* (New York: Norton, 1998), 137.

70 Ibid., 140.

71 I am referencing the version found in Jeremy Noakes and Jeffrey Pridham, eds, *Nazism, 1919–1945: A Documentary Reader*, vol. 1 (Exeter: University of Exeter: 1983), 14–16.

The program was a direct refutation of the postwar settlement and the actions of municipal, regional, and national governments since 1918. The first three clauses were explicitly revisionist, calling for the revocation of the treaties that ended the war, the return of German territory in Europe, and the return of Germany's lost colonies "to feed our people and settle our surplus population." Clause 22 called for the dismantling of the "mercenary army" and its replacement with a popular army. The program also reflects the near obsession with immigration issues current at the time. It called for the end of immigration, the social expulsion of immigrants, and, in clause 8, the physical removal of all immigrants who arrived after August 2, 1914. Finally, the drafters echoed popular concerns about profits, real and alleged, reaped by those who sought to benefit from the war and reconstruction. As Clause 12 claimed:

> In view of the enormous sacrifices of life and property demanded by any war, personal enrichment from war must be regarded as a crime against the nation. We demand therefore the ruthless confiscation of all war profits.

These were consistent themes in the early development of the party, and of the increasingly vocal extreme Right. In May, Hitler addressed the NSDAP faithful at the *Bürgerbräukeller*, a hall that the Nazis would three years later make famous as the site of the Beer Hall Putsch.[72] Hitler, who had not yet turned his attentions to the connections he perceived between Bolshevism and the Jews, instead drew his material from the economic program of groups like the *Schutz-und Trutzbund*.[73] He railed against the perfidy of English diplomacy, which he claimed was trying to destroy Germany's capacity to compete. He linked this to the disarmament clauses of the treaty. "The reduction of our military will only make us defenseless and dependent, leaving us at their mercy. They have forced upon us a mercenary army (*Söldnerheer*) that we cannot afford to support. On the other hand, all the other nations are arming themselves in force in spite of the lovely but hollow words of the League of Nations."

There is no denying that the Nazi program was startlingly radical in some respects. By establishing themselves as an explicitly anti-Semitic party, the DAP set itself clearly in the *völkisch* fringe. It is worth considering, however, that the rhetoric of these few racist beer-hall and barrack-room agitators was not really so distant from what was being heard on the streets in a variety of venues. The incessant references to the war, even to the point of back-dating a demand for the explusion of immigrants to the day hostilities began, points to the extraordinary sense of dislocation caused by the circumstances under which the war ended.

72 It is a mark of how marginal the Nazis were at this point that the Military Intelligence Section of the Bavarian Reichswehr, who had until recently been Hitler's employers, misspelled his name not once but twice in the report on this meeting. "Hittler" is hand-corrected to "Hitler." See Insitut für Zeitgeschichte FA-97.

73 See Kershaw, 152.

The *völkisch* movement drew from the camaraderie of the war years, real and imagined, and drew upon the domestic consensus of the war years as a reference point for their admittedly far more radical vision of community.[74] The DAP, like so many in Munich during those years, felt that reversing the changes of the past seven years, albeit in a decidedly particular and selective way, would expiate the shame of defeat and the unwelcome changes of demobilization.

While the Nazis' day was coming, they were still a marginal force in municipal politics in 1921.[75] They had powerful friends, a charismatic and talented emerging leader, and a message that resonated within the context of city and regional politics. While no study of postwar political life in Munich would be complete without them, they were simply one ingredient in the boiling stew of local political allegiance in the early 1920s. Even as groups like the DAP/NSDAP grew in size and status, they were still far from possessing the extraordinary drawing power of the representatives of older conservative ideas.[76]

On October 18, 1921, the deposed former King of Bavaria Ludwig III died in exile in Sárvàr, Hungary. His wife Maria Therese, who predeceased him by a year, was buried in Austria. Their son, the ambitious Crown Prince Rupprecht, was eager to hold a public burial in Munich's magnificent *Frauenkirche*, an occasion on which he hoped that the family's former subjects would loudly voice their desire for the monarchy's return. As Schwend has pointed out, this hope was in vain. As we have seen, even the notionally monarchist BVP was not really interested in re-establishing the Wittelsbach family.[77]

The monarchy had become an object of nostalgia. Given the tumultuous events of the past few years, many remembered the "*gute alte Prinzregentenzeit*" as a time of calm, order, and peace the like of which they had not seen since. The previous month, an informant wrote a report on a meeting of a savings club in the Westend district that had turned into an alcohol-fueled monarchist revel. "Our King was a good guy, but these Reds are bastards" (*unser Koenig war a guata Man und die Rot'n san Lump'n)* one participant had been heard to remark.[78]

The King's obituary in the *Münchener Neueste Nachrichten* emphasized his humanity and accessibility, in contrast to his preening predecessors and the vainglorious Kaiser whose martial ardor had brought about the Empire's collapse. "The ruler here was never some demigod, seen by the people only in theatrical poses." Instead, the king was remembered as a man who appeared in the streets

74 See George Mosse, *Fallen Soldiers: Reshaping the Memory of the World Wars* (New York: Oxford University Press, 1990) and Stanley Payne, *A History of Fascism, 1914–1945* (Madison: University of Wisconsin Press, 1995), 162.

75 Kershaw cites figures of 2,000 members by the end of 1920 and 3,300 by the next Fall. Kershaw, 149.

76 The party officially changed its name during late February, 1920. The party program still bore the name "German Workers' Party." Ibid., 18.

77 Schwend, 514–15.

78 "Etwas aus der Zeit." September 13, 1920. RWGrKdo 4, 347. BHStA IV.

and in the theaters of Munich. "His fate was deeply tragic because in his short period as monarch, which the war took from him, he did not have time to do all that he could and wanted to do."[79] The implication was clear: the monarch, in his absence, had become a symbol for the unrealized potential that, in the popular imagination, had been hindered by the end of the war. Ludwig was, in short, far more popular dead than he ever had been when he was alive.

The funeral of the king and queen, held just a few days after the King's death, has been little examined by historians, in large part because it was so devoid of any tangible political consequence. The day was fraught with meaning, however, for the evolving identity of the city as it moved temporally away from the disasters of war and internecine violence. It was by any measure a remarkable day, as the city welcomed back the bodies of the royal family who had fled a growing mob on a cold November night almost exactly three years before. The extraordinary constellation of political interests that, because of their positions in government, were compelled to greet the cortege as it arrived in the city from Prien am Chiemsee reflected the deep divisions and uncertainties that marked municipal life in the postwar years. The public display of political unity that surrounded the services masked real tensions, some of which revealed themselves in the attempted assassination of SPD leader Erhard Auer by unknown gunmen outside his home on October 27.[80] Still, the public display of nostalgia, curiosity, and affection demonstrated by the scope of the funeral highlighted the key role that memory, particularly of the war years, played in shaping the city's political culture in the early 1920s.

One of the parties emphatically not participating was the KPD, which encouraged its allies in the USP to protest against what they dismissively referred to as "the burial of 'their majesties'." Instead, the local KPD leadership suggested a joint celebration of the 1918 revolution, which fell within a few days of the planned funeral. There was little indication that any such counter-demonstration to the funeral ever got off the ground. Whether this suggests the effectiveness of police measures to prevent such demonstrations or the declining organizing power of the political Left in the city remains an open question.[81]

The funeral was one of the grandest events in the city during the early postwar years. More than 200 groups sent delegations of marchers, including many of the city's Catholic religious associations and most of the political parties. The procession began at the *Hofgarten* by the former royal residence, then processed up the broad nineteenth-century *Ludwigstrasse*, then west on a loop through the architectural fantasies of Ludwig I before returning to *Odeonsplatz* and south to the double towers of Munich's cathedral, where Cardinal Michael Faulhaber,

79 "König Ludwig III." *MNN*, September 19, 1921. Special.

80 Anschlag auf den Abgeordenten Auer." October 27, 1921 MInn 71525. BHStA II. Auer, you will remember, was shot and nearly killed on February 21, 1919 as he sat in the *Landtag* during an apparent misguided attempt to avenge the killing of Eisner hours before.

81 Clipping from *Neue Zeitung*, October 29, 1921. *Polizeidirektion* 4020. StaMu.

Archbishop of Munich and Freising, presided over the funeral. For Faulhaber, and those who agreed with him, this was an unprecedented opportunity to air their grievances.

Faulhaber, who would play a key role in Munich's religious life for almost the entire first half of the twentieth century, had joined the College of Cardinals that year. He was a committed anti-communist, aggrieved by the actions of successive postwar administrations in Munich and Bavaria.[82] Faulhaber's preparations for the funeral underscored his call to his fellow Bavarian clerics to make sure that the royal funeral "must lift itself up above Eisner's funeral parade, not only in terms of participation but also in its core beliefs"[83] If this was to be the last opportunity for those restorationists to make a public statement of their loyalty to their King, then the Archbishop had no intention of seeing the proceedings upstaged by the memory of the grandiose Eisner funeral.[84]

His eulogy on the day of the funeral barely concealed the extraordinary anger of this brilliant and frustrated cleric. Faulhaber chastised the assembled crowd. "King Ludwig was not King by the Grace of the people (*von Volkes Gnaden*), he was King by the Grace of God." These were powerful words, calling into question the legitimacy of the monarchy's ouster. Before he finished this brief but remarkable address, Faulhaber seethed: "The seeds of 1918 have not yet come to fruition. Our people have not yet drunk the dregs of this bitter chalice."[85] This message, delivered by a man whose position made him one of the most influential Catholics in Germany, suggests the implacable hostility of traditional conservative elements to the changed postwar order, and the potential for serious conflict over issues like Church schools that festered in the Weimar period.[86]

In marked contrast to the venomous energy of Faulhaber, Mayor Schmid's eulogy was succinct, probably to the point of rudeness. He praised the late King's devotion to science, art, and agriculture, while avoiding anything remotely

---

82 The Munich revolutionary experience was arguably extraordinarily influential in the future of the Catholic Church, since the *Nuncio* in Munich at the time was Eugenio Pacelli, later Pope Pius XII. Pacelli's personal experience with the chaos in Munich seems to have left him with an abiding fear of and distaste for political radicalism and may in turn have helped shape his response to Fascism and National Socialism. See John Cornwell, *Hitler's Pope: The Secret History of Pius XII* (New York: Viking, 1999).

83 Letter "an den bayerischen Episkopat" October 28, 1921. Found in Ludwig Volk, *Akten Kardinal Michael von Faulhabers, 1917–1945*, vol. 1 (Mainz: Matthias-Grünwald-Verlag, 1975), 223.

84 Ibid., lxii.

85 Rudolf Reiser. *Kardinal Michael von Faulhaber: Des Kaisers und des Führers Schutzpatron* (Munich: Buchendorf Verlag, 2000), 29. From the title, one can fairly readily deduce that this is one of the less flattering biographies of Faulhaber. Many others have seen Faulhaber as a key figure in state–Church relations in interwar Germany, most recently Daniel J. Goldhagen.

86 Marjorie Lamberti, *The Politics of Education. Teachers and School Reform in Weimar Germany* (New York: Berghahn, 2002), 151–95.

controversial. Schmid managed a brief feat of damning with faint praise, acknowledging that it was well known that the King "took extraordinary interest in providing the population with food and coal, especially during the terrible years of war." Given that one of the most damaging anti-monarchist rumors centered around the King's financial interest in the provision of foodstuffs and given Schmid's role in food control during the war, the mayor's comment clearly had an intended double meaning that would have been evident to his listeners.[87]

The royal funeral, held against the backdrop of violent politics, controversy over the future of the militia, and the growing power of the *völkisch* movements, emphasized the role of memory in shaping postwar politics in the city of Munich. While monarchism played an increasingly marginal role in the city's political life, it also acted as a convenient symbol for conservatives who could evoke the prewar world without any real chance that such a restoration would actually necessitate a return to monarchy.[88] It was a day, as the *Münchener Neueste Nachrichten* described it, "that would always remain memorable."[89]

As 1921 drew to a close, the processes that began with the erosion of domestic consensus toward the end of the First World War seemed to come full circle in Munich. The old order, which had found so few defenders in the chaotic days of November 1918 now served as an object of apparently harmless nostalgia. The forces that flexed their organizational and political muscle at the end of the war had lost most of their momentum, and political discussion had come to revolve around questions of restoring the rule of law and order.

The extraordinary events of the royal funeral should not be seen as a sign that Munich and its citizens wished to return to the days of the monarchy. Even the ostensible supporters of a restoration were not particularly receptive to monarchism in practice. Instead, the royal funeral and the events leading up to it demonstrate the marked disillusionment and frustration of many in the city toward the political, social, and cultural changes that they witnessed since the end of the war. This rejection of the war's legacy can be seen most clearly on the margins of political life. Lion Feuchtwanger, in the early years of his bitter exile from his home city, looked back on the early 1920s and captured this climate of political extremism through the struggle between fictional (although thinly-veiled) "True German" nationalists and their Communist enemies:

87 Draft of speech found in Bürgermeister und Rat 660/6, StaMu.

88 Rupprecht dabbled with the *völkisch* right, then moved toward the anti-Nazi conservative opposition when it became clear that the Nazis were not interested in restoring the monarchy. He was briefly considered as *Generalstaatskommissar* in an effort to head off a Nazi takeover of the Bavarian government. He eventually returned from exile and lived most of the rest of his life in the family palace at Berchtesgaden. He died in 1955. See Prinz, 475.

89 "Die Beisetzung des Königspaares." MNN November 5/6, 1921.

> They flayed each other mercilessly in the papers, spied on each other's doings and threatened to exterminate each other, but in the last resort they were like-minded; there as here, force was considered the ultimate solution of everything.... Since both parties were thus fundamentally as one, although they did not admit it, they used to go to each other's headquarters to look for somebody whom they could fight in the usual violent fashion of their country.[90]

Politically marginal interest groups in Munich, including radical Right, radical Left, and monarchist organizations, drew their strength from the general sense of disillusion with the status quo. Since it was generally understood that the war and postwar settlement were the wellspring of still unresolved issues of food, money, governance, and demographics, the events of 1914–18 were the basis for political discussion. The presence of armed paramilitaries, ranging from underground death squads to militia formations with nominal strengths several times greater than the notional size of the army of the new Republic, belied the very notion that German society was, in fact, demobilizing. As Feuchtwanger suggested, this culture of street fighting also legitimized the continued use of violence in the resolution of political disputes, effectively prolonging the armed struggle of the war years in an effort to recapture a version of wartime consensus by force.

The outpouring of anti-Semitic and anti-foreign feeling in the period after the restoration of order in Munich was also of crucial importance. Such expressions were not especially novel in postwar Munich, the central role played by Jews and foreigners in popular anger with postwar governments demonstrates just how polarizing the demobilization struggles could be. While it is certainly too simplistic to suggest that anti-Semitism was simply an instrumentalist device in the postwar period, there was certainly a sense at the time that Munich's Jews could be molded into any image that served the uses of agitators from across the political spectrum. The commonality between all of the uses of the image of the Jew was that, in the dreamscape of postwar political rhetoric, the Jews were the only ones not suffering ill effects from the postwar settlement, and therefore, were an acceptable target for resentment and jealousy.

These traits continued to define Munich's self-image in the years to come and played an important role in the complex history of the city and the region in the later 1920s. Still, it would be a mistake to look back at Munich in the early 1920s and read into it the violent events that defined the city a few years later. A reasonably informed citizen in 1921 might have been able to deduce that Munich would be a center for conservative thinking of all varieties, but no one could have predicted that the city would shelter the rise of what was then a growing fringe party into a mainstream political movement of remarkable appeal and durability. What we can see during those crucial years is that political legitimacy came to stem from repudiating the results of the war and that anything and anyone associated with the defeat or its aftermath was anathema to much of mainstream political life.

---

90 Feuchtwanger, 439.

Munich did not emerge from the war on a road to dictatorship, but the political choices that Munich's citizens made in the years to come are only explicable when viewed through the lens of the postwar years.

The events surrounding the Kapp Putsch and the royal funeral suggest some of the ways that the experiences of Munich, Manchester, and their respective national polities diverged and converged after the war. In both places, the language of reciprocity with its emphasis on tangible reward and the reiteration of wartime promises retained its power long after the guns fell silent. Victory or defeat proved to be of far less consequence than the legacy of the pervasive propaganda and debate that anchored civil societies to their wartime states. However, the ways in which those reciprocal relationships broke down in the wake of the war were very different. While Mancunians confronted a state, along with local government, which they believed could be convinced to live up to its wartime promises, Bavarians came to believe that it was their government that was the problem. The legacies of a wartime mobilization in which the state claimed sole responsibility for the well-being of its citizens while it managed the war proved to be unsustainable. Successive regimes found themselves trapped between Scylla and Charybdis, unable to abandon or fulfill the promises of their predecessors. The postwar constellations of 1919–21 came to power already weakened by a set of challenges already beyond resolution.

In 1921, the Munich Citizen's Council sent a letter to its constituents. In it, they outlined some of the key anxieties of middle-class Bavarians at this point, a list that suggests how central the continuing struggle over the terms of the demobilization of German society:

> Our situation is extremely grave. The *Diktat* of Paris, the sanctions, the unrest in Central Germany, the battle against the disarmament of the *Einwohnerwehr*, and the not fully realized socialization and communalization plans demonstrates our serious position.

For the Citizen's Council, and groups like it across Munich and Germany, the future looked grim indeed in those dangerous days of 1921. For middle-class Bavarians, like so many others, the wartime and postwar worlds were destabilizing and all too frequently terrifying. As a postwar political constellation emerged from the tumult of 1919, it became clear that a new order was emerging. That order proved fragile, but for observers who had lived through the preceding years, even a tenuous step into a world beyond the war was welcome. What they did not, and perhaps could not, know was that the future of Munich, Bavaria, and the German state would be seized by those who ultimately refused to demobilize. For them, the resentments of the war years catalyzed their antagonism toward what came afterward. That their story emerged from the story of Munich in the wake of the war should not blind us to the reality that there were a range of choices available in the early 1920s and many public figures and ordinary people eagerly sought solutions that would bring them safely out of the long years of war.

Conclusion
Ending and Beginning Again

The First World War, wrote the French psychologist Gustave le Bon in 1921, "has shaken the conceptions by which our human societies used to live and which, having betrayed their ineffectiveness, have lost their prestige. Ideas are appearing which are apparently new. They are in violent effervescence and endevour to impose themselves by force."[1] As the war ended, European societies were confronted with the extraordinary task of reorienting themselves after four years of unprecedented mobilization and physical and spiritual loss. Added to this imperative was a muscular, if protean, revolutionary ideology that seemed poised to threaten the very foundations of "bourgeois Europe."[2]

For le Bon and his contemporaries, the world had clearly changed after 1918. Violence and uncertainty were such an integral part of everyday life for four years that any possible return to *status quo ante bellum* seemed remote, if not impossible. But how much of that transformation was a direct outcome of the war and how much was the result of conditions that emerged from the conflict? While "the war" provided a convenient shorthand for the transformative element in European society, how can we demarcate between an armed conflict with an apparently fixed end point and the much longer and more complex aftermath of that struggle?

This study has considered the many and varied ways in which the transition from war to peace was planned and carried out in two European cities over the course of four years. Across the combatant states, there was a period of demobilization beginning during the last two years of the conflict and ending in the early 1920s, during which the central issues of political and cultural life centered on the rebuilding of European societies following the conclusion of hostilities. The period of demobilization was defined by a crisis of reciprocity in which competing claims to political legitimacy were based on assertions of wartime sacrifice and the need for tangible reward. The inability or unwillingness of authorities in defeated or victorious states to provide the profound reforms that had been envisioned during the war catalyzed social conflicts that had been bounded by wartime regulation and self-censorship.

Demobilization, I have argued, was not simply the reduction in the size of military forces and the resulting economic dislocation, but the process through which combatant states withdrew their legal claims on the material and human

1 Gustave le Bon, *The World in Revolt: A Psychological Study of our Times*. trans. Bernard Miall (New York: Macmillan, 1921), 12.

2 Charles Maier, *Recasting Bourgeois Europe: Stabilization in France, Germany, and Italy in the Decade After World War I*. (Princeton: Princeton University Press, 1975).

resources of the nation. Demobilization was not imposed upon European societies, but rather negotiated between states and civil societies. Various actors within those negotiations struggled to claim the rewards due to those who had sacrificed for the national good during the war. The result was a set of debates framed by these questions of sacrifice and just recompense.

This process of negotiation began in the last years of the war, in debates over the shape of the postwar world. With formal politics circumscribed by wartime regulations, much of this negotiation took place through informal channels or manifested itself in an assertive politics of the streets that frequently alarmed authorities. As armed conflict drew to a close, those who had participated, both at home and at the front, found new avenues through which to demand that their sacrifices be recognized and rewarded. Postwar debates centered on the idea of reciprocity, while authorities at all levels confronted the juxtaposition between wartime promises and the very real limits of postwar reform.

This multi-faceted and complex transition can best be understood by examining how states and civil societies responded to the challenges of mass industrial war. These challenges reflected national organizational and political cultures, but also the European experiences of urbanization, industrialization, and wartime mobilization. The Era of the World Wars in Europe was defined by the employment of large armies, almost always raised through conscription, and the integration of those armies within the economic and industrial capacity of dynamic European states. In the period of demobilization that followed the prolonged deployment of those human and economic resources, European societies faced a set of related crisis just as profound as those engendered by wartime mobilization.

We have seen the tremendous pressures engendered by this conversion and the extraordinary resentments that demobilization created and fostered. While the war continued to play a role in the lives of millions of Europeans for decades to come, the immediate postwar period was one during which the aftershocks of the conflict were widely and directly perceived in almost all manifestations of public life. The urban nature of societies in Western Europe in the early twentieth century, along with the particular demands placed on urban residents by the war, suggests that urban space is a good place to begin such an exploration of the mechanisms of demobilization.

As historians become more comfortable thinking about war in trans-national terms, we should also seek to understand the international dimensions of postwar situations. In the age of "total war," in which the population became both a vital asset of the state and a viable target for wartime violence, states pursued similar strategies of mobilization.[3] As the military, economic, and demographic costs of losing wars rose, the willingness of states to mobilize below their full capacity to do so decreased.

3 Stéphane Audoin-Rouzeau and Annette Becker, *14–18: Understanding the Great War*, trans. Catherine Temerson (New York: Hill and Wang, 2002), 29.

Both the initial process of wartime mobilization and the constant re-mobilization of combatant societies during wartime demonstrate the interplay between coercion, apathy, and a high degree of self-mobilization across the continent of Europe and beyond. Mobilization necessarily bore certain common features. Most of the participant nations employed conscription in 1914, and after 1916, all did so. While there were different judicial and bureaucratic cultures across Europe, no state was willing or able to resist legally managing industrial and agricultural production or placing limits on dissent.

While the geographic scope of physical destruction in Western Europe was relatively narrow, no society was spared the unprecedented death toll of the war. This left all participant states and civil societies with the financial and emotional burden of widows, orphans, the grievously wounded, and the invisible psychological damage suffered by warriors across the continent. At the same time, these societies faced the problems associated with transitioning between state-dominated wartime economies and postwar economies that would be responsive to consumer needs.

Historians have recently begun again to explore the factors that kept conscript armies in the field for more than four years. There is broad agreement that, until very late in the war, there were no mutinies or civil disturbances that targeted the legitimacy of the state, aside from the extraordinary experience of Russia.[4] If we accept the conclusion that European societies were willing to follow their governments into war and remain quiescent despite the growing carnage and the increasing restrictions on their daily lives, how do we explain the apparent collapse of that consensus so soon after the end of the war? What were the implications of this collapse in the 1920s, and what does the ubiquity of unrest tell us about the ways in which historians can conceptualize the experience of mass industrial war?

The answer lies in the interplay between state-directed coercive mobilization and the broader self-mobilization of European societies. It is clear that the war continued for as long as it did because of widespread belief in the rightness of the cause, the odiousness of the enemy, and the necessity of victory. The sacrifices demanded of combatant populations meant that, by 1917, the last of these was by far the most important. The success of mobilization both generated and was fueled by expectations that victory would come in time and that such an outcome would bring about reforms that would resolve the problems and contradictions of life in industrial Europe.

The tensions of mobilization and demobilization emerged from the radicalization of the war and were mediated by a triangular relationship between civil society, local authorities, and national governments. The growing juxtaposition between propaganda designed to foster and sustain mobilization and the reality of the situation on the ground resulted in a paradox that lies at the heart of the story of

4 One of the most thoughtful studies of the limits of mutiny in the First World War is Leonard Smith, *Between Mutiny and Obedience: The Case of the French Fifth Infantry Division in World War One* (Princeton: Princeton University Press, 1994).

demobilization: at the same time that the power of local and national governments reached their wartime zenith, the legitimacy of that authority was in precipitous decline. By asserting the right and duty of the state to intervene in the lives of citizens, while at the same time consistently failing to match the expectations of the citizenry, local and national authorities publicly associated themselves with a policy that appeared confused, inadequate, and doomed.

The demobilization of European societies failed to satisfy the vast majority of those who believed that they were owed a debt for their wartime service. Since wartime governments had encouraged, if not promoted, visions of rewards for the population's loyal service, expectations in all combatant states were high. Since groups within European societies, like workers and business-owners, often had opposing or contradictory visions of what postwar reform should look like, it was inconceivable that even the most stable and amply-resourced European state could have enacted reforms that would please the bulk of their population.

Why then did Germans, who had after all seen their country unexpectedly defeated in 1918, nonetheless still anticipate substantive reform in the postwar world? The answer lies in the same matrix of expectations created and fostered during the war. As we have seen, by 1917 wartime propaganda shifted in focus from the promise of a swift and imminent victory to encouragement simply to "hold on." Despite cracks in the domestic consensus like the January Strikes of 1918, millions of ordinary Germans continued to believe that sustaining the war would result in the sorts of tangible improvements that they had been promised. That we saw a similar shift in Britain at roughly the same time suggests the European dimensions of anxieties over the willingness of populations to continue the process of self-mobilization in the face of increasing privation and, by years' end, of a viable model of social revolution.

There was no "correct" way to demobilize a society after the experience of mass industrial war. It is not accurate to suggest that because Britain's democracy survived postwar challenges and Germany's ultimately did not, Britain was better able to manage its demobilization. As we have seen, for instance, the self-demobilization of the German army alleviated many of the pressures that were acutely felt in Britain. The fact that Britain was on the winning side of the conflict actually made demobilization more problematic because it seemed all the more realistic that the British government deliver on the promises that it had made during wartime. The extent of mobilization may have ultimately rendered the success of demobilization impossible. Because Europeans with very different visions of the future came to believe that the successful conclusion of the war would bring their ideas to fruition, demobilization was bound to prove disappointing to most, if not all, of them.

Demobilization, like mobilization, was a local, regional, national, and trans-national experience in which one level cannot be fully understood without the others. Demobilization occurred at the intersection of many layers of policy and contingency in which events geographically far removed from home had interesting and important consequences. Mass media made it relatively easy, even during wartime, to follow events taking place elsewhere. By examining the mechanisms of demobilization in two urban centers, I have shown the importance of the interaction between local institutions, bureaucracies, and the national state in shaping the lived experience of demobilization. Local bureaucrats, ultimately responsible for the maintenance of order in their localities, variously followed, resisted, or awaited directives from regional and national authorities, who were often themselves watching events going on elsewhere on the continent.

In the preceding chapters we have seen the manifold ways in which the tensions of mobilization persisted for years after 1918. In some cases, these problems were not resolved by the early 1920s and continued to fester long thereafter. Certainly, the struggles over how to commemorate the conflict were most heated during the interwar period, but have continued to be a subject of debate as the meaning of the war has shifted over the intervening decades.[5] Still, in the cases outlined herein, the period from 1918–21 saw sharp political and social conflict over the best ways to establish a new postwar order and can meaningfully be defined as a discrete period of demobilization.

This study has attempted to avoid the trap of treating the postwar history of Britain as the story of something that did not happen while regarding the history of Germany at the same time as something that did. While there is no question that the experience of losing the First World War profoundly limited the political and economic options of Germans in the wake of the war, it is equally clear that victory did not make the British experience appreciably easier. If social violence did not take place on a grand scale in post-1918 Britain, contemporaries certainly saw it as a grim possibility. Demobilization, in all of its facets and complexities, indelibly defined the years after war. Those choices, which originated in the last years of the conflict itself, helped to shape the world to come.

For much of the European continent, organized violence continued to be a part of everyday life long after November 11, 1918. Eastern and Central Europe endured years of fighting and civil war as the political solution to the problems of continental empires resolved themselves. Munich saw short but violent interludes of violence and the persistence of armed formations with only notional commitment to the rule of law. In Manchester, the civil war in Ireland spilled over spectacularly, reminding many observers of the conflict that had just recently ended. The war and its violence left an undeniable legacy to its participants, and we cannot understand attempts to demobilize warring societies without taking into account the persistence of violence in postwar life.

Is the word "postwar" sufficient to describe the political, economic, and social circumstances of European societies after November 11, 1918? In Britain, the wartime government managed to stay in office until 1922, while food rationing and elements of industrial and commercial control continued into the 1920s. Such distinctions are even more difficult to make in the case of Germany, where the British blockade continued until 1919 and where the violence of wartime seemed

5 Audoin-Rouzeau and Becker, 4–12.

at times to be replicated in the streets of the defeated postwar nation. Long after warfare ceased in Europe, the mechanisms of war continued even as they were gradually reduced in scale and scope. This period of neither war nor peace suggests that in the modern world the liminal boundaries between war and peace have been far more fluid than the neat periodization of conflict would seem to suggest.

We can use many of the same conceptual tools that have helped us to reconstruct how societies endured the trauma of war to better understand how the same societies dealt with the challenges of peace. The experiences of victory or defeat did not alleviate the demands of managing the transition from highly mobilized societies to new postwar situations. Long after the troops came home, European societies still faced the choices and consequences of demobilization policy.

Demobilization is a set of processes emerging from the experience of war, but by no means should it be seen solely as a topic for military historians. The specific processes of demobilization are rooted in the organizational culture of societies and in the ways in which those societies mobilized for war. However, the issues raised during demobilization, such as managing the return of troops, economic reorientation, the role of women in postwar society, and the provision of social welfare, are common among industrialized societies. The troubled transition from war to peace that followed the First World War was unprecedented in large part because the stresses placed on wartime societies during that conflict were unimaginable just a few years before.

Because of the centrality of the two World Wars in the story of Europe's twentieth century, historians need to better understand the ways in which those conflicts ended if we are to grapple with the legacies they left behind. If, as George Mosse suggested, Europeans saw the Second World War through a "lingering memory" of the First, then our understanding of that memory must include not just the events of the war itself, but the complex and perilous transition to peace that followed.[6]

The First World War mobilized European societies like no other conflict had before. The challenges that faced planners, bureaucrats, and ordinary Europeans in the wake of the war were as daunting as they were unprecedented. If the world after the war was better for some, it was far worse for others. As the continent and its people faced the challenges of the 1920s, they carried with them their expectations from the end of the war. The Great War was over, but the struggles of the next decades can only be understood fully if we consider the myriad ways that Europeans emerged from that defining conflict, internalized the momentous events that they had witnessed, and used what they had learned to face a new and uncertain world after the guns fell silent.

6 George Mosse, *Fallen Soldiers: Reshaping the Memory of the World Wars* (New York: Oxford University Press, 1990), 223.

Bibliography

Archives Consulted

Bayerisches Hauptstaatsarchiv
  Abteilung II (Neuere Bestände)
  Abteilung IV (Kriegsarchiv)
  Abteilung V (Nachlässe und Sammlungen)
Bundesarchiv/Militärarchiv (Freiburg)
Bundesarchiv Abteilung R (Berlin)
BMW Corporate Archive
Co-Operative Movement Archive (Manchester)
Greater Manchester Police Archive
Imperial War Museum Archive (London)
Institut für Zeitgeschichte
John Rylands Library, Manchester University
Manchester Central Library
Manchester Jewish Archive
Manchester Regiment Archive, Tameside Local Studies Centre
National Archives (Kew, Surrey)
National Archives and Records Administration (Washington, D.C. and College Park)
People's History Museum Archive (Manchester)
Salford Local Studies Center
Stadtarchiv München
Working Class Movement Library (Salford)

Contemporary Newspapers and Periodicals

Ammersee Post
Augsburger Postzeitung
Auf Gut Deutsch
Bayern-Kurier
Das Bayernland
The Co-Operative News
Gemeinde Zeitung
Labour Leader
The Times
Manchester Evening News
Manchester Guardian
Münchener Neueste Nachrichten

Münchener Post
National Food Journal
Neue Zeitung
Odds and Ends
People's Yearbook
The Sphinx
Wheatsheaf
The Young Socialist
Zeitschrift des bayerischen statistischen Landesamt

Published Sources

175 Jahre Oktoberfest. Munich: Bruckmann, 1985.

Abbenhuis-Ash, Maartje M. *The Art of Staying Neutral: The Netherlands in the First World War, 1914–18*. Amsterdam: Amsterdam University Press, 2006.

Ablovatski, Eliza. "Cleansing the Red Nest: Counterrevolution and White Terror in Munich and Budapest, 1919." PhD diss., Columbia University, 2005.

Adams, R.J.Q. *Arms and the Wizard: Lloyd George and the Ministry of Munitions, 1915–1916*. College Station: Texas A&M University Press, 1978.

—— and Phillip Poirier. *The Conscription Controversy in Great Britain, 1900–1918*. Columbus: Ohio State University Press, 1987.

Abbott, Willis J. *The Nations at War: A Current History*. New York: Snydicate, 1915.

Adams, Tony. "Labour Vanguard, Tory Bastion, or the Triumph of New Liberalism?" Manchester Politics 1900 to 1914 in Comparative Perspective," *Manchester Region History Review* XIV (2001): 25–38.

Allen, Ann Taylor. *Satire and Society in Wilhelmine German: Kladderadatsch and Simplicissimus*. Lexington: University of Kentucky Press, 1984.

Angell, Norman. *The Fruits of Victory*. New York: Century, 1921.

Angermair, Elisabeth. *Eduard Schmid (1861–1933): Ein Sozialdemokratischer Bürgermeister in schwerer Zeit*. Munich: Stadtarchiv München, 2001.

Armitage, Susan. *The Politics of Decontrol of Industry: Britain and the United States*. London: Weidenfeld & Nicholson, 1969.

Arnot, R. Page. *The Impact of the Russian Revolution in Britain*. London: Lawrence and Wishart, 1967.

Askwith, George. *Industrial Problems and Disputes*. London: John Murray, 1920.

Astore, William J. and Dennis E. Showalter. *Hindenburg: Icon of German Militarism*. Washington: Potomac Books, 2005.

Audouin-Rouzeau, Stéphane. *Cinq deuils de guerre*. Paris: edn Noêsis, 2001.

——. *La Guerre des enfants, 1914–18*. Paris: Colin, 2003.

—— and Annette Becker. *14–18: Understanding the Great War*. Translated by Catherine Temerson. New York: Hill and Wang, 2002.

Auer, Alois. *Krauss-Maffei: Lebenslauf einer Münchener Fabrik und Ihrer Belegschaft*. Körsching: 3K Verlag, 1988.

Ay, Karl-Ludwig. *Die Entstehung einer Revolution*. Berlin: Dunker & Humbolt, 1968.

Baedeker, Karl. *Baedekers Sudbayern, Tirol, Salzburg, usw.* Leipzig: Verlag von Karl Baedeker, 1914.

Balfour, Sebastian. *The End of the Spanish Empire, 1898–1923*. Oxford: Clarendon Press, 1997.

Barker, G. *Agony's Anguish*. Manchester: Alf Eva, 1931.

Bartov, Omer. *Mirrors of Destruction: War, Genocide, and Modern Identity*. Oxford: Oxford University Press, 2000.

Bauer, Richard. *Geschichte Münchens*. (Munich: C.H. Beck, 2005).

Bauer, Reinhard and Ernst Piper. *München: Die Geschichte einer Stadt*. Munich: Piper, 1993.

Bayer. Statistischen Landesamt. *Statistisches Jahrbuch für den Freistaat Bayern 1919*. Munich: BSL, 1919.

Bean, Ron. "Police Unrest, Unionization, and the 1919 Strike in Liverpool." *Journal of Contemporary History* 15 (1980): 633–53.

Beckenbauer, Alfons. *Ludwig III von Bayern, 1845–1921: Ein König auf den Suche nach seinem Volk*. Regensburg: Friedrich Pustet, 1987.

Becker, Annette. *La Guerre et la Foi: De la mort à la mémoire (1914–1930)*. Paris: Armand Colin, 1994.

——. "Du 14 juillet 1919 au 11 novembre 1920, Mort où est ta victoire", *Vingtieme Siècle*, 49: 31–44.

Behrends, Ivan T. *Decades of Crisis: Central and Eastern Europe Before World War II*. Berkeley: University of California Press, 1998.

Belcahm, John, ed. *Popular Politics, Riot, and Labour: Essays in Liverpool History, 1790–1940*. Liverpool: Liverpool University Press, 1992.

Bertrand, Charles, ed. *Situations Rèvolutionaires en Europe, 1917–1922: Allegmagne, Italie, Autriche-Hongrie*. Montreal: Centre Interuniversitaire d'Études Européenes, 1977.

Bessel, Richard. *Germany After the First World War*. Oxford: Clarendon, 1993.

Beyer, Hans. *Die Revolution in Bayern, 1918/19*. Berlin: VEB Deutscher Verlag der Wissenschaften, 1982.

Birn, Donald S. *The League of Nations Union, 1918–1945*. Oxford: Clarendon Press, 1981.

Black, Jeremy. *War and the World: Military Power and the Fate of Continents, 1450–2000*. New Haven: Yale University Press, 1998.

Blackbourn, David and Geoff Eley. *The Peculiarities of German History: Bourgeois Society and Politics in Nineteenth-Century Germany*. Oxford: Oxford University Press, 1984.

Boemeke, Manfred, et al., eds. *The Treaty of Versailles: A Reassessment After 75 Years*. Cambridge: Cambridge University Press, 1998.

——, Roger Chickering, and Stig Förster, eds. *Anticipating Total War: The German and American Experiences, 1871–1914*. Cambridge: Cambridge University Press, 1999.

Bonjour, E., ed. *A Short History of Switzerland*. Westport: Greenwood Press, 1985, 343–56.

Bosl, Karl, ed. *Bayern in Umbruch*. Munich: Oldenbourg, 1969.

Bourke, Joanna. *Dismembering the Male: Men's Bodies, Britain, and the Great War*. Chicago: University of Chicago Press, 1996.

Bourne, J.M. *Britain and the Great War*. London: Arnold, 1989.

Bronder, Dietrich. *Bevor Hitler Kam: Eine historische Studie*. Geneva: Marva, 1975.

Bucur, Maria, ed. *Gender and War in Twentieth-Century Eastern Europe*. Bloomington: Indiana University Press, 2006.

Butler, David and Jennie Freemen. *British Political Facts*. 3rd edn. London: Macmillan, 1969.

Cabanes, Bruno. *La Victoire Endeuillée: La Sortie de Guerre des Soldats Francais, 1918–1920*. Paris: Éditions du Seuil, 2004.

Cannadine, David. *History in Our Time*. London: Penguin, 2000.

Carr, E.H. *The Twenty Years' Crisis, 1919–1939*. London: Macmillan, 1940.

Cecil, Lamar. *Wilhelm II*, vol. 2. Chapel Hill: University of North Carolina Press, 1989.

Chambers, John Whiteclay, ed. *The Oxford Companion to American Military History*. New York: Oxford University Press, 1999.

Charlesworth, Andrew, et al., eds. *An Atlas of Industrial Protest in Britain, 1750–1990*. London: Macmillan, 1996.

Chickering, Roger. *Imperial Germany and the Great War, 1914–1918*. Cambridge: Cambridge University Press, 1998.

——. *The Great War and Urban Life in Germany, Freiburg, 1914–1918*. Cambridge: Cambridge University Press, 2007.

Chickering, Roger and Stig Förster, eds. *Great War, Total War: Combat and Mobilization on the Western Front, 1914–18*. Cambridge: Cambridge University Press, 2000.

—— and Stig Förster, eds. *The Shadow of Total War: Europe, East Asia, and the United States, 1919–1939*. Cambridge: Cambridge University Press, 2003.

Clarke, Peter. *Hope and Glory: Britain, 1900–2000*. London: Penguin, 1996.

Cline, Peter K. "Reopening the Case of the Lloyd George Coalition and the Postwar Economic Transition, 1918–1919." *Journal of British Studies*, vol. 10, no. 1 (November 1970): 162–75.

Cohen, Deborah. *The War Come Home: Disabled Veterans in Britain and Germany, 1914–1939*. Berkeley: University of California Press, 2001.

——. "Comparative History: Buyer Beware," *Bulletin of the German Historical Institute* 29 (Fall 2001): 23–34.

—— and Maura O'Conner, eds. *Comparison and History: Europe in Cross-National Perspective*. New York, Routledge, 2004.

Committee of the Police Services. *Report of the Committee on the Police Service.* London: HM Stationary Office, 1920.

Cornwell, John. *Hitler's Pope: The Secret History of Pius XII.* New York, Viking, 1999.

Davis, Belinda. *Home Fires Burning: Food, Politics, and Everyday Life in World War I Berlin.* Chapel Hill: University of North Carolina Press, 2000.

Dean, Eric. *Shook Over Hell: Post-Traumatic Stress, Vietnam, and the Civil War.* Cambridge: Harvard University Press, 1997.

DeGrazia, Victoria. *Irresistible Empire: America's Advance through 20th Century Europe.* Cambridge: Harvard University Press, 2005.

DeGroot, Gerard. *Blighty: British Society in the Era of the Great War.* London: Longman, 1996.

Desmarais, Ralph. "The British Government's Strikebreaking Organization and Black Friday." *Journal of Contemporary History*, vol. 6, no. 2 (1971): 112–27.

DiScala, Spencer. *Italy: From Revolution to Republic, 1700 to the Present.* 3rd edn. Boulder: Westview Press, 2004.

Dobson, Sean. "Authority and Revolution in Leipzig, 1910–20." PhD diss., Columbia University, 1996.

Donson, Andrew. "War Pedagogy and Youth Culture: Nationalism and Authority in Germany During the First World War." PhD diss., University of Michigan, 2000.

Dorondo, D.R. *Bavaria and German Federalism: Reich to Republic, 1918–33, 1945–49* New York: St. Martin's, 1992.

Dreesbach, Anne and Helmut Zedelmaier, eds. *"Gleich hinterm Hofbräuhaus waschechte Amazonen:" Exotik in München um 1900.* Munich: Dölling und Gallitz, 2003.

Dreiziger, N.F., ed. *Mobilization for Total War: The Canadian, American, and British Experience, 1914–1918.* Waterloo: Wilfred Laurier University Press, 1981.

Duffy, Eve. "Representing Science and Technology: Politics and Display in the Deutsches Museum, 1903–45." PhD diss., University of North Carolina at Chapel Hill, 2002.

Eley, Geoff. *Forging Democracy: The History of the Left in Europe, 1850–2000.* New York: Oxford University Press, 2002.

Englander, David. "Die Demobilmachung in Grossbritannien nach dem Ersten Weltkrieg." *Geschichte und Gesellschaft* 2 (1983): 195–210.

Evans, Richard. *Death in Hamburg: Society and Politics in the Cholera Years.* London: Penguin, 2005.

—— and Dick Geary, eds. *The German Unemployed.* New York: St. Martins, 1997.

Feldman, Gerald. *Die Erfahrung der Inflation / The Experience of Inflation.* Berlin: de Gruyter, 1984.

Fenske, Hans. *Konservatismus und Rechtsradikalismus in Bayern nach 1918.* Bad Homburg: Verlag Gehlen, 1969.

Ferguson, Niall. *The Pity of War*. London: Penguin, 1998.

Festa, Caroline. "Als BMW noch in den Kinderschulen Steckte: Die Schwierigen Anfänge eines Symbols der Deutschen Autoindustrie". MM Thesis, Université de Nice Sophia-Antipolis, 2001.

Feuchtwanger, Lion. *Success*. Translated by Willa Muir and Edwin Muir. New York: Viking, 1930.

Förster, Stig, ed. *An der Schwelle zum Totalen Krieg: Die militärische Debatte über den Krieg der Zukunft, 1919–1939*. Paderborn: Schöningh, 2002.

Fraser, W. Hamish. *A History of British Trade Unionism*. Houndmills: Macmillan, 1999.

Frevert, Ute. "Europeanizing German History." *Bulletin of the German Historical Institute* 36 (Spring 2005): 9–24.

Frobenius, Hermann, ed. *Militär-Lexikon: Handwörterbuch der Militärwissenschaften*. Berlin: Martin Oldenbourg, 1901.

Frow, Ruth and Edmund Frow. *The Communist Party in Manchester, 1920–26*. Salford: Working Class Movement Library.

Funck, Marcus and Roger Chickering, eds. *Endangered Cities: Military Power and Urban Societies in the Era of the World Wars*. Boston: Brill, 2004.

Fussell, Paul. *The Great War and Modern Memory*. London: Oxford University Press, 1977.

Furet, François. *The Passing of an Illusion: The Idea of Communism in the Twentieth Century*. Translated by Deborah Furet. Chicago: University of Chicago Press, 1999.

Gambone, Michael. *The Greatest Generation Comes Home: The Veteran in American Society*. College Station, Texas A&M Press, 2005.

Garner, Robert. "Local Labour Politics in Manchester and Salford and the Communist Question in the 1920s," *Manchester Region History Review*, vol. II, no.1, 1988: 21.

Garnet, Jim and Danny Mead. "The Struggles of the Lancashire Cotton Workers." Self-published. Undated. Working Class Movement Library, General Collection.

Gerstenberg, Günther. *Freiheit: Sozialdemokratische Selbstschutz in München der zwanziger und frühen dreiziger Jahre*. Munich: Ulenspiegel, 1997.

Gerwarth, Robert, ed. *Twisted Paths: Europe 1914–1945*. Oxford: Oxford University Press, 2007.

Geyer, Martin. *Verkehrte Welt: Revolution, Inflation, und Moderne in München, 1914–1924*. Göttingen: Vandenhoeck und Rupprecht, 1998.

Gleason, Arthur. *What the Workers Want: A Study of British Labour*. London: George Allen and Unwin, 1920.

Gould, Gerald. *The Lesson of Black Friday: A Note on Trade Union Structure*. London: Labour Publishing Company, 1921.

Grau, Bernhard. *Kurt Eisner, 1867–1919: eine Biographie*. Munich: C.H. Beck, 2001.

Graubard, Stephen Richards. "Military Demobilization in Great Britain Following the Great War." *Journal of Modern History* 19 (December 1947): 297–311.

Graves, Robert and Alan Hodge. *The Long Week-End: A Social History of Great Britain, 1918–1939*. New York: Norton, 1940.

Gregory, Adrian. *The Silence of Memory: Armistice Day, 1919–1946*. Oxford: Berg, 1994.

Griffiths, Trevor. *The Lancashire Working Classes, c. 1880–1930*. Oxford: Clarendon Press, 2001.

Grimmelshausen, Hans Jakob. *Simplicius Simplicissimus*. Translated by George Shulz-Behrend. New York: Bobbs-Merrill, 1965.

Grunberger, Richard. *Red Rising in Bavaria*. New York: St. Martins, 1973.

Gurney, Peter. "The Politics of Public Space in Manchester, 1896–1919." *Manchester Region History Review* XI (1997): 12–23.

Hagemann, Karen and Stephanie Schüler-Springorum, eds. *Home/Front: The Military, War, and Gender in Twentieth-Century Germany*, Oxford: Berg, 2002.

Hamilton, Richard and Holger Herwig. *Decisions for War, 1914–1917*. Cambridge: Cambridge University Press, 2004.

Hannington, Wal. *Unemployed Struggles, 1919–1936*. London: Lawrence and Wishart, 1936.

Hanna, Martha. *The Mobilization of Intellect: French Writers and Scholars During the Great War*. Cambridge: Harvard University Press, 1996.

Harding, Brian. *Keeping Faith: The History of the Royal British Legion*. London: Leo Cooper, 2001.

Hart, Peter. *The IRA at War, 1916–1923*. Oxford: Oxford University Press, 2003.

Hastings, Derek. "How 'Catholic' Was the Early Nazi Movement? Religion, Race, and Culture in Munich, 1919–1924." *Central European History* 36, no. 3: 383–433.

Havighurst, Alfred. *Britain in Transition*. Chicago: University of Chicago Press, 1985, 147–9.

Healy, Maureen. *Vienna and the Fall of the Hapsburg Empire: Total War and Everyday Life in WWI*. New York: Cambridge University Press, 2004.

Hecht, Ben. *A Child of the Century*. New York: Simon and Schuster, 1954.

Henry, Marilene Patten. *Monumental Accusations: The Monuments aux Morts as Expressions of Popular Resentment*. New York: Peter Lang, 1996.

Herbert, Michael. *The Wearing of the Green: A Political History of the Irish in Manchester*. London: Irish in Britain Representation Group, 2001.

Hermann, Wilhelm, *Dichter, Denker, Fememörder: Rechstradikalismus und Antisemitismus in München von der Jahrhundertswende bis 1921*. Berlin: Transit Buchverlag, 1989.

Hewitt, Eric. *A History of Policing in Manchester*. Didsbury: E.J. Morton, 1979.

Hillmayr, Heinrich. *Roter und Weisser Terror in Bayern nach 1918*. Munich: Nusser Verlag, 1974.

Hirschfeld, Gerhard, Gerd Krumeich, and Irina Renz, eds. *Keiner fühlt sich hier mehr als Mensch: Erlebnis und Wirkung des Ersten Weltkriegs*. Essen: Klartext, 1993.

—— et. al., eds. *Enzyklopädie Erster Weltkrieg*. Paderborn: Schoeningh, 2003.

Hitzer, Friedrich. *Der Mord im Hofbräuhaus*. Frankfurt a.M.: Röderberg-Verlag, 1981.

Höller, Ralf. *Der Anfang, der ein Ende war. Die Revolution in Bayern, 1918/19*. Berlin: Aufbau, 1999.

Horne, John. "'L'impôt du sang': Republican rhetoric and industrial warfare in France, 1914–18," *Social History*, vol. 14, 2 (May 1989): 201–23.

Horne, John, ed. *State, Society, and Mobilization during the First World War*. Cambridge: Cambridge University Press, 1997.

——. "Presentation." *14–18 aujourd'hui*, 4 (May 2002): 41–53.

——. "War and Conflict in Contemporary European Society, 1914–2004." *Zeithistorische Forschungen* no. 3 (2004): http://www.zeithistorische-forschungen.de/portal/alias__zeithistorische-forschungen/lang__de/tabID__40208266/Default.aspx.

—— and Alan Kramer. *German Atrocities, 1914: A History of Denial*. New Haven: Yale University Press, 2001.

Howard, Michael, *The Lessons of History*. New Haven: Yale University Press, 1991.

Howell, David. *The Politics of the NUM: A Lancashire View*. Manchester: Manchester University Press, 1989.

Hümmert, Ludwig. *Bayern von Königreich zur Diktatur, 1900–1933*. München: Ludwig Verlag, 1979.

Hürten, Heinz. *Deutsche Katholiken, 1918 bis 1945*. Paderborn: Schöningh, 1992.

Hylton, Stuart. *A History of Manchester*. Chichester: Phillimore, 2003, 183.

Hynes, Samuel. *A War Imagined: The First World War in English Culture*. London: Atheneum, 1991.

——. *The Soldier's Tale: Bearing Witness to Modern War*. New York: Viking, 1997.

Independent Labour Party. *Report of the Annual Conference*. London: ILP, 1919.

Janatkov, Alena and Hanna Kozinska-Witt, eds. *Wohnen in der Großstadt 1900–1939: Wohnen und Kultur in Östlichen Mitteleuropa*. Stuttgart: Franz Steiner, 2006.

Jessup, John and Robert Coakley. *A Guide to the Study and Use of Military History*. Washington, D.C.: Government Printing Office, 1982.

Jones, Bill. *The Russia Complex: The British Labour Party and the Soviet Union*. Manchester: Manchester University Press, 1977.

Jelavich, Peter. *Munich and Theatrical Modernism: Politics, Playwriting, and Performance, 1890–1914*. Cambridge: Harvard University Press, 1985.

Johnson, Paul Barton. *Land Fit for Heroes: The Planning of British Reconstruction, 1916–1919*. Chicago: University of Chicago Press, 1968.

Judt, Tony. *Postwar: A History of Europe Since 1945*. New York: Penguin, 2005.

Jungling, Elisabeth. *Streiks in Bayern 1889–1914: Arbeitskampf in der Prinzregentenzeit.* Munich: Neue Schriftenreihe des Stadtarchives München, 1986.

Kaes, Anton, Martin Jay, and Edward Dimendberg, eds. *The Weimar Republic Sourcebook*. Berkley: University of California Press, 1994.

Kaiser, David. *Politics and War: European Conflict from Philip II to Hitler*. Cambridge: Harvard University Press, 2000.

Kapfer, Herbert and Carl-Ludwig Reichert, eds. *Umsturz in München: Schriftsteller erzählen die Räterepublik*. Munich: Wiessman Verlag, 1988.

Keegan, John. *The Face of Battle*. New York: Viking, 1976.

——. *A History of Warfare*. New York: Knopf, 1993.

Kent, Susan Kingsley. *Sex and Suffrage in Britain: 1860–1914*. London: Routledge, 1990.

Kershaw, Ian. *Hitler 1889–1936: Hubris*. New York: Norton, 1998.

Keynes, John Maynard. *The Economic Consequences of the Peace*. New York: Harcourt, Brace, and Howe, 1920, 8.

Kidd, Alan. *Manchester*. Edinburgh: Edinburgh University Press, 2002.

Kiecel, Daniel. *Selbstbild und Image zweier europaischer Metropolen: Paris und Berlin zwischen 1900 und 1930*. Frankfurt a.M.: Peter Lang, 2001.

Klier, Johann. *Von der Kriegspredigt zum Friedensappell: Erzbischof Michael von Faulhaber und der Erste Weltkrieg*. (Munich: Neue Schriftenreihe des Stadtarchiv München, 1991.

Köglmeier, Georg. *Die zentralen Rätegremien in Bayern, 1918/19*. Munich: C.H. Beck, 2001.

Königsberger, Kurt. "Die wirtschaftliche Demobilmachung in Bayern während der Zeit vom November 1918 bis Mai 1919," *Zeitschrift des bayerischen statistischen Landesamts*, 52 (1920): 197.

Könnemann, Erwin and Gerhard Scholze, eds. *Der Kapp-Lüttwitz-Ludendorff Putsch: Dokumente*. Munich: Olzog, 2002.

Konrad, Helmut and Karin M. Schmidlechner, eds. *Revolutionäres Potential in Europa am Ende des Ersten Weltkrieges*. Vienna: Böhlau Verlag, 1991.

Krafft, Sybille, ed. *Zwischen den Fronten: Münchner Frauen in Krieg und Frieden, 1900–1950*. Munich: Buchendorf, 1995.

Krumeich, Gerd, ed. *Versailles 1919: Ziele, Wirkung, Wahrnehmung*. Essen: Klartext, 2001.

Lamberti, Marjorie. *The Politics of Education. Teachers and School Reform in Weimar Germany*. New York: Berghahn, 2002.

Landeshauptstadt München. *München wie geplant: Die Entwicklung der Stadt von 1158 bis 2008*. Munich: Landeshauptstadt München, 2007.

Laqueur, Walter. *Voices of Terror*. New York: Reed Press, 2004.

Large, David Clay. *The Politics of Law and Order: A History of the Bavarian Einwohnerwehr, 1918–21*. Philadelphia: American Philosophical Society, 1980.

——. *Where Ghosts Walked: Munich's Road to the Third Reich*. New York: Norton, 1997.

Laturell, Volker D. *Volkskultur in München: Aufsätze zu Brauchtum, Musikalische Volkskultur, Volkstanz, Trachten und Volkstheater in einer Millionenstadt*. Munich: Buchendorf Verlag, 1997.

Lawrence, Jon. "Forging a Peaceable Kingdom: War, Violence, and Fear of Brutalization in Post-First World War Britain." *Journal of Modern History* 75 (September 2003): 557–89.

le Bon, Gustave. *The World in Revolt: A Psychological Study of our Times*. Translated by Bernard Miall. New York: Macmillan, 1921.

Lee, Janet. *War Girls: The First Aid Nursing Yeomanry in the First World War*. Manchester: Manchester University Press, 2005.

Levy, Carl and Mark Roseman, eds. *Three Postwar Eras in Comparison*. Houndmills: Palgrave, 2002.

Liddington, Jill and Jill Norris. *One Hand Tied Behind Us: The Rise of the Women's Suffrage Movement*. London: Virago, 1985.

Lindemann, Albert. *The Red Years: European Socialism versus Bolshevism, 1919–1921*. Berkeley: University of California Press, 1974.

Lindenberger, Thomas. *Strassenpolitik: Zur Sozialgeschichte der öffentlichen Ordnung in Berlin 1900 bis 1914*,. Bonn: J.H.W. Dietz, 1995.

Lipp, Anne. "Friedenssehnsucht und Durchhaltbereitschaft: Wahrnehmungen und Erfahrungen deutscher Soldaten im Ersten Weltkrieg," *Archiv für Sozialgeschichte 36 (1996): 279–92.*

Liszewski, Stanislaw and Craig Young, eds. *The Comparative Study of Lodz and Manchester: Geographies of European Cities in Transition*. Lodz: University of Lodz, 1997.

Lloyd, David W. *Battlefield Tourism: Pilgrimage and the Commemoration of the Great War in Britain, Australia, and Canada, 1919–1939*. Oxford: Berg, 1998.

McHugh, Declan. "The Labour Party in Manchester and Salford Before the First World War: A Case of Unequal Development," *Manchester Region History Review* XIV (2001): 13–24.

Macionis, John J. and Vincent Parrillo, *Cities and Urban Life*, 4th edn, Upper Saddle River: Pearson, 2007: 212.

McKechnie, H.M. *Manchester in 1915*. Manchester and London: The University Press, 1915.

McKibbin, Ross. *Ideologies of Class: Social Relations in Britain, 1880–1950*. Oxford: Clarendon, 1990.

——. *Classes and Cultures: England, 1918–1951*. Oxford: Oxford University Press, 1998.

MacMillan, Margaret. *Paris 1919: Six Months that Changed the World*. New York: Random House, 2002.

Mahon, John. *Harry Pollitt: A Biography*. London: Lawrence and Wishart, 1976.

Maier, Charles. *Recasting Bourgeois Europe: Stabilization in France, Germany, and Italy in the Decade After World War I*. Princeton: Princeton University Press, 1975.

——. *The Unmasterable Past: History, Holocaust, and German National Identity*. Cambridge: Harvard University Press, 1988.

Malvern, Sue. Modern *Art, Britain, and the Great War: Witnessing, Testimony, and Remembrance*. New Haven: Yale University Press, 2004.

Màrai, Sàndor. *Embers*. Translated by Carol Brown Janeway. London: Penguin, 2003.

Marwick, Arthur. *Britain in the Century of Total War*. London: Bodley Head, 1968.

Masterman, C.F.G. *The Condition of England*. London: Metheun, 1909.

Mayr, Norbert J. "Particularism in Bavaria: State Policy and Public Sentiment, 1806–1906." PhD diss., University of North Carolina at Chapel Hill, 1988, 374.

Messinger, Gary. *Manchester in the Victorian Age: The Half-Known City*. Manchester: Manchester University Press, 1985.

Millman, Brock. "HMG and the War Against Dissent, 1914–18." *Journal of Contemporary History* 40, no. 3 (2005): 413–40.

Mitchell, Alan. *Revolution in Bavaria, 1818–1919*. Princeton: Princeton University Press, 1965.

Mommsen, Hans. *The Rise and Fall of Weimar Democracy*. Translated by Elborg Forster and Larry Eugene Jones. Chapel Hill: University of North Carolina Press, 1996.

Mommsen, Wolfgang. *Imperial Germany, 1867–1918: Politics, Culture and Society in an Authoritarian State*. New York: Arnold, 1990.

Morgan, Philip. *Italian Fascism: 1919–1945*. New York: St. Martin's Press, 1995.

Mosse, George. *Fallen Soldiers: Reshaping the Memory of the World Wars*. New York: Oxford University Press, 1990.

Mumford, Lewis. *The City in History: Its Origins, Its Transformations, and Its Prospects*. New York: Harcourt, Brace, 1961.

Münchner Stadtmuseum. *München – Hauptstadt der Bewegung*. Munich: Münchner Stadtmuseum, 2002.

Neal, Frank. *Sectarian Violence: The Liverpool Experience, 1819–1914: An Aspect of Anglo-Irish History*. Manchester: Manchester University Press, 1988.

Neubauer, Helmut. *München und Moskau, 1918/19*. Munich: Isar Verlag, 1958.

Nolte, Ernst. *Der europäische Bürgerkrieg*. Berlin: Propyläen, 1987.

Noakes, Jeremy and Jeffrey Pridham, eds. *Nazism, 1919–1945: A Documentary Reader*. Exeter: University of Exeter: 1983.

Ophir, Baruch Z. and Falk Weisemann. *Die jüdischen Gemeinden in Bayern, 1918–1945: Geschichte und Zerstörung*. Munich: Oldenbourg, 1979.

O'Sullivan, Michael. "Persevering Piety and Declining Devotion: Popular Catholicism, Secularization, and Everyday Religion in Western Germany, 1918–1965." PhD diss., University of North Carolina at Chapel Hill, 2006.

Panayi, Panikos. *The Enemy in our Midst: Germans in Britain during the First World War*. Providence and Oxford: Berg, 1991.

——. "The Lancashire Anti-German Riots of May, 1915." *Manchester Region History Review*, vol. II, no. 2 1988/9: 3–11.

Pankhurst, E. Sylvia. *The Suffragette Movement: An Intimate Account of Persons and Ideals*. London: Longman's Green, and Co., 1931.

Patel, Kiran Klaus. *Nach der Nationalfixierheit: Perspektiven einer transnationalen Geschichte*. Antrittsvorlesung: Humbolt-Universität zu Berlin, 2004.

Paxton, Robert. *Europe in the Twentieth Century*, 4th edn. Belmont, CA: Wadsworth, 2005.

Payne, Stanley. *A History of Fascism, 1914–1945*. Madison: University of Wisconsin Press, 1995.

Peukert, Detlev. *The Weimar Republic*. Translated by Richard Deveson. New York: Hill and Wang, 1992.

Phelen, Anthony, ed. *The Weimar Dilemma: Intellectuals in the Weimar Republic*. Manchester: Manchester University Press, 1985.

Pinon, Rene. *La Reconstruction de l'Europe Politique*. Paris: Perrin, 1920.

Pollard, Sidney. *Peaceful Conquest: The Industrialization of Europe, 1760–1970*. Oxford: Oxford University Press, 1981.

Portelli, Alessandro. *The Death of Luigi Trastulli and Other Stories: Form and Meaning in Oral History*. Albany: SUNY Press, 1991.

Porter, Bernard. *Plots and Paranoia: A History of Political Espionage in Britain, 1790–1988*. London: Routledge, 1992.

Powell, David. *British Politics and the Labour Question, 1868–1990*. London: Macmillan, 1992.

Prinz, Friedrich. *Die Geschichte Bayerns*. Munich: Piper, 2001.

Prost, Antoine. "Les représentations de la guerre dans la culture française de l'entre-deux-guerres," *Vingtième Siècle*. 41: 23–31.

——. *In the Wake of War: 'Les Anciens Combattants' and French Society, 1914–1939*. Providence: Berg, 1992.

Pugh, Martin. *The Making of Modern British Politics, 1867–1939*. Oxford: Basil Blackwell, 1982.

——. *State and Society: A Social and Political History of Great Britain, 1870–1997*. London: Arnold, 1999.

——. *The Pankhursts*. London: Allen Lane, 2001.

Purseigle, Pierre, ed. *Warfare and Belligerence: Perspectives in First World War Studies*. Leiden: Brill, 2005.

Raatjes, John. "The Role of Communism during the Munich Revolutionary Period, Nov. 1918–May 1919." PhD diss., University of Illinois, 1958.

Rae, John. *Conscience and Politics: The British Government and the Conscientious Objector to Military Service, 1916–1919*. London: Oxford University Press, 1970.

Read, D. *Peterloo: The Massacre and Its Background*. Manchester: Manchester University Press, 1958.

Reader, John. *Cities*. New York: Atlantic Monthly Press, 2004.

Redford, Arthur. *The History of Local Government in Manchester*. London: Longmans, Green, and Co., 1940.

Reiser, Rudolf. *Kardinal Michael von Faulhaber: Des Kaisers und des Führers Schutzpatron*. Munich: Buchendorf Verlag, 2000.

Renner, Hermann. *Georg Heim: Der Bauerndoktor, Lebensbild eines <Ungekrönten Königs>*. Munich: BLV, 1960.

Repington, Charles a Court. *After the War: A Diary*. New York: Riverside, 1922.

Roberts, Robert. *The Classic Slum: Salford Life in the First Quarter of the Century*. Manchester: Manchester University Press, 1971.

Rosenberg, Chanie. *1919: Britain on the Brink of a Revolution*. London: Bookmarks, 1987.

Rothstein, Andrew. *The Soldiers' Strikes of 1919*. London: Macmillan, 1980.

Royle, Edward. *Modern Britain: A Social History 1750–1997*. 2nd edn. London: Arnold, 1997.

Rüger, Jan. *The Great Naval Game: Britain and Germany in the Age of Empire*. Cambridge: Cambridge University Press, 2007.

Sackett, Robert. *Popular Entertainment, Class, and Politics in Munich, 1900–1923*. Cambridge: Harvard University Press, 1982.

Salvadó, Francisco J. Romero. *Spain 1914–1917: Between War and Revolution*. London: Routledge, 1999.

Sammartino, Annemarie. "Migration and Crisis in Germany, 1914–1922." PhD diss., University of Michigan, 2004.

Saunders, Nicholas J. *Matters of Conflict: Material Culture, Memory, and the First World War*. London: Routledge, 2004.

Schade, Franz. *Kurt Eisner und die bayerische Sozialdemokratie*. Hannover: Verlag für Literatur und Zeitgeschichte, 1961.

Schäfer, Michael. *Bürgertum in der Krise: Städtische Mittelklassen in Edinburgh und Leipzig, 1890 bis 1930*. Göttingen: Vandenhoeck und Rupprecht, 2003.

Schmid, Alois and Katharine Weigand, eds. *Die Herrscher Bayerns: 25 Historische Portraits von Tassilo III bis Ludwig III*. München: C.H. Beck, 2001.

Schumann, Dirk. *Politische Gewalt in der Weimarer Republik: Kampf um die Straße und Furcht vor dem Bürgerkrieg*. Essen: Klartext Verlag, 2001.

——. "Europa, der Erste Weltkrieg und die Nachkriegszeit: eine Kontinuität der Gewalt?" *Journal of Modern European History*, vol. 1 (2003): 24–44.

Schwaiger, Georg, ed. *Das Erzbistum München und Freising in der Zeit der nationalsozialistischen Herrschaft*. Munich: Schnell & Steiner, 1984.

Schwarze, Johannes. *Die bayerische Polizei und ihre historische Funktion bei der Aufrechterhaltung der öffentlichen Sicherheit in Bayern von 1919–1933*. (Munich: Neue Schriftenreihe des Stadtarchiv München, 1977.

Schwend, Karl. *Bayern zwischen Monarchie und Diktatur* (Munich, 1954), 143–50.

Seipp, Adam R. "Scapegoats for a Lost War: Demobilisation, the Kapp Putsch, and the Politics of the Streets in Munich, 1919–20." *War and Society* 25, no. 1 (May 2006): 55–76.

——. "A League of Youth: Boy Scouting, Youth, and War, 1907–1925." M.A. Thesis, University of North Carolina, Chapel Hill, 2001.

Senn, Alfred Erich. *The Russian Revolution in Switzerland, 1914–1917*. Madison: University of Wisconsin Press, 1971.

Sherman, Daniel. *The Construction of Memory in Interwar France*. Chicago: University of Chicago Press, 1999.

Showalter, Dennis. *Little Man, What Now?: Der Stürmer in the Weimar Republic*. New York: Archer, 1982.

Siegl, Manuela. "Aspekte einer Rezeptionsgeschichte der Russische Oktoberrevolution und der Bolschewismusbegriffs in Münchner Quellen von November 1917 bis Mai 1919." Magister Artium, Ludwig-Maximilians Universität, 1990.

Silkin, John, ed. *The Penguin Book of First World War Poetry*. 2nd edn. London: Penguin, 1991.

Silverman, Daniel. *Reconstructing Europe after the Great War*. Cambridge: Harvard University Press, 1982.

Simon, E.D. *A City Council from Within*. London: Longmans, 1926.

Sixteenth, Seventeenth, Eighteenth, Nineteenth Battalions: The Manchester Regiment (First City Brigade): A Record: 1914–1918. Manchester: Sherratt and Hughes, 1923.

Smith, Helmut Walser. *The Butcher's Tale: Murder and Anti-Semitism in a German Town*. New York: Norton, 2002.

Smith, Leonard. *Between Mutiny and Obedience: The Case of the French Fifth Infantry Division in World War One* (Princeton: Princeton University Press, 1994).

——. "The 'Culture de guerre' and French Historiography of the Great War of 1914–18." *History Compass* 5/6 (2007): 1967–1979.

Sneeringer, Julia. "The Political Mobilization of Women in Weimar Germany, 1918–1932." PhD diss., University of Pennsylvania, 1995.

Soames, Mary, ed. *Winston and Clementine: The Personal Letters of the Churchills*. New York: Mariner, 2001.

Sontag, Raymond. *A Broken World, 1919–1939*. New York: Harper, 1971.

Sperl, Gabrielle. *Wirtschaft und Staat in Bayern, 1914–1924*. Berlin: Haude & Spener, 1996.

Stadtarchiv München. *München und der Fussball: von den Anfängen 1896 bis zur Gegenwart*. Munich: Stadtarchiv München, 1997.

——. *München wie geplant*. Munich: Stadtarchiv München, 2006, 80.

Statistischen Amt der Stadt München. *Statistisches Jahrbuch der Stadt München*. Munich: J. Lindauersche Universitäts-Buchandlung, 1928.

Steinberg, Jonathan. *Why Switzerland?* 2nd edn. Cambridge: Cambridge University Press, 1996.

Steiner, Zara. *The Lights that Failed: European International History, 1919–1933*. Oxford: Oxford University Press, 2005.

Stephenson, Donald S. "*Frontschweine* and Revolution: The Role of Front-Line Soldiers in the German Revolution of 1918." (PhD diss., University of Kansas, 1997).

Stern, Harold Norman. "Political Crime and Justice in the Weimar Republic." PhD diss., Johns Hopkins University, 1996.

Stevenson, David. *Cataclysm: The First World War as Political Tragedy*. New York: Basic Books, 2004.

Sutterlein, Sigfried H. *Munich in the Cobwebs of Berlin, Washington, and Moscow: Foreign Political Tendencies in Bavaria, 1917–1919*. New York: Peter Lang, 1995.

Symons, Julian. *Horatio Bottomley*. London: Stratus, 2001.

The People's Year Book, 1920, Manchester, 1920.

The People's Year Book, 1922, Manchester, 1922.

Tawney, R.H. "The Abolition of Economic Controls, 1918–1921." *Economic History Review*, vol. 13, no. 1/2 (1943): 1–30.

Taylor, A.J.P. *English History, 1914–1945*. Oxford: Oxford University Press, 1965.

Ther, Philipp. "Beyond the Nation: The Relational Basis of a Comparative History of Germany and Europe." *Central European History* 36, no. 1: 45–73.

Thompson, F.M.L. *The Cambridge Social History of Britain*, vol. 1, *Regions and Communities*. Cambridge: Cambridge University Press, 1990.

Thoss, Bruno. *Der Ludendorff-Kreis, 1919–1923. München als Zentrum der Mitteleuropäischen Gegenrevolution zwischen Revolution und Hitler-Putsch*. Munich: Neue Schriftenreihe des Stadtarchives München, 1978.

Tilly, Charles. *Coercion, Capital, and European States, AD 990–1992*. Cambridge: Blackwell, 1992.

Uhle-Wettler, Franz. *Erich Ludendorff in seiner Zeit*. Berg: Verlagsgesellschaft Berg, 1996.

Vance, James E. Jr. *The Continuing City: Urban Morphology in Western Civilization*. Baltimore: Johns Hopkins University Press, 1990, 443–4.

Verhey, Jeffrey. *The Spirit of 1914: Militarization, Myth, and Mobilization in Germany*. Cambridge: Cambridge University Press, 2000.

Volk, Ludwig, ed. *Akten Kardinal Michael von Faulhabers, 1917–1945*. Mainz: Matthias-Grünwald-Verlag, 1975.

Walton, John K. *Lancashire, A Social History: 1558–1939*. Manchester: Manchester University Press, 1987.

Ward, James. "Between Right and Left: Ernst Niekisch and National Bolshevism in Weimar Germany." PhD diss., New York University, 1973.

Ward, Paul. *Red Flag and Union Jack: Englishness, Patriotism, and the British Left, 1881–1924*. Woodbridge and Rochester, NY: Royal Historical Society and the Boydell Press, 1998.

Watson, Janet S.K. *Fighting Different Wars: Experience, Memory, and the First World War in Britain*, Cambridge: Cambridge University Press, 2004.

Weber, Eugen. *The Hollow Years: France in the 1930s*. New York: Norton, 1994.

Weckerlein, Friedrich, ed. *Freistaat! Die Anfänge des Demokratischen Bayern, 1918/19*. Munich: Piper, 1994.

Weisbrod, Bernd. "Gewalt in der Politik: Zur politischen Kultur in Deutschland zwischen den beiden Weltkriegen." *Geschichte in Wissenschaft und Unterricht* 43 (1992): 391–410.

Wessler, Judith. *Lion Feuchtwanger's Erfolg: A 'Grosstadt' Novel*. New York: Peter Lang, 1989.

Whitehead, Ian R. *Doctors in the Great War*. Barnsley: Leo Cooper, 1999.

Whitley, J.H. "Works Committees and Industrial Councils" in *Labour and Industry*. London: Longmans, 1920, 7.

Williams, Bill. *The Making of Manchester Jewry, 1740–1875*. Manchester: Manchester University Press, 1976.

——. *Manchester Jewry: A Pictorial History, 1788–1988*. Manchester: Archive Publications, 1988, 75

Wilson, Captain S.J. *The Seventh Manchesters*. Manchester: The University Press, 1920.

Wilson, Trevor. *The Myriad Faces of War: Britain and the Great War, 1914–18*. Cambridge: Polity Press, 1986.

Winkler, Heinrich August. *Weimar, 1918–1933: Die Geschichte der ersten deutschen Demokratie*. Munich: C.H. Beck, 1993.

Winter, Jay. *Sites of Memory, Sites of Mourning : The Great War in European Cultural History*. Cambridge: Cambridge University Press, 1995.

—— and Jean-Louis Robert, eds. *Capital Cities at War: Paris, London, Berlin, 1914–1919*. Cambridge: Cambridge University Press, 1997.

—— and Emmanual Sivan, eds. *War and Remembrance in the Twentieth Century*. Cambridge: Cambridge University Press, 1999.

——, Geoffrey Parker, and Mary R. Habeck, eds. *The Great War and the Twentieth Century*. New Haven: Yale University Press, 2000.

Wirsching, Andreas. *Vom Weltkrieg zum Bürgerkrieg? Politischer Extremismus in Deutschland und Frankreich 1918–1933/39. Berlin und Paris im Vergleich*. Munich: Oldenbourg, 1999.

Woollacott, Angela. *On Her Their Lives Depend: Munitions Workers in the Great War*. Berkeley: University of California Press, 1994.

Wrigley, Chris, ed. *The Challenges of Labour: Central and Western Europe, 1917–20*. London: Routledge, 1993, 263.

——. *From Napoleon to the Second International: Essays on Nineteenth Century Europe*, New York: Viking, 1994.

——. *A Companion to Early Twentieth-Century Britain*. Malden: Blackwell, 2003.

Ziemann, Benjamin. *Front und Heimat: Ländliche Kriegserfahrungen im südlichen Bayern, 1914–1923. Essen: Klartext, 1997.*

Zimmerman, Werner Gabriel. *Bayern und das Reich 1918–1923. Der bayerische Föderalismus zwischen Revolution und Reaktion*. Munich: Pflaum, 1953.

Zofka, Zdnek. "Wahlen in Bayern, 1849–1994". http://www.stmuk.bayern.de /blz/web/archiv/landtag/artikel.html.

Index

Addison, Christopher 53, 84–5, 218
Addison (House and Town Planning) Act 217–18
advertising 106–7, 141–2
Angell, Norman 199
Arco-Valley, Count Anton 176
Armistice 2, 6
  durability of 1
  celebrations of 20
  German army and 181–2
  local authority and 128
  Manchester and 88–9, 131–2
  planning for 124
  unemployment and 151, 157
art 231
Ashton, Margaret 78, 82
Ashton-under-Lyme 72, 149
Asquith, Herbert 48, 134, 137
atrocity stories 68–9
Auer, Erhard 170–2, 175
  assassination attempts on 176, 255
Austro-Hungarian Empire 4

Bamberg Constitution 177–8
Bauernbund 40, 171–2
Bavarian Peoples' Party (BVP) 175, 179–80, 246, 254
Bavarian Revolution (1918) 169–173
  commemoration of 193
  as coup 117, 169
  legacies 175, 182, 235
  see also Eisner, Kurt; Ludwig III
Belle Vue 56,71, 203–4
Bethmann-Hollweg, Theobald 105
Black Friday, *see* Triple Alliance Strike
Blunden, Edmund 43
BMW (Bayerische Motoren Werke) 94, 117, 189
  women and 118
Bolshevism 76
  Co-operative Movement and 77
  consumer anxiety and 235–43
  dancing and 215
  in European perspective 44
  January 1919 *Landtag* elections and 175–6
  labor unrest 156–161
  peace and 116
bonds, *see* war bonds
Bottomley, Horatio 221, *see also John Bull*
Britain 1–9, 21
  Left in 34, 143
  postwar recovery 133
  reciprocity and 16, 134
  revolution and 143, 265
  see also conscription; demobilization; Manchester; mobilization
"Britain for the British" 82–3, *see also* Jews
British Legion 209, 216
Burgfrieden 110
Burnley 78, 146–9

Center Party 40
censorship 66, *see also* film
Churchill, Clementine 23–4, 219
Churchill, Winston 144
Church Army 210
church bells, melting of 98
Clarions 33
Clynes, J.R. 137, 204–6, 221, *see also* Ireland, Labour Party and
coal
  demobilization and 123, 132, 149, 191, 227–8, 236
  industry and 114, 146, 191
  mining in Lancashire 28–9, 134, 207, 212
  wartime shortages of 98, 100, 114, 122, 257
Co-operative Movement 60, 73–4, 76, 77
  elections and 135–6
  housing and 85
  postwar growth of 154–6

radicalism and 203
communism, *see* Bolshevism; Communist Party of Great Britain (CPGB); German Communist Party (KPD)
Communist Party of Great Britain (CPGB) 222–4, 226, 230
conscientious objectors 79–82
Alternative Service Guild and 137
conscription 78–82
comparative perspective on 44, 263
medicine and 67–8
see also conscientious objectors
Conservative Party 221, 229
Khaki Election and 134–7
"working class Toryism" and 32, 201, 221, 229
cotton industry
bolshevism and 160, 223
prewar 27–9, 31–2, 35
postwar recovery of 132, 134, 146, 148, 160, 207
unemployment and 212
women and 56, 72
wartime labor disputes 72–3, 87
Councils (*Räte*) 177, *see also* Eisner, Kurt
Bavarian coup and 170–73
demobilization and 168–9, 178–85
Republic (*Räterepublik*) 166–7, 177–8
CPGB, *see* Communist Party of Great Britain (CPGB)
crusade, First World War as 68, 106
culture de guerre 10

decontrol 146–7, 189, 200, 217
Triple Alliance and 227–9
Defense of the Realm Act (DORA) 50, 70, 73
demobilization 2–9, 128–31, 200–202, 261–6
Britain and 61, 84, 132–3, 138–41, 145, 163, 215, 229–30
definition of 8–9
demonstrations and 114–16
cultural history and 7
demobilization of the mind 12
Germany and 92–3, 168–9, 181, 259
paradox of 21
planning for 18, 43–4, 120–24
reciprocity 16–17, 261–2
self-demobilization 20, 169, 174
see also Britain, mobilization; Germany; Manchester; Munich; Soldiers' Strikes; Triple Alliance Strike; veterans
Desborough Commission 152–3
Deutschvölkische Schutz-und Trutzbund 192, 237, 252–3
Kapp Putsch and 247
DDP, *see* German Democratic Party (DDP)
dilution 57–8, 72–3, 219, *see also* women

education 50, 56–7, 65–6
improvement of 86
school closings 97–8
Socialist Sunday Schools 79–81, 86
Einwohnerwehr 185–6
complaints about 195–6
composition of 194–5
dissolution of 250–52
Kapp Putsch and 244–5
Eisner, Kurt 105
administration of 172–6
anti-Semitism and 192
assassination of 177–8
Bavarian autonomy and 184
councils and 181
coupled by 169–72
January Strike and 117–20
memory of 235–8, 256
origins of 117
"No Eisner, No Hitler" 167
elections 129
Manchester
prewar 29–32
Parliamentary Election (1918), *see* Khaki Election
Munich
Landtag by-election (1918) 169–70
Landtag election (1919) 174–6
Municipal election (1919) 178–80
prewar 39–40
women and 166
Employment Exchange 140–41, 145, 149
enemy aliens 53–5
Epp, Franz Ritter von 177–8
commemoration and 250

Ernährungsamt 101
Escherich, Georg 185, 245, 251, *see also* *Einwohnerwehr*

Faulhaber, Cardinal Michael 255–7
Feuchtwanger, Lion 195, 233, 257–8
film 66–9, 105–6
food 9, 19, 72, 105, 175
 demobilization planning and 122, 227
 demonstrations and 54–5, 72–3, 111, 114–15, 203–7, 237–42
 ersatz 96–102
 food control 45, 47–8, 59–65, 90, 99–102
 Jews and 82–3, 237–42
 Kapp Putsch and 247
 shortages 71, 190
 substitute 62, 125, 99–100
 see also Ernährungsamt; prices; Schimd, Eduard; temperance
Fox, Tom 218–19
Frauendemonstration (1920) 240–3, *see also* women; Jews
Frick,Wilhelm 235, 247

General Strike (1926) 223
Germany 1–9, 35, 81, 92, 116–17, 125, 163, 166, 189, 190, 244–5, 259, 265
 blockade of 61, 91, 94, 236, 255–6
 economy of 96
 patriotism and 107–8, 111–12
 reciprocity in 15–16
 see also demobilization; mobilization; Munich
German Communist Party (KPD) 183, 193–4, 255
German Democratic Party (DDP) 179
Gleason, Arthur 134
Graves, Robert 1
Groener, Wilhelm 110, 115–16, *see also* *Kriegsamt*

Hallsworth, Joseph 135
Haig, Douglas 228
 British Legion and 210
 Manchester and 145
"Hands Off Russia" 159–60, *see also* Russia
Hannington, Wal 213
Heaton Park 49, 67, 141, 144
Heim, Georg 40
Hellingrath, Philipp von 116, 124
Hindenburg, Paul von 181, 193
 celebration of (1917) 108–10
 Hindenburg Program 109
 film about 105–6
Hitler, Adolf 167, 237, 252–3, *see also* Nazi Party
 education and 187–8
Hoffman, Johannes 176–7, 196
 resignation of 243–6
hospitals 66–8
housing 14, 16, 17–18, 22
 Manchester and 30–31, 84–5, 217–20
 Munich and 36, 190–91, 236–8
 postwar reform and 22
 social reformers and 26, 86–7
 wartime 95–6, 128–9
 see also Ministry of Reconstruction; slums; *Wohnungsamt*
Hungary 4, 157, 244

Independent Labour Party (ILP)
 demobilized soldiers and 161
 "Hands Off Russia" and 158–60
 support for 75–8
 origins of 33
 Peterloo and 153
 political education and 155–8
immigration
 demobilization and 210–11
 nineteenth century 14, 26, 29–30, 35–6
 Irish 29–30
 Jewish immigration to England 30
 postwar anxieties and 236–8, 242, 247, 253
 see also Jews, Ireland, Russia
Independent Social Democratic Party (USPD)
 commemoration and 193–4
 coup and 169–73
 Einwohnerwehr and 195–6
 Landtag election (1919) and 175
 meetings of 175–6, 194–5
 municipal elections (1919) and 179–80, 195

Neue Zeitung and 180
origins of 104
wartime labor unrest and 115, 117–19
see also January Strikes; Eisner, Kurt; *Neue Zeitung*
inflation, *see* prices
internment, *see* enemy aliens
IRA, *see* Irish Republican Army (IRA)
Ireland
civil war in 200, 223–4
immigrants from
nineteenth century 29–30, 32
wartime employment and 52, 75
Irish Self-Determination League 161, 224
Labour Party and 203–6
Republicanism 161–2
Royal Irish Constabulary, *see* Royal Irish Constabulary (RIC)
terrorism and 225–6
postwar politics and 226
Irish Republican Army (IRA) 225–6
Italy 5, 138

January Strikes 116–19
Jews 173–4, 192–3, 236–9, 241–3, 247, 257–8
Bolshevism and 160–61, 253
immigration of 30, 37–8, 53–5
wartime experience of 82–3, 113–14
see also Bolshevism; *Deutschvölkische Schutz-und Trutzbund*; Eisner, Kurt, anti-Semitism and; immigration; *Thule Gesellschaft*
John Bull 221

Kahr, Gustav Ritter von 243, 246, 248, 251
Kapp Putsch 21, 243–9
reciprocity and 259
right-wing politics and 249–52
Keynes, John Maynard 127
Khaki Election (1918) 134–8, 161, *see also* elections
KPD, *see* German Communist Party (KPD)
Kriegsamt 110, 115–16, 121
Kriegsanleihe, *see* war bonds
Krupp Cannon Works 95, 101–2, 117

Labour Party 32–4
Co-operative Movement and 156
Clynes, J.R. and 203–6
Khaki Election and 135–8
radicalism and 221–4
Lager Lechfeld 187
Landauer, Gustav 176
murder of 178
Lehmann, Julius (J.F.) 107, 192–3
Liberal Party 29–33, 48, 221
Khaki Election and 134–8
Lloyd George, David
as Minister of Munitions 52–3, 69
as Prime Minister 84, 89–90, 134
Ludendorff, Erich 194
as counter-revolutionary 249–50
Ludwig III 41–2
death and funeral of 254–7
overthrow of 172
war aims of 42
Lusitania 54–5

Manchester 14–16, 20–22, 46, 129, 200–201
Armistice in 131–63
demobilized military personnel in 138–45
economic demobilization in 145–50
economic mobilization of 49–59
food supply in wartime 59–65
housing and demobilization in 217–20
industrial disputes during wartime in 70–83
military personnel in 67–9
postwar election in 134–8
prewar 27–34
radical politics in 156–62, 204–5, 220–30
unemployment in 150–52, 207–10, 213, 216
Manchester Area Armaments Output Committee 71–2
Manchester Evening News 61, 63, 66, 74, 83, 87, 135, 143–4, 148, 150, 203, 209, 214
Manchester Guardian 31, 112, 151
Triple Alliance Strike and 206, 226–8
"Manchester Martyrs" 161–2, 224
Manchester Regiment 49

demobilization of 138–9, 142
Manchester University 71, 78–80, 85
Mann, Thomas 38, 172
Mayr, Karl 187
Metropolitan Police Strike 152–3, *see also* police
migration, *see* immigration
Ministry of Labour 74, 139
unemployment and 149–51
Ministry of Reconstruction 84–5, 139–41, 217–18
Ministry of Munitions 52–3, 57, 71–6, 83
mobilization 1–3, 10–11, 125, 128–9, 234, 259, 262–4
as complex phenomenon 6–7
Britain and 47–9, 89–90, 132–3, 163
cultural history and 7
demobilization and 7–9
Germany and 92–3, 98–9, 102, 108–9, 116–17
propaganda and 18–19
remobilization 44
self-mobilization 3, 15–16, 70–71, 107, 263
semi-mobilization 84
strategies for 16–17
see also Britain; demobilization; Germany; Manchester; Munich
Möhl, Arnold von 177–8, 187
Kapp Putsch and 245
monarchism 249, 257
morality 45
demobilization and 22
entertainment and 66–7
immigration and 236
temperance and 64
unemployment and 149–50, 212–16
see also film; sexuality
MSPD, *see* Social Democratic Party (SPD)
Münchener Neueste Nachrichten 98, 102, 104–5, 106, 116, 255, 257
Munich 14, 19–20, 21–2, 46, 128–9, 201, 233–4
economic demobilization in 188–91
economic mobilization of 93–9
end of war in 169–73
demobilized military personnel in 174, 180–83
food protests in 235–43
food supply in wartime 99–102
industrial disputes during wartime in 111–19
invasion of by anti–revolutionary forces 177–8
postwar elections in 174, 178–80
prewar 34–42
radical politics in 192–7, 243–7, 252–4, 258–9
unemployment in 189–90
Munich Chamber of Commerce (*Handelskammer*) 124, 169, 178
Munitions of War Act 50

National Federation of Discharged and Demobilised Soldiers 73, 211
National Aircraft Factory 52, 147
National Shell Factories (NSF) 52, 58
National Union of Miners 221
Nazi Party 20
origins of 192–3
party program (1920) 252–4, 167
see also Hitler, Adolf
Netherlands 5, 100–101
Neue Zeitung 180, 237
NSDAP, *see* Nazi Party
Nürnberg 35, 93, 101, 117, 190
nursing 66–8

Oberste Heeresleitung (OHL) 109, 116, 181
Oktoberfest 188

Pacifism 78, 89, 178, *see also* Independent Labour Party (ILP)
Pankhurst, Sylvia 33, 54
Peacock, Robert 61, 75, 79
Peterloo 31, 159
centenary of 153–4
Pmf Dachau 94–7, 190
women and 97, 190
Pöhner, Ernst 235–6, 240
police
industry and 74–5, 146–7
sources on 23
surveillance by 46, 55, 62–3, 77–8, 112, 170, 171, 174

see also Desborough Commission; food; *Frauendemonstration* (1920); Metropolitan Police Strike; Peacock, Robert; Pöhner, Ernst
Potter, Alexander 47
prices 59–60, 63–5, 95–102, 116, 188–9, 227, 236, 239–41, *see also* food
Prinzregentenzeit 35–9
nostalgia and 254

Räterepublik, *see* Councils (*Räte*)
rationing, *see* food
reciprocity
Britain and 90, 130, 144, 230
crisis of 3
definition 15–16
disabled veterans and 208–9
Germany and 105, 115, 116–17, 165, 179, 200, 234, 259
international dimensions 16–18, 129–30, 261–2
wartime labor disputes and 72–3, 88
Reichskommissarat für Übergangswirtschaft 122
Reichswehr 188, 196, 237–9, 245
conversion of 183–7
Rhonnda, Lord 204
Roberts, Robert 41, 51, 59
politics and 157
Robinson, Annot 153, 159
Robinson, Wright 72–3, 78–80, 223
as parliamentary candidate 136
Rochdale 52, 56, 58, 149
Royal Irish Constabulary (RIC) 152
Russia 2, 81–2
immigrants from 37, 55, 82–3
see also "Hands Off Russia"
Russian Revolution 6, 115–16, 158–60, 234–6
Eastern Front and 182–3
political language and 19–20, 44–5, 76–7, 80–81, 86
Soldiers' Strikes and 143–4

Salford 27–8, 49, 64–5
local politics in 32–3, 137, 157
Schmid, Eduard 99, 179–80, 257–8
schools, *see* education
Scotland Yard 152, 222–3
Scott, C.P. 31, 131, 133
Segitz, Martin 121–3, 174
sexuality 23, 45, 67, 213, *see also* morality
Simon, E.D. 133, 208, 213
reform and 218–19
Simplicissimus 1, 38–9, 112
slums 30
abolition of 155, 217–20
Smethurst, Thomas 59
Snowden, Philip 153, 161
Social Democratic Party (SPD) 104
Bavarian coup and 168–71, 175
Frauendemonstration (1920) and 241–2
Kapp Putsch and 243–6
Kurt Eisner and 117
Landtag election (1919) and 175
Municipal elections (1919) and 179–80
prewar 40–41
wartime labor disputes and 115–16
Soldiers' Strikes 142–5
Sonderweg 23
Spain 5
SPD, *see* Social Democratic Party (SPD)
Switzerland 112
postwar politics and 5

Taylor, A.J.P 27
temperance 74–5
Thule Gesellschaft 174–6, 192, 252
Times, The (London) 112, 160, 162, 222, 224
Tories, *see* Conservative Party
Toller, Ernst 104, 119, 177, 235
Tory Party, *see* Conservative Party
total war 5, 55, 93, 109, 123
definition of 16–17
international dimensions of 262
transnational history 12–15
Triple Alliance Strike 206, 212–13, 226–9

unemployment 10, 20–22, 128–9
cotton industry and 146
demonstrations and and 150–51, 203–8
military personnel and 140–41, 150–52, 209–11
morality and, 215–16

National Conference of the Unemployed 213
postwar planning and 85–7, 87–8, 120, 139
war industries and 146–7, 189–90
women and 151, 189–90
see also coal; cotton industry; decontrol; demobilization; women
University of Munich 96
USPD, *see* Independent Social Democratic Party (USPD)

veterans
disabled 149–50, 165, 214–15
image of 208–9
organizations for 142, 150, 210–11, 216–17
parade in Munich (1920) 250–51
radicalization of 20
Soldier's Charter 161
Triple Alliance Strike and 227
see also advertising; British Legion; *Einwohnerwehr*; unemployment
Vollmar, George von 41, 169–70

war bonds 5
Britain 69–70, 79
Germany 107–8, 111
War Ministry (Bavaria) 94, 98, 101, 104
demobilization planning and 120–21, 174, 181
West Gorton 52
Wigan 58
Wohnungsamt 95–6, 190
women
demonstrations of 36–7, 91–2, 153
industry and 55–8, 60, 71, 95, 97, 114–15, 118–19, 131–2, 141
prewar 33, 36–7
unemployment and 147, 151, 189–90, 212, 215
voting and 16, 136–7, 174–5, 179–80
see also dilution; food; *Frauendemonstration* (1920); nursing; Peterloo; Pankhurst, Sylvia
Würzburg 93, 171

Yapp, Arthur 61
YMCA 149, 216

Zentrum, *see* Center Party